THE UNDISCOVERED DEWEY

THE UNDISCOVERED DEWEY

Religion, Morality, and the Ethos of Democracy

Melvin L. Rogers

COLUMBIA UNIVERSITY PRESS ☒ NEW YORK

COLUMBIA UNIVERSITY PRESS
Publishers Since 1893
New York   Chichester, West Sussex

Copyright © 2009 Columbia University Press

Library of Congress Cataloging-in-Publication Data

Rogers, Melvin L.
    The undiscovered Dewey : religion, morality, and the ethos of
democracy / Melvin L. Rogers.
        p.   cm.
    Includes bibliographical references and index.
    ISBN 978-0-231-14486-5 (cloth : alk. paper) —
    ISBN 978-0-231-51616-7 (ebook)
    1. Dewey, John, 1859–1952.   I. Title.

    B945.D44R59   2008
    191—DC22

                                        2008022221

∞ Columbia University Press books are printed on permanent and
durable acid-free paper.

This book is printed on paper with recycled content.

Printed in the United States of America

c 10 9 8 7 6 5 4 3 2 1

DESIGN BY VIN DANG

TO MY PARENTS,
YVONNE & ROOSEVELT ROGERS

CONTENTS

PREFACE

This book offers a new perspective on the foundations of John Dewey's philosophy and so tilts our understanding of his religious, ethical, and political reflections in a novel direction. This assertion may seem a bit cavalier. After all, in the past two decades the field of Dewey scholarship has greatly expanded. Influential books have been written by Cornel West, Robert Westbrook, James Kloppenberg, Alan Ryan, John Patrick Diggins, and Steven Rockefeller, making the field a crowded one. Yet even in these important contributions Dewey is consistently understood as a child of the Enlightenment in regard to his appreciation for scientific inquiry. Despite his consistent rejection of philosophical and theological certainties, he seems inescapably wedded to a progressive view of experience, making him an unlikely guide in these politically uncertain times. Indeed, all of these contemporary thinkers are united by a singular worry: Dewey's conception of inquiry denies the fragility of life that a thoroughgoing experimentalism demands.

While there is much to recommend in the work of these scholars, their view of Dewey has the effect of obscuring the significance of his philosophy for understanding ourselves under modern conditions. All of these scholars miss or diminish in various ways the profound influence of Charles Darwin's account of evolution on Dewey's notion of inquiry and the corresponding ideas of contingency and uncertainty it introduced. By focusing on this influence, I show that for him, our cognitive abilities are both stimulated and potentially frustrated by contingency, and that this beginning point guides even as it humbles the significance of human action. While he retains the humanistic and political hopes of the Enlightenment, those hopes are cautiously advanced and defended, given the background of contingency from which they derive. The result, as Dewey himself explains in his 1910 essay, "The Influence of Darwin on Philosophy," is that Darwin "introduced a mode of thinking that in the end was bound to transform the logic of knowledge, and hence the treatment of morals, politics, and religion." To follow this line of inquiry, as this book does, is to encounter the undiscovered Dewey.

My purpose in this book is twofold: to investigate and reconstruct the historical framework in which Dewey's appreciation for Darwin is located, on the one hand, and to interpret and distill his understanding of its epistemological and normative importance in guiding human life, on the other. I trace the way in which the former—as articulated through the themes of inquiry and contingency—informs and appropriately directs the latter as revealed in his engagement with religious, moral, and democratic commitments. The book encompasses a large swath of his writings, while holding in view and exploring the different dimensions of the connection between inquiry and contingency for managing modern life.

This helps explain my selection of texts throughout this book. After all, the reader may worry that the texts I have used have been cherry-picked to suit the overall interpretation being advanced here. Moreover, one might object that the differences between this work and those of the commentators I criticize arise solely from selection of texts. In all respects, I avoid this problem by (a) employing the same texts that Dewey's critics use and (b) using a thematic approach to my analysis that relies on and shows continuity among a variety of Dewey's writings. In this regard, I try to do justice to the larger argument of this book while keeping in view the peculiarities of Dewey's specific works. And I largely work in his middle and later works, beginning roughly in the 1890s, since these texts are developed outside of his previous and deeply held Hegelian commitments and are instead located more firmly within a Darwinian framework.

The line from Dewey's essay on Darwin, then, provides not only a rejoinder to critics, but also the outline, interpretative goals, and organizing structure for this book. The text is divided into two parts. In part I—"From Certainty to Contingency" (chapters 1 and 2)—I analyze the importance of contingency in Dewey's philosophy of action, and the precise relationship between that account and what he says about inquiry. This requires that we turn our attention, as intellectual historians, to the ascendancy of Darwin's notion of evolution within the context of the nineteenth-century liberal Protestantism with which Dewey is often allied. The project attempts to understand better than we now do how each—that is, liberal Protestantism and Dewey—appropriates Darwin's vision of evolution.

What emerges is a startling and vital distinction, the result of which will orient the reader differently to the very foundations of Dewey's philosophy. While his liberal Protestant counterparts exploit evolution as a story about progress, he argues that inquiry proceeds from and must not presume to overcome the uncertainty that characterizes human action. Dewey separates the meaningfulness of inquiry from a larger metaphysical story about human development, while simultaneously opening our commitments to reflective reevaluation and public contestability in the context of our ongoing social practices. There is a guiding insight at work in this account to which scholars have paid little or no attention, but which this project uncovers for readers: Dewey's account of inquiry attempts a transformation in the modern self-understanding that simultaneously encourages a Promethean intervention in managing our social and natural environments, but constrains action by highlighting its intimate relationship to uncertainty. That the Enlightenment gave birth to Dewey's outlook cannot be denied, but in his hands that vision has reached maturity.

In part II—"Religion, the Moral Life, and Democracy" (chapters 3–5)—the book is more explicitly philosophical. I explore and explicate the relationship between inquiry—now understood as preceding from a more contingent foundation—and Dewey's religious, moral, and political philosophy. As I argue, he does not seek to abandon religious commitments, as many scholars have thought, but rather to redescribe their place within the context of democracy. He is thus sensitive to modern pluralism, especially the absence of a dominant theological or ethical horizon that would otherwise guide the substantive content of our lives. And he seeks to provide an answer to the following question: In the absence of unifying theological commitments, how do we go about the business of managing democracy while simultaneously paying respect to religious commitments? His answer, I argue, awakens us to the importance of our religious commitments from the outset. We honor and pay due respect to those commitments not by blindly deferring to them, but by elucidating their place in sustaining and ennobling human existence. This elucidation places our pious allegiances within the everyday discourse of giving and asking for reasons and so allows us to invite our fellow citizens to partake in the richness of our lives.

This sensitivity to pluralism in religious matters makes Dewey very attentive to the presence of moral conflict. To be sure, inquiry does seek to achieve resolution among conflicting moral claims, but Dewey acknowledges that the result of reflection may be to reveal the incommensurability of values. Too often, however, we are seduced into believing that the very fact of pluralism and the inevitability of conflict imply some deeper crisis in normative evaluation. We are told that the world is disenchanted because we are without a nonhuman background to which we can appeal to adjudicate between moral conflicts. Yet Dewey shows us that even amid conflict there still exist resources within our social practices to guide and assess moral reflection. We are beings for whom it is natural to be moral and this implies a normative character to our entrance into the world at birth and participation in social practices throughout life. As Dewey argues, the question is not whether we will be moral agents and so engage in evaluation of right and wrong, good and bad, but rather with what skill will we exercise that agency.

The unifying theme throughout much of Dewey's reflections on religion and the moral life turns on a certain way of understanding inquiry, how it opens us up to the possibility of transformation even as it places us in positions where we court danger and so come to acknowledge the limitations of human existence. Yet again and again we come back to a kind of anti-authoritarian impulse—a vision that rejects the claim that some few have privileged access to truth and so are beyond the practice of giving and asking for reasons. This view informs and profoundly shapes Dewey's democratic philosophy. After all, given the specific connection he draws between inquiry and modern science, we worry (and rightfully so) that his view invites epistemic elitism. And yet it is precisely his specific understanding of inquiry and its cooperative character, I argue, that provides us with an appropriate way to think about the relationship between experts and the larger public so that epistemic power does not lapse into domination. In fact, if we take seriously the relationship between contingency and action that is the backdrop of democracy, Dewey helps us see the inescapable incompleteness of democratic politics. For him, democracy is that regime that instantiates reason-giving as the fundamental principle for legitimating its ongoing affairs, even as that principle always already points beyond any final settlement of democratic practices and institutions.

These discrete, but connected accounts revolve around the centrality of the reflective and contestable character of inquiry. They are seen, in this study, as emerging from a mature vision of human enlightenment—an account that demands intervention on our part and cautions humility at every turn.

That I have framed this work partly as an engagement with Dewey scholars should not obscure the fact that I find much of their work compelling. In engaging their works, I hope I have been steady and careful in my judgments, that my inferences have not been carelessly drawn, and that once complete, these thinkers would see this book as a complement to rather than an attempted refutation of their own hard intellectual work. I make this point explicit so that the reader can properly receive the book and understand where it hopes to stand among others like it. In doing so, my central goal is to say that there remain untapped resources in Dewey that can help us navigate our very complex individual and collective lives.

My engagement, then, with Dewey scholars and the elucidation and defense of his work is about so much more. It is about a certain way of seeing ourselves as human beings under modern democratic conditions attempting to realize the good in life. In this respect, the book is consistent with Dewey's deepest belief that philosophies are "not colorless intellectual readings of reality, but men's most passionate desires and hopes, their basic beliefs about *the sort of life to be lived*" (PD [MW 11:44 (emphasis added)]). The defining feature of Dewey's philosophy—and an outlook that we are desperately in need of cultivating in these uncertain times—is an understanding of humility that does not extinguish hope. We build better than we know, and worse than we could ever imagine. The first encourages our forward-looking outlook as we engage each other and the natural world that we inhabit, while the second demands that we not become too sure of ourselves, that we reject the presumptive belief that justice and right are on our side, and that we alone have a claim to truth beyond contestability.

ACKNOWLEDGMENTS

Acknowledgments can never communicate the true depth of one's appreciation. With that in mind: The manuscript has benefited greatly from the insights of Ian Shapiro, Steven Smith, Brain Garsten, and Seyla Benhabib. During my stay at Princeton University (2004–2005), both Jeffrey Stout and Cornel West provided a great deal of intellectual assistance on this project. Their joint course on contemporary pragmatism that I visited intermittently was of profound importance for my thinking about the ethical and religious significance of pragmatism. Additionally, Thomas Alexander, Raymond Boisvert, William Caspary, Vincent Colapietro, Michael Eldridge, Jill Frank, Hans Joas, James Kloppenberg, Colin Koopman, Todd Lekan, Eric MacGilvray, John Shook, John Smith, Bob Pepperman Taylor, and Robert Westbrook provided helpful insights and/or comments for thinking about the arguments in this book.

During my time as a student at Bowdoin and Amherst College, then as a graduate student at Cambridge and Yale, and a faculty member at Carleton College and now the University of Virginia, I have incurred a great deal of intellectual debt. Jean Yarbrough and Paul Franco sparked my interest in political theory and nurtured my ideas. Jeffrey Ferguson, Robert Gooding-Williams, and James Martel supported and encouraged my intellectual ambitions. Melissa Lane served as a helpful advisor to my first set of reflections on Dewey. John McCormick has been a steady voice of encouragement and guidance. In recent years, Carleton College and members of the political science department there have provided generous support. In particular, Laurence Cooper, Kimberley Smith, Barbara Allen, Angela Curran, and Harry

Williams have been amazing colleagues and friends. Thanks must also be extended to my new colleagues at the University of Virginia, especially Lawrie Balfour, Colin Bird, George Klosko, and Stephen White.

Although many people have provided support to this endeavor, reading one or two chapters or simply listening to my thoughts on Dewey, there is one person who deserves special mention, Eddie S. Glaude. He first sparked my interest in Dewey and read several versions of this project. He helped me improve its overall quality and direction. But most important, it was with his guidance during my undergraduate time at Bowdoin, after I transferred to Amherst, and during my graduate career that I discovered my most enduring and important intellectual habits. He has been my walking buddy on every intellectual adventure. If my parents nurtured my habits for managing life, then it seems appropriate to say that he has nurtured my habits for the life of the mind. We can repay such debts only through the quality of the life we live and the work we produce. I hope this work complements his important book, *In a Shade of Blue: Pragmatism and the Politics of Black America*.

For their friendship and dialogue during the process of writing this book, I am especially indebted to Kevin Wolfe, Jack "Chip" Turner, Michelle Tolmin Clarke, Ethan Lieb, and the students in my classes at Carleton, especially Ryan McLaughlin, Terin Mayer, and Colin Bottles.

Thanks must also be extended to Columbia University Press. Wendy Lochner, senior executive editor, showed steadfast support for this book from the beginning. The comments I received from her and the anonymous reviewers helped me to improve the overall quality of the book. I hope I have done justice to their important insights. Finally, I must say thank you to my copy editor, Kerri Cox Sullivan, who substantially improved the book.

All that I am and may yet become I owe to my family: my parents, Yvonne and Roosevelt Rogers; my sisters, Crystal Rogers, Tiffany Rogers, Aisha Rogers, and Bunnie Rogers; my brothers, Jonathan Rogers and James Rogers. I love them so very much. To Esther Saver and Sandra Unger: words cannot capture the place you occupy in my heart. That I have included both of you, my former high school teachers, among family should be no surprise. You have nurtured me during my times of disappointment and cheered me on throughout my moments of triumph. Chance may have introduced us, but choice underwrites your steadfast encouragement! To close friends Cindy, Toyce, Eddie, Willie, and Shawn, either in word or deed, you all provide a break from the mundane. And to my partner, Frederick: I find both purpose and hope in your company, and with you my failures are never final but only reasons to try again and much harder.

I thank *Transactions of Charles S. Peirce Society* for allowing me to reprint material originally published in their pages. An early version of chapter 2 was published as "Action and Inquiry in Dewey's Philosophy," *Transactions* 43, no. 1 (2007): 90–115.

ABBREVIATIONS

All references to Dewey's works appear in-text unless otherwise noted. Citations will include first the essay or book abbreviation, then series abbreviation with volume number, and last the page number(s) (e.g., PP [LW2:214]).

CLT   "Challenge to Liberal Thought" (1944)

DAP   "The Development of American Pragmatism" (1925)

DE   *Democracy and Education* (1916)

DEA   "Democracy and Educational Administration" (1937)

DR   "Dr. Dewey Replies" (1933)

E_1 "Ethics" (1904)

E_2 *Ethics* (1908)

E_3 *Ethics* (1932)

ED   "The Ethics of Democracy" (1888)

EKV   "Experience, Knowledge, Values: A Rejoinder" (1939)

EN   *Experience and Nature* (1925)

ENR   "Experience and Nature: A Re-Introduction" (1948)

EPD   "Emerson—the Philosopher of Democracy" (1903)

ETK   "The Experimental Theory of Knowledge" (1910)

EWLP   "The Existence of the World as a Logical Problem" (1915)

F   "Freedom" (1937)

FC   *Freedom and Culture* (1939)

HNC   *Human Nature and Conduct* (1922)

HWT_1 *How We Think* (1910)

HWT_2 *How We Think* (1933)

IB   "I Believe" (1939)

IDP   "The Influence of Darwin on Philosophy" (1910)

IM   "Intelligence and Morals" (1910)

ION   *Individualism, Old and New* (1929)

L   *Logic: Theory of Inquiry* (1938)

LCM   "Logical Conditions of a Scientific Treatment of Morality" (1903)

LFW   "Lessons from the War—in Philosophy" (1941)

LJP   "The Logic of Judgment of Practice" (1915)

LSA   *Liberalism and Social Action* (1935)

MPL   "Maeterlinck's Philosophy of Life" (1911)

NG   "Nature and Its Good: A Conversation" (1910)

NRP   "Need for Recovery of Philosophy" (1917)

OTE   "Outlines for a Critical Theory of Ethics" (1891)

P   "Progress" (1929)

PAL   "Philosophy and American National Life" (1904)

PD   "Philosophy and Democracy" (1919)

PFSA   "Philosophy's Future in Our Scientific Age: Never Was Its Role More Crucial" (1949)

PIE   "The Postulate of Immediate Empiricism" (1905)

PLT   "Present Position in Logical Theory" (1891)

PME   "Psychological Method in Ethics" (1903)

POF   "Philosophies of Freedom" (1928)

PON   "The Principle of Nationality" (1917)

PP   *The Public and Its Problems* (1927)

PPI   "Introduction" to *The Public and Its Problems* (1946)

PWHS   "The Philosophical Work of Herbert Spencer" (1904)

QC   *The Quest for Certainty* (1929)

QT   "Qualitative Thought" (1930)

RE   "Reality as Experience" (1906)

RIP   *Reconstruction in Philosophy* (1920)

ROS   "Religion and Our Schools" (1908)

RPO   "Review of Public Opinion" (1922)

RPP   "Practical Democracy. Review of Walter Lippmann's *The Phantom Public*" (1927)

SLT   *Studies in Logical Theory* (1903)

SSM   "Science as Subject-Matter and as Method" (1909)

SSSC   "Social Science and Social Control" (1931)

TIM   "Three Independent Factors in Morals" (1930)

TIM$_2$ "Three Independent Factors in Morals: Introductory Remarks and Discussion" (1930)

VEK   "Valuation and Experimental Knowledge" (1922)

WIB   "What I Believe" (1930)

WJ   "William James" (1910)

WPP   "What Pragmatism Means by Practical" (1916)

THE UNDISCOVERED DEWEY

INTRODUCTION

John Dewey's writings are widely recognized as an important contribution to democratic theory. As Robert Westbrook writes in his seminal intellectual biography, *John Dewey and American Democracy*:

> Dewey was the most important advocate of participatory democracy, that is, of the belief that democracy as an ethical ideal calls upon men and women to build communities in which the necessary opportunities and resources are available for every individual to realize fully his or her particular capacities and powers through participation in political, social and cultural life.[1]

This characterization is further crystallized in recent interpretations that locate Dewey firmly on the side of deliberative democracy.[2] Interpreters identify the normative content of his conception of participation, thus distinguishing it from the narrower descriptions of democratic politics that can be found in Walter Lippmann or Joseph Schumpeter.[3] In Dewey's view both representative government and deliberation among the citizenry are fundamental interacting features of democracy. The connection between the two binds political accountability and justification and foregrounds the intersubjective or cooperative character of legitimate political action. Political action is instrumental in that it aims to solve specific problems. But for Dewey political action also includes the transformative intentions that we have come to associate with deliberative democracy.[4] For him, democratic deliberation is fundamentally about crafting policy decisions that seek to be of benefit to the community at large rather than to just a single-party interest.

Yet fruitful retrieval is undercut by a long-standing criticism that centers on his attempt to link what he calls the "scientific method" to democracy (SSM [MW6:69–80]; L [LW12: pt. IV]). In brief, Dewey extends to democracy the model of science as it embodies publicity, fallibilism, and testing hypotheses against expected consequences. But the connection, or so his critics argue, does much more: it suggests that if we only extend the methods of science to social life, then will we be able to engineer a form of society that can manage the problems of collective organization and thereby eventuate in moral and political progress. This much Bertrand Russell has in mind when, in 1910, he writes: "Pragmatism appeals to the temper of mind which finds on the surface of this planet the whole of its imaginative material; which feels confident of progress, and unaware of non-human limitations to human power; which loves battle, with all the attendant risks, because it has no real doubt that it will achieve victory."[5] John Patrick Diggins makes a similar remark, linking Dewey to the Enlightenment tradition: "Although Dewey has been hailed for ridding philosophy of epistemology in order to bring it into the modern world . . . he appears to be returning to the eighteenth-century French Enlightenment in his conviction of a rational world responsive to scientific manipulation."[6] One who follows Dewey's outlook, Diggins says earlier, "identifies knowledge with control rather than understanding, with mastery rather than meaning."[7]

Diggins' worry over Dewey's faith in progress and the corresponding belief that it will come about by the use of the "scientific method" has an underlying meaning that cannot be understated. It is motivated, like Russell's criticism, by the thought that Dewey lacks a sense of our limitations—an appreciation for the looming sense of catastrophe, whether it be in the form of power or sin. Connecting him to the Enlightenment, then, is meant to remind us that amid Dewey's criticisms of certain aspects of modernity, he nonetheless appears to succumb to its hubris. This point is strongly asserted in Patrick Deneen's recent book *Democratic Faith*, in which he argues, among other things, that what is missing from Dewey's account is a sense of humility. For him, Dewey has bequeathed to us an orientation toward the world in which we move between an elevated sense of human possibilities and an intractable sense of despair that results from a confrontation with recalcitrant dimensions of the human condition.[8]

This general concern with the primacy of method, progress, and the lack of epistemic modesty and therefore humility in social action lends itself to two more specific criticisms. Hilary Putnam worries that in moral and political matters, Dewey seems unable to recognize genuine conflicts among human values—conflicts that bespeak the limits of inquiry.[9] As Eric Mac-Gilvray recently remarks in agreement with him: "To be sure, social conflict exists, but they appear in Dewey's political thought as symptoms of a kind of self defeating ignorance or blindness."[10] Dewey's desire for reconciliation through intelligence—a residue of his earlier Hegelian commitments, as Mac-Gilvray explains—obscures the possibility of irresolvable tension. C. Wright Mills, Christopher Lasch, and others argue that Dewey's privileging of science ironically lends itself to an elitist conception of democracy, which blocks ordinary citizens from engaging in deliberation about matters of collective concern.[11] Modeling democracy after scientific communities, coupled with greater levels of complexity in modern society, seemingly shrinks the number of knowledgeable participants that can and should comprise the space of political reflection. As such, Dewey seems unable to address the potential eclipse of the public by a form of power that is grounded in expert knowledge and harnessed by political elites.[12]

AVOIDING THE CRITICISM:
DEWEY'S DARWINIAN ENLIGHTENMENT

To be sure, there are differences among Dewey's critics. Nonetheless, their various worries are linked by two underlying claims. The first of these relates to ontology or metaphysics.[13] MacGilvray summarizes its content when he says: "Dewey's own faith in the experimental ideal rests upon three related assumptions about the nature of reality: that it has a fundamentally rational character, that its rational character can be grasped by unaided human reason, and that we can ultimately (and perhaps only) grasp its rational character in common."[14] These are striking assertions; Dewey appears to be less Darwinian and more Newtonian in both his reading of reality and his aspirations regarding inquiry.

In this context the second underlying worry emerges. This is the sense that the ontological claim is bound up with epistemological aspirations. If Dewey is saying what MacGilvray attributes to him, then any Deweyan inquirer will always already interpret the difficulties of life as resulting from a failure to think clearly or gain more information, a problem which can then be surmounted only if we delineate the demands of the scientific method and adhere to it consistently. Such a position, if this reading is accurate, merely relocates the source of human salvation, rather than abandoning how we understand that term altogether. Here we have a psychological orientation that raises the level of expectation, one that is on par with the optimism of the Enlightenment. Indeed, all of the criticisms above can be drawn back to this ontological claim and its epistemological aspirations in one way or another.

The previous sentence is advanced with care. After all, I am placing both sympathetic and unsympathetic interpreters of Dewey under a single umbrella. Although the reader may concede that criticisms by Diggins and Deneen for example may well presuppose the description above, surely the same cannot be said of someone like Putnam or, as I shall suggest later, Cornel West and Dewey's most thoughtful reader, Westbrook. I will come back to the texture of these thinkers' views later, but at this juncture two points need to be observed. First, these thinkers often disagree about how the rational character of reality displays itself in Dewey's philosophy. For Diggins, in Dewey's philosophy reality is bent and manipulated by human will so as to affirm the will's aspirations. At crucial moments in Putnam and Westbrook's readings of Dewey, reality seems *always already* conducive to inquiry.[15] Second, there are differences in the emphases these thinkers place on the hubris of inquiry. Putnam and Westbrook are thus very careful in laying out Dewey's sensitivity to the problems in experience and the role of experimentalism therein. Indeed, I see my views as continuous with theirs in some crucial respects. Yet when they examine his moral philosophy in particular, Dewey's account of inquiry seems far more ambitious and less attentive to moral conflict and value pluralism. An important question emerges. What is his lack of or inconsistent attentiveness to moral conflict meant to tell us about his philosophy? For these thinkers, I suggest, it means that Dewey presupposes that a rational and harmonious character for reality is always achievable. Here, the epistemological aspiration seemingly reveals both itself and the ontology from which it proceeds.

These criticisms invariably trade on a misconception. They assume that Dewey's faith in our ability to change our circumstances for the better blinds him to (1) the inability of human beings to completely control their environment, and therefore (2) the necessity of cultivating an orientation of responsiveness to the complexities of the modern world that chastens and conditions how we understand human intervention. To be clear, the differences among sympathetic and unsympathetic interpreters of Dewey will affect how this misconception is seen to play itself out, but this does not preclude the fact that this misconception is at work.

If the fundamental criticism hinges on his account of inquiry and the presumed self-assertion it encourages, we need a richer narrative that will allow us to receive Dewey in a different light. The overriding theme of this book is that his conception of inquiry—particularly as it functions as a guide for life—is based on a balanced and defensible criticism of modern thought. As Dewey sees it, modern thought, at least as it comes to expression in the Cartesian and Newtonian quest for certainty, wrongly characterizes the relationship that obtains between human beings and the natural world. Indeed, there are key overlaps between the theological vision of certainty and modern thought more generally. But this mischaracterization emerges most clearly, I suggest, if we examine the problematic intersection of religious certainty and Darwinian evolution in late-nineteenth-century America—an intersection that captures a number of concerns with which Dewey is preoccupied at the beginning of the twentieth century.

I have no doubt that Dewey advances ontological claims. He devotes an entire book—*Experience and Nature* (1925)—to the subject. For him, it is unlikely one can offer a social and political philosophy without a vision of what it means to be a human being and to exist within the natural world. But these commitments are far weaker than his critics believe, owing to the importance of Darwin to his thought. If, as Ralph Ketcham notes, the first Enlightenment had as its exemplar "Newtonian guidelines of order, balance, and harmony," and the second, which includes Dewey, has "Darwinian guidelines of struggle, competition, and indeterminacy," then the Promethean possibilities that attend inquiry should proceed from a standpoint of humility.[16]

I do not attempt to offer a historical narrative in this book regarding the two Enlightenments, except where Dewey's work itself implies such a distinction. Yet the distinction that Ketcham articulates cannot be understated and deserves modest elucidation. Newtonian guidelines of order, balance, and harmony (aspirations that Descartes shared) persisted into the nineteenth century and contributed then, as they had in the seventeenth century, to a desire to reconcile reason and faith, science and religion. The new science of the seventeenth century developed out of a practical engagement with the natural world that did not expunge God from the universe. In this context, the global distinction between some key rationalists and empiricists (which holds true along several lines) often belies a more subtle consensus. As Jonathan Israel explains in his exhaustive study, *Enlightenment Contested*, Descartes, Newton, Locke, and Kant believed in the force of reason precisely because "man . . . [dwelt] in a divinely ordered universe."[17] This string of names comprises a very complicated and deep intellectual history that Israel recently dubbed as the "moderate Enlightenment," and which I identify as the Cartesian and Newtonian Enlightenment. But Israel's use of "moderate" contains an important paradox; it denotes a circumspection of reason that *seemingly* acknowledges its limits, but only because reason belongs to a universe that declares the splendor of God. The power accorded to reason, whose conceptual development we have come to associate with thinkers as diverse as Descartes and Hegel, contains more than a hint of the divine.

This is something that Dewey equally highlights in his classic 1929 Gifford Lectures, *The Quest for Certainty*, partly to indicate the more radical character of his own experimentalism. As he explains, the belief in a divinely ordered universe has been central to "modern spiritualistic philosophies since the time of Kant; indeed, since that of Descartes, who first felt the poignancy of the problem in reconciling the conclusions of science with traditional religious and moral beliefs" (QC [LW4:33]). But this approach, as Dewey goes on to argue in that work, often led to a bifurcation between *theoria* and *praxis*, and a relative inattentiveness to the internal uncertainty of the latter. Although the new science made experimentalism central to its outlook, the metaphysics of nature in which it was located meant that the experimental approach could only be half-hearted. The desire for reconciliation along with this half-hearted experimentalism played itself out no less in the late-nineteenth-century debates over religion and science, specifically evolution, helping to explain why, in America, Darwin disrupted what was otherwise an amicable relationship.[18] Darwin centralized contingency, as opposed to order, harmony, and regularity, as the essence of existence, and Dewey exploited its significance to outline a vision of human enlightenment that at once encouraged self-assertion and cautioned epistemic and practical humility.

I begin, then, with an emphasis on the nineteenth-century debates over religion and evolution in the United States because this background will help to centralize the Darwinian horizon that figures so prominently in Dewey's philosophy. Indeed, it allows us to disrupt the strong ontological claim attributed to him so that the other specific worries cited above will no longer seem viable. In the following, I want to argue for the importance of my beginning point and outline the argumentative moves it makes possible. In doing the latter I will indicate how my argument differs from other interpretations of Dewey's philosophy.

REDIRECTION:
RELIGIOUS CERTAINTY AND THE QUEST FOR MEANING

In the latter of half of the nineteenth-century, America underwent dramatic social and political changes. Unlike earlier generations, Americans could no longer retain the belief in their special status—that of a chosen people—the view that God had ordained the United States as that nation which would usher in a new world through its religious commitments, political tradition, and fluid class structure. The Civil War, for example, had pointed to the limits of America's political tradition—that it was not a nation beyond hypocrisy and violence. Industrialization and urbanization underscored differences of wealth, which, although not enshrined in a class structure akin to feudalism, nonetheless embodied divisions that cut against the belief that class boundaries were in fact fluid. Between the years 1870 and 1920 the otherwise amicable relationship discussed earlier between science and religion changed dramatically.[19] Charles Darwin's 1859 work *The Origin of Species* marked an important advancement in theories of evolution, the result of which, however unintended, was to weaken religious orthodoxy. While it would be inaccurate to exaggerate the importance of this development above all the rest of the era, it nonetheless figures prominently because it shook the framework within which one might address the other concerns. In the minds of many Americans, slavery and the persistence of racism that followed after the Civil War were connected to the economic changes that undermined social responsibility and the persistence of a truly egalitarian society because both signaled a deficiency in America's moral compass.

Nowhere is the concern over Darwin's impact more explicit than among some of the most important theologians and preachers of the time.[20] Charles Hodge, professor of theology at Princeton Seminary and founder of the popular *Princeton Review,* is of singular importance in this regard. He stands as the most appropriate proxy for a more general worry and provides perhaps the clearest articulation of the perceived problem.[21] In brief, like others of the time, Hodge worried about the radical contingency that informed natural selection. It denied the divine goodness that was otherwise attached to the unfolding of both the world and the lives of its inhabitants. As James Kloppenberg remarks on just this point: "If evolution proceeded by means of random variations and competition for scarce resources, then Darwin's ideas made nonsense of theological arguments from design" and of the claim that the meaningful character of the moral and political universe rested on something more certain than mere social volition.[22] Natural selection implied a genuine unpredictability to life independent of one's knowledge of antecedent conditions, defying other goal-directed notions of evolution found in Jean-Baptiste Lamarck, Robert Chambers, and Herbert Spencer. While Darwin lamented his use of "selection" because it implied intent, "natural selection" nonetheless meant that chance rather than necessity determined the adaptive viability of variations. There was no *telos* toward which those changes aimed and no essence of which they were expressive. And this scientific reality, in Hodge's view, could not exist alongside the belief in an ordered universe constructed by God. More important for Hodge, in lacking the object of one's piety—i.e., God—Americans would be without a sense of purpose and commitment to self and society.

Still others amended Darwin's insights so as to sustain the larger faith in America's special place and retain the belief in progress that it implied. Here I am referring to liberal Protestants such as Henry Ward Beecher, Lyman Abbott, John Fiske, and James McCosh.[23] Indeed, the use of the qualifier "liberal" means to signal those who felt that an amicable relationship between religious commitments and science was nonnegotiable and indeed essential. But this second response, often articulated in Darwin's name, merely reconceptualized the theory by abandoning the view of contingency that was so central to it in order to reaffirm a vision of epistemic certainty that provided guidance at the moral and political levels of existence. One vision languished in the disappointment and despair that it attached to the ascendancy of Darwin's theory, while the other expressed a cosmic optimism about human abilities precisely because of it. This is but the barest sketch of a more complicated account to which we shall return in chapter 1.

To suggest, however, that Dewey's writings constitute a third way in this debate might seem altogether misguided. We find no explicit reference to this debate in his corpus. Nor does he discuss (if he does at all) the work of these thinkers in any substantive detail. From Dewey's perspective, among the three founding pragmatists, it was William James who concerned himself with the relationship among moral life, science, and religious commitments. This much Dewey explains when he says that James sought to give shape to "a *via media* between the natural sciences and the ideal interests of morals and religion" (WJ [MW6:96] [original emphasis]). But James, Dewey continues, was alone in his task.[24]

Moreover, Dewey's mature philosophical position—a move away from Hegelian idealism to pragmatism in the 1890s—is characterized by a shift in venue from the University of Michigan, where he was actively involved as a member of the Congregational Church, to the University of Chicago, where we find no record of his participation in organized religion. Looking back over his earlier period, Dewey remarks in 1930 that he had "not been able to attach much importance to religion as a philosophic problem; for the effect of that attachment seems to be in subordination of . . . thinking to the alleged but factitious needs of some special set of convictions" (AE$_1$ [LW5:153]). Many commentators take this point seriously, thereby leaving me with very little upon which to stake my claim.

There is reason then to question my beginning point, given that Dewey never seems to address or acknowledge the problem identified above. To be sure, if we treat the crisis of religious certainty as merely a theological debate among academics about the existence of God, the importance of supernaturalism, or how we should interpret scripture and doctrinal obedience, then we conclude rightly about Dewey's lack of philosophical interest. He should therefore not be read as contributing to a set of debates and discourses from which he explicitly abstains.

But this conclusion, too, depends on whether we have accurately described the moment. For as D. H. Meyer writes, these issues were merely placeholders for something more: "Although the formal intellectual issue was the existence or non-existence of God, the God-question was really only a convenient symbol for the growing feeling that, as Nietzsche put it, the highest values were losing their value, and that certainty was no longer possible in matters of ultimate concern."[25] The worry was that without inalterable foundations all beliefs lose their meaningful quality and claim on us. Indeed, this theme figured prominently in Max Weber's classic reflections on disenchantment and rationality, which, like Hodge's arguments, elevated the issue to a problem of the cognitive attitude of modern individuals.[26] Of course, there was a difference between the two: Hodge's worry was limited to his analysis of Darwin whereas Weber's concern emerged from an interpretation of the internal logic of the modern scientific tradition. Still, the issue was the same: In the absence of a sacred bedrock, how could we find one value or end more compelling than another? Although more attention is given to how this question emerged in the American context, it should be observed that it extended beyond both the precinct of theological seminaries and America largely because it went to the very heart of the modern imaginary, suggesting that the crisis of religious certainty implied a crisis of normative evaluation.[27] Indeed, all these thinkers were animated by a constellation of ideas and concerns despite not explicitly engaging one another.

These common problems are more than sufficient to justify placing Dewey in conversation with them; this will also elucidate Dewey's philosophy. We are able to discern in his writings an attempt to contribute to the cognitive and practical health of modern societies, for his philosophy principally seeks to reorient us to our values—that is, to acknowledge their socially constructed character, the way their meaning is indexed to the likely consequences that follow in negotiating the world and so are therefore in need of justification, and their inescapable fragility. The necessity of reorientation comes about in part because of the larger worry Darwin sparks, suggesting a more fundamental connection to the debate above. As Dewey says, the genuine tension was not between "science on the one side and theology on the other," but the more lasting issue of whether we will believe that our values emerge from "the mutual interaction of changing things" or look for "them in some transcendent . . . region" (IDP [MW4:6]). The first of these, says James in 1907, "turns away from abstraction and insufficiency, from verbal solutions, from bad *a priori* reasons, from fixed principles, closed systems, and pretended absolutes and origins. . . . It means the open air and possibilities of nature."[28] While James was seemingly alone in his attempt to find a manageable relationship among science, religion, and morals in the nineteenth century, Dewey rightly adds that his approach was a siren call that changed the "temper of imagination" in the twentieth century (WJ [MW6:96]).[29] The content of this changed imagination, in my view, comes in significant part from Dewey's philosophy.

His is a third way between spiritual sickness or disenchantment and Protestant self-assertion precisely because all three positions engage the same underlying existential concerns and generate reverberations that affect our moral, religious, and political outlooks. This much he suggests in a commencement address, "Philosophy and American National Life," given at the University of Vermont in 1904. We shall return to this address in the next chapter, but it is worth noting here that he highlights the need for philosophical reflection in order to be attentive to the intractable features of ordinary existence. And he remarks on the need to refashion our vision of the self and its orientation toward the natural world. Here, in rudimentary form, we find the concern for articulating an alternative position:

> If our civilization is to be directed, we must have such a concrete and working knowledge of the individual as will enable us to furnish on the basis of the individual himself substitutes for those modes of nurture, of restraint and of control which in the past have been supplied from authorization supposedly fixed outside of and beyond individuality. (PAL [MW3:75])

This emphasis on the individual does not bespeak a form of subjectivism, but rather a recentering of the human subject as the source from which meaning in life and its authorization spring. Meaning and authorization emerge not from exclusive appeal to antecedent phenomena as we find in both Hodge and liberal Protestants, but from consequent transactions between us and the larger natural environment (DAP [LW2:12]). Our continuity with nature as organic beings means that interaction and change are always about us, but when an interaction "intervenes which directs the course of change, the scene of natural interaction has a new quality and dimension.

This added type of interaction *is* intelligence" (QC [LW4:171] [original emphasis]). This position, as Dewey well knows, courts danger. As he says in *Experience and Nature*:

> Everything that man achieves and possesses is got by actions that may involve him in other and obnoxious consequences in addition to those wanted and enjoyed. His acts are trespasses upon the domain of the unknown. . . . While unknown consequences flowing from the past dog the present, the future is even more unknown and perilous; the present by that fact is ominous. If unknown forces that decide future destiny can be placated, the man who will not study the methods of securing their favor is incredibly flippant. In enjoyment of present food and companionship, nature, tradition and social organization have cooperated, thereby supplementing our own endeavors so petty and so feeble without this extraneous reinforcement. Goods are by grace not of ourselves. (EN [LW1:44])

There is a two-pronged argument at work in this passage. In the first instance, Dewey does not deny that ours is a narrative that includes important advances in scientific developments. As he argues in both *Reconstruction in Philosophy* of 1920 and *The Quest for Certainty* of 1929, these advances bespeak an underlying method capable of avoiding the worst in our quest for the better (RIP [MW12: chap. 3]; QC [LW4: chaps. 3–6]). This is what the Enlightenment, whether in its Newtonian or Darwinian variants, has bequeathed to us. In his 1916 article "Progress" he writes the following of modernity: "[F]or the first time in history mankind is in command of the possibility of progress" (P [MW10:237]).

Here we sense at work the cognitive attitude Weber discerns in modern science that brings about disenchantment, the belief that there are no "mysterious incalculable forces that come into play" and that "one can, in principle, master all things by calculation."[30] But as the passage above from *Experience and Nature* makes clear, this emphasis on progress exists alongside a fundamental uncertainty—a new repository of the mysteries of existence—that characterizes action and is more consistent with his Darwinian commitments. Our experiences of the world, on Dewey's account, do not exhaust the complexity and mysteries of our natural and social horizons. My earlier use of the adjective *fundamental* is more than appropriate precisely because Dewey is keen to emphasize that the goods we seek depend on a grace "not of ourselves." But for him the term denotes a grace that is bound up with the natural world to which we belong. Herein lies the problem of modern life: the experimentalist approach that he recommends for creating "new ideals and values" simultaneously implicates us in an unknown future that threatens our efforts (EN [LW1:4]). And for him there is little we can do, to borrow from Weber, to rid ourselves of those "mysterious incalculable forces." This is precisely why Dewey argues that "humility is more demanded at our moments of triumph than at those of failure. . . . It is the sense of our slight inability even with our best intelligence and effort to command events; a sense of our dependence upon forces that go their way without our wish and plan" (HNC [MW14:200]).

There is a crucial underlying difference that distinguishes Dewey from these other thinkers. Stephen White helps us capture this difference with his recent distinction between strong and weak ontological commitments—a distinction, I should add, that roughly lines up with the Newtonian and Darwinian Enlightenments discussed earlier. As he argues in *Sustaining Affirmation*, strong ontology, typically that of premodern and modern times, offers a vision of how the world is, the meaning of human nature, or visions of what God is and the responsibilities we have in relation to God.[31] But a strong ontology not only is articulated through revelation and the existence of the divine, but equally lends itself to the idiom of scientific investigation. With both, there exists in experience or outside of it self-justifying and credible characteristics that ground all claims of knowledge and serve as the final destination for epistemic adjudication. On a moral and political level, these fixed truths anchor institutions and identities in ways that ignore or suppress, under the pretense of control, uncertainty and the possibility of tragedy. As Dewey remarks in "The Influence of Darwin on Philosophy" of 1909, a strong metaphysics treats "change and origin as signs of defect and unreality" from which we must escape (IDP [MW4:5]). And he attributes this to both the eschatological narratives and the modern, philosophical quests for certainty.

A weak metaphysics, however, is different. As White remarks on this point:

> Ontology figures our most basic sense of human being, an achievement that always carries a propensity toward naturalization, reification, and unity, even if only implicitly. A weak ontology must possess resources for deflecting this propensity at some point in the unfolding of its dimensions. Its elaboration of fundamental meanings must in some sense fold back upon itself, disrupting its own smooth constitution of a unity. In a way, its contestability will thus be enacted rather than just announced.[32]

Ontological commitments are not neutral regarding identity and the natural world.[33] Dewey agrees on just this point: "Every social and political philosophy will be found upon examination to involve a certain view about the constitution of human nature: in itself and in its relation to physical nature" (FC [LW13:72]). So a weak ontology does not avoid articulating descriptions of self and world, it only prevents those descriptions from receding so far into the background that they are beyond revision and contestability. As Charles Peirce says: "Every man of us has a metaphysics, and has to have one; and it will influence his life greatly. Far better, then, that that metaphysics should be criticized and not be allowed to run loose."[34] Dewey's acknowledgment of contingency and emphasis on inquiry intends to prevent our metaphysics from running loose. This is his intention when he employs the words of Oliver Wendell Holmes in *Experience and Nature*:

> "That the universe has in it more than we understand, that the private soldiers have not been told the plan of campaign, or even that there is one ... has no bearing on our conduct. We still shall fight—all of us because we want to live, some, at least, because we want to realize our spontaneity and prove our powers, for the joy of it, and we may leave to the unknown the supposed final valuation of that which in any event has value to us. It is enough for us that the universe has produced us and has within it, as less than it, all that we believe and love. If we think of our existence not as that of a little god outside, but as that of a ganglion within, we have the infinite behind us. It gives us our only but our adequate significance." (EN [LW1:313])

To my mind, this cautionary note underwrites the reflective power of inquiry and constrains the ends to which it aims, whether those ends relate to religion, morality, or politics. This book attempts to follow this logic and its multifaceted character.

THE PLAN OF THIS BOOK

Let me say a bit more about my argument here and simultaneously indicate the differences between my position and other interpretations. After all, critics will no doubt wonder about the extent to which my account adds value to our understanding of Dewey. Does it justify such a cavalier title as *The Undiscovered Dewey*? There is a wealth of scholarship on Dewey, and it would be a mistake to say that my view constitutes a wholesale rejection of it all. By way of analogy you can think of this book as a piece of music of which the elements are familiar but stunningly different because of the arrangement. And as with music, the arrangement has the effect of providing the listener with a new way of experiencing the music; it unleashes moods within the listener and orientations toward the music that had gone untapped. Of course, it is true that the music is familiar, but it is in the arrangement that one experiences the music anew.

So my claim in making Darwin central to Dewey's later outlook is that important dimensions to Dewey's philosophy will emerge—aspects that have nonetheless been *overlooked, underappreciated,* or *denied.* As a result, we have not until now fully understood the resources he provides us for thinking about our religious, moral, and political commitments. I have sought in this work to provide a new arrangement—a way of appreciating and accepting these other aspects of Dewey's philosophy—so that we may experience his work anew. And if I am successful, it too will unleash moods within the reader and orientations toward his work that had otherwise gone untapped.

Isolating specific differences, in this regard, between my argument and the existing scholarship must therefore occur in the unfolding of the book. However, there is a group of thinkers (some more widely known than others) who cannot go ignored even at this early juncture, and so require explicit attention in the forthcoming outline. This is all the more important because they are sympathetic readers of Dewey, but readers whom I will nonetheless disagree with at critical junctures. Among these are Robert Westbrook, Steven Rockefeller, Alan Ryan, Raymond Boisvert, Michael Eldridge, James Campbell, Hilary Putnam, William Caspary, and Eric MacGilvray.

The book is divided into two parts. Part I, "From Certainty to Contingency," situates Dewey's appropriation of Darwin for understanding inquiry in the context of the crisis of religious certainty or modern disenchantment in the late nineteenth century. Part II, "Religion, the Moral Life, and Democracy," explores the way inquiry functions in the context of these respective dimensions of his philosophy. Although I proceed in an order different from the one he sketches, I am merely following Dewey's claim that Darwin "introduced a mode of thinking that in the end was bound to transform the logic of knowledge, and hence the treatment of morals, politics, and religion" (IDP [MW4:3]).

In chapter 1, I turn specifically to the impact of Darwin on America's religious imagination. I argue that this impact eventuates in a crisis that disrupts the moral economy of self and society, leading to spiritual sickness or disenchantment. Although my focus is largely on the American context, I have found it necessary to extend that analysis at several junctures via Weber's writings. This is largely because of the similarity among those who worry about the influence of Darwin on religion and Weber's own lament about the effects of modern science on the spiritual and moral foundations of existence. Moreover, employing Weber helps us to see that the worry expressed by Americans is not idiosyncratic, but rather taps into the deeper currents of modernity. Placing Dewey against this backdrop allows us to read his philosophy as an alternative to both the spiritual sickness that Hodge and Weber worry about and the cosmic optimism of some liberal Protestants. Dewey's alternative view, which emerges through his experimentalist approach to understanding knowledge formation and corresponding naturalistic account of human values, rejects the connection between meaning and certainty that is at work in these other positions. I go on to outline in the latter half of that chapter the general shape of this response.

This chapter will read more like a work of *stylized* intellectual history than of philosophy proper. And it is decidedly tilted away from Dewey. But I ask the reader to bear with me, for the story matters precisely to the extent that it casts into relief Dewey's alternative response. What I provide there has ample support from historians, but I am not a historian. I employ the historical framework and the questions therein to tease out similar concerns in Dewey. History, in this sense, is meant to inform but not wholly constrain, to direct but not wholly determine the philosophical resources and possibilities contained within Dewey's philosophy. It is above all else the possibilities of his philosophy with which this book is concerned, even though it will selectively employ history to access them.

In proceeding this way—that is, in showing how Dewey differs not only from Hodge and Weber but also from his liberal Protestant counterparts—I disagree slightly with Rockefeller's interpretation, which ironically links Dewey to liberal Protestantism. After all, to say, as he does, that Dewey humanizes Christianity implies a form of utopianism that must be then funneled through his account of inquiry. At the very moment when Rockefeller seemingly staves off the tendency to read Dewey as installing inquiry as the new key to the pearly gates, we read the following:

> [Dewey] views faith and love as flowers that bloom naturally when all the conditions are right—conditions of body, mind, and environment. Human beings should concentrate on using their intelligence to improve the natural conditions of moral and spiritual growth like diligent gardeners who trust their seeds, fertile soil, and the sun. His approach assumes the immanence of a divine creativity in nature, including human nature.[35]

Unfortunately, in Rockefeller's view, this divine creativity is identified with intelligence as such. With this, we easily lapse back into the critique advanced earlier. Dewey's faith in intelligence never seems tinged with the kind of uncertainty that distinguishes him from liberal Protestantism. Rather, he becomes their secular variant.[36] But this view overlooks the way Dewey rearticulates the meaning of inquiry and religious experience, distinguishing himself from the larger historical context with which he is often identified.

Focusing primarily, although not exclusively, on such works as "The Influence of Darwin on Philosophy," *Experience and Nature,* and *The Quest for Certainty,* chapter 2 argues that when we examine Dewey's experimentalism, the subtleties of inquiry come into focus—subtleties that seek to make us sensitive to the complexities of the horizon in which inquiry functions. This is because contingency saturates the domain of practical action; it stimulates the necessity of reflection and potentially frustrates or undermines its goals. The desire to escape peril as it relates to the moral life discussed in chapter 1 is a piece of what Dewey calls the quest for certainty that I set out to explain in chapter 2, and which he believes is central to the classical and modern outlook found in thinkers like Descartes, Newton, and Kant. Both obscure an appropriate understanding of our being-in-the-world, and this includes the extent to which value and meaning are coextensive with existence.

While such an account of inquiry bespeaks the fragility of life, it does not lead to a kind of spiritual malaise regarding the meaningfulness of the objects of inquiry.[37] Dewey's appropriation of Darwin helps him to locate value within the evolving transactions between self and world, giving human action an overall aesthetic and creative quality.[38] As he says in his major work on aesthetics in 1934: "Art is prefigured in the very processes of living" (AE$_2$ [LW10:30]). Yet his use of Darwin suggests a potential discontinuity between the aims of human action and what the world will allow. This discontinuity is grounded within the same contingent horizon that makes possible opportunities for creatively transforming our environment for the better in the first instance. Given this general framework, Dewey articulates a modest psychological profile in which the epistemic status we accord inquiry's productions is no longer bound up with the quest for certainty.

To be sure, inquiry as Dewey understands it does involve methodological elements. But given the field of value in which inquiry is located, especially in matters relating to moral and political governance, it cannot simply be a crass method. When read through a Darwinian framework, Dewey's understanding of inquiry resuscitates and expands Aristotle's notion of practical reason to all domains of human reflection. Inquiry's legitimating character draws from two different directions, the character of the individuals confronted with specific ruptures in experience on the one hand, and the larger social background in which both they and the problem are located on the other. As such, it involves fallibility, the willingness to engage in revision, and responsiveness to the larger horizon in which one is located.

This legitimating character is realized through the discursive medium of giving and asking for reasons for proposals or plans of action, and this constrains the radical aestheticism of human action that we see expressed by Richard Rorty.[39] But this view also begins to shed light on the normative resources of human self-understanding that are called into question by Hodge and Weber in the absence of a sacred foundation. In my view, Dewey's fundamental insight is that modernity read through Darwin raises the level of reflexivity to such an extent that to be a modern individual is at once to acknowledge the sources of a meaningful existence, the way they naturally direct our lives and generate obligations, and to understand that such sources are in no way shielded from critical reflection because their foundation is contingent. The result is that the anti-authoritarian character of inquiry—the sense that we are answerable to each other independent of wealth, birth, or intellectual endowment—exercises enormous influence over his reflections on religion, morality, and politics in modern life.

This anti-authoritarian character is not a value to which Dewey independently subscribes, but is bound up with his conception of situated intelligence. For him, the sociocultural contexts in which human reflection functions are subject to the vagaries of time. This means that there are no human-independent authorities that can adjudicate once and for all between rival claims, thus making any claim always contestable by others. Contestability simply means that because our beliefs about how to act in response to specific problems seek to be the best beliefs we can have, they are reason-responsive. In this sense, authority, whether it functions within our religious, moral, or political lives, is not divinely ordained or provided by intuition but rather emerges from a cooperative enterprise among human beings attempting to realize the good and avert the worse.

In many respects, the emphasis on contingency as distilled from Dewey's interpretation of Darwin is not new. We find this link articulated by Boisvert and Campbell.[40] And they emphasize, as I do, the way in which Dewey's turn to Darwin helps him to undermine the appeal to essences or some fundamental teleology. But they underappreciate the sheer unpredictability that informs human action. It is no wonder that Boisvert, in particular, can say that Dewey's emphasis on inquiry seems to have no sense of limitations.[41] The problem is that too much attention is given to inquiry's aim and not to the background domain of action from which it emerges and to which it must return for assessment. Shifting our attention to the latter holds in view the potential success as well as failure of inquiry. To be sure, there is still talk of human progress, but in my view it is consistently understood as a claim about historical possibility rather than ontological fact.

Understanding inquiry along these lines prepares the way for an examination of its connection to Dewey's religious, moral, and political philosophy in part II. Chapter 3 explores his religious naturalism by focusing primarily, although not exclusively, on *A Common Faith* (1934). The fundamental question here is the following: If contingency saturates the horizon from which inquiry proceeds, how are we to understand our religious commitments in the context of democracy? Here I focus on the relationship between inquiry and the moral virtues of piety and faith. In many ways, this chapter attends to the epistemic ethos that underwrites democracy. I reveal Dewey's profound sensitivity to modern pluralism, especially the absence of a unifying theological framework, and so begin to give texture to the anti-authoritarian character of his outlook. Similar to the approach taken by Ralph Waldo Emerson before him, Dewey argues for a view of self-reliance, but one that stands in between an account of identity that is exhausted by any one allegiance and one that denies the hold of allegiances altogether.

Indeed, he acknowledges that we must show pious allegiance to traditions, whether they derive from specific religions or from elsewhere. As he understands the matter, our ability to give meaning to the present would be crippled without piety. Precisely for this reason his position does not entail a constraint, as we see in John Rawls' *Political Liberalism*, on the source to which we can appeal in public debate even though he shares Rawls' aversion to philosophic and religious dogmatism and the place it could come to occupy in political life if left unchecked.[42] Rather, he maintains that the immediacy of those traditions and their relevance emerges because they are held up against the critical lens of reflection in the light of different experiences. His is a critical piety that blocks the past from having a permanent claim on how we move forward even as he acknowledges the inescapable importance of the past.

Here too his understanding of faith is grounded in his experimentalism. Our cognitive abilities do not necessarily outstrip the complexities of the world in which our religious ideals are located. Unlike piety, faith is primarily forward looking. Although I mention it in passing in chapter 2, I take up the character of experimentalism more completely in the context of Dewey's religious proposal. To be sure, experimentalism involves attentiveness to an existing state of affairs, but it is also about imaginatively transforming the present to guide action. Commitment to religious ideals is not necessarily exhausted by the existing state of evidence that may exist on their behalf. This does not, as one might think, place religion beyond the pale of inquiry, for the giving and accepting of reasons continues to function as we assess what affect our allegiance to those commitments will have on our current state of existence. The reflective capacity involved in belief-formation and ideal-formation is the same, but the two are distinguishable in Dewey's view by the fact that the latter produces a more comprehensive transformation in one's orientation in life.

Here my disagreement is not with Rockefeller, as one might think, but rather with Eldridge. To contend, as he does, that Dewey should have dropped the language of faith and piety because it departs from traditional accounts narrows the range of religious descriptions and therefore overlooks altogether Dewey's transformative intentions. If the account of chapter 1 is accurate, then Eldridge's argument seems overdrawn. To say that Dewey articulates his "secular project in religious language" makes him seem disingenuous and not interested in religious commitments at all.[43] This claim, however, is difficult to sustain. A more plausible view is that he seeks to articulate the democratic framework in which religious claims exist, and to explain how that framework partly conditions the functioning of those commitments. Dewey's claim, then, is quite similar to that expressed most recently by Jeffrey Stout: "The mark of secularization . . . is rather the fact that participants in a given discursive practice are not in a position to take for granted that their interlocutors are making the same religious assumption."[44]

In chapter 4 I turn to Dewey's moral philosophy to address two distinct but related issues. The first relates to the considerations of chapter 1. For Hodge, Weber, and the liberal Protestants, without a sacred foundation moral life is emptied of its evaluative compass. Second, this crisis of normative evaluation frames the discussion when critics argue (as indicated above) that Dewey does not seriously entertain value pluralism and the moral conflicts that invariably emerge. We might say, then, that it is the absence of the first (that is, an evaluative compass) that leads to the conflicts expressed by the second (that is, value pluralism). Focusing on works such as *Human Nature and Conduct* (1922), "Three Independent Factors in Morals" (1930), and his *Ethics* (1932), I tease out the ways in which Dewey is profoundly sensitive to moral conflict owing to his Darwinian commitments and thus provides an evaluative framework in which to locate and think about conflict.

Like Weber and contemporary moral theorists who emphasize the fact of modern pluralism, Dewey argues that conflict now arises with greater frequency because traditional attitudes, what he calls "customs," no longer determine the beginning and ending of one's self-understanding. This, for him, is the determinant social horizon in which we exist; it makes central the necessity of reflection. This tilts how we should understand moral deliberation. For him, it is a process in which we both imaginatively and discursively trace out courses of action and their potential consequences for settling conflicting demands. "It is," writes Dewey, "an attempt to uncover the conflict in its full scope and bearing," to reveal the "qualitative incompatibilities" of proposed decisions in search of a more inclusive option (HNC [MW14:150]). In its ideal form, deliberation seeks to manage conflict so that the final decision is more inclusive than either competing vision. What is at stake in this process, he contends, "is not a difference of quantity, but what kind of person one is to become, what sort of self is in the making, [and] what kind of world is [in the] making" (HNC [MW14:150]).

Yet Dewey is quite clear that this reflective moment may potentially (because its outcome is uncertain) deepen our sense of conflict, implicating us in feelings of loss or regret. These two positions—*resolution as harmony* and *resolution as tragic choice*—are potentialities of deliberation. In making this claim, I disagree with Westbrook, Putnam, Caspary, and MacGilvray, who either underappreciate Dewey's sensitivity to conflict or deny it all together. As Westbrook remarks, "Dewey's ethics, at its worst, suggested that one could always find a synthetic resolution that harmonized competing values."[45] But this confuses the ideal aim of deliberation with the actualities of moral life; the latter, as Dewey argues, may present us with a conflict of goods that defy harmonization.[46]

But there is a more radical position here aside from his sensitivity to conflict. For Dewey, managing our moral lives and the conflicts that emerge involves a kind of responsiveness that makes us attentive to the claims of others and the larger environment in which we exist. Although he does not deny that the ethical content of our identities is bound up with specific narratives of experience, he nonetheless seeks to explain the resources within our identities that allow for moral evaluation and growth. But where, we should ask, does this responsiveness come from, in Dewey's view? His answer is that it is coextensive with our *natural* introduction into social life as such. We are moral agents just insofar as we are antecedently participants in social practices, and this implies a character to moral evaluation that makes us attentive to self, other, and the natural world, if evaluation is to make sense at all. We might say, as Dewey does, that our *first*, biological, nature is developed and enhanced by our *second*, acquired, nature (HNC [MW14:60–65]). His argument is of significant importance because he shows us that absent a sacred horizon—*pace* Hodge, Weber, and the liberal Protestants—we can still speak intelligibly about what it means to be a moral agent. Normativity is not externally imposed on nature, but is nature's gift to us.

This form of naturalism shifts attention away from defending the proposition that the human world is *always already* a normative world to elucidating the perceptual and emotional resources that are part and parcel of the space of moral reflection. Thus, when Dewey discusses inquiry in the context of the moral life he emphasizes the way it allows us to see widely and feel deeply about the situations in which we are located. It not only involves a willingness to engage in revision, but an ability to consider the importance of normative principles and their limitation, and a kind of sympathetic outlook that feeds into the content of evaluation. Absent such features, the moral life would be unintelligible, for we would be without the basic features to render moral deliberation meaningful or explicable to ourselves and our fellows.

In chapter 5 I revisit the anti-authoritarian character of Dewey's understanding of inquiry, but now in the context of his democratic theory as articulated in *The Public and Its Problem* (1927) and his other political writings. The connection he draws between inquiry and democracy is rightfully interpreted as a theory of political justification and legitimacy. It is Dewey's appeal to inquiry as a method for justifying beliefs that feeds directly into and underwrites democratic deliberation. We find this articulated by Putnam, Caspary, Westbrook, and Ryan, yet none of these thinkers makes explicit the way Dewey's understanding of the relationship between inquiry and democracy can be recast as a preoccupation with power and domination.[47] This is made all the more striking when we concede an inequality in knowledge and epistemic skill among the citizenry on the one hand, and the complexity of modern societies on the other. As Weber, Lippmann, and Mills knew, this combination points away from expanding the domain of deliberation. If this interpretation is accurate, Dewey's emphasis on the importance of inquiry to democratic action may unintentionally point toward an epistemic guardianship that will inevitably lead to power inequity.

As I argue, Dewey's account of the relationship between inquiry and democracy is based on the claim that without having a say in decision-making, citizens leave their development or lack thereof open to arbitrary rather than directed control. Viewed from this perspective, he worries about the way power becomes domination insofar as knowledge employed for decision-making comes unhinged from broad mechanisms of accountability and inclusion. If we are to be affected by political decisions that most assuredly will involve systems of expertise in a complex democratic society, as Lippmann rightly highlights, then for Dewey those decisions cannot be distinguished from judgments about how to direct and assess reliance on such systems. It is the desire to block power from becoming domination that partly underwrites his presumptive commitment to inclusion.

But if Dewey rejects Lippmann's democratic elitism (while accepting pieces of his and others' understanding of modern complexity), I argue that he would equally find Sheldon Wolin's defense of democratic radicalism unconvincing. For Wolin, democracy is best thought of as an anarchic impulse that displays itself against the constraining force of institutional forms. In this view, political or representative democracy is a contradiction in terms, for it implies that democracy can be embodied in institutions without sacrificing rule by the people.[48] To be fair, Dewey rejects the reduction of democracy to institutions and he encourages eternal vigilance on the part of citizens. He is attentive to the ways in which institutions may ossify to the disadvantage of democracy, and in such instances he embraces a kind of radicalism akin to Wolin. Comparing Wolin to Dewey, then, helps us see the way in which the latter's vision does contain a radical impulse. Yet Dewey is not hostile to the existence of modern representative institutions as such. Indeed, political democracy, for him, provides the structural mechanisms to manage power relations so that they do not lapse into domination.

These structural mechanisms, however, proceed from a deeper level of uncertainty, which is at the core of democracy for Dewey. Precisely because the democratic public emerges from the intimate connection between contingency and practical activity, the institutions that are expressive of that public can never finally solidify and so the "we" that constitutes the public can never be permanently settled. In fact, his account cautions against fixing the identity of the public sphere. To say, then, that the practice of giving and asking for reasons is central to how democracy legitimizes itself is to say that at the very least it provides resources for overcoming (although not permanently) its own specific limitations. This outlook allows Dewey, I argue, to defend a view of the public sphere that is internally differentiated. This differentiation accounts for the smooth substantive inclusion of the demands of specific publics into the administrative apparatus of the state, even as it defends publics that emerge in a more oppositional relationship to state power.

If the course of this study is followed from beginning to end, what emerges is an account of Dewey's philosophy that demonstrates that it circumscribes inquiry, is less dismissive of religion than normally assumed, can aid us in understanding and seeing the immanence of normativity in our social practices, is sensitive to conflict and the inability to achieve resolution, and is concerned with defending a view of democracy that blocks power from becoming a dominating force. If this vision is sustainable, as I believe it is, we will have not only responded to Dewey's critics but discovered resources with which to critically engage the complexity of our modern lives. It is above all else this last issue with which this book and Dewey's philosophy are principally concerned.

FROM CERTAINTY TO CONTINGENCY

Where hope is unchecked by any experience, it is likely that our optimism is extravagant.

CHARLES S. PEIRCE, "The Fixation of Belief"

In a merely human world without a God, the appeal to our moral energy falls short of its maximal stimulating power. Life, to be sure, is even in such a world a genuinely ethical symphony; but it is played in the compass of a couple of poor octaves, and the infinite scale of values fails to open up. . . . When, however, we believe that a God is there, and that he is one of the claimants, the infinite perspective opens out. The scale of the symphony is incalculably prolonged.

WILLIAM JAMES, "The Moral Philosopher and the Moral Life"

When the future arrives with its inevitable disappointments as well as fulfillments, and with new sources of trouble, failure loses something of its fatality, and suffering yields fruit of instruction not of bitterness. Humility is more demanded at our moments of triumph than at those of failure. For humility is not caddish self-depreciation. It is the sense of our slight inability even with our best intelligence and effort to command events; a sense of our dependence upon forces that go their way without our wish and plan.

JOHN DEWEY, *Human Nature and Conduct*

PROTESTANT SELF-ASSERTION AND SPIRITUAL SICKNESS

Few deny the extraordinary influence John Dewey exerted during the first half of the twentieth century. His time at Columbia University, beginning in 1904, overlapped with a number of movements interested in laying out a social theory to underwrite political transformation. Both the Social Gospel and the Progressive movements of the previous century reached maturity in the twentieth, attempting on the one hand to elucidate the social commitment of Christianity as the only road to God and sustain the integrity of moral agency, and on the other to harness the power of institutions and the rising social sciences to improve human welfare against a willful and economically exclusive liberalism. In this context, Dewey addressed problems relating to economic and industrial life first in Chicago and then in New York. He sought to redefine the meaning of liberal democratic politics in order to sustain a society of free individuals without the deleterious impact such an account has if left unchecked by a vision of social responsibility.[1]

But Dewey's preoccupation with reform and persistent talk of the importance of science to political action prompts some of his admirers and critics to see him as an exemplar of self-assertion. Dewey, it is argued, synthesized the theological commitments of Protestantism with his theory of inquiry; he carried forward the commitment of his time to reformism based on a carefully worked out epistemology that leads to social engineering. The most important and sympathetic of these accounts has come in Steven C. Rockefeller's

John Dewey: Religious Faith and Democratic Humanism.[2] But its extension has taken a more critical turn, I believe. "The spirit of revelation [in Dewey]," Hans Joas writes disapprovingly, "is . . . 'sublated' in scientific inquiry, as the incarnation of God in man is 'sublated' in the democratic community."[3] In his *A Nation of Agents*, James Block extends the claim by connecting it to the larger horizon of twentieth-century America: "[Dewey's] vision of a progressively and transcendently realized liberal society invested early twentieth-century liberalism with the powerful cultural legacy of Protestant millennialism."[4] Such readings are continuous with a series of attacks that see Dewey as hopelessly optimistic regarding inquiry and his conception of experience (à la Cornel West and Richard Rorty), as encouraging self-assertion over and against humility (à la Reinhold Niebuhr and John Patrick Diggins), as unable to makes sense of the tragic dilemmas at the heart of our moral lives (à la Hilary Putnam and Raymond Boisvert).

These readings, I believe, go wrong at the level of ontology; they imply that Dewey misrepresents fundamental features of human existence through his account of inquiry, mistaking the irreducible circumstances of life for pathologies that can be surmounted rather than negotiated. But if we interpret his philosophy only as an analogical but secular application of liberal Protestantism, then we miss how his work undermines hubris and encourages humility. To put it crudely, we obscure the fact that inquiry-talk for Dewey is not doing the same work as God-talk does for liberal Protestants. In fact, Dewey's response to liberal Protestantism and the crisis of religious certainty indicates a thinker more circumspect about the ambitions of inquiry and more attentive to the spiritual sickness that closes the nineteenth century and opens the twentieth. It is to this moment that we must turn.

The image of the period that comes to mind, although in need of some qualification, is one William James offers us. In his 1902 Gifford Lectures, *The Varieties of Religious Experience* (1902), we find the following description of the sick soul:

> But there are others for whom evil is no mere relation of the subject to particular outer things, but something more radical and general, a wrongness or vice in his essential nature, which no alteration of the environment, or any superficial rearrangement of the inner self, can cure, and which requires a supernatural remedy.[5]

The description is arresting; here we have an account of individuals who long for comfort that outstrips temporal existence, and for whom the Jamesian voluntaristic outlook is unsatisfactory.[6]

James' description, however, is not readily transparent. Admittedly, he often speaks of the sick soul more as a temperament or character-type and less as a description of the age.[7] But in the context of late-nineteenth-century America spiritual sickness has a more expansive designation. The longing for a supernatural remedy is coeval with the sense that no such cure exists. Spiritual sickness thus denotes not estrangement from a unified and stable cosmological order—a state of mere sinfulness in the presence of God—but a full acknowledgment of its absence.[8] Spiritual sickness should be read as a forerunner to Max Weber's now famous account of disenchantment—an image in which science profoundly alters the outlook of individuals because it erodes the religious roots that sustain both them and society. Prefiguring Weber's description, in which science eviscerates meaning from nature, James writes the following in the latter part of *Varieties*:

> The Darwinian notion of chance production, and subsequent destruction, speedy or deferred, applies to the largest as well as the smallest of facts. It is impossible, in the present temper of the scientific imagination, to find in the drifting of the cosmic atoms, whether they work on the universal or on the particular scale, anything but a kind of aimless weather, doing and undoing, achieving no proper history, and leaving no result. Nature has no one distinguishable ultimate tendency with which it is possible to feel sympathy. . . . The bubbles on the foam which coats a stormy sea are floating episodes, made and unmade by the forces of the wind and water. Our private selves are like those bubbles,—epiphenomena, as Clifford, I believe, ingeniously called them; their destinies weigh nothing and determine nothing in the world's irremediable currents of events.[9]

Like Weber's view of modern science, James often expresses ambivalence about how we ought to orient ourselves to Darwinian evolution and what it means for our religious and moral lives. For both him and Weber, if the world looks increasingly alien, if our destinies weigh and determine nothing in the world, it is because the scientific transformations in modern life have reached the level of metaphysics.

Prominent theologians such as Charles Hodge write in agreement. For Hodge, Darwinian evolution erodes purpose in the world and a sense of moral commitment to self and society by denying individuals the object of their piety—namely, God. Liberal Protestants, such as Henry Ward Beecher, Lyman Abbott, James McCosh, and John Fiske, weed out the contingency Darwin's theory implies in order to sustain a conception of piety that can underwrite human agency. The religious framework thus renders intelligible and legitimate both humans and the world in which they live. The preoccupation of liberal Protestants with certainty and progress remains, but it finds expression through a divinely sanctioned vision of *self-assertion*.[10]

The word "self-assertion" does some work for us precisely because it carries implications often attributed to Dewey's philosophy. At one level, it denotes an image of humans as artisans whose intervention is applied to humanity, society, and nature to mold a world for human purposes. In its theological guise, this vision retains the belief that a fully meaningful view of the world must continue to draw on a metaphysical source of creation. But liberal Protestants give salvation a decidedly historical character that underscores self-assertion's formative powers.[11] Self-assertion rejects the existential threat posed by the sick soul precisely because it affirms (a) a vision in which the accent is placed on the ability of humans to fashion a world for use and comfort, along with (b) a view of the world, in its materiality, as wholly amenable to human purposes. This description dissolves a humble orientation toward acting in the world in favor of a strong presumption of the world's openness and encouragement of human aims and aspirations. It is therapy in the form of spiritual reedification.

This is the problematic and complex context in which to locate Dewey and to which he should be read as responding. This context includes a decline in the importance of a religious ethos and an ascendancy in the belief that human action is completely arbitrary and uncertain and that one's identity, conduct, and political institutions are thus without a moral compass.[12] Dewey's mature philosophy—which emerges in the early 1890s[13]—develops at the very moment in which the stability of the self is disrupted ontologically and the epistemological framework to which individuals appeal seems less plausible. The crucial point, however, is that his intervention leaves him with neither recourse to Hodge's pessimism nor the reconciliation that liberal Protestants' proffer.

We can thus read Dewey, without this appearing anachronistic, as accepting Hodge's contention that the naturalization of human development severs the connection between a divine Creator as the ultimate source of allegiance and what this reveals to us regarding human agency. But he rejects the claim that such a position leads to paralysis of will or ethical nihilism. In taking seriously the biological anthropology of Darwin's theory and its constitutive features of change and contingency in grounding human development, Dewey also punctures the conceit of liberal Protestants regarding the relationship between human beings and the natural world. For him, where reliance on God or natural law is now in doubt, the untidiness of human existence cannot simply be folded back into an unfolding story of progress. Rather, this untidiness serves as the wellspring from which inquiry and identity flow—in short, the foundation of human agency. Only at the end of this chapter will we get a brief outline of this account and its importance.

DARWIN, SCIENCE, AND
THE MORAL ECONOMY OF SELF AND SOCIETY

The relationship between religion and science during the late nineteenth century gradually undergoes an important transformation in the United States, in part because of Charles Darwin's theory of evolution. As historian Herbert Hovenkamp notes, science initially found a home among Protestant theologians in America.[14] Yet Darwin's *The Origin of Species* of 1859 and subsequent *Descent of Man* of 1871—particularly with its emphasis upon change, process, and struggle in understanding human development—called into question the religious foundations of social and political life in ways that were absent from previous accounts of evolution.[15] What distinguishes Darwin's theory from earlier evolutionary doctrines is the specific place given to chance, which, when placed in the context of religion, undermines the entire project of Ultimate Design.[16] As Keith Ward explains, unlike in other theories of evolution the "irony is that the theory of natural selection has virtually no predictive power. It makes the existence of presently known facts highly improbable, rather like the outcome of the National Lottery."[17]

Darwin's language points in this direction. Diversity in an organism's development, he maintains, can potentially aid survival and thus be passed on to the next progeny. As he states: "[A]s natural selection works solely by and for the good of each being, all corporeal and mental endowments will tend to progress towards perfection."[18] At this juncture we must exercise caution. To be sure, enhancements that result from an organism's adaptation to its environment are possible. Such adaptations that affect groups of organisms allow for diversity in taxonomic status, even though they are genetically tied to a single organism. This explains the origination of species by descent with modification from a shared ancestry.

Darwin underscores, however, that such transfers are merely the result of chance. The transfers could potentially not have taken place at all largely because they depend on a number of other unpredictable variables—namely, various environmental factors—that could be at variance with survival conditions.[19] Even here, Darwin doubts that natural selection can produce an absolutely perfect organism, for what is "perfect" in regard to survival abilities is relative to other species that exist in the same ecosystem, and is constantly in jeopardy of being rendered "injurious" because of "changing conditions of life."[20] For this reason, he does not subscribe to a law of necessary development where that denotes change in a specific direction resulting from fundamental elements that exist in a latent or immature state.

This is only a bare sketch of some of Darwin's claims. Consider, however, one negative interpretation of this account that assumed primacy in the late nineteenth century among theologians such as Hodge. Here I mean only to briefly articulate this interpretation, turning explicitly in the next section to Hodge's language. To the extent that Darwin's theory is credible, the story goes, arguments from Ultimate Design are rendered problematic. From the perspective of natural selection, nature appears ruthless. Natural selection empties the world of mercy and justice, once believed to have been invested by God at the moment of creation. This equally throws into doubt the belief that human conduct is sanctioned by a higher power.

We find echoes of this perspective outside the American context, directed at the larger scientific horizon to which Darwin belongs. Weber, for instance, reaches a conclusion quite similar to Hodge, albeit derived more directly from his analysis of modern science. In a Weberian framework, Darwin is merely the outgrowth of the naturalization of all norms and values that result from science's engagement with the natural and social world. What is left, argues Weber, in the wake of modern science's encounter with the sacred sources of existence is an unanchored subjectivism.[21] If God is dead, to whom should one turn for guidance? The self seems more autonomous to be sure, but the lightness of being is seemingly unbearable.

It is at this point that the theological framework of justification by faith comes under assault. Beliefs no longer seem grounded in a fixed benevolent reference point—an unchangeable divinely ordained universe—but are the contingent result of humans attempting to cope with a treacherous and wasteful world. To employ the language of "contingency," "chance," "fortune," and variations of the same, is to underscore the unpredictability that inheres in nature. Recourse to God, in whose image one's identity is concretized and given purposeful direction, seems problematic because the world God seemingly provides works against human efforts.[22] Moreover, Scripture as a point of adjudication and assessment at the level of metaphysics (i.e., the study of Being) and epistemology (i.e., the study of knowledge with respect to truth) no longer seems viable for many when read through the lens of Darwin's theory of evolution. As we shall see in a moment, natural selection symbolizes for a number of theologians an attack resulting from modernity's development on the place religion occupies in American society.

Few terms have as many incompatible uses and meanings as "modernity." The notion provokes much debate, to which I do not want to contribute. But I employ the term to call attention to a change that begins in the seventeenth century and reaches its zenith in the nineteenth century: individuals come to understand nature in a more scientific way that stimulates the construction of *rational* techniques to penetrate, interpret, and ultimately control nature in its totality. The term "rational" is doing more work than we might think, for it denotes a conflation of reason with a conception of scientific certitude. To apply rationality, then, to the study of natural, social, and political affairs is thus to seek out certain or exact knowledge regarding their functioning.[23] This change in orientation draws a strong connection between science and progress that in turn extends to human affairs. But it takes the form that it does not because scientific advances spark an epistemological crisis, but rather because of the larger theological-political conflicts. The religious and political affairs of the seventeenth and eighteenth centuries thus stimulated the application to the study of human affairs of a mode of reasoning based on science, creating a tension between religion, understood as an "*un*provable and accordingly *un*certain" faith, and science, perceived as that which discloses clear, distinct, and certain ideas.[24] This understanding of modernity is thus coextensive with the philosophical and political developments of the Enlightenment.[25]

In characterizing modernity and the Enlightenment in this manner, however, we need to take note of the internal complexity that, in a pre-Darwin era, rendered intelligible the positive relationship between science and religion in the United States. After all, both Hodge and liberal Protestants understand themselves as heirs to the Enlightenment. So although the tension described above did exist, this is not the complete story. Natural philosophy was not always employed over and against religion, but often as empirical support. While we often emphasize the tension between the two, few can deny that thinkers as diverse as Bacon, Descartes, Newton, Locke, and Kant sought to elucidate the appropriate relationship between reason and faith. As Jonathan Israel skillfully explains in a passage worth quoting at length:

> Most men had no more desire to discard traditional reverence for established authority and idealized notions of community than their belief in magic, demonology, and Satan. Doubtless, this is true of both elites and common people.... Even those relatively few in society sufficiently swayed by the Cartesian intellectual revolution to adopt mechanistic explanation and mathematical logic as the new general criterion of truth rarely sought to apply it to everything. Just as Descartes with his two-substance dualism created a reserved area for spirits,

angels, demons, and miracles, and Boyle and Locke with their emphatic empiricism similarly ring-fenced miracles, spirits, and the core Christian "mysteries,"
so the intellectual elite of Europe mostly sought one or another intellectual ex-
pedient for having it both ways—that is reconciling the new mechanistic criteria
of rationality not just with religion and theological doctrine but also with social
norms.[26]

Israel's point is that a cognitive orientation, infused by a belief in an enchanted background, served as the site for the development of modern philosophy
and the new science. Even in Newton's world of inert matter, human purpose
continued to appear ennobled by something other than creative wills, making the motion of human and celestial bodies more than contingent. If these
thinkers are sometimes thought of as articulating a science of humanity,
for them, as Israel explains, it is only because there was an authority to give
that science direction. That the reconciliation often encountered conceptual
problems and contradictions in no way diminishes the attempt that these
thinkers made. This explains why American theologians so often understood
themselves as working within the Enlightenment tradition, albeit the Cartesian and Newtonian variant. They interpreted that tradition (and with good
reason) as committed to a cosmic horizon in which human purpose and reason were affirmed within a distinct soteriology. To be sure, their approach
involved a less mystical analysis of religion, as we will see below, but it was an
approach that did not deny the mysteries of the divine or that God was necessary to live a morally upright and meaningful existence.

Confining ourselves for a moment to the American context, then, what was
troubling in relation to Darwin was not simply that his arguments *seemed* to
deny the existence of God because scientific investigation and evidence do not
warrant God's existence. This problem was an issue from the time of Hume.
The threat Darwin posed was more specific, relating to the absence of moral
purpose in existence. This is the conclusion that scholars such as Hodge at-
tacked. But others, such as some liberal Protestants we shall consider in a
moment, attempted to redefine this feature of Darwin's theory altogether.
My contention is that Dewey is attentive to both the worry that precipitated
Hodge's challenge and the attempt by liberal Protestants to recast Darwin
and escape the potential frustration of human energies. He sought a path
between the religious traditionalism and lamentation that we find in Hodge
and the overconfidence of Protestantism. This third way has profound implications for his philosophical outlook; Dewey retained the humanistic and
political hope of both the Newtonian and Darwinian Enlightenments to be

sure, but he located it in a more humble understanding of knowledge acquisition that is sensitive to the primacy of contingency.

HODGE AND THE PROBLEM OF
HUMAN AGENCY IN THE WAKE OF EVOLUTION

Many American theologians during the period in question saw themselves as engaged in a genuine scientific enterprise in their elucidation of Christian commitments, and so viewed their activities as consistent with the Enlightenment. However, they believed that their conception of the field of inquiry was far more expansive in the context of Darwinian evolution. Thus Charles Hodge remarked that scientists in the wake of Darwin did not acknowledge "the strength with which moral and religious convictions take hold of the minds of men."[27] For that reason, Hodge continues, such convictions should "be accepted as facts" susceptible to analysis. Failure to acknowledge the intuitive power of these facts, he argues, will leave us morally adrift.[28] As Mark Noll and David Livingston remark: "The heart of Hodge's interest [is] the Augustinian picture of human salvation."[29]

The image of humans as morally adrift is crucial to understanding the nature of Hodge's worry. For him, Darwin's theory provided a scientific foundation for a life and culture that increasingly defined itself in the absence of God. As Hodge explains in his classic *What Is Darwinism?* (1874), belief in our abilities to sustain ourselves in God's absence is tantamount to "atheism."[30] We might consider Hodge's formulation of the matter this way: Is Darwin's theory of natural selection a doctrine that can accommodate Christian beliefs without those beliefs ceasing to be true? For him the answer is a resounding "no." He explains the reason for this in his well-respected *Systematic Theology* (1872–73), where he lays out the meaning of Scripture's claims based upon the same methods of inductive reasoning championed by Francis Bacon and exalted by Newton. As he writes of his method, "it agrees in everything essential with the inductive method as applied to the natural sciences."[31] For that reason, he continues, "[t]he Bible is to the theologian what nature is to the man of science. ... In theology as in natural science, principles are derived from facts, and not impressed upon them."[32] If Darwin's theory is accepted, Hodge reasons, the Bible as a reservoir of facts must be rejected because natural selection is intelligible only if we accept its "ateleological" character.[33]

Hodge's philosophical move follows from the very popular commitment to commonsense realism and the exaggerated Baconian outlook regarding induction. Indeed, many relied on this union as a way to reconcile genuine religious belief in God and divine purpose with scientific methodology.[34] In Hodge's case, it allowed him to underscore the hypothetical nature of Darwin's theory, and as a result deny it the status of a fact. For what distinguishes the scientist from the theologian is not, in Hodge's view, their methodology, but the content of what is investigated. Darwin's methodology as it relates to his "rules of evidence," Hodge argues, makes his conclusions the object of attack.[35]

Here Hodge is extending the commonsense realism articulated by Thomas Reid.[36] What Theodore Bozeman writes of Reid can equally be applied to Hodge: "[I]f efficient causal agency in nature is beyond sensory reach, then the scientific investigator properly may deal with its visible effects."[37] God, in Hodge's view, is in essence the nonempirical connector between what lies beyond sensory reach and the visible effects that give Biblical data credibility. Systematic theology, then, is a further effort at classifying and eliminating wrong correlations within the Bible so that factual generalizations regarding conduct and right living can be sustained. "The law," writes Hodge, "is revealed in the constitution of our nature, and more fully and clearly in the Written Word of God."[38] This is the claim noted earlier, in which principles are derived from facts rather than being impressed upon them. The point, however, is that for Hodge facts assume greater weight over theories because the latter are necessarily tentative and dependent on facts for evidential support. But facts, Hodge tells us, "are determined by the wisdom and will of God. To deny facts is to deny what God affirms to be true."[39] Hodge contends that since Darwin's theory lacks sufficient support and the evidence offered contradicts the wisdom of God, it should be rejected.

In saying this, we must be clear that Hodge does not oppose science as such. He is very clear, as are many American theologians, that Christians have often adjusted themselves to scientific truths that are then hermeneutically related back to and affirmed by the Bible. "The Bible," he remarks, "has stood, and still stands in the presence of the whole scientific world with its claims unshaken."[40] But he adds: the "theologian . . . acknowledges that the Scriptures must be interpreted in accordance with established facts. He has a right, however, to demand that those facts should be *verified beyond the possibility of doubt*."[41] Such an account of the relationship between reason and faith, science and religion, was not antithetical, even if not identical, to the much earlier positions staked out by Descartes and Newton.[42] Hodge's aim, no less than these thinkers before him, was to offer a more moderate picture, in which human rationality matters in our negotiations with the world, but which nonetheless does not expunge God from the universe.

There is a running together of several distinct claims worth mentioning that no longer seem viable in the wake of Darwin, but to which Hodge and others subscribe. The first is that intuition is an objective feature of our psychological profile given by God.[43] Second, within this framework we comprehend and experience the divine, since it is here that the moral laws are inscribed. Third, Biblical facts become further proof of God's existence, but more significantly provide evidence from which axioms for conduct are drawn. Here we see a metaphysical horizon against which one's claims to knowledge are located and rendered intelligible. Hodge's worry is that once this background disappears, piety no longer makes sense. The result would be that we become, in a moral sense, individuals without direction, and the possibility for commitment to self and society would equally become unintelligible.

The urgency was all the more pressing because the crisis of religious certainty extended beyond the bourgeois intelligentsia. Precisely because those individuals who sided with Darwin were more thoroughly bound up with the strands of popular culture, the growing erosion of religious belief developed alongside a crisis of certainty that extended beyond the academy and America.[44] In this context we should observe, as did Hodge, a framework that questioned the possibility of an objective horizon in which to locate one's beliefs. Moreover, the significance of sincerity for self-identity—that is, a state of being free from personal dissimulation—was unpleasantly cast into relief. For Hodge, the evaluative stance that one assumes toward actions presupposes an independent reference for its own assessment that is beyond contingency. For him and others, absent this independent reference point, our moral and political lives are open to arbitrariness and chance.

The significance and historical scope of Hodge's worry cannot be understated. Weber expressed the same concern years later in his 1918 address "Science as a Vocation," which is worth mentioning in this context. After all, his account is the most famous description, even if not the first, of the mood with which we have been concerned and continues to serve as a touch-point for contemporary reflections. For Weber, disenchantment has two distinct but related components: a psychological dimension, and an institutional aspect that centers on a specific deployment of the scientific paradigm in modern democratic life. As I mentioned earlier, Weber shared Hodge's worry not because of an analysis of Darwin, but because he believed that he discerned within the larger scientific tradition to which Darwin belonged a logic that eroded the religious and teleological roots of the moral life. This erosion, he argued, followed simply from the cognitive attitude of the scientific stance— namely, that all could be known, that there was no limit to human knowledge and so no mysteries in nature.[45] Nature may well be a problem, but no longer a mystery. Ironically, it is the sense of a mysterious nature that implies forces at work "not of ourselves"—forces that provide comfort and a point of epistemic and moral adjudication in the management of our lives. For Weber, as Lawrence Scaff explains, disenchantment denotes the "disruptive sense of disengagement, abstraction, alienation, homelessness, and the 'problem of meaning' that begins to gnaw at the vital core of modern experience and social philosophy."[46] But there is another—more institutional—dimension to Weber's analysis that outstrips Hodge's reflections. Science's quest to understand reality by "increasingly precise and abstract concepts," coupled with the growing complexity of modern societies, will inevitably lead to a reduction of politics to mere calculation and a displacement of the citizen by the expert.[47] We shall come back to this second dimension in chapter 5, since it relates directly to how Dewey seeks to reconcile the relationship between experts and the public in the context of democratic decision-making.

If we focus for a moment on this first dimension, however, a crucial question emerges that is explicitly at work in Hodge's account. If Christian beliefs—principally in the existence of God—are in fact a sham, what beliefs can one confidently commit oneself to? Here the issue of sincerity rears its head for Hodge as it did years later for Weber. In other words, in the face of Darwin's theories and the modern scientific stance, the objective correlate to which faith attaches comes undone. The agency-enabling element that supports and guides the construction of individual identity and social cohesion disappears.

The results of this are twofold. The first is the emergence of competing and conflicting value commitments—a theme most clearly at work in Weber's analysis. On this view, the crisis of religious certainty contributes, if not wholly produces, the crisis in normative evaluation that continues to animate thinkers as diverse as Jürgen Habermas and John McDowell.[48] The crisis in normative evaluation informs Hodge's worry about the disappearance of an objective horizon to guide life. How, in other words, do we adjudicate between conflicting value commitments? What are the normative resources available to modern individuals if a thoroughgoing naturalism is accepted or inescapable?

The second result is a kind of perpetual doubt regarding one's commitments. As James puts the matter: "Now our Science tells our Faith that she is shameful, and our Hopes that they are dupes; our Reverence for truth leads to conclusions that make all reverence a falsehood."[49] Along these lines, for Hodge, the certainty that theological beliefs find justification in something beyond what is distinctively human is fundamentally tied to and sustains the faith one accords them. Indeed, it is what makes both purposefulness and commitment possible. Man, writes Hodge, "has desires, aspirations, and necessities for which the world does not furnish the appropriate object."[50]

If, however, the background of meaning implicates one in self-deception because an infallible criterion of knowledge cannot be had, any acceptance of belief thereafter, Hodge reasons, will be experienced not merely with caution, but with corrosive skepticism.[51] Theologian Theodore Munger laments all this before offering a more positive alternative when he observes that such individuals "cannot make the transition from that which no longer feeds and satisfies to the fresher conceptions that can. Hence it is largely an age of arrested belief, dangerous to all, fatal to many."[52] We hear of a similar concern across the Atlantic, this time from Matthew Arnold in 1852, a feeling of "[w]andering between two worlds, one dead, the other powerless to be born."[53] But in the context of Darwinian evolution, Arnold comes to lament the emerging world. This much he indicates in his 1867 poem, "Dover Beach":

> The sea of faith
> Was once, too, at the full, and round earth's shore
> Lay like the folds of a bright girdle furl'd;
> But now I only hear
> Its melancholy, long, withdrawing roar,
>
> . . . .
>
> Ah, love, let us be true
> To one another! for the world, which seems
> To lie before us like a land of dreams,
> So various, so beautiful, so new,
> Hath really neither joy, nor love, nor light,
> Nor certitude, nor peace, nor help for pain;
> And we hear as on a darkling plain
> Swept with confused alarms of struggle and flight,
> Where ignorant armies clash by night.[54]

The upshot is the following: Darwin's theory throws into doubt the foundation of existence and does not equally provide a suitable replacement that answers the question of central importance: "What shall we do and how shall we live?"

This question, offered first by Leo Tolstoy and then by Weber,[55] is intimately bound up with Hodge's lament: "Without the Bible we are without God and without hope. The present is a burden and the future a dread."[56]

That the future is a dread I take to be both a psychological and sociological claim. Regarding the psychological aspect, Hodge seeks to save individuals who are without firm ground upon which to stand by underscoring the incompatibility between theological facts and the scientific hypothesis of evolution, and then retreating to the former. This serves, he believes, as the only genuine answer to the crisis in normative evaluation—that is, do not abandon God or the Word of God. But here Hodge differs dramatically from Weber, since the latter views the modern condition as irreversible—"the fate of our times" as he says—and so rejects otherworldly solutions.[57] In fact, as Eyal Chowers explains, the only explicit response Weber offers to the "crisis of the modern self" is that the solution should be "sought for 'each person by herself.'"[58] But this only sends us back to a kind of subjectivism, groping after what both Weber and Hodge take the modern self to be longing for and in need of—namely, a comprehensive view that serves as a foundation for adjudication in our moral and political lives.

Hodge fleshes out the sociological implications of his approach with its political undertones when he remarks: "[Darwinism] does not meet the religious and moral necessities of our nature."[59] For him, we need something of substance that is beyond the precinct of the human to bestow meaning and direction on our lives.[60] In this train of thought Hodge's concern is with a hidden and much greater threat that prefigures the political, to be sure, but also sustains and orients it. The ability to see beyond our subjective experiences to the experiences of others as objects of concern and thus ennoble our existence is made possible only if we travel down a road that ends in God's company and grace. The possibility for positive redemptive political action depends on a prior metaphysical commitment to God in order to guide life. This is precisely why, for him, we perceive but do not create moral laws.[61] To rely exclusively on our rational capacities will lead to a proliferation of evil and deny to us the possibility of salvation that is bound up with faith.

Hodge's point, one which comes out in *Systematic Theology*, is that a turning away from God—that is, a renouncing of one's piety—renders unintelligible the moral faith that orients our conduct and sustains political life. To him, our individual and collective lives are wholly impoverished and crippled once we have accepted the Darwinian stance. The conclusion, then, is that at the heart of spiritual sickness lies paralysis of will. In this context, Hodge remarks: "[T]heism is the basis of jurisprudence as well as morality."[62] This suggests that his psychological claim is always accompanied by the worry that political life apart from acknowledgment of God will be equally emptied of normative force and direction.[63]

RECONCILIATION AND THE QUEST FOR CERTAINTY

In contrast to Hodge's pessimism, liberal Protestants were far more open to Darwin's conception of evolution and the scientific milieu to which it belonged. This openness was necessary in order to reconfigure God's relationship to humanity and categories such as original sin, redemption, and progress. By using the term "liberal" to describe one branch of American Protestantism, I mean it to refer to a theological outlook not simply friendly to evolution and modernity, but even, more significantly, optimistic in its orientation toward the world because of this amicable relationship. While Hodge argued incompatibility, others believed they need only adjust features of the theological account. For them, these adjustments did not harm the metaphysical or epistemological dimensions of belief, and in fact reasserted a more resilient notion of human action. The classics of this genre, we might say, are works like Munger's *The Freedom of Faith* (1883), John Fiske's *The Destiny of Man Viewed in the Light of His Origin* (1884), Henry Ward Beecher's *Evolution and Religion* (1885), James McCosh's *The Religious Aspect of Evolution* (1890), and Lyman Abbott's two works, *The Evolution of Christianity* (1892) and *The Theology of An Evolutionist* (1897).

The issue of human agency, specifically in it social context, was central to their outlook. If the developing partnership between science and Protestantism aimed to realize progress and deepen social harmony, then the elements of purposefulness and commitment would seem untouched. Thus on the heels of Munger's earlier lament, he quickly rebounded, asserting a spiritual optimism: "There is, however, this sure ground of hope that the great body of mankind will not long live without a faith."[64] Reconciliation between Protestantism and evolution did not rest merely on a semantic distinction, nor was it simply an argument about the appropriate understanding one should take regarding humanity's relationship to the divine. This latter view worked within the traditional framework, where, although humans are estranged from God, there is an unquestioned assumption that God exists. The matrix of justification was not at issue.

More subtly, however, liberal Protestantism was about the meaning of the divine as such. Precisely because of the ensuing crisis, liberal Protestants were more anxious to find confirmation for the divine and corresponding moral beliefs in the reconciliation of science and religion. The upshot of this position was that to accept Darwinism did not necessarily lead to disenchantment. We cannot deny that the objective of liberal Protestants was to respond to traditional problems within the Christian worldview, but this was because those problems, given the tension between religion and evolution, hindered a more robust attempt to renew faith in the existence of God, which could in turn serve as a basis for one's actions and commitments. Of course, they often spoke in the name of Darwin, but could not remain completely consistent with his theory. It is precisely the element that Hodge worries about—natural selection's ateleological character—that falls away when read through the reconciliation thesis.

James' description of the "healthy-minded temperament" captures the nature of this reconciliation. As James writes, the healthy-minded temperament is one which has a "constitutional capacity for prolonged suffering, and in which the tendency to see things optimistically is like a water of crystallization in which the individual's character is set."[65] This description, in which progress and certainty become possible in this world because one's character is placed beyond the crippling reach of suffering, most resembles the aspirations of liberal Protestants. This account mingles with an activist will, resulting in self-assertion. But once self-assertion and a commitment to progress replace humility, sin undergoes a radical transformation that relocates it from the level of ontology to history.

In his 1882 article, "Progress of Thought in the Church," Henry Ward Beecher, a popular Brooklyn pastor, gives us a taste of this developing sensibility. "There is a strong and growing tendency," Beecher explains, "to enlarge the sphere of Divine Revelation by adding to the Bible the revelation of Nature, and of man's reason and moral consciousness, which are a chief part of Nature."[66] Historian and philosopher of religion John Fiske gives this vision greater clarity when he observes that the story of evolution "shows us Man becoming more and more clearly the image of God, exercising creative attributes, transforming his physical environment, incarnating his thoughts in visible and tangible shapes all over the world."[67]

For Beecher and others, nature's revelation through evolution need not be inconsistent, and indeed is essential to understanding God's work and our moral nature. This much we see when Beecher makes an understanding of human nature the bedrock upon which one manages and realizes a moral government:

> Now, let us see what government is. It is the science of managing men. What is moral government? It is moral science, or the theory upon which God manages men. What is the management of men, again, but a thing founded upon human nature? So that to understand moral government you are run right back to the same necessity. You must comprehend that on which God's moral government itself stands, which is human nature.[68]

But the unfolding of our nature, as he goes on to say, reveals itself through evolution. To deny evolution misses what our nature reveals about how we ought to conduct ourselves in society. Evolution is thus an exemplary process of moral self-disclosure that informs collective self-governance. The two— moral self-disclosure and collective self-governance—are intimately linked, with the former serving as the center of gravity for the latter. Through the unfolding of humanity's moral biography we come to desire rightly, with the belief that insofar as our actions are based on those desires, we may act rightly as witnesses to God's kingdom in this world.

On this matter, of course, we should be clear. Beecher concedes in his sermons of 1885, *Evolution and Religion*, that evolution is a hypothesis that makes the origins of man "uncertain and debatable."[69] But this is not something that leaves much doubt in his mind, as it had done with Hodge. Notwithstanding the hypothetical character of natural selection, Beecher goes on, what should not be in doubt is that our earlier beginnings when compared to now are proof of an "incubation" period in which we developed those "social and moral elements which would make it possible for men to understand the moral character of God."[70]

Beecher, Fiske, and others thus give salvation a decidedly historical character. This undercuts the world-weariness and angst that are bound up with visions of redemption through an impersonal God. This perspective displaces Hodge's worries precisely because once we see evolution as an expression of the union between religion and science it is possible to take comfort in a view of the world that *seems* to be ruled by chance—a world where the image of fortune *appears* to find naturalistic grounding.

The result of all this was a transformation of evolution into eschatology, for evolution was thus seen to work on the level of epistemology to influence the moral and political levels of existence. This eschatological view provided the model in which the forward movement of history embodied in evolution was made possible, and which at no point denied its consummation in time. This is because evolution was considered a process of extrapolating and perfecting from within an organism in response to the larger environment.[71] In this thinking, evolution always already orients one in time as it refers back beyond to that eternal locus that underwrites reality and secures human self-redemption. Liberal Protestants were thus representational realists for whom moral knowledge was mediated through humanity's evolution. As an independent source, God was responsible for the substance of moral knowledge, but the human grasp of this independent reality came through evolution.

Thus conservative Protestants who clung to a narrow reading of Scripture, especially in the wake of Darwin, Beecher argues, misconstrued the relationship between humanity and God. Indeed, they diminished the importance of a purposeful existence because of the way they defined the object of humanity's loyalty. As such, they consigned humanity to a world of "infinite sin and suffering."[72] With Luther, Calvin, and Jonathan Edwards our ability to partake of God's complete nature is prevented by our disobedience; God's image must forever remain vague and unclear, obstructed by the veil of knowledge beyond which we can never see. Temporal existence, in this view, is thus devoid of meaning. Augustine's morality, much like that of Calvin, Luther, and Edwards, is one in which goodness in the world becomes a mechanism by which we exalt God and are allowed to experience a realm of transcendence. But this exaltation of God is independent of the question of whether it leads to social improvement, indicating in essence the inconsequential nature of human purposes to God. Our purposes are ennobled through our commitment to God, as we are simultaneously reminded of the diminutive human horizon that grounds those purposes. This description, Beecher explains, understands the fall as an ontological description—that is, as an event that results in God imposing an eternal condition on humanity's existence in the world. The implication is that God transmits "to the whole human race, through all time, the degradation . . . [and] suffering of [the] divinely destroyed experimentalists of Eden."[73]

Instead, Beecher likens man's evolution to acquiring the fundamentals of reading and writing, which begins with learning the alphabet. Analogously, he reasons, the earlier stages of Christian development were trial-and-error attempts in gaining first letters, words, and a vocabulary with which to decipher God's work and understand precisely the importance of man's development.[74] Hence his earlier description of Adam and Eve as "experimentalists" admits fallibility to be sure, but more significantly bespeaks our ability to revisit and correct the errors of the past in future activity. Because sin becomes a historical event redemption is equally made temporal in character.[75] The image of Adam and Eve as experimentalists implies that humans should hold in reserve the ability to impose themselves upon nature as a way to prevent regression or the replication of error that would stifle evolution. In redefining through evolution the proper object of religion as man rather than God, liberal Protestants placed greater emphasis on humanity's moral transformation, yet it was a transformation that looked backward in defining *to* humanity God and forward in reconciling humanity in this world to the image of its Creator. Human nature and human institutions became the new repository of the redemptive power once properly tied to Christ's spiritual intervention.[76]

I do not want to exaggerate the importance of the scientific discovery of evolution for Beecher, Abbott, and others. That is to say, we must be careful not to obscure the role of the ministry in this philosophical context. For to rely completely on facts gained from science was to miss precisely the importance of those facts. They revealed more than an empirical world subject to investigation, but rather a connection to divinity and knowledge upon which to stake humanity's claim to the future. Man's self-disclosure through evolution was seen as an education *to* human nature in which the species "comes under the law of the human,—that is, under the law of God, under the law of right and wrong."[77] To proceed in this way, liberal Protestants believed, both rescued humanity from the older Manichean conception of Christianity and staved off the suggestion that evolution destroyed God. To ensure this conclusion, Beecher adds: "[W]e are in danger of having the intelligent [i.e., scientific] part of society go past us, [for] the study of human nature is not going to be left in the hands of the church or ministry."[78]

We must parse this claim carefully largely because it attempts to define what an appropriate recognition of our dependence on God should look like, blurring, as did Hodge, the metaphysical presupposition of God with epistemological claims regarding right action in the world. To begin, Beecher's philosophical idiom restates the implication of Hodge's worry regarding the collapse of the moral economy of self and society, although the ateleological character of evolution that concerned Hodge is missing. And Beecher agrees with him regarding the importance played by theology in educating us to human nature; science's disclosure of evolution alone does not meet the moral and religious demands of our nature. Moral guidance and locating its legitimation in a larger horizon thus remained the essential principle of religion in ways that resembled the concern of Hodge: "the moral structure of the human mind is such that it must have religion."[79]

But if the study of human nature was not to be left in the hands of the Church because of its failure to engage evolution, and yet the moral structure of the human mind must have religion, what conclusion should we reach? We are to conclude that for liberal Protestants something of primacy in human life would be lost. For that reason, Beecher says elsewhere, "if ministers do not make their theological systems conform to facts as they are, if they do not recognize what men are studying, the time will not be far distant when the pulpit will be like the voice crying in the wilderness."[80] The image of wilderness that he invokes conjures up a darker vision—a site potentially populated by unwieldy beasts, incapable of displaying the traits of human agency. The taming of the wilderness is thus a copartnership between God and man:

"Though [God] works through laws and a continuity of laws, yet there is a large commonwealth of liberties by which a man can produce effects through God, that *cannot be produced in any other way*."[81] Beecher's attempt, like that of his fellow liberal Protestants, was to satisfy the psychological and sociological aspirations of theologians like Hodge through the language of evolution, and in doing so to stave off the concern he expresses regarding the appropriation of evolution in the first instance.

The vision of self-assertion expressed above was inextricably linked to belief in a normative reality independent of human beings and their practices. The result was an oscillation between questions of epistemology and claims about moral and political direction. Evolution filled the gap that separated human action from an independent God-sanctioned reality, therefore justifying self-assertion and locating progress within time. Liberal Protestants connected their optimism about humanity's potential to their ecstasy about the immanence of God. Their conceptions were predicated on the elevation of the self that paradoxically occurs through an incessant preoccupation with God as the self-affirming source of human existence.

There is, however, an irony to the foregoing account that must be acknowledged. The meaning of this reconciliation belied its inner secrets: religious self-understanding agonizes over the melancholy it rejects. "In early affairs," James McCosh (president of what would later be named Princeton University) contends, "there may be greater glory in suffering and sorrow than in prosperity and dazzling splendor."[82] The reconciliation gestures, as indicative of McCosh's remark, toward sickness. We will obscure the darker undercurrent of the very notion of spiritual loss in this period if we interpret McCosh and others purely through a theological framework. In the context of Darwin we must render differently the inner turmoil of the self no less than its impact on society. At one level it refers back to God, and at another it bespeaks the absence of the divine altogether. On the one hand, the self exists in the presence of the divine, and on the other, it is simply thrown back on itself.

The worry Hodge captures was thus part of the motivating force that generated the quest for reconciliation by liberal Protestants. The healthy-minded temperament expressed by the reconciliation grew out of the same worries over spiritual sickness that we find in Hodge and that came to define the modern era in Weber's work. This is because the sick soul (as with the implied feelings of despair, melancholy, anxiety, suffering, and sorrow) takes on new meaning in the context of modernity. "It [melancholy] arises," Charles

Taylor remarks in his recent commentary on James' *The Varieties of Religious Experience*

> in a world where the guarantee of meaning has gone, where all its traditional sources . . . can be cast in doubt. It therefore has a new shape: not the sense of rejection and exile from an unchallengeable cosmos of significance, but rather . . . a definitive emptiness, the final dawning of the end of the last illusion of significance. It hurts, one might say, in a new way.[83]

The Jamesian sick soul existed, then, in a darker universe than did the Augustinian self because it embodied Hodge's and Weber's worry. This concern stimulated a need for reconciliation and conditioned the particular way it framed itself. The union between science and theology thus reconfigured the religious possibilities through an activist spirit that recognized human imperfection, but which, as William Clebsch argues, "assure[d] the spirit of its relevant engagement with reshaping the universe" by taking up a "program of reform."[84] Protestantism thus rationalized its creed, and liberalized its approach, as it engaged social and political relations to sustain that optimism regarding worldly progress. In this account, the contingency of life must be perpetually denied. The result, however, was that Adam and Eve's reluctant naturalism could produce only a half-hearted experimentalism.

DEWEY AND THE MEANINGFULNESS OF MODERN LIFE

The worries of Hodge and liberal Protestants, including the positions they assumed, received serious attention throughout Dewey's mature career. We can thus read Dewey's critique of the varieties of foundationalism—philosophic, scientific, and theistic—that he developed after 1900, along with his constructive projects during the period, as an attempt to respond to the crisis of agency. The full significance of this account will have to await our investigation in later chapters, but a substantive overview is necessary to show how Dewey negotiated the crisis. In this regard, we should turn immediately both to the importance he attributed to our embodied existence, and to the centrality of change and uncertainty in his philosophy. What work were these doing for Dewey's overall philosophical outlook? In answering this question, I want to highlight his views on the emergence of knowledge, and on the dynamic process of our encounters with the world.

The approach by liberal Protestants, on Dewey's view, led to a false promise regarding the relationship between human agents and the natural world. There was in it a strong presumption of an articulable world that provided fixed reference and guidance markers, which were nevertheless independent of human perspective and indeed legitimized human action. For him, to treat known elements within experience as causally connected to something beyond it was to insert a suspicion of sense perception that seemed unwarranted, even if one conceded that this was all we had to go on. For knowledge would always appear, in this view, as a revelation—indeed, one that was true and untarnished. The conclusion, then, would have to be that if integrity of agency in relation to Darwinian evolution depended on the old way of thinking, we would, in effect, have to view agency as emptied of normative force because the entire project was conceived through a structure *corresponding* to something fixed and outside of experience.

In Dewey's reading of Darwin, the notion of stasis is rejected in favor of the empirical belief in change and contingency in constituting human development. Dewey's point was that there is a transactional relationship among self, other, and the world—resulting from the movement of and disruptions in life (what he often calls "problems")—that generates and structures frameworks of meaning. We are connected to the world and others in a more fundamental way before the question of the absence of agency can even arise in the first instance (see, for example, EWLP [MW8:83–98]).[85] Dewey takes as his starting point an unquestioned belief in our embodied existence in social relations as the primary datum of investigation. Or to say it differently, Dewey's claim is that if we understand the question of agency not as a logical problem—an attempt to ascertain its vitality in relation to objects that precede it in a causal but nonexperiential chain—but rather as an issue of social psychology, then the problem as here defined dissolves.

Of course, as made clear in Hodge and Weber above, this standpoint must raise another issue relating to the objective status of morality. As Weber put the matter, a form of human inquiry modeled after science "is not the gift of grace of seers and prophets dispensing sacred values and revelations, nor does it partake of the contemplation of sages and philosophers about the meaning of the universe."[86] How, then, do we retain the very notion of objectivity when, in James' famous words, "the trail of the human serpent is thus over everything?"[87] Notwithstanding this issue, which we take up most directly in Part Two, for Dewey any account of moral objectivity will have to be internally situated within social life, as an emergent corollary to our engagements with the social world. That is, the point is not to get in touch with something that bestows normative guidance and provides objectivity from without, but to understand how these elements inhere in our social practices from the start if we are to make sense of how they function.

Situated inquiry, for Dewey, is always coextensive with the fact of contingency. The primacy of contingency, he argues, is brought home to us by Darwin. Recognition of contingency is the beginning point for understanding our biological anthropology, and by this I mean an empirical account of the nature and origins of, and ways of maintaining, human existence. This empirical account, since it takes its point of departure from experience, disrupts the traditional structures in which knowledge claims are grounded. This is the frame to Dewey's philosophical outlook, and its reverberations can be identified throughout his religious, moral, and political philosophy.

One result is a relocation of knowledge claims. At one end, knowledge cannot be the result of impingement of external things on a passive mind, since this is merely to speak the language of revelation. But nor is knowledge wholly spun from the mind's formative powers independent of external things. For in both cases knowledge appears to preexist: either the senses distort it, needing the mind's formative powers, or the senses accurately perceive it (SLT [MW2:298–337]; RE [MW3:101–107]; ETK [MW3:107–128]; PIE [MW3:158–168]).[88] Both perspectives, Dewey argues, preclude knowledge from being an "affair of the intercourse of a living being with its physical and social environments" (NRP [MW10:6]). For him, it is the flux of our environments and the indeterminate pressures they place on us that generate responses in which knowledge emerges. This is precisely why inquiry is situated.

Although scholars often get sidetracked by Dewey's explicit criticisms of classical thinkers, especially Aristotle, we should nonetheless read him as rehabilitating practical intelligence, or *phronēsis*, through a Darwinian outlook. Thus Dewey refers to "experience in its vital form [as] experimental, an effort to change the given; it is characterized by projection, by reaching forward into the unknown" (NRP [MW10:6]). He presupposes a chastened account of inquiry, given its generative structure in experience. But this means that unlike Aristotle's division between theoretical and practical action, inquiry becomes the central practice that underwrites and connects both. Dewey's aim, then, is not simply to lay out a method, narrowly conceived, but to articulate the way inquiry makes us sensitive to the complexities and potential disruptions that emerge in our natural encounters with and negotiations of the world. Whereas Aristotle, Dewey argues, seemingly confined this sensitivity to ethical and political life (BE [MW3:89]), he extends it to all aspects of the human condition precisely because the contingency that Darwin highlights runs all the way down. His approach is thus a modified Aristotelianism, with a difference attributable to the pervasiveness of contingency he discerns (via Darwin) in nature.

How does this sort of account help us with the question of human agency? How is one to proceed given the prior commitment to the substantiality of the self articulated by the liberal Protestants and Hodge? Here the worries of these thinkers meet the concerns of contemporary theorists. If human agency rests on a prior commitment to something fixed for its legitimation, how do we hold on to this substantive account of the self after we have abandoned the prior commitment—that is, after the world has become disenchanted? The question is particularly acute in our own time, serving as the backdrop of both Richard Rorty's liberal irony, on the one hand, and Charles Taylor's concept of the self on the other.

For Rorty, the question is itself based on confusion: "[It] ask us to believe that . . . the springs of private fulfillment and of human solidarity are the same."[89] "The vocabulary of self-creation," argues Rorty, "is necessarily private . . . while the vocabulary of justice is necessarily public and shared."[90] As such, we must abandon the presumption that there is a connection. There is a fundamental anxiety in Rorty's philosophy—that is, he seems to acknowledge that our socio-linguistic practices and frameworks demand that we see the world as ethically infused, and yet this seems to be in tension with his strongly aestheticized notion of self-formation. In Rorty's philosophy there is a structural analogue to the problem we have preoccupied ourselves with: If spiritual sickness implies that we have to drop truth as correspondence to a reality independent of us, then we must provide a radical picture that divinizes the self through exalting its self-creative powers. This radical picture of self-assertion runs up against the boundaries of social life, leading Rorty to assert: "The [I]ronist . . . worries that the process of socialization which turned her into a human being by giving her a language may have given her the wrong language, and so turned her into the wrong kind of human being."[91] Taylor's account of the self, however, hovers between presupposing a theistic framework and the straightforward point that our social practices generate allegiance and commitments that take hold of us in a deeper sense than is often thought.[92] In both cases the question remains: once we acknowledge the contingent-laden character of human development and values does this mean that we must partition what is most important to the self from the motivation needed to sustain political life? Can we no longer speak meaningfully and coherently about the world we inhabit and the people with whom we associate, without lapsing back into a theological story about the primacy of a background independent of human perspective that affirms "the human" (à la Taylor) or saying that the only valuable kind of determination is that which is self-determining in the strong sense (à la Rorty)? Dewey's answer consists of a complex set of points to which we must now turn.

Any attempt to salvage a meaningful view of agency must, in Dewey's view, confront the sense of longing expressed by the sick soul and what this implies about the self's relationship to the natural world and the web of social relations. As such, he wants us to take seriously the implication of Darwin's theory in our understanding of human agency: "The subject is that which suffers, is subjected and which endures resistance and frustration; it is also that which attempts subjection of hostile conditions; that which takes the immediate initiative in remaking the situation as it stands" (EN [LW1:184]). The sick soul, then, is a commentary on, as much as it is a product of, a vision of human existence that entails a kind of resistance and frustration from which we cannot be permanently relieved once a personal God is thrown into doubt. But unlike Hodge's response, this carries the beginning of a richer self-understanding concerning the source of the attachments and values that sustain us and provide direction. In placing *transactionalism* at the core of our biological anthropology, Dewey attempts to make us feel comfortable with a picture of ourselves as beings that do and suffer, resist and are frustrated. With our doing this, the art of living is defined not by our ability to escape our condition, but rather how well we can successfully navigate and improve it.

The background of Dewey's commencement address "Philosophy and American National Life," delivered at the University of Vermont in 1904, articulates this position. We have already referred to this essay and the following passage, but let us take a look at it once more, now in the light of the concerns delineated above. Here Dewey brings into focus the problems of the self in modern times:

> If our civilization is to be directed, we must have such a concrete and working knowledge of the individual as will enable us to furnish on the basis of the individual himself substitutes for those modes of nurture, of restraint and of control which in the past have been supplied from authorization supposedly fixed outside of and beyond individuality. (PAL [MW3:75])

The passage raises a crucial question suggested, I think, by the direction of liberal Protestantism: Can Dewey provide an answer to the problem he describes without domesticating contingency? Can he resist the worry, expressed by William Connolly, that because of a preoccupation with human mastery we will simply "experience modern life . . . [as being] . . . conducive to [a] faith in the responsiveness of the world to human organization?"[93] For Dewey, the use of the word "faith" makes sense only over and against the potential for that faith to go unrealized, just as accentuating the world's responsiveness only means that it does not *necessarily* work against us. As we shall see in the next chapter, he favors a more Aristotelian view of practical rationality that is bound up with a "sense of our dependence upon forces that go their own way without our wish or plan" (HNC [MW7:200]).

Against this backdrop, the passage from "Philosophy and American National Life" takes on a different meaning. We must first look to the use of the word "substitutes," which can have two meanings. The first would suggest that we are finding substitutes for x, where x is understood to be fixed but simply relocated within rather than outside of the self. This accentuates the interiority of the self as being the most authentic light by which we ought to guide ourselves. But this formulation often courts a strong vision of human mastery and threatens to camouflage the extent to which "we are beings who suffer" (BE [MW3:84]). In other words, it obscures the possibility of frustration and so distorts what Dewey takes to be an appropriate psychology of expectation under modern conditions. So when he says that the substitutes are furnished on the basis of the individual, he must mean something other than this romantic view.

My claim here and throughout the book is that Dewey's intentions are more complicated. On the one hand, he refers to and seeks to nurture an aestheticized notion of human action in crafting a meaningful existence. But (and this is crucial) he divorces the implications of what the self creates from some stronger claim about its metaphysical status in or beyond nature (BE [MW3:84]). This separation means that the substitutes are not cordoned off from future consideration, in which case our self-fashioning, at both the individual and collective levels of existence, does not presume that we are merely little Gods. The substitutes are fallible. As Hilary Putnam keenly observes: "Fallibilism does not require us to doubt *everything*, it only requires us to be prepared to doubt *anything*—if good reason to do so arises!"[94] But there is a stronger point here. Dewey wants to keep in view the extent to which we remain answerable to the world of social and natural phenomena and so engage in an *objective* affair, without also making the more dubious claim about corresponding to the real. This view, which Dewey shares with contemporary thinkers such as Brandom, McDowell, Sabina Lovibond, and Jeffrey Stout, is nicely crystallized by Cheryl Misak when she writes: "An objective area of inquiry must be such that its beliefs are sensitive to something that can speak for or against them."[95]

To verify my understanding of Dewey's intentions, consider the following. In his 1906 address "Beliefs and Existences," Dewey expresses sympathy with a desire to have an authorization that precedes existence and is fixed. But he is clear in that essay that "the progress of intelligence . . . has evolved a procedure of knowledge that renders untenable the inherited conception of knowledge" (BE [MW3:92]). For Dewey, this inherited conception—which he takes up in a number of works and identifies with the modern revolutions in philosophy and science initiated by Descartes and Newton—is founded on a procedure that aims to establish beliefs that are incontrovertible and certain (QC [LW4]). In his view, this fails to address the existential despair at the heart of spiritual sickness: that perhaps order is not inherent in nature, that there is no sanction that precedes the human and which justifies and guides our conduct. As with Hodge and Weber, Dewey is no stranger to what may potentially follow from this, for as he writes in "Religion and Our Schools" of 1908: "There is undoubted loss of joy, of consolation, of some types of strength. . . . There is manifest increase of uncertainty; there is some paralysis of energy" (ROS [MW4:168]). To be sure, this essay reflects on the growing tensions between religious belief and the secularization of public schools, but underlying this is a deeper attentiveness to the existential crisis that saturates the historical moment.

The crucial starting point, in Dewey's view, is that rather than understanding the sick soul as *the* diagnosis of the modern age—Hodge's and Weber's claim—we should see it as a pathological mood within modernity for which he *wants* a diagnosis. Here he immediately rejects what appears in our time as a kind of apocalyptical postmodernism that falls prey to the belief that without a strong metaphysics all that is left is a constant play of signs. But unlike some communitarians, Dewey does not run in the opposite direction, by defending a strong vision of identity, the good, and community to serve as a substitute for a unifying religious or ethical framework. In fact, his analysis parallels Nietzsche's description of the advent of nihilism that follows from the eclipse of the transcendent. And he articulates, as did Nietzsche, a new religious sensibility bound up with our worldliness.[96] "It may be," Dewey remarks, "that the symptoms of religious ebb as conventionally interpreted are symptoms of the coming of a fuller and deeper religion" (ROS [MW4:176]). Of course, Dewey's account, in contrast to Nietzsche's philosophy, is at home with democracy and eschews viewing the romantic quest for individual greatness or genius as the paradigmatic expression of modern life. His notion of natural piety, which he mentions in this essay but takes up fully in *A Common Faith* (1934), is an attempt to retrieve the religious impulse from the strong metaphysical frameworks in which it previously functioned:

Yet nothing is gained by deliberate effort to return to ideas which have become incredible, and to symbols which have been emptied of their content. . . . Bearing the losses and inconveniencies of our time as best we may, it is the part of men to labor persistently and patiently for the clarification and development of the positive creed of life. (ROS [MW4:168])

If spiritual reedification is a pathology that persists in the context of modernity, so too, Dewey argues, is the existential despair of spiritual sickness. Individuals who assume either position are like artists who have imagined the ideal painting of a human being but are disheartened by the many pictures they or others have painted. Such renditions do not exemplify the model. The fault, Dewey maintains, is with the ideal itself. It is not simply an incorrect model, but in being so, it incorrectly shapes that which is most vital to the model: piety, human purpose, and commitment to self and society. These positions—spiritual reedification and spiritual sickness—then are two sides of the same coin. Dewey's wager—the hope of laboring persistently and patiently, as he says—is that the first of these is not essential for a meaningful existence, and that the paralysis of the second need not be the final conclusion. The upshot, then, is that moral life does not have to connect piety to a strong metaphysical structure to avoid spiritual sickness or Rortyan irony. There must, in Dewey's view, be a third way. A unifying theme in his writings is the effort to paint a different picture in which human agency is still intelligible.

From the points Dewey articulates in "Philosophy and American National Life," "Beliefs and Existences," and "Religion and Our Schools," we discern the importance of his religious naturalism. Put another way, he finds a way for us to speak and act seriously regarding our fundamental commitments, while simultaneously holding at bay the tendency to reify them. At bottom Dewey seeks to articulate a new psychological posture—that is, to supply substitutes, even as we acknowledge their contestability. He refers to this natural piety in *A Common Faith* not as blind deference; such an account would make sense only if one accepted the older model of knowledge as correspondence. Rather, natural piety is an appropriate posture toward the sources of a meaningful existence; they aid us in moving through life, but are open to critical engagement. Prospectively, religious naturalism means that our orientation to the world is such that our aspirations and ideals—what Dewey calls faith—ought not to be excluded out-of-hand, but still must be reconciled with reality.[97] We shall turn to Dewey's specific language in chapter 3, but I use the words "appropriate posture" here to signal something about his approach. His third

way is an articulation of the psychological disposition humans ought to cultivate and nurture as they attempt to negotiate and sustain political and ethical
life. This foregrounds the importance he attributes to inquiry and the contingency of our practical lives that it implies.

Dewey's approach tilts our understanding of metaphysics in a different
direction. Because the experiential dimension of human existence constitutes
stimulated inquiry, structured and directed by an assessment of the consequences of action, it generates traits that we employ in future inquiry. Metaphysics thus consists, he argues, in positing constructs derived from experience that we believe will help us fruitfully manage the world we encounter. It
becomes an empirical metaphysics. The potential failure of these constructs
is not the beginning point but rather one forced upon us by their inability to hold up in the battleground of everyday life. We weakly embrace our
metaphysical commitments, Dewey maintains, not because we do not take
them seriously. It seems an inaccurate picture of our moral world to imply
that a critical disposition toward our commitments implies a diminution of
their meaning. Instead, we weakly embrace such commitments because we
acknowledge that our projections into the world and reception of what exists may fall short of what we intend for them to do for us.[98] Thus the line
by Dewey quoted earlier, referring to the precariousness of practical activity,
concludes with the following observation: "Judgment and belief regarding
actions to be performed can never attain more than a precarious probability" (QC [LW4:6]). This claim is obviously the background commitment to
Putnam's account of fallibilism.

If this is so, Dewey's realism is provisional, evolving, as it does, out of
the impasses that stimulate inquiries aimed toward human flourishing.
"[J]udgment appears," Dewey writes, "as the medium through which the
consciously effected evolution of Reality goes on. . . . Reality is thus dynamic
or self-evolving" (SLT [MW2:296]). Science generally, but inquiry in human
life specifically, works in a piecemeal fashion wherein the facts upon which
we work are coextensive with, evolving out of, the process itself. For Dewey,
this is more than enough reason to believe in the growth of knowledge, even
as the structure and ground from which inquiry flows tell us that there is no
necessary reason to believe that such growth will occur. The results of inquiry
form an interlocking web of warranted beliefs—that is, beliefs assessed on the
basis of their consequences in action—upon which we stand as we move forward and further engage the world. This is one aspect of Dewey's much larger
reflections on experimentalism and the anti-authoritarianism it expresses;
he deploys it in his understanding of religion, morality, and democracy. But I

mention it at this juncture because it stipulates features that provide expansive psychological and emotional direction in our practical judgments. This is the reason Dewey often speaks of human existence as requiring courage: "An empirical method which remains true to nature does not 'save'; it is not an insurance device nor a mechanical antiseptic. But it inspires the mind with courage and vitality to create new ideals and values in the face of the perplexities of a new world" (EN [LW1:4]; cf. HNC [MW4:163]).

The sources of a meaningful existence do not precede what it means to be a human being or the contingencies of human experience. Rather, they are the result of a more primordial encounter that leads to a constructivist account of our relationship with self, other, and the world. Here is the positive extension of Darwin's impact; it resists the despair of spiritual sickness because the religious content is relocated to an experiential domain presupposed by a web of social relations that is plural in its offerings. This domain works in turn to condition an aestheticized vision of the self that if completely unhinged or totally opened to transformation will slowly erode our connections to others both morally and politically. This also provides resources to hold at bay a strong communitarianism that if left unchecked equally threatens to make us unresponsive to the claims of others. Both private aestheticism and strong communitarianism block us from engaging in the practice of giving and asking for reasons that is, in Dewey's estimation, so central to legitimacy and justification in the modern world—the anti-authoritarian legacy of modernity.

The lectures that comprise *A Common Faith*, writes Dewey to a soldier in 1943, were "meant for those whose religious beliefs had been abandoned, and who were given the impression that their abandonment left them without any religious beliefs whatever. I wanted to show them that religious values are not the monopoly of any one class or sect and are still open to them."[99] If we map his preoccupation with the problems of the self onto the crisis of religious certainty, then we can see that his mature philosophy is a sustained attempt to articulate what he expresses in this letter.[100]

In referring to his understanding of our embodied existence and its connection to inquiry and knowledge formation, his appreciation for contingency and continuity in experience, his account of religious naturalism and its attending psychological orientation, and the central weight he places on a view of legitimacy grounded in a practice of giving and accepting reasons, we hit on a deeper claim. Dewey is offering a way to see ourselves in relation to each other and the natural world in which human agency can still find a home. He attributes significance to these concepts and worries, as did Hodge and liberal Protestants, about their fate. His approach is an attempt to rescue their meaning from metaphysical exaggeration and therefore the confusion or evisceration that results from spiritual sickness. Yet he rearticulates human agency through a specific view of the practical limitation of being-in-the-world. The question is not whether we can hold on to the substantiality of the self, but rather how it looks once we take this existential background seriously.

Another way of putting this matter is the following: Dewey is attempting to answer a question regarding the fate of human agency; the answer to that question is either no longer satisfying or wholly nonexistent in the wake of modernity, but its importance persists nonetheless. His response continues to affirm self-assertiveness, to be sure, but it is mingled with humility born out of our encounter with self, other, and world. If we return to the view of self-assertion articulated in the introduction, we might say, then, that he accepts proposition (a), that we must encourage human intervention in order to realize the better and advert the worse. But he rejects proposition (b), since he affirms that just because the world is there for us to encounter does not ipso facto mean that it is wholly amenable to human aims and aspirations. To explore the meaning of these points we need to understand, as I argue in the next chapter, the precise importance Dewey attributes to contingency and the connection to practical action that it presupposes. What, in other words, is the significance of moving from philosophical and religious quests for certainty to an acceptance of contingency? The answer to this question will help us clarify Dewey's understanding of inquiry and tease out its all-important normative character.

AGENCY AND INQUIRY
AFTER DARWIN

The argument of the previous chapter focused on the crisis of religious certainty in late-nineteenth-century America and its impact on perceptions about human agency. In this context, Dewey's approach (as noted at the end of chapter 1) sets him apart from thinkers like Hodge, who reject Darwin out of hand, and the liberal Protestants, whose reformulation of evolution leads to a reluctant experimentalism. Liberal Protestantism's description of evolution underwrites an expansive conception of self-assertion. In contrast, for thinkers like Hodge, "spiritual sickness" is not merely a shorthand description of Darwin's impact on the American religious imagination, but more profoundly a belief that experience is emptied of meaning altogether because of its connection to contingency. Spiritual sickness thus prefigures the disenchantment thesis that we have come to associate with Max Weber. My final argument of the previous chapter was that Dewey's account of self-assertion is more circumscribed than that of the liberal Protestants because he accepts the contingency that Darwin reveals, but it is not as crippling as spiritual sickness because he rejects the original connection between meaning and epistemic certainty. There are three questions that must orient and guide our analysis here.

> *First*, what is Dewey's precise understanding of Darwin in comparison to his liberal Protestant counterparts?
> *Second*, what is the specific usage to which Dewey puts Darwin, especially in relation to his account of human agency and inquiry?
> *Third*, how does the answer to the second question stave off the worries advanced by Hodge and Weber?

In seeking to answer these questions, this chapter examines the connection between contingency and action in order to clarify for us Dewey's understanding of inquiry. The charge, after all, is that his conception of inquiry is based on an ontology that orients the self to the world in a way that cuts against a belief in the fragility of life that a thoroughgoing experimentalism demands. Dewey seemingly, the argument goes, flattens the otherwise rough terrain of the natural world we inevitably confront, and simplifies the cognitive resources he most certainly intends for us to use. The accuracy of this criticism, however, has to do with the weight Dewey accords contingency in what I refer to as his philosophy of action,[1] and the precise relationship between that account and what he says about inquiry. If we are to short-circuit the criticisms directed at inquiry, then we must first understand better than we currently do his philosophy of action, in which inquiry functions.[2] This will clear the way for us to examine in part II how Dewey envisions the role of inquiry in our religious, ethical, and political lives.

I begin in the first section with an interpretative claim, one which I advanced in passing in the last chapter: *Dewey favors a more Aristotelian view of practical rationality that is bound up with a "sense of our dependence upon forces that go their own way without our wish or plan"* (HNC [MW14:200]). This implies that inquiry must not be perceived as a crass form of proceduralism—a set of rules to be followed in order to yield answers to very clear problems. On the contrary, inquiry is something far more complex. Of course, my placing Dewey and Aristotle in closer proximity will strike some as odd.[3] After all, among all the ancient thinkers, it is Aristotle against whom Dewey often directs his harshest criticism. But this observation obscures the fact that Aristotle's formal categories of knowledge—*epistēmē* (scientific knowledge), *phronēsis* (practical wisdom), and *technē* (technical knowledge)—undergo an important usage and modification in Dewey's philosophy. This modification captures the complexity of inquiry as well as the epistemic status he believes we can accord the knowledge that inquiry produces.

We can extrapolate from Dewey's texts against the backdrop of Aristotelian categories in a way that is consistent with what Dewey intends to convey when he discusses inquiry. In doing so, we are positioned to see that inquiry extends the status of practical wisdom, and the contingency it implies, beyond the ethical and political realm, in which Aristotle locates it exclusively. For Dewey, all domains of human inquiry provide a truth about what is probable. The suggestion for pursuing this line of investigation comes from Dewey in a striking passage from *Experience and Nature* (1925): "Aristotle perhaps came the nearest to a start in [the direction of naturalism]. But his thought did not go far on the road, *though it may be used to suggest the road which he failed to take.* Aristotle acknowledges contingency, but he never surrenders his bias in favor of the fixed, certain and finished" (EN [LW1:47] [emphasis added]).[4]

In order to make good on this interpretative claim—the suggestion provided above by Dewey—we need to ask, as I do in the second section below, the following: What is the greatest obstacle to recognizing the reach of contingency in action? This question is central not only to his essay "The Influence of Darwin on Philosophy" (1910), but to one of his most important books, *The Quest for Certainty* (1929). In both works he turns to the history of Western metaphysics and epistemology. He focuses on the distinction between theory (*theōria*) and the practical domain of ethical and political life (*praxis*). He rejects a description that perceives knowledge of human values to be independent from our practical transactions with the social and natural world. This distinction implies that theory can lay claim to a nonexperiential realm—the "antecedently real," as Dewey refers to it (QC [LW4:14, 193])—that can direct our experiences in the world. The quest for certainty, features of which we will recognize from the last chapter, produces a view of agency that is always retrospective and singular, and denies the reach of contingency.

But as Dewey points out, the quest for certainty actually implies that the content of one's commitments develops through action. Our commitments thus have a socially constituted, constructed, and contingent character. His philosophical anthropology reveals that the distinction between theory and practical action presupposes that the latter is the primary point of departure for inquiry. The quest for certainty thus obscures our original relationship to this sphere; it blocks from view a clearer and more productive account of the relationship between contingency and action.

This relationship is the subject of the third section. There I explicate Dewey's positive appropriation of Darwin in "The Influence of Darwin on Philosophy." Whereas earlier the analysis only opens space for examining the relationship between contingency and action, here I explore the precise connection between the two. In short, Darwin helps Dewey undermine the quest for certainty, collapse the distinction between theory and practice, and understand the reach of contingency in human action. Here I focus on several elements key to Dewey's philosophy of action—that is, its *existential dimension*, its *function in constituting the self*, its *temporal quality*, and what I call the *psychological orientation of expectation*—and the place of contingency therein. In brief, contingency becomes the paradigm in which action and knowledge (that is, of both self and world) are emergent environmental properties, potentially defying human mastery and control. This description makes his philosophy of action a descendent of Aristotelian naturalism, but with a difference attributable to the more thoroughgoing experimentalism of Dewey's scientific milieu.

The relationship between action and contingency frames the role of inquiry discussed in the final part of this chapter. The Aristotelian connection explicitly returns. Precisely because of the centrality of contingency to experience, coupled with the collapse of theory and practice, inquiry functions as that paradigmatic social practice in which knowledge emerges. This presents a problem precisely because for Aristotle *theōria*, in contrast to *praxis*, produces a kind of knowledge that is universal and unchangeable (*epistēmē*).[5] The knowledge of *praxis*—namely, practical wisdom—however, involves a capacity to act, rather than a kind of knowledge; it requires more than the application of universals to particulars, but the ability to understand, discern, appraise, and manage the complexities of specific situations.

But for Dewey, knowledge claims are experimental at their core, and therefore fallible and revisable in the context of experience. To be sure, although he emphasizes the procedural structure of inquiry, he intends much more. His aim is to underscore the fact that when we say a person (e.g., scientist, craftsman, or citizen) displays practical wisdom, we are reading their judgments within a complex horizon, wherein success as judgments requires alertness, cultivation of perception and imagination, and discernment of salient features in response to a demanding environment. As I argue, for him, the structure of action places demands on the function of inquiry such that individuals must be sensitive to and perceptive of the particularity of the situation in which they operate in order to make an informed judgment.

There is a corollary to understanding action and inquiry in this way. The conception of metaphysics to which Dewey subscribes can only be weak. In other words, inquiry acts as a limiting condition relative to traditional ways of understanding metaphysics that had previously been bound up with the quest for certainty. For him, inquiry can only provide access to a world in which the meaning-content of our practices is retained, but not in the rigid, nonexperimental form suggested by the quest for certainty. This is because the logic of inquiry incorporates the theoretical tools that allow metaphysics to remain critically aware of the contingent circumstances under which it functions, thus limiting its descriptive reach.

INQUIRY AND *PHRONĒSIS*:
DEWEY'S MODIFIED ARISTOTELIANISM

Since the Second World War we have witnessed a revival in the use of Aristotelian categories to reinvigorate a philosophy of practice that is sensitive to the complexities of our moral and political lives. Thinkers with whom this revival is commonly associated include Hannah Arendt, Hans Georg-Gadamer, and Leo Strauss.[6] Given the list, it is no wonder that Dewey has been overlooked as a potential contributor. Writing as they do amid the vertigo of disenchantment and instrumental reason, these later thinkers turn to Aristotle to undercut the assimilation of ethical and political life into science. As they argue, the result of this assimilation exaggerates what we can expect from human action when it is guided by science. Dewey's language of instrumentalism and inquiry seems to make him one of the forces we should struggle against.

Dewey is in fact much closer to the Aristotelian line that includes Hegel and Marx and that undergoes a transformation as a result of the evolutionary biology of Darwin. This line stands in contrast to the thinkers cited at the outset of this section, all of whom owe, in some significant degree, their analysis to Martin Heidegger's narrow conception of modern science and technology. Here I am interested only in elucidating the way Dewey's account of inquiry modifies Aristotelian categories and their meaning and so provides us with a more complete naturalism; I have no intention of exploring the comparisons above. My aim is to put us on track to see the complexity and dynamism of inquiry.

In book 6 of the *Nicomachean Ethics*, Aristotle lays out his all-important categories of knowledge: *epistēmē*, *phronēsis*, and *technē*.[7] Since I have already described the first of these, we can focus on the other two categories. For Aristotle, *phronēsis* denotes a performative quality of practical action, while *technē* signifies a qualitative evaluation of action based on its productive results.[8] To say that *phronēsis* is displayed in practical action means for Aristotle that it is inseparable from the person who displays it—that is, it cannot be distilled as a formula to be learned, used, and appropriated in the same way the craftsman teaches his trade. The success that practical action seeks is internal to itself. Action-specific judgments have remainders that are not reducible to the formal structure of deliberation. This is because *phronēsis* belongs to the ethical and political practices relating to human goods that admit of change and variation.[9] Aristotle is clear that *phronēsis* and *technē* correspond to ontological distinctions and therefore do not refer to different accounts of action proper.[10] That both are a kind of action aiming at a goal he admits. But for him they are not one and the same kind of action.

For Dewey, to locate inquiry against the backdrop of contingency foregrounds the pressures under which living well takes place—the extent to which humans are always both agents and patients. Here, we find our point of positive contact between Dewey and Aristotle: action denotes a kind of performance that is constitutive of the agent of inquiry. Individuals display wisdom, a kind of cumulative experience, in their judgments throughout life that make them an object of respect. His understanding of the proper functioning of inquiry in any given case can thus be read as including Aristotle's account of *phronēsis*.

What needs to be observed, however, is that while Aristotle confines *phronēsis* to moral and political deliberation, in Dewey's view, this is also part of the fundamental character of human action in toto. The entire process of inquiry seeks to make the agent attuned to the uniqueness of the situation and potential disruptions. We might call this inquiry's *internal good*; it is bound up with the individual's character and conditions her outlook, providing insight into both the concrete situations and their existential background. For Dewey, this undermines the commitment to a permanent set of beliefs that are thought to be applicable to all situations, and, instead, emphasizes prudence and experimentation in constructing judgments.

If the process of inquiry makes the agent sensitive to the uniqueness of and complexities within situations, it does so for Dewey because it seeks *external goods*. Here he departs from the ontological claim upon which Aristotle bases his distinctions in at least three ways that constitute the modification. First, inquiry is always enacted with an end-in-view: "[I]ntelligence develops within the sphere of action for the sake of possibilities not yet given" (NRP [MW10:45]; cf. LJP [MW8:48]). Inquiry thus realizes goods that are external—observable products that extend beyond the agent. The result of this, however, is that Dewey collapses the rigid distinction between *phronēsis* and *technē*. For him, it is a person's attentiveness to context and sensitivity to the existential background that combine in a formal process that potentially bears fruit in experience. The bearing of fruit will at once refer to the internal good that is bound up with the agent—a kind of excellence of character, we might say—but also external goods that we appraise and judge. External goods in this sense become the legacy of the individual.

Second, Dewey believes that these previous remarks regarding internal and external goods apply to all domains of human endeavor: science, art, and moral and political reflection. It would be odd in Dewey's view to speak of someone as displaying practical wisdom and therefore successfully engaging in inquiry, if they consistently made bad choices or were subject to constant misfortune.[11] In fact, we would begin to make judgments about their character, their intellectual abilities, and their insensitivity to the complexities of the situations in which they find themselves.[12] Understood this way, a crucial dimension to realizing the end-in-view, for him, is the extent to which one commands the skill to engage in the entire performance—the art of living.

On careful inspection, Dewey's outlook intentionally dissolves the meaning behind *epistēmē*. As he says in emphatic engagement with Aristotle in his 1906 essay "Beliefs and Existences," noting both the possibilities and limitations of an Aristotelian outlook:

> We recall Aristotle's account of moral knowing, and his definition of Man. Man as man, he tells us, is a principle that may be termed either desiring thought or thinking desire. Not as pure intelligence does man know, but as an organization of desires effected through reflection upon their own conditions and consequences. What if Aristotle had only assimilated his idea of theoretical to his notion of practical knowledge! (BE [MW3:89])

This passage is critical because it brings us to the third crucial point of difference. Continuity between action and production for Dewey is the origination of knowledge, which, in turn provides points of departure for future encounters with the world that either reaffirm that knowledge or throw it into question. This is what it means, as Dewey says above, to reflect upon one's own conditions and consequences as materialized in experience. Here he takes his cue from the nineteenth-century science of human development with its corresponding reliance on probability. In short, the Darwinian paradigm becomes the framework in which he works. As Robert Brandom remarks, this framework emphasizes "situated narratives of local, contingent, and mutable . . . reciprocal accommodations of particular creatures and habitats" in which the expected is coeval with the unexpected.[13]

Of course Dewey concedes that the knowledge of the craftsman or physical scientists is often "more precise and more technical," in contrast to the complexity and imprecision of knowledge associated with ethical and political life (QC [LW4:158–159]). But this is not an ontological difference, and so for Dewey, Aristotle needed only to extend the internal dynamism of moral knowing to knowing as such. As he points out, the "object of specifically physical knowledge is the same thing as being an object of operations that discriminate definitely fundamental relations of the experienced world from others, and that deal with them in their discriminated character" for engaging other aspects of the world (QC [LW4:158–159]). "The objects thus known," he contends, "lay no claim to be final. When used as factors for inquiring into phenomena of life and society they become instrumental" (QC [LW4:158–159]). In his reading, he does what he perceives Aristotle to be unable to do—that is, Dewey assimilates *epistēmē* to *phronēsis*, transforming knowledge once thought certain and unassailable into knowledge that is fallible. In Dewey's hands, the latter is informed by the experimental method he discerns in the modern self-understanding, rather than its other—problematic—quest for mathematical precision.[14] The latter view is often premised on a more structured and purposive view of nature.

Dewey's underlying claim is that experience constitutes the beginning and terminal points for both the "normative" and "empirical" sciences, giving the actions of both a logical form and experimental character for which explanation and defense can be provided. What hypothesis we should endorse or ideal we should follow equally unfolds against the background of past experiences and future expectations relative to a specific problem. The validity of the hypothesis is no clearer before action than the normative ideal, and so both must be tested by way of action. The difference lies not in the operation responsible for the emergence of knowledge, but rather in the scope of such knowledge: "The more complex the conditions with which operations are concerned . . . the more significant . . . is the resulting knowledge" (QC [LW4:159]).

He does not deny that we can continue to speak of technical or scientific knowledge, thus marking off the distinctions between art and science for functional purposes. Rather, the acquisition of such knowledge is not qualitatively distinct from the knowledge of ethical and political life. We would want the agent of inquiry, the craftsman, and the scientist to be capable of responding to the vicissitudes of life that confront them in their respective domains. This allows us to say when they are successful that they have skill or a knack for making good judgments.[15] We long to be the apprentice or to use them as models of good conduct, with the hopes that something of what they have might "rub off" on us.

To read Dewey this way provides us with the all-important methodological clue for using the Darwin essay to highlight the importance of practical action to human self-understanding, while texts such as *How We Think* (1910/1933), *Experience and Nature* (1925), and *The Quest for Certainty* (1929) in particular elucidate various features of practical action, its connection to contingency, and the role of inquiry. Indeed, *The Quest for Certainty: A Study of the Relation of Knowledge and Action* announces in its very title the continuity with Aristotle and thus circumscribes its subject matter as a philosophy of practice.

Thus far I have meant to deal only with the relationship between Aristotle's distinctions and what Dewey has in mind when he discusses inquiry. We should now turn to what he believes is the obstacle to appreciating the importance and centrality of contingency to human action. This will allow us to answer more directly the questions set for ourselves at the outset.

THEORY, PRACTICE, AND THE QUEST FOR CERTAINTY

The obstacle to understanding the importance of contingency to human action is what Dewey calls the quest for certainty. By this he means an attempt within the philosophical and theological discourse of the West to shield ourselves from the intrusion of uncertainty, contingency, or fortune. In his view, the quest for certainty often takes the form of an epistemological project, but it dramatically alters our psychological orientation to the world, as expressed in the rigid distinction between theoretical reflection and practical action. In both "The Influence of Darwin on Philosophy" and *The Quest for Certainty*, Dewey engages in a strategy of selective historiography, one that seeks to isolate the original motivation behind the quest for certainty and to liberate it from the distorting framework in which it is located. He often uses the language of "recovery" or "reconstruction" in his recounting of the history of philosophy largely because he sees himself as retrieving that primordial motivation as it has emerged out of a confrontation with the recalcitrant dimensions of the human condition. As we shall see in this section, recounting this story allows Dewey to critically reappropriate the past, imbue the present with purpose and meaning, and humbly guide the future without overstating the possibilities and limitations that attend human intervention.

In §I of "The Influence of Darwin on Philosophy," Dewey writes the following: "In . . . treating the forms that had been regarded as types of fixity and perfection as originating and passing away, the *Origin of Species* introduced a mode of thinking that in the end was bound to transform the logic of knowledge, and . . . treatment of morals, politics and religion" (IDP [MW4:3]). Darwinian evolution is a protest against a static conception of species, that is, a belief that there are latent traits to which development can be referred. Dewey's interest in this is important. The model exemplifies not simply a way of understanding the development of species, but a view of knowledge acquisition that links the Platonic-Aristotelian tradition to the Christian tradition and then to the modern debates among rationalists and empiricists (QC [LW4: chaps. 3–4]). For Dewey, species variation, as Darwin uses it, is evidentiary support that undermines the more traditional account and with it the vision of knowledge it advances.

His claim is not that we ought to jettison teleological constructions (as if that were possible). After all, theories of nature or life processes that seek to realize goods and projects can scarcely be thought problematic in themselves. But for him a teleological vision that presupposes a reference point of permanence and one that does not will look very different. Each will configure our relationship to the landscape in fundamentally different ways and each will offer a different account of our cognitive abilities. This distinction is important because Dewey wants to retain the teleological orientation of human life, but without reifying its content. Reification, as we will see, often follows from a specific understanding of the sources of our teleological orientations.

What are the implications of Darwin's account of species for understanding "the cause and the import of the sharp division between theory and practice" (QC [LW4:5])? Dewey's answer works on two distinct levels. The first relates to a theory of knowledge and the second, although connected, has to do more with "ontological security"; by this I mean the intellectual and emotional foundations of practical consciousness that respond to fundamental existential questions regarding self-understanding and the narrative of experience in which it emerges.[16]

In §II of the Darwin essay, Dewey provides us with a very clear statement of the early notion of species, taking the Greek tradition as his primary point of departure:

> The conception of species . . . a fixed form and final cause, was the central principle of knowledge as well as of nature. Upon it rested the logic of science . . . Genuinely to know is to grasp a permanent end that realizes itself through changes, holding them thereby within the metes and bounds of fixed truth. Completely to know is to relate all special forms to their one single end and good: pure contemplative intelligence. Since, however, the scene of nature which directly confronts us is in change, nature as directly and practically experienced does not satisfy the conditions of knowledge. Human experience is in flux, and hence the instrumentalities of sense-perception and of inference based upon observation are condemned in advance. Science is compelled to aim at realities lying behind and beyond the processes of nature, and to carry on its search for these realities by means of rational forms transcending ordinary modes of perception and inference. (IDP [MW4:6])

This conception of knowledge is understood as analogically derivative of the notion of species. To know is to grasp the permanent, that which exists in and through change. Knowledge is understood as a fixed reference point to which the object of study is referred. The most immediate example to which Dewey refers is Aristotle's conception of matter as the embodiment of purpose, whose final shape comes into view through growth (EN [LW1:53]). The underlying model is that of a vertical axis: the process of change is understood within a purposive framework and so excludes the possibility of contingency.

Because change and "the scene of nature" are inextricably linked in this view, our practical experience of the world will always fall short of the demands of knowledge. Dewey frames this issue more precisely in *The Quest for Certainty* when he writes: "Practical activity deals with individualized and unique situations which are never exactly duplicable and about which, accordingly, no complete assurance is possible" (QC [LW4:6]). Dewey associates this negative view of practical activity with the Greeks, arguing that for them, self-sufficient knowledge "was ideal and eternal, independent of change and hence of the world in which men act and live, the world we experience perceptibly and practically. 'Pure activity' was sharply marked off from practical action" (QC [LW4:5]).

On this view, Dewey maintains, we cannot elicit from our reflections on practical experience any meaningful features to orient life. As such, "experience [of the world] and thought [about the world] are antithetical terms" (NRP [MW10:6]). To speak, for example, of crafting tools or instruments to refine and enhance knowledge makes little sense. Science will have to be of a special kind, conducted quite differently from the technique of using practical experience as an experimental domain to arrive at knowledge.

Dewey believes that this traditional model of knowledge, experience, and science is the fundamental contribution of Greek thought to the Western philosophic and religious traditions (QC [LW4:22]). In later empiricism and rationalism, he argues, knowledge is understood through an a priori lens. In both cases the experiential dimension of life is disparaged. This may seem odd, at least from the perspective of empiricism, but even there he notes, the term does not mean attentiveness to experience as producing knowledge, but only refers to the belief that sensations are the true place of our "first hand intercourse with reality" and knowledge (QC [LW4:88, 90–91]; cf. LJP [MW8:58]).[17]

The point above is important in the light of the earlier distinction drawn in both the introduction and chapter 1 between the Cartesian and Newton Enlightenment on the one hand and the Darwinian Enlightenment on the other. Dewey's point is not that experimentation and judgment do not take place for empiricists and rationalists, but that these processes are secondary to and not originative of knowledge. Even in Newton, says Dewey, "scientific conceptions are valid in the degree in which they are revelations of antecedent properties of real Being and existence" (QC [LW4:153; cf. 93–95]). Indeed, when placed in this framework, he argues, the radical character of the modern experimental method is undermined. Its distinctive importance is defined by science's ability to drive to the core of reality and access fundamental laws or first principles (QC [LW4:83, 112–113; cf. chap. 8]).[18]

This is not to suggest that the new science, with its emphasis on experimentation, did not involve a latent transformation in metaphysics. As Dewey explains, it made the "realm of change which had been the subject of opinion and practice . . . the sole and only object of natural science" (QC [LW4:76]). "But—and this 'but' is of fundamental importance—in spite of the revolution, the old conceptions of knowledge as related to an antecedent reality and of moral regulation as derived from properties of this reality, persisted" (QC [LW4:76–77]).[19] Hence the motivating force, for example, behind Descartes' retention of God as a founding property in his system is no different than what we find in Newton, despite the many other substantive differences between them. This much Dewey explains regarding their underlying agreement:

> Since science has made the trouble [between itself and religion], the cure ought to be found in an examination of the nature of knowledge, of the conditions which make science possible. If the conditions of the possibility of knowledge can be shown to be of an ideal and rational character, then, so it has been thought, the loss of an idealistic cosmology in physics can be readily born. The physical world can be surrendered to matter and mechanism, since we are assured that matter and mechanism have their foundation in immaterial mind. (QC [LW4:33; cf. 93–95])

Why should the notion of understanding knowledge as something which human beings simply discover, whether it be by intuition, reason, or revelation, make us worry? The problem is that this formulation partitions our encounter with the world into theory and practice. In focusing as he does on this distinction, Dewey makes central to his investigation the problem concerning philosophical certainty and social practice. This is a problem which is central to Greek philosophy; it is transformed in the Christian figuration of the two cities, Hegel's critical assessment of Kant, and Dewey's own abandonment of Hegel's nonnaturalized account of history's movement. The distinction emerges out of a confrontation with uncertainty and a desire to be placed beyond risk. Dewey refers to this as one of two responses to uncertainty, which seeks a "method of changing the self in emotion and idea" (QC [LW4:3]; cf. IDP [MW4]). By this he simply means that the distinction between theory and practice carries a psychological orientation toward contingency—a belief that one can contain or avoid it altogether.

For him, this is especially acute within the Western philosophical and theological discourses on moral and political life. Hence he remarks that the Greek tradition sought to "develop a method of thought and knowledge which while purifying tradition should preserve its moral and social values unimpaired" (RIP [MW12:89]). This reappears in the Christian and modern traditions, finding its grandest formulation, Dewey notes, in Kant. "[Kant's] revolution," says Dewey, "was a shift from a theological to a human author-ship; beyond that point, it was an explicit acknowledgement of what philoso-phers in the classic line of descent had been doing" (QC [LW4:230, 242–243]; cf. DE [MW9:345]). Here he is referring to Kant's description of the moral law as borrowing nothing "from experience or from any external will," and to his epistemology, which distinguishes between things as they appear (*phenomena*) and things as they are in themselves (*noumena*).[20] The tran-scendental framework, as Dewey well knows, saddles us with the unfortunate thought that we partake of a supersensible reality that is independent of our conceptual and discursive activities.

The premise behind Dewey's account is that uncertainty carries ethi-cal import. It potentially "involves us in peril of evils," leaving both our fate and values in doubt (QC [LW4:4]). "[T]here is the enforced recognition," he says, "of the peril and frustration in the actual world of meanings and goods most prized, a matter which makes men ready to listen to the story of a higher realm in which these values are eternally safe" (QC [LW4:62]; cf. BE [MW3:87]). In these formulations, Dewey is already noting the socially constituted character of our values, which, because of their conduciveness to order, stability, and human flourishing in navigating a hazardous world, are reified by the quest for certainty.

Retrospectively, however, the quest for certainty misdescribes the origins of such values. Our prospective orientation regarding right conduct is defined through attentiveness to *known* elements:

> As far as [philosophy] occupied itself at all with human conduct, it was to su-perimpose upon acts ends said to flow from the nature of reason. It thus di-verted thought from inquiring into the purposes which experience of actual conditions suggest and from concrete means of their actualization. It translated into a rational form the doctrine of escape from the vicissitudes of existence by means of measures which do not demand an active coping with conditions. (QC [LW4:14])

This passage and many others like it in his work indicate that he is deeply concerned about the distinction between theory and practice as such, and not simply in its modern incarnation in Kantian rationalism. For the distinc-tion implies that values are not generated through life; we do not speak of them, in Dewey's view, as being forged, but rather as discovered or revealed, and this shifts our focus to mere application. Motivated by a quest to escape practical insecurity we ironically run headlong into cognitive certainty (QC [LW4:28]).

Here, he suggests, lies the fatal flaw, one that recalls the problem of the last chapter. At one extreme, certainty becomes the standard by which practical action is assessed and directed independent of its contingent and historical character. At the other extreme, practical activity is left to languish in the vicissitudes of existence. Descriptions such as "corrupt" and "deprave" become not moments in action, but define the very character of action. Can we not see, in this context, a resemblance to the therapeutic reedification and spiritual sickness of the last chapter? In a vivid passage obviously meant to unsettle, Dewey gives us little doubt of the connection:

> Men move between extremes. They conceive of themselves as gods, or feign a powerful and cunning god as an ally who bends the world to do their bidding and meet their wishes. Disillusioned, they disown the world that disappoints them; and hugging ideals to themselves as their own possession, stand in haughty aloofness apart from the hard course of events that pays so little heed to our hopes and aspirations. (EN [LW1:313])

As in the Darwin essay, Dewey's language in this passage from *Experience and Nature* is doing a couple of things. He refers us to the specific character that philosophy gives to our orientation toward the world. Although this orientation, he maintains, casts into relief the messiness of existence, it nonetheless pays very little heed to our hopes and aspirations. The relationship between theory and practice is thus the "most practical problem of life. For it is the question of how intelligence may inform action, and how action may bear the fruit of increased insight into meaning" (QC [LW4:224]; cf. LJP [MW8: §§III–IV]). If what we originally cared about—that is, managing and navigating a treacherous world—stimulated the distinction between theory and practice, but now is ironically neglected by our approach, Dewey attempts to return us to the original ethic of care.[21] His claim is that if we define our socially constituted condition as an imperfection from which we must escape, then the art of living will have been misunderstood from its inception. What is crucial, then, is not escaping this condition, Dewey contends, but orientating ourselves to it differently—coming to terms with ourselves as beings that enjoy, love, suffer, and die. Coming to terms is not a note of resignation or toleration, but an act of realizing the historicity of the lived relations in which human possibility, fragility, and defeat emerge.

There is yet a bolder message to Dewey's account. In this traditional view, agency is always retrospective, its object singular, and its method coercive. Both purpose and the strength of our ethical commitments are assessed in relationship to how closely one aligns him or herself to Being. Perversions of practical experience "are to be corrected and controlled through adoption of methods of conduct derived from loyalty to the requirements of Supreme Being" (QC [LW4:205]). "Only the single," he says elsewhere, "the uniform, assures coherence and harmony" (DE [MW9:274]). For the "intervention of initiative and invention, of individuality are counted contrary to reason as well as to sincerity and loyalty" (EN [LW1:166]). Thus, "[t]he world of experience can be steadied and ordered, [but] only through subject[ion] to its law of reason" (DE [MW9:274]). To be responsible to the world of action does not mean attentiveness to specific problems and the conflicts of opinion regarding their resolution, nor does it orient us to refinement of how we engage such quandaries. It does not encourage, in Dana Villa's apt phrase, "end-constitutive debate," but the "mechanical application" of the antecedently real to practical activity.[22]

When Dewey argues that the distinction between theory and practice diminishes the latter at the expense of the former, he maintains that both the prospective character of agency and the world of plurality to which it belongs are emptied of normative worth. That is to say, in the older view, practice, by virtue of its ontological description, cannot generate values to orient and guide life. The existence of a world of plurality from which inquiry emerges and to which the products of inquiry must return for assessment always implies an uncertain dependence on forces beyond our control. To display agency, however, in the traditional model, is to be unhinged from the uncertainty that otherwise attends practice. It describes freedom as a romantic vision of mastery over the forces that threaten us by referring the agent to a realm beyond what is the source of concern in the first instance. Such an account of freedom, as Isaiah Berlin reminds us in a line that sounds very Deweyan, "derives from the wish on the part of the individual to be his own master. I wish my life and decisions to depend on myself, not on external forces of whatever kind."[23] In Berlin's formulation of this radically romantic notion of "positive" liberty we find the quest for certainty. I say radically romantic because, as we will see, Dewey also advances an account of positive freedom, but one that does not fall prey to the worry being advanced. Notwithstanding, he and Berlin argue that in venturing on this quest we ironically cultivate hubris rather than humility, and overstate what human intervention can achieve. Linking practical action, as Dewey does, more precisely to contingency is an attempt to cultivate humility by making us aware of the fragility of the objects of inquiry. But if this is his goal, as I believe it is, then we must understand more clearly the dynamics between action and contingency before approaching his conception of inquiry.

THE EXPERIENCE OF LIVING:
ACTION AND THE PRIMACY OF CONTINGENCY

Having laid out this account, Dewey turns to Darwin in §§III and IV of that essay for reconstructive purposes—"reconstructive" in the sense that Darwin helps him, in contrast to his liberal Protestant counterparts, dispense with permanence. In contrast to what is the case for Hodge, Darwin also helps Dewey foreground the world of practical action as the primary locus in which the acquisition of knowledge is meaningfully possible. This is because he provides an alternative model capable of preserving, he argues, the productive and aesthetic aspects of practical action while keeping in view its limitations. He thus refers to practical action in *The Quest for Certainty* as the second "constructivist" response to uncertainty.

In §III of the Darwin essay, Dewey underwrites his philosophical anthropology with a precise statement of Darwin's positive contribution: "If all organic adaptations are due simply to constant variation and the elimination of those variations which are harmful in the struggle for existence that is brought by excessive reproducing, there is no call for a prior intelligent causal force to plan and preordain them" (IDP [MW4:9]). His point here is straightforward. Darwin's empirical work, we recall from the last chapter, indicates that the generative structure of species' development is a function of varying and unpredictable pressures on existence resulting from the external environment.[24] This shifts attention away from belief in some prior directive force in or outside of nature. Instead, the biological paradigm indicates that since we encounter nature in experience, direction—that is, ways of coping, dealing, enduring, and surviving—emerges out of that transaction. Analogously, cognition becomes an emergent moment relative to specific demands in nature that we experience.

The impact of Darwin's account is threefold. First, the specific conception of knowledge that was, as previously discussed, a derivative of the earlier model of species falls away. "Philosophy," Dewey argues in this regard, "forswears inquiry after absolute origins and absolute finalities in order to explore specific values and the specific conditions that generate them" (IDP [MW4:10]). Knowledge comes to fruition within nature as an "affair of the intercourse of a living being with its physical and social environment" (NRP [MW10:23]).

Second, philosophy no longer sets itself up to prove that "life *must* have certain qualities and values—no matter how experience presents the matter—because of some remote cause and eventual goal" (IDP [MW4:12]). The meaningfulness of life does not hang on a logical argument of causal antecedents that are thought to be enchanted or in which determinate goods are identified. Instead, philosophy orients itself positively to the plurality of life, taking this as its starting point for yielding qualities and values that sustain and direct human conduct. The analogue here, one that relates to the first point, is that when we say that an object is "known," we do not mean this to refer to its antecedent properties, and so do not mean to make a claim about its putative origin. Rather, we mean "known," Dewey argues, as devolved from its consequent use in experience. To know an object is thus to have experience of its function in this or that way. That there may be intermediates between the object and us or cherished values and us, such as other individuals, institutions, stories, and the like, in no way undermines the notion that the original knowledge results from experience with this or that object. From this perspective, we are positioned to become more reflective vis-à-vis traditionally sacred hierarchies or political arrangements, exposing them to potential reconsideration and alteration.

Third, it introduces responsibility, but not one determined exclusively by how well the agent adjusts to extant knowledge, but rather one that is capable of elucidating a "method of locating and interpreting the more serious of the conflicts that occur in life . . . a method of projecting ways for dealing with them" and accepting the consequences that follow (IDP [MW4:13]; cf. DE [MW9:153]). Inquiry is prospective and experimental rather than retrospective and submissive; it seeks to elucidate and engage in "a method of moral and political diagnosis and prognosis" (IDP [MW4:13]). That Darwin's account introduces responsibility among agents is to say, with Eric MacGilvray, that the "appeal to experimental intelligence is egalitarian in the sense that all may reasonably be thought capable of developing this faculty more fully and profiting thereby."[25]

What, then, is the precise character of this second—constructivist—response to uncertainty, what Dewey refers to as "doing and making" (QC [LW4:3, 26])? We risk obscuring what he says in his positive project regarding the role of inquiry if we do not attend carefully to what he means in connecting contingency to action. Even some of Dewey's more careful interpreters have underappreciated the importance of contingency to his philosophy. Cornel West, for example, misrepresents the matter when he argues that Dewey does not maintain a "delicate balance between excessive optimism and exorbitant pessimism regarding human capacities."[26] Raymond Boisvert adds to West's mischaracterization when he suggests that "sensitivity to inherent natural limitations is decidedly underemphasized" in Dewey's work.[27] But how can West and Boisvert—sympathetic interpreters—make such claims? This is especially surprising considering the latter's treatment of Darwin's importance to Dewey.[28] Essentially, what they argue is that inquiry presupposes a description of the relationship between action and nature (broadly conceived) which obscures the uncertainty that connection involves.[29]

Unfortunately, Dewey fuels such indictments with a number of remarks in *Reconstruction in Philosophy* (1920) that seemingly suggest that our only limitation is failure to apply the scientific method to the problems of life (RIP [MW12:102]). On close analysis of that work, argues Boisvert, limitation of human capacities does not capture the classic vision of fortune Machiavelli worries about—a vision in which fortune's potential intrusion is ever present.[30] Limitation for Dewey seems to be one of application and is therefore methodological, while the latter Machiavellian view regarding fortune seems to be an ontological claim. These moments in *Reconstruction in Philosophy* (or others like them) are employed by Boisvert and others as part of a much larger indictment, suggesting that unlike Hannah Arendt, for example, Dewey is unable to see the "futility, boundlessness and uncertainty of outcome" that attends action.[31] Whatever the differences between Machiavelli and Arendt (and there are many), they seem to share a sense of the contingency of human affairs that is seemingly missing from Dewey. He lacks, it is argued, a tragic sensibility.

This critique will return in later chapters, specifically when we are examining Dewey's moral philosophy. At this stage, we need only consider it as a broad phenomenological challenge to his project. In my view, critics understate the importance of contingency to his philosophy of action, and in so doing overlook the way it positively informs and circumscribes what Dewey can reasonably attribute to inquiry. His conception of inquiry will be operative in the background of this account, but I want to focus attention *only* on the contours of action—that is, its existential dimension, its function in constituting the self, its temporal quality, and what I will call the psychological orientation of expectation. These themes are crucial to *Experience and Nature*, but also to his work in education as found in *How We Think* (1910/1933) and *Democracy and Education* (1916), the social psychology of his *Human Nature and Conduct* (1922), and his ethical theory in "Psychological Method in Ethics" (1903) and *Ethics* (1932).

THE EXISTENTIAL DIMENSION OF ACTION

In linking the world of action to uncertainty, Dewey is referring to something very specific about our relationship to the environment. Action in this instance does not mean the commonsensical notion of movement or series of movements. That action is this for him cannot be denied, but action for him also equals organized activity to achieve ends. Hence the examples he offers of the world of practical activity: "Man constructs a fortress out of the very conditions and forces which threaten him. He builds shelters, weaves garments, makes flame his friend instead of his enemy, and [this] grows into the complicated arts of associated living" (QC [LW4:3]; cf. DE [MW9:146]). The relationship between action and uncertainty reveals the self-reflective character of identity. Human beings find themselves located within problematic environments and the potential correctives to those situations are partly dependent on how those individuals respond.

There is, however, another revelatory dimension to action. This refers to the intentionality of consciousness as realized through action that orients individuals to the larger context (e.g., nature, other individuals, and social arrangements). The self is not focused on its needfulness, but rather on the problematic situation that generated the need from the outset. Action thus discloses to us a world that is unfinished, in the process of becoming, and which demands a response. The "stimulus to thinking . . . implies that the situation as it stands is, either in fact or to us, incomplete and hence indeterminate" (DE [MW9:158]; cf. PD [MW11:50]). An uncertain world thus impinges on and provokes the self, bringing action into existence. The dual dimension of action exposes the self and creates space not simply for commendation and condemnation or critique and affirmation by other individuals. In doing so, action also opens up the possibility for uncertainty to emerge. We do not know how the world will respond to us, both in its natural movement and in the reactions by others who inhabit the world. When Dewey speaks, for instance, of the complicated arts of associated living he is referring, in particular, to the uncertainty implied by the presence of other human beings.

THE EXISTENTIAL DIMENSION OF ACTION AND THE CONSTITUTION OF THE SELF

What is important to note is that contingency and action are coextensive and so are constitutive of identity formation. For Dewey, we do not think about being creatures of action, constructing ways of managing and navigating our environment. This is simply what we are in a primordial sense. "We are," he says, "active beings from the start and are naturally, wholly apart from consciousness, engaged in redirecting our action in response to changes in our surroundings" (LJP [MW8:52 n. 16]). Our sense of the world and ourselves

comes to us through action and therefore has a determined character by virtue of its generative structure in specific situations. Action thus discloses the
contours of reality and the commitments of our agency. Obviously, this claim
rejects the Cartesian thinking subject as the appropriate beginning point of
analysis, since this thinking subject is prefigured and constituted by specific
problems. Nor does this account embrace the romantic notion of the sover-
eign self as indicated earlier, since the reflexive dimension of action bespeaks
our sustained dependence on the external world. Thus knowledge of self and
world does not, Dewey contends, just come intuitively, we must do something
to achieve it—we must act.

At this juncture, critics often emphasize the progressive view of Dewey's
account, arguing that embedded in his conception of action is the assumption of a world, open to human intervention, waiting to be bent and altered
to human desire. Recall John Patrick Diggins' remark: "Although Dewey has
been hailed for ridding philosophy of epistemology . . . he appears to be returning to the eighteenth century. . . . Enlightenment in his conviction of a rational world responsive to scientific manipulation."[32] The implication is that
the obstacles to human intervention for Dewey have nothing to do with the
world as such—that is, the impediments do not inhere in the subject matter.

But we move too quickly if we ignore the subtlety of his claim and its underlying realism. Of course his philosophy of action is coextensive with a theoretical framework that is progressive and reformist in orientation, much in
keeping with the Progressive movement of his time. But progress is a socio-
scientific possibility, not an ontological fact. He retains, without contradiction or subterfuge, the cautionary note at the heart of his philosophy—namely, that a thoroughgoing experimentalism "is not an insurance device nor a
mechanical antiseptic . . . it inspires the mind with courage and vitality to
create new ideals and values in the face of the perplexities of a new world"
(EN [LW1:4]; cf. HNC [MW14:163]). If action allows the self to control and
understand the world, to disclose the possibility within life and the poten-
tiality of one's own life, then action can equally make clear and deepen the
contingent dimension of human projects.

In this description, we see the priority of action for the formation of character. Action is the site for the emergence of a shared world in which the self
is constituted and from which it distinguishes itself. Dewey shares this position with both William James and George Herbert Mead and discusses it in
several places in his writings (HNC [MW14: pts. I, IV]; cf. EN [LW1: chaps.
6–7]; E$_3$ [LW7: chap. 15]).[33] As he says in *Human Nature and Conduct*,
character is formed through and constituted by habituation: "For it makes

us see that character is the name given to the working interaction of habits" (HNC [MW14:31]). And he argues that upon honest reflection, we realize that "habit has this power [that is, disposes us to act in certain ways] because it is so intimately a part of ourselves. It has a hold upon us because we are the habit" (HNC [MW14:21]). When someone says of another, "I know his character," what is known is the way in which a configuration of habits disposes him to act. Or, when we say of a person that "she is not acting like herself," we are able to utter and make sense of this claim because of our capacity to connect dynamic actions across a temporal landscape to say something consistently about who she understands herself to be, and the ways in which she can be expected to act in the light of certain situations. We are reminded of that wonderful Biblical dictum: "By their fruits ye shall know them."

Dewey can accept this claim provided we understand it to assert two points. The first is that character is intelligible (that is, can be assessed and understood) through action. The second point is that the very constitution of character is linked to and informed by the layered connections among previous experiences. This forms the basis of *phronēsis*—that is, the wisdom we draw on in our engagement with the world and its various parts. He speaks along these lines in his defense of his use of the term "habit":

> The word habit may seem twisted somewhat from its customary use when employed as we have been using it. But we need a word to express that kind of human activity which is influenced by prior activity and in that sense acquired; which contains within itself a certain ordering or systematization of minor elements of action; which is projective, dynamic in quality, ready for overt manifestation; and which is operative in some subdued subordinate form even when not obviously dominating activity. (HNC [MW14:31]; cf. EN [LW1:213])

There is interdependency then between action and self-understanding in that the former helps constitute the latter, which in turn allows us to transform the world we engage. As Dewey explains, "[s]ince habits involve the support of environing conditions, a society or some specific group of fellow-men, is always accessory before and after the fact. Some activity proceeds from a man; then it sets up reactions in the surroundings" (HNC [MW14:16]). For this reason he writes in his *Ethics* that "there is no such thing as a fixed, ready-made, finished self. Every living self causes acts and is itself caused in return" (E$_3$ [LW7:306]).

His claim is quite similar to those of contemporary thinkers who emphasize the narrative dimension of action.[34] So for him, we cannot tell a story about the identity of agents and ourselves without reference to the context in which the individuals find themselves. Our identity comes into view in relation to a past that we do not make and a future that we do not completely control (HNC [MW14: pt. I]). This simply means that the social world forms a temporal-spatial horizon; it embodies funded experiences that extend around the self in both time and space. It exists before and after the fact in the sense implied by intersubjectivity, through which institutional structures, symbols and their meaning-content, and the consciousness of persons emerge (L [LW12: chap. 12]).

Dewey thus understands the social world as forming a narrative background of experience in which the self is initiated and from which she draws linguistic and conceptual resources to engage in interpretation. This initiation involves the acquisition of what Dewey, and most recently John McDowell, calls a "second nature"—that is, the habits and sensibilities that accrue to our cognitive capacities and that open us up to the demands of social life as such (HNC [LW14:65]).[35] Of course, in attempting to understand a person's actions we must examine the individual in question, but Dewey quickly adds that "to convert this specific reference into a belief of exclusive ownership [by the individual] is . . . misleading" (HNC [MW14:15]; cf. EN [LW1:170–172]). It implies an atomistic psychology that betrays the sociological and narrative character of our situated existence.

We must be careful here. To say that these two, action and self-understanding, are interdependent must not be taken to mean, for Dewey, that they are completely equal. "Personality," he writes, "selfhood, subjectivity are *eventual* functions that emerge with complexly organized interactions" (EN [LW1:162 (emphasis added)]). "Subjectivity," he says more precisely, is thus "a novel reconstruction of a pre-existing order" (EN [LW1:168; cf. 170–171; 187–188]). Self-understanding emerges during breaks in what is otherwise the continuous connection between self and its context. These breaks mark off the points where we speak of the uniqueness of selves. Dewey specifically intends to capture the meaning of uniqueness in its political and ethical dimension, highlighting the resources of identity that serve to reconstitute and transform the larger social world:

> The point in placing emphasis upon the role of individual desire and thought in social life has in part been indicated. It shows the genuinely intermediate position of subjective mind: it proves it to be a mode of natural existence in which objects undergo directed reconstitution. Reference to the place of individual thought in political theory and practice has another value. Unless subjective intents and thoughts terminate in picturesque utopias or dogmas irrelevant to constructive action, *they are subject to objective requirements and tests.* . . .

Thinking and desiring, no matter how subjective, are a preliminary, tentative and inchoate mode of action. They are "overt" behavior of a communicated and public form in process of construction, and behavior involves change of objects which tests the meanings animating behavior. (EN [LW1:171 (emphasis added)])

These reflections from chapter 6 of *Experience and Nature,* "Nature, Mind and the Subject," are critically important because they begin to shed light on what I have referred to as the normative dimension of self-understanding for Dewey. They encapsulate his belief that practical action both regulates and liberates. What he intends to capture in the passage above goes some way toward avoiding the concern expressed by Hodge and Weber that without a sacred foundation we lapse into a radical subjectivism. I will not try to do complete justice to the point in this context and will instead return to it in chapters 3 and 4, but it is helpful to initiate the discussion. In elucidating Dewey's argument, I will also make reference to two other thinkers, namely, Brandom and McDowell, who advance similar claims that help capture the force of his position.

For Dewey, practical action regulates in the sense captured by the habitual dimension of identity, which, although flexible, nonetheless narrows and steadies the self—a self about which claims can be made, from which fulfillment of commitments can be demanded, and to which obligations can be owed and settled. The regulating or constraining dimension comes into view in *Human Nature and Conduct* when Dewey says: "A general liberation of impulses may set things going when they have been stagnant, but if the released forces are on their way to anything they do not know the way nor where they are going" (HNC [MW14:115]); he mentions this in the context of explaining the importance to freedom of social institutions and conventions. Such impulses will appear as mere behavioral spasms inexplicable within and unconstrained by the norms of the community. This is what he means when he says, in the passage quoted earlier: "Unless subjective intents and thoughts terminate in picturesque utopias or dogmas irrelevant to constructive action they are subject to objective requirements and tests."

The use of "objective" in this instance functions in precisely the way Brandom speaks about "constraint": "Being constrained by or subject to norms is a matter of belonging to a community, and that is a matter of being *taken* to be a member by the rest of the community."[36] If the relationship between practical action and self-understanding in Dewey's philosophy that I have been describing is correct, then it means that constraints are internally generated by virtue of our entrance into a social world. The constraints are immanent to a specific community, to be sure, but as I read Dewey and Brandom, the very *idea* and *existence* of constraints transcends all communities in the sense that we understand actions *qua* actions as that for which reasons may be provided, criticized, and assessed. This harmless view of transcendence, as McDowell explains, does not have as its aim the desire to escape the world, the "illusion that though we aim our thought and speech at the world from a standpoint constituted by our present practices and competences, we must be able to conceive the conformity of our thought and speech to the world from outside any such standpoint."[37]

Notice that on this account we remain completely located in the natural world, even as our extra-natural world (that is, of norms and their conceptual content) is emergent from it. Hence Dewey says in chapter 8 of *The Quest for Certainty*, "The Naturalization of Intelligence," that the "intelligent activity of man is not something brought to bear upon nature from without; it is nature realizing its own potentialities in behalf of a fuller and richer issue of events. Intelligence within nature means liberation and expansion" (QC [LW4:171]). Herbert Schneider provides us with a very animated, but helpful description of Dewey's position: "Mind is simply nature feeling her way, groping in her own darkness by her own light, trying herself out, finding out for herself what she can and cannot do."[38] Indeed, for Dewey the second, extra-natural, world functions as a normative constraint in the same way that the first, natural, world functions as a causal constraint. Naturalizing intelligence in this way, to quote McDowell once more, "removes any need to try to see ourselves as peculiarly bifurcated, with a foothold in the animal kingdom and a mysterious separate involvement in an extra-natural world of rational connections."[39]

Practical action also liberates in precisely the way Dewey is suggesting above. It provides the self with the very social world that potentially becomes an object of reconstruction.[40] "Habit," he explains, "is more than a restriction of thought. Habits become negative limits because they are first positive agencies. The more numerous our habits the wider the field of possible observation and foretelling" (HNC [MW14:123]). The idea of the social world, then, is meant to be taken expansively, so that acquiring habits to engage in communal practices includes resources for the development of new habits for managing and negotiating the world. Remember, Dewey discusses the importance of institutions and conventions in the context of freedom to describe not merely how they constrain, but what they make possible. And what they make possible, in this instance, is a novel reconstruction of a preexisting order. This much he says in his *Ethics*: "No argument about causation can affect the fact, verified constantly in experience, that we can and do learn, and that the learning is not limited to acquisition of additional information but extends to remaking old tendencies" (E$_3$ [LW7:305]). This is precisely why he goes on to say that "positive freedom"—what Brandom calls "expressive freedom" and McDowell refers to as "responsible freedom"—"is not a native gift or endowment but is acquired" (E$_3$ [LW7:306]).[41] Once more, it is worth turning to Brandom at length; he makes the same point in the context of human languages:

> One has not learned the language, has not acquired the capacity to engage in the social practices which are the use of the language, until one can produce *novel* sentences which the community will deem appropriate, and understand the appropriate novel utterances of other members of the community. . . . This emergent expressive capacity is the essence of natural languages. We ought to understand this creative aspect of language use as the paradigm of a new kind of freedom, *expressive* freedom. When one has mastered the social practices comprising the use of a language sufficiently, one becomes able to do something one could not do before, to produce and comprehend novel utterances. One becomes capable not only of framing new descriptions of situations and making an indefinite number of novel claims about the world, but also becomes capable of forming new intentions, and hence of performing an indefinite number of novel *actions*, directed at ends one could not have without the expressive capacity of language. . . . Without a suitable language there are some beliefs, desires, and intentions that one simply cannot have.[42]

I cite Brandom here because his account of the expressive capacity that accrues to language acquisition can be read (although I am not sure he would agree) as a more general explication of what Dewey means by the positive agencies that attach to practical action. For both, the conceptual substance needed to render intelligible to ourselves and others our desires, beliefs, and intentions (even novel ones) would not be possible without the prior *content-ful* restrictions of a social horizon. Hence Dewey explains in a letter to James in 1907: "I cannot help feeling that an adequate analysis of activity would exhibit the world of fact and the world of ideas as two correspondent objective statements of the active process itself. . . . It is this transcendence of any objectified form, whether perceptual or conceptual, that seems to me to give the clue to freedom, spontaneity, etc."[43] Expressive freedom does not simply fall out of the acquisition of our second nature, but is constitutive of it in the sense that it makes our entrance into and negotiation of the social world something more than mere imitation.

THE EXISTENTIAL DIMENSION OF
ACTION AND ITS TEMPORAL QUALITY

Precisely because action is revelatory it implies a condition of possibilities that may attend specific situations. Following James, Dewey notes in *Experience and Nature* that experience is "a double-barreled word . . . in that it recognizes in its primary integrity no division between act and material, subject and object but contains them both in an unanalyzed totality" (EN [LW1:18]).[44] But what does he mean here? To begin, although there is a revelatory dimension to action, it would be inaccurate to say that all experience is of this quality. Consider our everyday interactions with the world. We constantly employ habits and ways of doing things that do not disclose anything about the environment or us. To confront the loss of a loved one, to experience the excitement of an event, to drive and adhere to the rules of the road—each implies cognitive awareness, to be sure, but such experiences, in Dewey's view, are not primarily reflective. Our daily encounters are not necessarily an adventure in self-discovery; in fact, the habitual character of life saves us from having to reflect all the time. In this way we are not fundamentally creatures of thought.

This does not mean that reflection has never taken place, but rather that habits move to the background of reflection after having been formed through a process of reasoning in context. So when Dewey refers to experience as an "unanalyzed totality" or as "primary," he does not mean "any aboriginal stuff out of which things are evolved," for this stuff "is already overlaid and saturated with the products of the reflection of past generations and by-gone ages" (PIE [MW3:166]). He continues in *Experience and Nature*: primary experience "is filled with interpretations, classifications, due to sophisticated thought, which have become incorporated into what seems to be fresh naïve empirical materials" (EN [LW1:140]). Habits only *appear* to be pre-reflective, as simply part of the narrative in which we are implicated and to which we adhere by virtue of the choices we continually make. These choices help redeem the relevance of the narrative. To say that we build a storehouse of habits that allow us to engage our environment intelligently does not mean we are going through the motions outright. Nor does it make a claim in Dewey's view about the indeterminacy of the environment or the putative search for knowledge. Habit acquisition is not an adventure in discovery, even as the habit itself denotes that such an adventure has taken place.

Yet to refer to experience as "unanalyzed totality" or "primary" means that there are distinct reflective moments—that is, experience when analyzed and secondary—in which action emerges in relationship to the temporal horizon that makes the experience of agents purposive, meaningful, and an object of knowledge. The self is poised in an immediate way in the problematic or needful *present* between a *past* that provides resources (i.e., accumulated habits) discordant with the present, and a *future* in which the present event may be settled.[45] The self takes cognitive control to realize and determine some possibilities, while interpreting and avoiding others within the same temporal field that indicates the problem in the first instance. The intervention of action will effect a modification in two ways. First, there is a reconstruction and extension of past elements to create something novel that seeks to restore continuity (the view of expressive freedom discussed above)[46]; second, if continuity is restored the self is related differently to the experience previously understood as problematic.

The line of argument we have been pursuing indicates a more fundamental point about Dewey's philosophy that is rarely emphasized. His account of action should be read as also making a phenomenological claim that our cognitive capacities do not inherently or necessarily grasp the complex and elusive dimensions of the experiences they engage. "[W]e live forward," he says, "we live in a world where changes are going on whose issue means our weal or woe" (NRP [MW10:9]; cf. EN [LW1:18]; DE [MW9:146]). In a critically important passage in *Experience and Nature*, one which has parallels elsewhere in his work, he states this point and its implication clearly:

> The visible is set in the invisible; and in the end what is unseen decides what happens in the seen; the tangible rests precariously upon the untouched and ungrasped. The contrast and the potential maladjustment of the immediate . . . with those direct and hidden factors which determine the origin and career of what is present, are indestructible features of any and every experience. We may term the way in which our ancestors dealt with the contrast superstitious, but the contrast is no superstition. It is a primary datum in any experience. (EN [LW1:44–45]; cf. CIF [MW4:83]; HNC [MW14:145]; QC [LW4:6])

This passage is drawn from chapter 2 of *Experience and Nature*, "Existence as Precarious and as Stable." He uses the designation of "precarious" as part of that title to define one dimension of the world of action. If this claim is so rarely the primary object of Dewey's analysis, it is not because he discounts it, but rather because he takes it for granted. If, however, we centralize precariousness, and we understand action and the realization of values as organically related, then Dewey must be saying that precariousness saturates the whole of human experience. Contingency thus determines not merely the origin, but more critically the career of what is present (i.e. had, enjoyed, loved, valued).

His point is that the end toward which action aims is potentially resistant to mastery. The qualifier "potentially" is important: we do not know the consequent impact of our actions, "ends-in-view," as Dewey says, until they have played themselves out. In action, says Dewey, we put the "world in peril and no one can wholly predict what will emerge in its place" (EN [LW1:172]). This unpredictability—what Arendt would later call the "capacity for action"[47]— does contain within itself the possibility of settling needs, demands, problems. But for both Dewey and Arendt it equally places us in a position where we court adverse consequences. Action and the absence of complete mastery are coextensive; this means, to quote Arendt once more, that the "capacity for action does not harbor within itself certain potentialities which enable it to survive the disabilities of non-sovereignty."[48] If the term "adverse consequences" used a moment ago is to do justice to what Dewey means by linking contingency to action, it must denote the multifaceted composition of the natural world (including the agent), which may very well undermine action.

To identify the agent as a potential site for the display of contingency follows from Dewey's claim that our character is expressed through action. The self potentially becomes an obstacle to the settlement of the issue to the extent that "a desirable trait of character does not always produce desirable results" (HNC [MW14:36]). We are reminded of those unfortunate souls in Greek tragedies: they never realize the extent to which they become the source of their own demise or that of the people they most cherish. This is not usually because of their vices, but more tragically the way in which commitment to specific virtues obscures other factors of consideration. Hence Dewey's remark: "[E]ven when proper allowances are made [regarding the complex relationship between character and consequences], we are forcing the pace when we assume that there is or ever can be an exact equation of disposition and outcome" (HNC [MW14:36]).[49] As Patchen Markell explains in a different context, there is thus a potential vulnerability built into the temporal structure of action that "involve[s] the *doubling back* of some human capacity upon itself—a recursivity, in which a source of possibility also operates as its own limitations."[50]

The dual dimension to Dewey's account of action must therefore always be kept in focus, lest we obscure the character of action altogether. His point is captured nicely by Jean-Pierre Vernant in his discussion of Greek tragedy:

> From a tragic point of view then, there are two aspects to action. It involves on
> the one hand reflection, weighing up the pros and cons, foreseeing as accurately

as possible the means and the ends; on the other, placing one's stake on what is unknown and incomprehensible, risking oneself on a terrain which remains impenetrable, entering into a game . . . not knowing whether, as they join with one, they will bring success or doom.[51]

Much akin to Vernant's language, Dewey fundamentally understands living as a gamble. His language replicates the complexity of action to which Arendt, Markell, and Vernant draw our attention:

> Man finds himself living in an aleatory world; his existence involves, to put it baldly, a gamble. The world is a scene of risk; it is uncertain, unstable, uncannily unstable. Its dangers are irregular, inconstant, not to be counted upon as to their times and season. . . . It is the darkest just before dawn; pride goes before a fall; the moment of greatest prosperity is the moment most charged with ill-omen, most opportune for the evil eye. (EN [LW1:43])

The enabling relationship between contingency and action potentially contains disabling features that may undermine action.

THE PSYCHOLOGICAL ORIENTATION OF EXPECTATION

The foregoing remark is a crucial insight that has considerable value for understanding not only political and ethical life, but also scientific activity. Many, from Aristotle to Machiavelli to Arendt, have developed this insight in thinking about political action. For them, as for Dewey, it implies that the moral and political domains of life cannot wholly be captured or systematized under a covering law of universalism. Similar to these thinkers, for Dewey this chastened outlook does more, the substance of which goes to the very heart of our self-understanding. There is an internal tentativeness—a specific psychological orientation regarding expectation—to his conception of action that distinguishes his reflections from the traditional quest for certainty. For this reason the optimism-pessimism distinction does not capture the complexity of his position. He is clear that he rejects optimism as an appropriate stance toward the world of practical action, for "optimism has been the consequence of the attempt to explain evil away" (RIP [MW12:181]). And he equally abandons pessimism, for in "declaring the world is evil wholesale, it makes futile all efforts to discover the remediable causes of specific evils" (RIP [MW12:181]). Instead, the position of the practical actor is that of the meliorist—that is, "the belief that the specific conditions which exist at one moment, be they comparatively bad or comparatively good, in any event may be bettered" (RIP [MW12:181–182]). The auxiliary verb "may" in this formulation denotes caution. That we are creatures in time subject to all sorts of miseries equally means that we are capable of bringing into existence that which will sustain us through time. As Thomas Alexander keenly observes, Dewey's universe is one in which "action matters because tragedy is real."[52] The upshot is that the relationship between action and contingency for Dewey refers to that which is unprepared for because it is unanticipated or unexpected. But this, as he understands the matter, is nonetheless a presupposition for the unfolding dimension of life.

CONTINGENCY AND THE PLACE OF INTELLIGENT ACTION

Thus far the argument has advanced several steps. First, we examined the appropriate fit between Aristotle's categories of knowledge and the way in which Dewey's account of inquiry generally transforms those categories. In that context, the emphasis was placed on the importance of contingency not only to ethical and political life as found in Aristotle's thoughts, but more broadly to human action, as Dewey argues. Here we answered the first two of the questions with which we began, questions relating to his understanding of Darwin in contrast to his liberal Protestant counterparts and the precise usage to which he puts Darwin's theory. Second, we examined his account of the philosophical obstacle—namely, the quest for certainty—to seeing the importance of contingency to human action. And third, we explicated how Darwin helps him undercut the quest for certainty. This opened space to explore the relationship between contingency and the contours of Dewey's philosophy of action. Here we found resources to hold at bay the worry advanced by Hodge and Weber regarding spiritual sickness or disenchantment. These three steps were necessary in order to understand Dewey's perspective on inquiry's proper functioning.

There are several conclusions we must now keep in mind as we transition to an explication of inquiry. If certainty cannot be had, Dewey's aim is to structure inquiry such that the judgments we reach are the products of a bit more than luck. His conception of inquiry is therefore unintelligible unless it proceeds via sensitivity to particulars and the potential for disruptions. This works on two levels:

First, there is the character of the agent—the experiences and habits that feed into and comprise his character.

Second, there is the complexity and salience of the situation of concern—the unavoidable rough terrain of life.

Inquiry works best as Dewey describes it when there is a dialectical relationship between these two dimensions. The well-functioning inquiry is not merely a matter of proceduralism, but must also include appreciation for just those features of a situation that ought to engage a person in order for us to be able to say that they have made an informed decision. This description, I argue, solidifies the connection that we have stipulated in general terms between Dewey's notion of inquiry and Aristotle's account of *phronēsis*.

There are two additional points we should remember as we examine inquiry. First, I have referred to inquiry as a social practice. Given the discussion above, this means that it is functionally assessed in the flow and reconstruction of problematic experiences to which others are privy. We should remember that while there is a larger context (i.e., institutions, symbols, persons) in which inquiry derives its significance, the connection between action and contingency means that this context cannot be so unshakable as to prevent future deployment of inquiry. Second, I have referred to Dewey's account of inquiry as setting limiting factors that allow for a *weak* metaphysics. That is, the proper functioning of inquiry orients the self not merely to the material objects of the world but also to the potential pressures that are emergent in our connection with the world. Dewey often reads as a cartographer with his use of the language of maps to explain what inquiry does and the way it helps navigate the world of practical action. Precisely because of the primacy of contingency, he understands the fundamental need to revisit the map's construction. A weak metaphysics thus has an open-ended, evolving, and therefore experimental dimension. This must mean, as Richard Bernstein notes, that "such a metaphysics makes no claim to reveal a reality which is beyond all experience and is known only in an *a priori* fashion. It is an *a posteriori* metaphysics, descriptive and hypothetical."[53] These two points—inquiry as a social practice and inquiry as a limiting factor on metaphysics—represent analytic distinctions, but are coextensive at the moment of intelligent action.

DEWEY'S MODIFIED ARISTOTELIANISM REVISITED

Let us return to Aristotle for a moment in order to focus our analysis. When Aristotle refers to *phronēsis* as an intellectual virtue, he indicates that it is a "reasoned and true state of capacity to act with regard to human goods," and when so exercised it "issues commands, since its end is what ought to be done or not to be done."[54] What Aristotle means by this statement is captured by the relationship between *phronēsis* and the moral virtues. The virtue of generosity, for example, means that, when applied, it will be for the correct reason in the right context. But exactly how are individuals to know the right context if not because they have cultivated a level of sensitivity to particular situations that helps render the use of generosity intelligible. "Sensitivity" is a compact word in this instance; it means that one has assessed the situation that suggests the need for generosity; one has ruled out the particular need for another virtue as a settlement of the issue, and one has made a judgment that generosity fits the need. Individuals build up a storehouse of cases throughout their lives that provides them with the information to allow them to deal with other situations that are similar in structure, although not identical in substance. Aristotle expresses this point by making deliberation a vehicle through which *phronēsis* is expressed: "Deliberation is concerned with things that happen in a certain way *for the most part*, but in which the event is obscure, and with things in which it is indeterminate."[55]

That Aristotle views *phronēsis* as the completion of a deliberative process does not preclude error or the intervention of things about which we could not have been aware. It presupposes the relationship between action and contingency suggested above by Dewey's account. Aristotle presents *phronēsis* as the completion of a process to capture its fundamental aim. Thus, he understands *phronēsis* as reasoning well about ethical life generally as connected through particular actions.[56] The claim is simply this: whether one displays the virtue of generosity, courage, or justice, all require one and the same *phronēsis*.

As already noted, I read Dewey as expanding the reach of *phronēsis* via Darwin. In the first instance, the reliance on Darwin helps him highlight that contingency is a fundamental part of the world as such. This allows us to recast Aristotle's statement regarding deliberation from Dewey's perspective: inquiry into natural phenomena—broadly conceived—is concerned with "things that happen in a certain way for the most part, but in which the event is obscure, and with things in which it is indeterminate." In the second instance, Dewey interprets all cases in which we make a judgment of action as sharing the same intellectual structure. That some of these judgments are closer to or further away from the contours of one's identity (say, for example, moral decisions as oppose to scientific ones) is important in assessing the scope and consequences of those judgments, but does not transform their underlying intellectual structure. If moral and scientific judgments are radically different, in Dewey's view, the difference can be in terms of neither the intellectual structure that underwrites them nor their potential fallibility.

Another way to state my point is to say that *phronēsis*, for Aristotle, is to the moral virtues, what inquiry, for Dewey, is to human action in toto.[57] The claim is not, as indicated in the first section of this chapter, that *phronēsis* and inquiry are the same, but rather that if the latter is to function properly, it must, in my reading of Dewey, include the content of what we mean when we refer to the former. As a social practice, then, inquiry is exercised relative to a particular context and embodied in actions, the content of which exists at the crossroads between various experiential factors and reasons and the way the agent determines them.

If we turn to Dewey's formal structure of inquiry, we can see the dialectical relationship between the two levels mentioned earlier at work. He provides a precise statement of this in *How We Think*:

> (i) a felt difficulty; (ii) its location and definition; (iii) suggestion of possible solution; (iv) development by reasoning of the bearings of the suggestion; (v) further observation and experiment leading to its acceptance or rejection; that is, the conclusion of belief or disbelief. (Dewey, HWT$_1$ [MW6:236]; cf. LJP [MW8:15-23], L [LW12: pt. 2])

The felt difficulty means that the situation exerts pressure that demands a response. The continuity within experience is fractured, opening up the necessity for reflection so as to achieve restoration. But here, and this point is crucial, the fractures indicate the exhaustion of existing habits such that the problem requires creative valuation. What is needed is a judgment of action, something to be done in which the problem acts as a guiding marker in moving us through the other stages of our reflection.

The feeling of the difficulty requires us to localize and define the problem. The issue may require several propositional formulations before the clarity of the problem comes into view. We will often need to take counsel with others, for example. So there may be a subclass of formulations that are constitutively connected to articulating the precise problem to be addressed. "Their subject-matter," writes Dewey, "implies that the proposition is itself a factor in the completion of the situation, carrying it forward to its conclusion" (LJP [MW8:16]).

Obviously this is an intermediate stage—an attempt to clarify the situation so as to move to other aspects that will settle the problem. But even at this juncture, Dewey's language indicates that there are *better* or *worse* descriptions of the problem if we are to potentially arrive at a solution. "Better" or "worse" indicates that unless the situation is descriptively impenetrable,[58] it must contain elements that refer to a multitude of other—different—situations that indicate in abbreviated form how this situation should roughly look whether we are responsive to those elements or not. Now, the better or worse is not, properly speaking, derived from objective criteria regarding the specific case—no such criteria exist. Rather, better or worse is derived, as Brandom says, from the "holistic objective regularities of performance[s]" in relation to these various other elements that are salient.[59] Inquiry thus works, in Dewey's view, as a culling mechanism that registers content from the intersubjectively formed social world that extends beyond the epistemic authority of the self. Our ability to make reference to comparable features of the social world allows us to understand these *objective* regularities to which we appeal in making claims about better or worse.

Responsibility for describing the situation—crystallizing its contours or distorting them altogether—lies with the agent. That one takes counsel with others, as Dewey often emphasizes in his explication of the cooperative character of inquiry, is based on the belief that others may very well see the matter differently because their particular experiences shape their perceptual abilities in ways unlike our own (EN [LW1:135]). This is particularly so, he insists, in moral and political matters, but is no less apparent in empirical science. For in all cases what is needed is a sense of "sympathy which carries thought out beyond the self and which extends its scope . . . it is sympathy which saves considerations of consequences from degenerating into mere calculation, by rendering vivid the interests of others [or other factors] and urging us to give them weight" (E$_3$ [LW7:270]). McDowell, for instance, writes nicely on this point; his thoughts are much akin to Dewey's outlook: "The deliverances of a reliable sensitivity are cases of knowledge; and there are idioms according to which the sensitivity itself can appropriately be described as knowledge: a kind person knows what it is like to be confronted with a requirement of kindness. The sensitivity is, we might say, a sort of perceptual capacity."[60]

But honing this perceptual capacity, as Dewey and McDowell argue, will often involve us in significant exchanges with others. The kind of collaboration, then, suggested by intersubjectivity involves an underlying normative claim that we readily employ and usually take for granted—namely, that there are instances in which persons can incur blame for relying insufficiently or too heavily upon themselves when assessing complex terrain in which a judgment of action is necessary. The sensitivity here, Dewey explains, consists in just the extent to which we engage in a "broad, just, sympathetic survey of situations" to register relevant data in forming our judgments (HNC [MW14:144]). Dewey, no less than Aristotle before him and McDowell after him, views this not as blind deference, but rather as individuals allowing an authority that they acknowledge to participate in the formation of their own judgments.

What Dewey is drawing our attention to is the explicability of action that makes discursive negotiation central. This theme figures prominently in Brandom's normative pragmatics, Jeffrey Stout's attempt to distill the ethical and political implications of such a pragmatics, and Jürgen Habermas' discourse ethics.[61] For all these thinkers, to say some actions as opposed to others proceed from inquiry is to evaluate their reasons as appropriate because of the context in which they function. The agent is prepared to justify why that action is done rather than some other—which is simply to say, action is explicable in terms of the reasons we offer on its behalf. We understand ourselves to be offering cause or basis from a background of potential reasons that embody attentiveness to just those various considerations one could offer given the situation of concern. When a hypothesis or norm is advanced as a response to a problem situation, we usually justify our choice to other individuals by reference to competing alternatives that for one reason or another fail to sufficiently take into account important considerations which would otherwise make them the best projected options. Practical actions, then, have a linguistic counterpart—that is, they are responses to "why-questions" in a practice of giving and asking for reasons (HNC [MW14: chap. 14]; EN [LW1: chap. 5]).[62] This form of mutual responsiveness is reflected more clearly in the social psychology of Dewey and Mead. For both of them it grounds moral life proper (see the first section of chapter 4 below), and in Dewey's philosophy in particular it provides the framework from which democracy proceeds and in which it finds support (see the first section of chapter 3, and chap. 5).

The reason-giving character of inquiry rests on two separate tenets of Dewey's philosophy that we have considered thus far. The first relates to viewing experience as a potential experimental domain. And the second is Dewey's specific account of the way in which self-understanding emerges in a social network, with its liberating and constraining aspects. Inquiry and communication are thus coextensive. The result of this is that action and language are equi-primordial as well as publicly accessible: "[D]eliberation . . . regards the end-in-view . . . as tentative and permits, nay encourages the coming into view of consequences which will transform it and create new purpose and plan" (HNC [MW14:149]). He remarks elsewhere: "When communication occurs, all natural events are subject to reconsideration and revision whether it be public discourse or that preliminary discourse termed thinking" (EN [LW1:132]).

Yet what determines whether the problem is clearly described is something other than the formal process of inquiry, and is rather bound up with the shape of one's receptivity from upbringing. This much Dewey suggests:

"Habit does not preclude the use of thought, but it determines the channels within which it operates. Thinking is secreted in the interstices of habits" (PP [LW2:335]; cf. HNC [MW14:142]). Habits open the self to receiving considerations that inform inquiry's functioning, and those habits shape our understanding of those considerations. When we say a person is diligent, focused, attentive to others, cold, unimaginative, dramatic, careless, we are delineating character traits that will direct and condition both incoming data and information and outgoing responses and proposals (cf. E_3 [LW7:256–258]). We are reminded of situations in which individuals exclude or fail to take into consideration factors that might otherwise clarify the issue of concern. Our utterances often take the form of: "Did you consider X?" or "Did you look at Y?" In some cases these utterances will simply bring to light information that guides inquiry; they are not claims about a person's character. This is because the individual is appropriately sensitive in precisely the way I identified above. But in other cases these questions are asked because we know the agent to be just the sort of person who would not consider such factors. Or we know that because of various features of a person's character—traits such as the ones listed above—they simply cannot see the way in which those considerations ought to engage them given the problem.

These two previous statements advance different but important claims. The first suggests that one's character is of such a nature that given the situation a person simply ignores factors that any other competent inquirer in the situation would usually consider. The issue is not what we will say to the individual, but what we will say about their genuine desire to inquire—by elucidating the various epistemic virtues they refuse to employ. Such individuals, we might say, avoid having to address objections raised about their position or considerations that are contrary to their own beliefs. They are not interested, at least in this context, in offering beliefs or hypotheses that aim at being the *best* beliefs or hypotheses they could have. The second claim suggests that the considerations simply do not engage the person, independent of a desire and willingness to ignore them. Here we may be more interested in how they may become better attuned to the world. But neither claim necessarily means for Dewey that transformation within the self's outlook is closed off, for we recall that the self is relatively stable, not fixed.

To say that others can recognize and assess the content that feeds into inquiry simply identifies individuals as sharing modes of perception, senses of significance, parallel cases, interests, and desires—in short, forms of life. This allows us not only to identify better or worse characterizations of the problem situation, but, more significant, to indicate that there is a *best achievable state* of the agent regarding sensitivity to just those reasons and factors that help define the situation from the outset (see the first two sections of chap. 4).[63] What to do is parasitic on how the situation looks, and this requires, as Dewey understands the matter, a proper appreciation for those features which are constitutive of the present moment, but which can only be received based on the character of the self. Construal of the situation will always be something more than proceduralism, even as these independent dictates guide inquiry to fruitful destination points. If my reading is correct, it would show that for Dewey these independent dictates given the situation of concern are to be identified with inquiry—that is, practical wisdom and inquiry completely interpenetrate.

Dewey's third and fourth phases relate to the suggestions of possible solutions and reasoning from those suggestions. These two stages are critically important because they imply the launching into the unknown. He often refers to these stages as involving the "art of inference":

> Every act of human life, not springing from instinct or mechanical habit, contains it; most habits are dependent upon some amount of it from their formation, as they are dependent upon it for their readaptation to novel circumstances. From the humblest act of daily life to the most intricate calculations of science and the determination and execution of social, legal, and political policies, things are used as signs, indicates, or evidence from which one proceeds to something else not yet directly given. (LJP [MW9:69])

Inference does not function in the way that we would usually find articulated by statisticians; it does not simply refer to induction and deduction but also to what Charles S. Peirce calls abduction—that is, "studying facts and devising a theory to explain them. Its only justification is that if we are ever to understand things at all, it must be in that way."[64] As Norwood Hanson explains of Peirce's position, although it applies equally to Dewey's account: "Deduction proves that something *must* be; Induction shows that something *actually is* operative; Abduction merely suggest that something *may be*."[65] That inference is an art for Dewey (as well as for Peirce) means, among other things, that there is a level of imprecision in our attentiveness to the relationship between information gathered and the hypothesis inferred and proposed. "A keen eye and a quick ear," says Dewey, "are not in themselves guarantees of correct knowledge . . . but they are conditions without which knowledge cannot arise" (E_3 [LW7:268]). So inference here must be understood broadly to denote a kind of sensitivity to the salient elements of an intricate situation. We move back and forth between these features, at first only imaginatively envisioning the proposed consequences and then ultimately following their course in the domain of experience. But in this back and forth (a discursive-reflective equilibrium, we should note) we are reasoning and making judgments, taking hold of some set of factors that allow us to move to some other set, while ruling out others—all of which suggests that inference is a messy affair.

The fact that this process is not explicable in clearly stated rules does not undermine its importance. In the end, the suggestion is simply that we make inferences within the context of the problem, not external to it, so that the judgments made implicate us in the resolution or irresolution of the situation.[66] For this reason our conjectures, suggestions, or beliefs potentially carry an attached risk that is located at two different levels. The first level is the relationship between agent and context. Here the self constitutes a fundamental datum in arriving at a solution. The second level is the relationship between proposal and context. As Dewey says: "[T]hrough inference men are capable of a kind of success and exposed to a kind of failure not otherwise possible" (LJP [MW8:71]).[67]

The emphasis Dewey places on inference sheds some light on his thinking about the creative character of inquiry. Consider, for a moment, the section heading and subheading Dewey uses in chapter 6, "Examples of Inference and Testing" to the 1933 revised version of *How We Think*: "II. Inference to the Unknown" and "Inference Involves a Leap" (HWT$_2$ [LW8:190–191]). The titles are more than suggestive. But we do not infer blindly; the unknown is not meant as such largely because the problem guides the structure of the inquiry. This is also evident by the preposition he uses: something is already known from which we move *to* ascertain something unknown. As he says in "The Logic of Judgments of Practice": "[I]nference takes absent things as being in certain real continuum with present things, so that our attitude toward the latter is bound up with our reaction to the former as parts of the same situation" (LJP [MW8:71]; cf. NRP [MW10:15], VEK [MW13:10 n. 7]).

Inference as a phase in inquiry is clearly the moment of transformation and creativity. Transformation thus means that the thing known is related differently to the incomplete space that constitutes the problem situation. Our apprehension of the thing known—that is, the meaning-content—is different from what it was before inquiry began. The creativity of this moment rests with the settlement of the problematic situation, making the meaning of the experience richer than before, which becomes the new content that we use in other related experiences. Precisely because our inferences have their career in some present situation and set of facts and reasons we are able to defend against claims that our proposals or hypotheses are mere illusions or unrealistic.

The confirmation of phases three and four rests with the last stage, that of further observation and testing, on which Dewey places particular emphasis. *"What is important is that every inference be a tested inference; or that we discriminate between beliefs that rest upon tested evidenced and those that do not, and be accordingly on our guard as to the kind and degree of assent or belief that is justified"* (HWT$_2$ [LW8:92 (original emphasis)]; cf. L [LW12:14–15]). As Dewey explains in his *Logic* of 1938, we are thus warranted in asserting a belief, the accuracy of a proposed plan, or the appropriateness of this or that virtue if it settles the experience that stimulated the inquiry (L [LW12:15–17; cf. 156–161]). It is important to understand that in certain cases we will have suspended other beliefs that are ancillary to the hypothesis tested. That is, there will be an array of factors that we will need to take for granted but which contextualize the hypothesis under consideration. As Peirce reminds us, we will most certainly find it very hard to think at all if we stopped taking a great many factors for granted. But if this is so, as Dewey believes, acceptance of a hypothesis means that it settles the problem, that it can withstand new experiences and arguments if they arise, and that in some sets of cases (usually the most important ones) it coheres with other settled and suspended beliefs (L [LW12:343]). This last point merely carries through Dewey's initial commitment to experience as the beginning and terminal point for inquiry, where "terminal" denotes a potentially different temporal moment from the one in which the hypothesis originally settled the matter.[68]

The general account of inquiry we have been pursuing as well as the connection drawn between Aristotle and Dewey raises a concern worth considering. The worry is that Aristotle specifically wants to distinguish between cases in which one employs inquiry for the acquisition of some skill to achieve some given end, for example, and cases in which the end itself is determined in the process of deliberation. If assimilated, the argument might go, we risk obscuring the noncodifiable nature of *phronēsis*. If applied to the art of living, it implies that the purpose of human existence must be as fixed as the goal of acquiring and using a skill or form of technical knowledge.

Here the relationship between *phronēsis* and *technē* returns, but now it works as a critique against Dewey. It appears that Dewey's conception of inquiry is concerned only about means to some defined end, but is unable to reach and potentially transform the end sought after or create a new end altogether. When his account of inquiry is challenged for being instrumental, this is often one of the lines pursued. There is, however, an interesting argument presented by Julia Annas in her reading and expansion of Aristotle's thoughts.[69] In brief, she argues that there is a unifying logical structure that underwrites the acquisition of both skills and virtues. As she writes of this, "to consider our *telos* as a fixed point to guide our thoughts about the virtues is to get matters wrong way round. It is not the object of the skill but the structure and unification of the skilled reasoning that is the crucial point of analogy for ethical reasoning."[70] Dewey anticipates Annas' move in his account of inquiry:

> If thinking is the art by which knowledge is practiced, then the materials with which thinking deals may be supposed, by analogy with the other arts, to take on in consequence special shapes. The man who is making a boat will give wood a form which it did not have, in order that it may serve the purposes to which it is to be put. Thinking may then be supposed to give its material the form which will make it amenable to its purposes—attaining knowledge, or, as it is ordinarily put, going from the unknown to the known. (LJP [MW8:65–66)

There is a clear sense in which a skill can easily be taught and appropriated, but which in no way seems to depend on the practical wisdom of the maker. But this, argues Dewey and Annas, wrongly imports the determinate end back into the intellectual structure needed to originally arrive at the end and subsequently bring it to fruition again. If an instrument made to sail the boat-maker safely from one shore to another looked very much like what we call a boat, but seemed to sink immediately upon entering the water or was unable to last long enough in moving from one shore to another, we would scratch our heads in bewilderment. As Dewey says, however, in fixing our attention on the belief that the construction of objects such as boats requires "mere repetition [of a procedure] or literal loyalty" to a model, we obscure the extent to which the individual must "take account of" or "reckon with" factors that are not mere repetition, such as assessing, for example, "the grain and strength of the wood" (LJP [MW8:67]). This formulation immediately prompts us to ask: "How much should we take account of?" or "To what degree must we reckon with various factors?" If I understand Dewey correctly, the answer to these questions will often take the form: "You have to see for yourself." We can make use of and slightly amend Annas' language to serve Dewey: "As with any skill we can give rules to help the learner, but obviously there is no foolproof recipe or guarantee of success. And so with [the practice of inquiry]—success is not mechanical; there are many incalculable failures of temperament or intellect that may thwart the right decision."[71] Understanding this point, to employ Annas' language once more, keeps us from being tempted to see in Dewey's thought the "ideal of a purely mechanical decision-making procedure, one which would do the work for us and leave no role to individual deliberation."[72] Thus Dewey concludes: "To say that something is to be learned, is to be found out, is to be . . . believed, is to say that something is to be done. Every such proposition in the concrete is a practical proposition. Every such proposition of inquiry, discovery and testing will have then the traits assigned to the class of practical propositions" (LJP [MW8:65]).

There are two points we can draw from the line of reasoning we have pursued thus far that address the extent to which inquiry is also concerned about ends. First, the intellectual structure need not imply a substantive character to the end, as the example of boat-making suggests. It need only claim that the assessment of the end implies that its career begins and terminates in experience, the result of which often means that the agent is doing more than merely following a formal decision-making procedure. Recall the importance of inference in Dewey's account. There is a creative moment here that draws on funded experiences, but which is not reducible to such experiences. Second, this does not rule out those cases in which the means used to settle some problem or demand in experience transform and define what determinate judgment we make. Recall that the character of the agent, as well as context, influences considerations and factors at various stages of the overall inquiry, so that a subclass of outcomes will often reflexively impact the original intentions and outlook of the agent.

Dewey crystallizes this point in the context of our moral lives where end-constitutive debate is at issue. He writes the following: "The more completely the notion of the model is formed outside and irrespective of the specific conditions which the situation of action presents, the less intelligent is the act" (LJP [MW8:38–39]). In such cases, says Dewey, "[t]he man who is not accessible to such change in the case of *moral situations* has ceased to be a moral agent and become a reacting machine" (LJP [MW8:39]). Dewey's claim is obviously wide enough to account for reflection about what is to count *as* the end. But in order to say anything meaningful about ends, we need a much richer narrative about the communities involved, their ethical and political commitments, and their willingness to subject their decisions to scrutiny and revision. This should immediately signal that for Dewey whatever our ends are, they are subject to constraints, which contain normative implications that can potentially transform how we navigate through our religious, ethical, and political landscapes. To say, then, that control of our physical environment, the acquisition and successful deployment of skills, and the art of living share the same intellectual structure is only to point to a shift, Dewey believes, away from "forming ideas and judgments . . . on the basis of conformity to antecedent objects, [and rather] to constructing . . . objects directed by knowledge of consequences" (QC [LW4:217]).

Of course this explication of inquiry raises a number of issues, not the least of which pertains to the relationship between belief, evidence (old and new), and context, on the one hand, and the status and place of impartiality and objectivity, on the other. I have touched on some of these issues here, but we will take them up in the coming chapters as part of a reconsideration of the character of inquiry. In this chapter, I have intended only to explicate Dewey's conception of inquiry in the context of his philosophy of action, and to make a gesture toward the complexity this suggests. What this account ultimately commits us to can be discerned only through a consideration of the specific subject matter of religion, ethics, and politics. For the moment, the above account will suffice.

INQUIRY AND WEAK METAPHYSICS

We may now turn to the issue of metaphysics. At the outset we should acknowledge that Dewey departs from the standard usage of the term. Many Dewey scholars have tended to focus on that part of *Experience and Nature* that attempts to lay out the "generic traits of existence" (EN [LW1:50]). This vague phrase, to which Richard Rorty and others attach themselves, makes it appear as if Dewey seeks to articulate traits of existence prior to experience of them.[73] But if experience is our primary touch point, how can we be sure of the persistence of these traits? Surely, they will appear just as foundational as any other piece of traditional metaphysical reflection, beyond the testing reach of inquiry. There is an industry of commentary on this formulation of Dewey's that makes him the problem, rather than framing investigations into Dewey from the perspective of the problem he seeks to address.[74] To approach him from the latter perspective, as suggested throughout, redirects our attention in *Experience and Nature* to figuring out metaphysics' meaning for him. It takes seriously the narrative of the last chapter and its connection to the account in this one.

To begin, in chapter 3 of *Experience and Nature*, "Nature, Ends, and Histories," Dewey writes the following: "Poets who have sung of despair in the midst of prosperity, and of hope amid darkest gloom, have been the true metaphysicians of nature" (EN [LW1:96]). But what does Dewey mean by this formulation? Why is the poet—the artist—considered the true meta-physician of nature? This imagery of art comes back again where he notes that metaphysics provides a "ground-map of the province of criticism" (EN [LW1:309]). As he tells us in the unfinished introduction to an intended reis-sue of *Experience and Nature*, "experience [acts as a] cautionary and direc-tive word . . . to remind us that the world which is lived, suffered and enjoyed as well as logically thought of, has the last word in all human inquiries and surmises" (ENR [LW1:372]). "This is," he adds, "a doctrine of humility but it is also a doctrine of direction" (ENR [LW1:372]).

When Dewey's philosophy is criticized, these challenges are animated by the frustration that somehow his project and reflections on inquiry lack a certain gravitas that life demands. But if we combine the image of the artist or poet with that of the ground-map as a meeting point through inquiry, we find that his vision of what metaphysics is in fact achieves the opposite. It provides a figuration of the experiential world that serves not only as a source of direction, but also as one of caution, as he says. Inquiry makes us aware of nature's "impressive and irresistible mixture of sufficiencies, tight complete-nesses, order, recurrences which make possible prediction and control, and singularities, ambiguities, uncertain possibilities, processes going to conse-quences as yet indeterminate" (EN [LW1:47]). This is precisely why practical wisdom becomes important to inquiry, making the latter more than a mere inflexible procedure. Dewey acknowledges Aristotle's attentiveness to contin-gency, and so he notes continuity between his naturalistic metaphysics and what we find in Aristotle. But alas, he argues, Aristotle is unable to abandon a fundamental essentialism that installs a realm of Being and makes the world of practical action *appear* fallen—a sick world from which we are alienated (EN [LW1:47–49]).

For Dewey, humility is the gift of inquiry. Inquiry ascertains meanings otherwise not there and satisfies fractures in human life, but also may fail to do so—that is, our projections into the world may fall short of what they attempt to satisfy, manage, or negotiate. For an object may, says Dewey in *Experience and Nature*, "endure *secula seculorum* and yet not be everlast-ing; it will crumble before the gnawing tooth of time, as it exceeds a certain measure. Every existence is an event" (EN [LW1:63]). But we ought not to lament. The fact is "something to be noted and used. If it is discomfiting when applied to good things, to our friends, possession and precious selves, it is consoling also to know that no evil endures forever" (EN [LW1:63–64]). Recall the image of the poet who sings of despair at the moment of joy, and hope in the darkest hour. Retaining both of these images allows us to see that inquiry reins us in as well as spurs us on; it encourages self-assertion and cautions humility. So inquiry provides us access to a kind of metaphysics about human beings and the natural and social world they inhabit that simultaneously opens us to precisely those elements within experience that structure our future encounters. Opening us to elements in experience potentially points to the limitation of the foundations on which we rely from the outset. Stephen White provides some direction here in his elucidation of the contemporary turn in political theory to weak ontology against the background of two pressing issues:

> First, there is the acceptance of the idea that all fundamental conceptualizations of self, other, and world are contestable. Second, there is the sense that such conceptualizations are nevertheless necessary or unavoidable for an adequately reflective ethical and political life. The latter insight demands from us the affirmative gesture of constructing foundations, the former prevents us from carrying out this task in a traditional fashion.[75]

The upshot is that inquiry works to keep us critically aware of this in the sense suggested by the frame of mind it puts us in regarding expectation. When read through Dewey, I take this to mean that our conceptualizations of self and world are not placed beyond reevaluation. Recall the meliorist! The words that come to mind here include: watchful, wary, receptive, perceptive, and alert. Dewey provides an important passage worth citing at length that acknowledges and prefigures White's point:

> Fidelity to the nature to which we belong, as parts however weak, demands that we cherish our desires and ideals till we have converted them into intelligence, revised them in terms of the ways and means which nature makes possible. When we have used our thought to its utmost and have thrown into the moving unbalanced balance of things our puny strength, we know that though the universe slay us still we may trust, for our lot is one with whatever is good in existence. We know that such thought and effort is one condition of the coming into existence of the better. As far as we are concerned it is the only condition, for it alone is in our power. To ask more than this is childish. (EN [LW1:314])

Cornel West, for example, reads this passage as a wonderful example of what I referred to in the last chapter, following William Connolly, as the domestication of contingency.[76] No matter what fate may befall the products of inquiry, we can be sure, the passage seemingly says, that good is on our side and the better is coming into existence. If this is right, then Dewey will have fallen into a version of the problem that afflicted liberal Protestantism.

We should not conclude on this note so quickly. The question underlying this passage is the following: Where do we stand once we have sincerely deployed inquiry, come up with a course of action, and acted upon that decision? For Dewey, we confidently believe that our decision, our lot as he says in the passage, is on the side of whatever is good in existence—that is, what will sustain us—though the universe may slay us nonetheless. And perhaps we discover that we were wrong, or better still, we were right, but something befalls the plan and undermines our aims. Dewey's point is that if we do not at least assume the position that good possibilities may accrue to inquiry's productions, then it is unclear why we would employ it to begin with. We would, in other words, have fallen prey to pessimism. For this reason he argues, assuming the thought that inquiry can do *some work* in realizing the better is *one* of the conditions for the good coming into existence. Since this is all we have, he concludes, inquiry alone is in our power.

It is a mistake to ask for much more. The point is that Dewey seeks to engender an outlook toward the art of living that transforms the emotional and intellectual course one takes into any one particular issue in life. In his estimation, this is the framework of our metaphysical projects when they take their point of departure from the world of practical action. Our hubris is revealed by an inability to embrace the goods realized because we are unable to make a strong claim about their epistemic status or the extent to which they find affirmation in something nonhuman in character. This, I suggest, frames not only Dewey's reflections on religion in *A Common Faith*, but his ethical and political outlook as well.

RELIGION, THE MORAL LIFE, AND DEMOCRACY

And further, I will not dissemble my hope, that each person whom I address has felt his own call to cast aside all evil customs, timidities, and limitations, and to be in his place a free and helpful man a reformer . . . who must find or cut a straight road to everything excellent in the earth, and not only go honorably himself, but make it easier for all who follow him, to go in honor and with benefit.

RALPH WALDO EMERSON, "Man the Reformer"

Whether a God exist, or whether no God exist, in yon blue heaven above us bent, we form at any rate an ethical republic here below. And the first reflection which this leads to is that ethics have as genuine and real a foothold in a universe where the highest consciousness is human, as in a universe where there is a God as well.

WILLIAM JAMES, "The Moral Philosopher and the Moral Life"

At the present time, almost all important ethical problems arise out of the conditions of associated life. . . . That the present is a time of social change such as have been mentioned is a commonplace; the mere existence alone of democratic government, for example, raises social issues for moral decisions which did not exist for most men and women so long as government was autocratic and confined to a few.

JOHN DEWEY, *Ethics*

CHAPTER

3

FAITH AND
DEMOCRATIC PIETY

In the last chapter we examined the possibilities and limitations of inquiry as evidenced in Dewey's philosophy of action. By making practical action central and simultaneously connecting it to contingency, Dewey identifies inquiry as the source of knowledge. Inquiry thus retains, in his view, Aristotle's sensitivity to contingency as embodied in practical wisdom, but is nonetheless capable of serving as the determinant process for acquiring knowledge in all domains of life. Since inquiry emerges out of fractures or problems in experience, the products of inquiry are judged as effective responses within that horizon. The meaningfulness of human agency, questioned by Hodge in the wake of Darwin, is a function of effective action, and does not hinge on our ability to achieve epistemic certainty or to connect to something supernatural in character. This approach, however, makes central to inquiry the practice of giving and asking for reasons and so must contain normative resources to resist the problem of radical subjectivism. This completes Dewey's initial response to the problem identified in chapter 1. The aim of part II is to reconstruct his understanding of religion, morality, and political life in the light of these claims. We begin, in this chapter, with his reflections on religion.

We must now ask the following: How should we conceive of our religious lives given that our fundamental orientation proceeds from the domain of practical action? This is the question behind Dewey's 1934 Terry Lectures, *A Common Faith*, which he delivered at Yale University; it directs our attention away from the traditional questions within the history of theology. What this means for religion he indicates in his 1933 review of *Is There a God? A Conversation* by Nelson Wieman, Douglas Clyde Macintosh, and Max Carl Otto:

Separating the matter of religious experience from the question of the existence of God . . . I have found—and there are many who will corroborate my experience by their own—that all of the things which traditional religions prize and which they connect exclusively with their own conception of God can be had equally well in the ordinary course of human experience in our relations to the natural world and to one another as human beings related in the family, friendship, industry, art, science, and citizenship. *Either then the concept of God can be dropped out as far as genuinely religious experience is concerned or it must be framed wholly in terms of natural and human relationship involved in our straightaway human experience.* (DR [LW9:224] [original emphasis])[1]

This passage encapsulates Dewey's understanding of *religious naturalism*: nature—broadly conceived—can generate both a sense of piety and a guiding faith in life without requiring a supernatural source for their intelligibility. These themes run throughout Dewey's philosophy in various forms between 1900 and 1935. The major difference is that, in 1934, he turns in *A Common Faith* to self-consciously distilling its import through the idiom of religion, suggesting a more genuine interest in the latter than otherwise thought.[2]

In this chapter I focus then on Dewey's *A Common Faith* in order to explore the conversation it generates between religious experience and political life. The focal point is the kind of self that is at work, the character it entails, and the implications for social life. Dewey already begins to flesh out these implications when he writes of the term "religious" that "as a quality of experience [it] signifies something that may belong to all these experiences . . . aesthetic, scientific, moral and political" (CF [LW9:9]). This indicates a difference from his earlier claim in "The Influence of Darwin on Philosophy." In that essay, we recall, Dewey explains that once inquiry is freed, it can then be applied to morality, politics, and religion. But his intention, at least from the perspective of *A Common Faith*, is more radical and can be stated as such. Religious experience is subject to the reach of inquiry because it is potentially an aspect of any dimension of practical action.

In the first section below I argue that Dewey's perspective is not new in this respect. Ralph Waldo Emerson is most clearly the model, rather than Peirce or James, both of whom seem far more reluctant than Dewey to embrace religious naturalism.[3] Emerson's goal is to awaken the primordial element at the core of democratic life that exalts our everyday transactions with nature. His religious naturalism articulates a vision of self-reliance, to be sure, but one whose originating and constraining elements emerge from a kinship with nature. Similarly, Dewey's philosophy of practical action emphasizes the importance of the *ordinary*, where that term denotes the everyday space of shared currency—a site of transactions among others by virtue of which the art of living develops. In keeping with Emerson, then, Dewey wants to cultivate a more reflective sense of dependence—that is, to give an account of the democratic core of self-reliance.

Because this first section of the chapter is both lengthy and elaborate, I must give a clear explanation of why it should serve as a preface to our discussion of *A Common Faith*. At the heart of *A Common Faith* is an investigation of the relationship between inquiry and the categories of piety and faith. But this is parasitic, I argue, on a larger concern about the socio-psychological presuppositions of a vibrant democratic community. The importance of those presuppositions to political and moral deliberation is only gestured to here, but taken up fully in chapters 4 and 5. Notwithstanding, what is at stake in this context is the "ethos" of democracy under the conditions of modern pluralism: the relationship between a democratic framework and the activities that go on inside, "the manner in which citizens understand themselves as members of a political community," the responsibilities that emerge in the context of responding to common problems, and how they understand the emergence and maintenance of their respective commitments, which are now devoid of epistemic certainty.[4] The most immediate intellectual ancestor to whom Dewey connects his thinking on these matters is Emerson. This background makes more explicit the democratic ethos at the heart of his religious naturalism and conditions the explanation Dewey offers of religious experience. To turn to *A Common Faith* without this preparatory work invites confusion.

In the second section I explore the two important themes of *A Common Faith*—namely, piety and faith. Precisely because Dewey seeks to develop an account of democratic self-reliance, piety cannot mean blind deference as we traditionally understand the term. Rather, piety is a critical but retrospective assessment of the narrative of experience we inhabit and on which we depend; it allows us to deepen our apprehension of the present. Dewey refers to this with his term "habit" (as noted in the third section of chap. 2). But as previously indicated, habits denote the layered dimension that underwrites identity and thereby provide the starting points for future judgments and behavior. To speak of habits as constituting a narrative of experience is to see them in the form of traditions that we come to assess, employ, and honor. Jeffrey Stout refers to this conception of piety as a "just or appropriate response to the sources of one's existence and progress through life."[5] What makes piety a "just or appropriate" response in Dewey's philosophy is its entailment of inquiry—a position that carries political ramifications for how we appeal to religion in the context of public discourse.

For Dewey, if piety is a virtue where the posture of reflection is retrospective, faith is primarily forward-looking. This explains the distinction he makes in *A Common Faith* between "Religion" and "the Religious" (CF [LW9: chap. 1]). For him, the category of "Religion[s]"—that is, the institutions, practices, and beliefs that comprise religion—can no longer lay claim to absolute certainty, and so leaves individuals without certain answers to questions about life's ultimate meaning. But because of this, Dewey argues, individuals are opened to the possibility of ideals being continuous with, rather than external to, actual existence. This is Emerson's point in his provocative 1838 "Divinity School Address": "[L]et the breadth of new life be breathed by you through the forms already existing."[6] The metabolic imagery denotes, in Dewey's language, the transmutation of experience into a vision of the ideal through the inferential dimension of inquiry. He describes this facet of inquiry as the imagination.[7]

From the perspective of *A Common Faith*, the fractures or problems in experience to which inquiry repeatedly responds are now described as the attempt to achieve a *whole* or *harmonious* self. Although this configuration of one's ideals from actual existence orients the self in practice, Dewey is clear that it can only unify in imagination. The disjunction between actions that result in pursuit of ideals and what the world will allow explains his use of the term "faith." Defined this way, faith is always operative whenever a hypothesis of action is to be tested in experience. But what makes this description peculiarly religious is the all-inclusive nature of the ideal vis-à-vis the demands of practical action in toto. What we have hit upon in Dewey's philosophy is the intimate relationship of inquiry to the moral virtues of piety and faith.

DEMOCRATIC SELF-RELIANCE:
EMERSON, DEWEY, AND NIEBUHR

What are the concerns that *A Common Faith* addresses? Dewey speaks directly to this issue in a 1935 letter to the Unitarian humanist Max Otto: "My book was written for the people who feel inarticulately that they have the essence of the religious with them and yet are repelled by the religions and are confused."[8] He reiterates this point four years later in a rejoinder to reflections on his writings when he says: "*A Common Faith* [is] not addressed to those who are content with traditions in which 'metaphysical' is substantially identical with 'supernatural.' It [is] addressed to those who have abandoned supernaturalism, and who on that account are reproached by traditionalists for having turned their backs on everything religious" (EKV [LW14:79–80]). If we recall from chapter 1, these passages indicate Dewey's attentiveness to the crisis of religious certainty that partly developed out of the encounter with Darwinian evolution. But these passages also indicate his attempt to explain that religious experience does not require special obedience to specific beliefs or institutions or, by implication, commitment to their permanence.

This characterization of Dewey's intentions yields an important claim that explains how we ought to receive his Terry Lectures. *A Common Faith* is an exhortation to embrace a kind of character in the modern world—to be a self-reliant individual. As such, he signals the tentativeness of his project in "Religion and Our Schools" of 1908, when he says of the emergence of religious naturalism that it "may be" the coming into existence of a "fuller and deeper religion"; if so, he adds, "I do not claim to know" (ROS [MW4:168]). And again in *A Common Faith* he shows caution in stipulating the existence of this fuller and deeper religion largely because his own work attempts to bring this account of religious naturalism to fruition:

> History seems to exhibit three stages of growth. In the first stage, human rela-
> tionships were thought to be so infected with the evils of corrupt human nature
> as to require redemption from external and supernatural sources. In the next
> stage, what is significant in these relations is found to be akin to values esteemed
> distinctively religious. This is the point now reached by liberal theologians. The
> third stage *would* realize that in fact the values prized in those religions that
> have ideal elements are idealizations of things characteristic of natural associa-
> tion, which have then been projected into a supernatural realm for safe-keeping
> and sanction. (CF [MW9:48] [emphasis added])

As the passage makes clear, Dewey is cautious about claiming that this third stage exists, even as he attempts to describe what it might require and how it might orient us to the world. In other words, the third transformative stage is not one of fact, but rather a suggestion to be tested. To say this is not to deny that Dewey believes the historical milieu in which he writes is ripe for this transformative stage. But what this fully requires has yet to be stipulated. *A Common Faith*, then, must be read as a proposal—a picture of life we may well want to inhabit.

The use of self-reliance to describe Dewey's project may seem odd at this point. In what sense is this implied by his vision? On my reading, he means to capture the revolutionary orientation at the core of that term. As Emerson says of self-reliance, it works "in all offices and relations of men; in their religion;

in their education; in their pursuits; their modes of living; their association; in their property; in their speculative views."[9] The workings of self-reliance in our daily functioning make more explicit its existential dimension—that the absence of permanence in matters of religion requires and invokes courage, a willingness to forsake certainty for the insecurity of discovery. This under-standing of courage underwrites Dewey's account of faith; it is precisely what makes faith difficult, as he says. However, this conception of faith is a constitu-tive part of the *moral* dimension of self-reliance—that is, a state of dependence that entails responsibility. The relationship between courage and dependence, self-reliance and democracy stimulates self-assertion, but also tempers its meaning; without this self-assertion would easily slide into hubris.

DEMOCRACY AND SELF-RELIANCE

In Dewey's 1908 essay "Religion and Our Schools" the themes of democracy and self-reliance are already present. He argues for a suspension of religious training in public schools; the reason, he explains, that the American tradi-tion is opposed to any connection between church and state relates to the "diversity and vitality of the various denominations, each fairly sure that, with a fair field and no favor, it could make its own way" (ROS [MW4:168–169]). He does not want us to ignore the reality that the life of the state, "the vitality of the social whole, is of more importance than the flourishing of any segment or class" (ROS [MW4:169]). Here he voices a theme dominant throughout much of American political discourse, even if not always expressed in prac-tice. The worry is that in losing sight of the social whole, we court domina-tion by mingling state authorization with some class of interests, religious or profane, that claims to speak in the name of *truth*. This much he says of dogmatic faiths: "The characteristic of religion from their point of view, is that it is—intellectually speaking—secret, not public; peculiarly revealed, not generally known; authoritatively declared, not communicated and tested in ordinary ways" (ROS [MW4:173]). Dewey repeats this anti-authoritarian claim in *A Common Faith*: "The method of intelligence is open and public. The doctrinal method is limited and private" (CF [MW9:27]). From the per-spective of the doctrinal method, we move dangerously close to making our religious faith a hindrance to the political life we expect it to sustain—a po-litical life that aims for openness and general accessibility, and is based on discursive evaluation and public experimentation. Dewey's aim is to contrib-ute to a conversation in which, as Alexis de Tocqueville remarks with a note of overconfidence, "the spirit of religion and the spirit of freedom . . . [are] united intimately with one another."[10]

Dewey is not naïve, however. He recognizes the uncertainty that attends a framework of religious plurality and voluntary deference, especially where epistemic certainty is abandoned for a more humble, although still fleeting, sense of security. "I do not suppose," he says in *A Common Faith*, "for many minds the dislocation of the religious [as an orientation] from a religion [that is, a specific set of religious beliefs and institutions] is easy to effect" (CF [MW9:11]).[11] In a passage from "Religion and Our Schools," already quoted in chapter 1, we find the following remark: "There is undoubted loss of joy, of consolation, of some types of strength. . . . There is manifest increase of uncertainty; there is some paralysis of energy" (ROS [MW4:168]). But he quickly adds: "Bearing the losses and inconveniences of our time as best we may, it is the part of men to labor persistently and patiently for the clarification and development of the *positive creed of life implicit in democracy*" (ROS [MW4:168] [emphasis added]).

We get our clue to Dewey's appreciation for religious plurality and voluntary piety from his talk of democracy and the social whole. This undoubtedly prompts a moment of pause. Does this not cut against his presumed appreciation for individuality? Hans Joas voices this complaint in his reading of *A Common Faith* when he writes: "[Dewey] skips over the particularism of each individual experience and lands . . . in an empty universalism of the democratic ideal, the motivating force of which remains unfathomable."[12] Alan Ryan makes a similar point, although as a more general gloss on Dewey's political philosophy: "It is hard to repress the thought that Dewey may simply have been asking too much of democratic politics and that a moderate degree of alienation from one another is the price we pay for a liberal society and its virtues of privacy and diversity."[13] If Joas and Ryan are correct, we should rightly scold Dewey for wrongly describing democracy as the only source of spiritual enrichment.

We should not conclude on this note so quickly, however. The criticism, I believe, misses its mark by attributing to Dewey an overly romantic conception of democracy's role in the life of its citizens. There is a more subtle argument here. As I read him, Dewey does not mean to obscure the importance of individuality, let alone the religious commitments that particular individuals hold. Rather, he seeks to explain individuality's proper place in the context of democratic life. The "social whole" must mean something other than a strong communitarianism.

He points to the meaning of the term in his *Liberalism and Social Action* of 1935, published one year after *A Common Faith*: liberal democracy is "committed to an end that is at once enduring and flexible: the liberation of individuals so that realization of their capacities may be the *law of their life*"

(LSA [LW11:41] [emphasis added]; cf. DEA [LW11:217–218]). This requires development of "a social organization that will make possible effective liberty and opportunity for personal growth in mind and spirit in all individuals" (LSA [LW11:41]). The "social whole" thus refers to the sharing of common elements (i.e., goods, virtues, practices) that bring individuals together, allowing each to find something of themselves in others. This is a necessary factor for being able to bestow singular consideration on each other in the context of shared concerns, without compromising one's developing self-understanding (E$_3$ [LW7:345]). He is careful, then, not to conflate this vision of shared identity—in which our natural tendency for communal living is emphasized and becomes the object of contestation and evaluation—with the kind of collective will idea that comes to mind when we think of communion (PP [LW2:243–247]; cf. HNC [MW14: chaps. 5 and 26]).[14] As Dewey says in his 1927 work, *The Public and Its Problems*, publics "consist of all those who are affected by the indirect consequences of transactions to such an extent that it is deemed necessary to have those consequences systematically cared for" (PP [LW2:245–246]).

This is not a postulate, but rather an argument about how we *ought* to understand democracy as a form of social practice. He is clarifying and developing, to use his language, what the positive creed of life implicit in democracy means for the goods we seek. As far as he is concerned, and in keeping with his Protestant counterparts, the issue is not about whether the goods within life will stand in a supporting relationship to democracy, but rather how to envision and manage that relationship. From "the ethical point of view," says Dewey, "it is not too much to say that the democratic ideal poses, rather than solves, the great problem: How to harmonize the development of each individual with the maintenance of a social state in which the activities of one will contribute to the good of all others" (E$_3$ [LW7:350]).

In his view, the historical emergence of democracy stipulates a problem, the management of which it attempts, in principle, to confront. Consider the image of democracy Dewey conceives in thinking about our religious lives: "Whether or not we are, save in some metaphorical sense, all brothers, we are at least all in the same boat traversing the same turbulent ocean" (CF [LW9:56]). This image means to call to mind an important relationship between the activities within a democracy, on the one hand, and the relationship between those activities and democratic life, on the other. Like Neurath's boat, the democratic state is adrift at sea. The boat makes possible the activities and goods the crew enjoys; those activities have an autonomy, which, although not reducible to the maintenance of the boat, do not intend to sink it. In fact, it is what allows the crew to call the boat home and to see each other as fellow crew members in the light of their common vulnerability. Analogously, democracy provides a framework in which religious experiences (among others) develop and are negotiated, but democracy is not to be identified with the goods of those experiences as such or vice versa.[15] In keeping with the metaphor, we do not presume that the activities of citizens attempt to sink the ship, but rather seek to enhance the quality of life it provides. For Dewey, the motivation for sustaining our commitment to democracy is the goods it manages and makes possible, rather than replaces.[16]

The subtext to the "Religion in Our Schools" essay of 1908, *A Common Faith*, and the letters that follow is Dewey's account of the subject; he believes a new account of individuality emerges with the modern revolt against monarchical and ecclesiastical authority, which foregrounded the necessity of political accountability and demystifying political legitimacy. We have already encountered Dewey's understanding of identity formation in his philosophy of action. But in that context, identity formation emerged in his attempt to excavate both the possibilities and the limitations that attend our everyday practical encounters with the world once freed from the philosophical constraint he called the quest for certainty. Here, his philosophy of action doubles as a narrative of the emergence of the modern subject—an account that is presented in less systematic form in Emerson—in which the meaning-content of individual identities is not exhausted by their functional location in society. As such, individuals are no longer positioned to assume that within the social practice of democracy, their fellow citizens share the same private ethical assumptions—that is, assumptions relating to the meaning-content of their identity.

This is the undercurrent to *The Quest for Certainty*, and it becomes a central theme in the essays that comprise Dewey's 1930 *Individualism: Old and New*. Just as the quest for certainty, in Dewey's view, no longer exhausts the possibilities of philosophy and the importance of practical action to human well-being, religious authority and hierarchical structures in posttraditional societies no longer provide the *primary* source of self-understanding for individuals. His articulation of the creativity of practical action bespeaks the emergence of a new, albeit ambivalent, conception of subjectivity that his work tracks and attempts to support. Sounding much like Hodge or Weber, Dewey writes in the appropriately titled chapter 4 of *Individualism: Old and New*, "The Lost Self": "The significant thing is that the loyalties which once held individuals, which gave them support, *direction and unity of outlook on life*, have well-nigh disappeared" (ION [LW5:67] [emphasis added]).

This remark, which seemingly reads as a lamentation, appears in a work that is ostensibly addressing the rugged individualism of laissez-faire capitalism that is an obstacle to social transformation. But what does this have to do with the issue of religion? To begin, Dewey argues that the response to America's economic problems cannot simply be distributive. Merely extending "to all individuals the traits of economic initiative, opportunity and enterprise" is, to him, insufficient (ION [LW5:81]). That these are important cannot be denied, since a robust vision of freedom should acknowledge the necessity of, and access to, external resources on which one must rely. Effective freedom, as Dewey describes it, denotes the capability of persons to realize their life projects, a capability that most certainly requires economic resources (E_3 [LW7:305–309]; ASC [LW11:130–145]). But we cannot, he argues, leave untouched the understanding of the self that underwrites twentieth-century America, lest we transform institutions and practices without the appropriate psychology to sustain, nurture, and provide for their extension. The character type that has achieved currency, Dewey tells us, is that of an individual who seeks to "go west"; to be adventurous without concern; and to slough-off all traditional ties and remake himself wholly by his own devices without reliance on what is held in common.

In response to this development, he argues for "a new psychological and moral type" that reconfigures character in a democratic idiom (ION [LW5:67]).[17] Here Dewey negotiates a vision of individual identity, as Emerson did in the 1830s and 40s in response to a similar form of moral crisis that crass individualism posed to democracy. They do not want identity exhausted by traditional commitments, but nor do they wish to run headlong in the opposite direction of the unencumbered self that fuels what Dewey calls the "industrial oligarchy" (ION [LW5:66]). For both Emerson and Dewey, rugged individualism feeds "a system of selfishness . . . of distrust, of concealment, of superior keenness, not of giving but of taking advantage."[18] The fact that the intimation of spiritual sickness appears in a context so obviously about economic degeneracy should not be too difficult to understand. For if spiritual sickness bespeaks the emptying out of moral life then laissez-faire capitalism in the 1930s may well appear to be its partner. Dewey's contention is that the response must begin with a mood shift, the articulation of which, he believes, is one step to bringing it to fruition.

This new psychological type is grounded in an appreciation of the ordinary that connects Dewey to Emerson. For Dewey this is a positive attribute of Emerson's philosophy:

> [Emerson's] ideas are not fixed upon any Reality that is beyond or behind or in any way apart, and hence they do not have to be bent. They are versions of the Here and the Now, and flow freely. The reputed transcendental worth of

an overweening Beyond and Away, Emerson, jealous for spiritual democracy, finds to be the possession of the unquestionable Present. When Emerson ... designated the There and Then as "wild, savage and preposterous," he also drew the line which marks him off from transcendentalism—which is the idealism of a Class. ... It is such disinherited of the earth that Emerson summons to their own. "If man is sick, is unable, is mean-spirited and odious, it is because there is so much of his nature which is unlawfully withholden from him." (EPD [MW3:190])

So if the identity of individuals no longer centers on nor is *wholly* directed by tradition, class, or eschatological understandings of the world, they may be able to lay claim to that part of their nature which is "unlawfully withholden" from them, and which, once active, can creatively reinvigorate and socially bind. But how so? Is this what Dewey is trying to describe with the term "spiritual democracy"? Consider the classic passage from Emerson's 1836 *Nature*, where he waxes lyrical on precisely this point:

> Crossing a bare common, in snow puddles, at twilight, under a clouded sky ... I have enjoyed a perfect exhilaration. Standing on the bare ground—my head bathed by the blithe air and uplifted into infinite space—all mean egotism vanishes. I become a transparent eyeball; I am nothing; I see all; the currents of the Universal Being circulate through me; I am part or parcel of God.[19]

The poetic renderings yield an important claim about our shared lives that maps onto Dewey's philosophy of action. By "Universal Being" Emerson does not mean traditional Christianity's God. It is the nature that is at once "NOT ME," that is "all other men and my own body," but of which I am a part.[20] The self is not extinguished in this passage, nor in the case where it is distinguished from the "NOT ME," the partiality that selfhood can display. Hence the individual that vanishes is not the expression of egotism proper, the other part of the Universal Being that Emerson calls "the Soul," but of a "mean egotism."[21]

But egotism proper implies a form of self-regard that implicitly acknowledges dependence on social practices, what Dewey refers to in the last chapter as the complicated arts of associated living. "Conduct," he writes, "is always shared. ... It is not an ethical 'ought' that conduct *should* be social. It *is* social, whether bad or good" (HNC [MW14:16] [original emphasis]). As I indicated in the last chapter, this is the sense in which our extra-natural world implicates us in a normative world and thus contains liberating and constraining aspects. In Emerson's and Dewey's view, individuals are accountable to the socially constituted present, wherein they carve out forms of life. But this present equally contains the socially constituted future, wherein they reconfigure or maintain those forms of life. In this context of an implicit solidarity the partiality of selfhood, both present and future, is made both possible and circumscribed.

I do not mean to suggest that for Dewey this solidarity is not forged and discursively negotiated through social life; it rests on what can be described only as a form of mutual responsiveness. Recall the way habits recede into the background, appearing prereflective. Thus he writes: "To learn to be human is to develop through the give-and-take of communication an effective sense of being an individually distinctive member of a community" (AE$_2$ [LW10:332]).[22] What Emerson provides, as Dewey understands, is the philosophical scaffolding that points to the appropriate function of self-regard. The point here is that both he and Emerson are attempting to make *explicit* the social-psychological standpoint democratic life uncovers and relies upon. Making explicit this solidarity allows mean egotism to be challenged—that is to say, the display of one's egotism functions as something for which it is proper to offer and inquire after reasons—thus making it answerable on common ground. We make explicit, says Dewey, "some more comprehensive point of view from which the divergence may be brought together"—that is, where conflicting outlooks may be assessed and resolved from the critical dimension of where perspectives overlap (DE [MW9:336]). This comprehensive point of view is possible because the forms of life we pursue are not wholly independent from or reducible to the practices in which we pursue them. But this is not to say that the comprehensive point of view cannot be the subject of criticism in some later context.

Of course the critic will ask: Can we sincerely push this connection between Emerson and Dewey through the language of self-reliance? At first blush self-reliance appears to underwrite the kind of individualism or romantic conception of the self that is prevalent in Jackson's and Hoover's America.[23] It is Emerson's "mean egotism," and what Dewey refers to in *A Common Faith* as militant atheism: "The essentially unreligious attitude is that which attributes human achievement and purpose to man in isolation from the world of physical nature and his fellows" (CF [LW9:18]).

Both Emerson and Dewey (more emphatically) are too sociologically sophisticated to accept this position, but they want the fact of social life to register appropriately in one's life. They want to address the following observation that Stout has recently captured—namely, that human "pride being what it is, it will not be easy to think for oneself, in the pursuit of self-critical but genuine piety, without succumbing to the temptation of denying the very conditions of one's own existence or otherwise masking from oneself the sources on which critical thinking depends."[24] Consider Emerson's response in his essay "Man the Reformer"; it nicely extends the implication of *Nature* while simultaneously approximating the language Dewey comes to use:

> And further, I will not dissemble my hope, that each person whom I address has felt his own call to cast aside all evil customs, timidities, and limitations, and to be in his place a free and helpful man, a reformer . . . who must find or cut a straight road to everything excellent in the earth, and not only go honorably himself, but make it easier for all who follow him, to go in honor and with benefit.[25]

For Dewey's part, the narrower understanding of the self often associated with liberalism mistakenly reads the liberation of the individual from traditional moorings back into its philosophy as an *ontological* (rather than *normative*) claim about subjectivity.[26] From Dewey's perspective, this account is unable to make the enlargement or curtailment of freedom or authority an emergent issue within a practice of giving and asking for reasons. Modern selfhood is thus oddly expressed in a negative injunction that places freedom and authority in opposition, thus obscuring the normative resources already at work in our social practices. This is the ambivalence of the new conception of selfhood referred to earlier.[27] The vision of self-reliance Emerson and Dewey have in mind is therefore epistemic with practical intent, where the issue is the appropriate posture the self ought to take toward that on which she depends, taking for granted that dependence is her condition. Of course we must acknowledge dependence, but for them, we should also realize that without self-reliance, all allegiances may become invitations to epistemic blindness or, worst, injustice and cruelty.[28]

Dewey does not deny that theological frameworks, traditions, or even class identifications may psychologically integrate the individual. He accepts that they provide unity to one's identity and a narrative of meaning, making us, as Michael Sandel puts it, "encumbered selves."[29] Indeed, after noting in *A Common Faith* the difficulty in cultivating critical independence from one's religion, Dewey says: "Tradition and custom, especially when emotionally charged, are a part of the habits that have become one with our very being" (CF [MW9:11]). Unlike Sandel, however, he cautions against embracing a "strong view" of community, a position that makes "*sociality* a term of moral honor beyond criticism" (FC [MW13:8]).[30]

And here we ought to follow. For Dewey, without being able to critically say what our relationship is to these powerful identity-spheres, how they allow us to move fluidly within the flowing stream of life, the result is either "dogmatic fundamentalism . . . or private estheticism" (ION [LW5:72]). The former, the vision of community Sandel seemingly embraces, often translates into a strong and blinding sense of belonging and devotion that blocks from view a critical piety, while the latter confuses self-reliance with a lust for originality or novelty.[31] It makes self-creation an ethical goal, as one often sees in Nietzsche and Rorty, but obscures the relevance and demand of the context in which such an aspiration is rendered intelligible and sustained.

Dewey discourages the inclination in either direction, and in so doing crystallizes his understanding of the positive dimension of the modern subject:

> The new centre is indefinite interactions taking place within a course of nature which is not fixed and complete, but which is capable of direction to new and different results through the mediation of intentional operations. Neither self nor world, neither soul nor nature (in the sense of something isolated and finished in its isolation) is the centre, any more than either earth or sun is the absolute centre of a single universe and necessary frame of reference. (QC [LW4:232]; cf. EN [LW1:325–326])

The context of this passage is the emergence of knowledge, including self-understanding, as the result of transactions in and through experience. His point is that precisely because the center is shifting under the conditions of modernity, we must be careful before moving too quickly in assuming that our frame of reference is the *necessary* starting point. We must not assume that our reference point exists at the level of phenomenological fact, untouched by the contingency that is part of its development.

COURAGE AND DEPENDENCE:
REINHOLD NIEBUHR REVISITED

We have seen that for Emerson and Dewey a democratic ethos under modern conditions demands that individuals walk with less certainty about the commitments they hold, while simultaneously acknowledging the fact of sociality. The first curbs the high epistemic demand individuals attach to their commitments, but also mitigates the tendency toward dogmatism in their encounters with others. The second constrains "Promethean triumphalism" and a romantic conception of independence, which would otherwise lead individuals to believe that the vision of life they fashion has nothing more at its base than their own individual wills.

This picture of Emerson, and especially Dewey, seems strangely at odds with the basic understanding that we have of them. After all, the account offered here makes humility far more constitutive of their democratic politics. In the context of American political thought it is not Emerson or Dewey with whom we associate humility, but rather Reinhold Niebuhr. Indeed, the comparison is critically important because of the frequency with which Niebuhr is identified as being far more attentive than Emerson, Dewey, and liberal Protestants to the failings of human nature in ethical and political life. We often read Niebuhr's Augustinian stance as a diagnosis of the weakness of the American imagination, with its tendency toward pride and self-absorbed desire. For him, the Christian worldview humbles our pretension toward believing that our frame of reference is total in its comprehension and therefore can save us from a more definitive uncertainty. Of course, one cannot do justice to the complexity of Niebuhr's arguments in this comparison, but I think there is an important line of inquiry here that is worth pursuing and not wholly beyond reflection, given what has been said thus far. Indeed, it reveals a theological precommitment that undermines Niebuhr's realism in politics and falls short of the kind of courage self-reliance demands.

In his review of *Liberalism and Social Action* in 1935, Niebuhr criticizes Dewey for ignoring "a constitutional weakness in the liberal approach to politics."[32] But what is the source of this error, in Niebuhr's view? He provides us with the answer in his Gifford Lecture of 1941, *The Nature and Destiny of Man: A Christian Interpretation*, where he takes up Dewey's 1935 work once more: "Not a suspicion dawns upon Professor Dewey that no possible 'organized inquiry' can be as transcendent over the historical conflicts of interest as it ought to be to achieve the disinterested intelligence which he attributes to it."[33] What Dewey misses, Niebuhr contends, is the inescapable sin that contaminates intellectual intervention and which social life exacerbates. Niebuhr's reading of Dewey is mistaken, however, since inquiry itself is emergent out of specific problems that structure its movement. Inquiry, in other words, is never disinterested. But the reason-giving quality of inquiry helps explain how our interests are formed and, contra Niebuhr, how they may be transformed in the context of other conflicting claims. Dewey guards against an antecedent individuation of subjects (prevalent in rational choice theory today) that renders us blind to the formation of differentiated interests among those subjects.

There is something more at issue between the two than Niebuhr's mischaracterization of Dewey's position. What is interesting about Niebuhr, especially in the context of his political activism, is his aversion to the ordinary, which reveals his Christian orientation.[34] In this context, Michael Eldridge argues that the disagreement between Dewey and Niebuhr is over "the scope of intelligence in human affairs."[35] But Niebuhr, too, endorses pragmatism's method of justification, which prompts individuals to reexamine their presuppositions as they manage life.[36] So while I think Eldridge's inclinations are correct, the difference between Dewey and Niebuhr must give rise to another disagreement that prefigures the extent to which intelligence functions in the management of life. Each understands differently the ground from which intelligence proceeds, affecting how we relate to the sources of our existence.

In this context, Niebuhr's Christian traditionalism is tied to the meaning he attributes to "constitutional weakness" in his philosophy.[37] This term has ontological implications about human nature that cut against his experimentalism. After all, the charge of constitutional weakness is not levied merely against liberal theory, as he suggests, but against human intervention as such. What defines Nieburh's ontology then is the doctrine of sin, through which "one may understand that . . . there is no level of human moral or social achievement in which there is not some corruption of inordinate self-love."[38] This is precisely why, for him, pride (read as mean egotism) *always* mingles with reason to the detriment of individual and collective life. The result, as he argues in Hobbesian fashion in *Moral Man and Immoral Society*, is a "perpetual state of war."[39] Yet Niebuhr rejects Hobbes' authoritarian—but worldly—conclusion.[40] Indeed, his is the standard Christian response: "The man who searches after both meaning and fulfillments beyond the ambiguous fulfillments and frustrations of history exists in a height of spirit which no historical process can completely contain."[41]

Here is the downside for democrats like Emerson and Dewey: The urgency of acting in the world, and the responsibility it entails, is in danger of losing its gravity. If all is "going to Hell," why act? Or, if one believes that meaning exists beyond the ambiguous fulfillments of history, to whom is one accountable? When one's commitments exist beyond the pale of nature or are defined as clandestine emanations, the "inhibition of responsibility" is in jeopardy.[42] But when one looks beyond the world, nature itself will seem terribly empty and mundane. We will encase ourselves in our dreams as the world about us loses its luster, never thinking for a moment that our failure to act is the source of the world's diminishing glow. Under this interpretation, Niebuhr's realism dissolves, and Dewey is well aware of why: "Belief in the supernatural as a necessary power for apprehension of the ideal and for practical attachment to it has for its counterpart a pessimistic belief in the corruption . . . of natural means. . . . [T]his apparent pessimism has a way of suddenly changing into an exaggerated optimism" (CF [MW9:32]).[43] Biographer Richard Fox is correct to note that the "progression of [Niebuhr's] thought went from humanity to God . . . not from God to humanity."[44] But this is because humanity, on the level of ontology, always leaves something to be desired.[45]

Emerson and Dewey do not subscribe to Niebuhr's bias; they nurture an appreciation for the ordinary, but without installing it as an untouchable God. After all, Niebuhr's worry is that we do not respect the fundamental boundary between the perfection of God and the imperfections of this world. The result is to overstate what we are capable of achieving. Yet inquiry does not presume to imitate the creative production once attributed to God precisely because contingency is more thoroughly embedded within practical action. For "nature," Emerson says in *The Conduct of Life* of 1860, "is no sentimentalist,—[it] does not cosset or pamper us."[46] In this regard we should recall Dewey's meliorism, which argues that the world we confront daily is neither the best nor the worst possible, but may be subject to improvement through human action. A melioristic outlook generates caution; it acts to circumscribe our efforts and prevents us from conflating inquiry's possibilities with facts about nature, as when he says in *A Common Faith*: "The outcome, given our best endeavor, is not with us" (CF [LW9:17]; cf. EN [LW1:326]).[47] The claim encompasses not simply the wrath of physical nature, but the individuals that are part and parcel of nature and who may well reveal their mean egotism.

There is a positive upshot here, however. Dewey distills a moral interpretation of life, as does Emerson, that generates hope from the fact of social existence. The difference between Niebuhr and them is not simply that of two dissimilar ways of orienting ourselves to the world—one that emphasizes a redeeming God and the other, a redeeming intelligence—both of which seem to be merely an act of willing oneself to believe without evidence or support. Commitment to a redeeming intelligence read through Emerson and Dewey has something more at its core than volition. This much Emerson explains:

> We have all a certain intellection or presentiment of reform existing in the mind, which does not yet descend into the character, and those who throw themselves blindly on this lose themselves. Whatever they attempt in that direction, fails, and reacts suicidally on the actor himself. This is the penalty of having transcended nature. For the existing world is not a dream, and cannot with impunity be treated as a dream; neither is it a disease; but it is the ground on which you stand, it is the mother of whom you were born. Reform converses with possibilities, perchance with impossibilities; but here is sacred fact. *This also was true, or it could not be: it had life in it, or it could not have existed; it has life in it, or it could not continue.*[48]

Choosing to orient ourselves to the world in the way Emerson suggests is not a leap of "personal volition," a kind of "moral magic" as Dewey says, but rather a "humbler exercise of will to *observe* existing social realities and to *direct* them according to their own potentialities" (ION [LW5:74] [emphases added]). This is Emerson's point in the passage: the existing world is not a disease, and should not be treated as such. There are, as Dewey says, existing social realities on which we rely, however unstable and contingent. Emerson pushes further, gesturing not merely toward the possibility of reform within the world—or what Dewey denotes with his term "direct"—but its naturalness. There is a refined materialism to their account that justifies the subjunctive mood, lest we suffer the penalty of trying to transcend the uncertainty of nature; it demands courage, but nothing less. To invoke Paul, we may well be "perplexed" by human frustrations, "but not unto despair." Hence the last two lines of the passage.

The exchange among Emerson, Dewey, and Niebuhr need not reach a philosophical and practical impasse.[49] Dewey's rhetorical formulation is cast such that the positive upshot of the term "direct" is reflected through a sensibility of humility, thus allowing him to accommodate at least some of Niebuhr's worries. Dewey's and Emerson's preoccupation with the ordinary goes in the direction of their critics, placing them in closer proximity to the realism otherwise attributed to Niebuhr without abandoning a healthy sense of hope. Dewey's realism cashes out differently depending on what dimension of his philosophy one explores. Here, it represents a thoroughgoing experimentalism that completes the trajectory of liberal Protestantism charted in chapter 1. Dewey's experimentalism, however, neither backslides, as in the case of Hodge, nor loses something of its courage, as in the case of liberal Protestants. Echoing Emerson, Dewey says as much:

> Religious faith which attaches itself to the possibilities of nature and associated living would, with its devotion to the ideal, manifest piety toward the actual.... Respect and esteem would be given to that which is the means of realization of possibilities, and to that in which the ideal is embodied if it ever finds embodiment. Aspiration and endeavor are not ends in themselves; value is not in them in isolation but in them as means to that reorganization of the existent in which approved meanings are attained. Nature and society include within themselves projection of ideal possibilities and contain the operations by which they are actualized. *Nature may not be worshipped as divine even in the sense of the intellectual love of Spinoza. But nature, including humanity, with all its defects and imperfections, may evoke heartfelt piety as the source of ideals, of possibilities, of aspiration in their behalf, and as the eventual abode of all attained goods*

and excellences. (QC [LW4:244] [emphasis added]; cf. EN [LW1:312–315]; CF [LW9:36])[50]

Note the use of nature in this passage. In its *undifferentiated* form, nature denotes the whole, the totality of that which exists. But I take the passage also to mean, indicated by the claim that nature may be the "eventual abode of all attained goods and excellences," that the whole does not exhaust what may exist. Have we not found an opening for wonder and faith in things unseen? Do we not sense, even if its experienced character remains uncertain, the opening of the infinite horizon of meaning? Are we not enticed by and seduced into continuing on, albeit with a humble mind and heart? Perhaps, but at this juncture the *differentiated* form of nature is the result of treating it as a testing ground—that is, allowing one's naturalism to run all the way down without a note of pessimism (à la Hodge, Weber, and Niebuhr) or exaggeration (à la liberal Protestants) about what the encounter with nature will produce.[51] As Dewey is aware, our tendency to move in either direction conspires against our best wishes to be realistic and measured in our valuations.[52]

READING *A COMMON FAITH*

We have considered at some length the way democratic considerations and their relationship to Emersonian self-reliance are part of a much larger argument about character, our stance toward commitments, and identity for Dewey. There are several conclusions we must now keep in mind as we make the transition to *A Common Faith*. First, self-reliance stands in between a vision of identity that is exhausted by any one object of allegiance and one that denies the hold of allegiances altogether. Second, this middle position evokes both courage and dependence, since the care of the self is dependent both prospectively and retrospectively on the seen and unseen of nature. Third, the result is a vision of religious experience that is plural, but which always must square itself with democratic life. The issue to which we must now turn is the precise way these considerations animate the themes of *A Common Faith*, namely, piety, faith, and their relationship to imagination and ideals.

Properly understood, *A Common Faith* attempts to articulate a naturalistic outlook that is religiously inflected, but which does not threaten from its inception to run roughshod over the communal dimensions of our nature. Dewey offers a way for individuals to conceive of their spiritual projects that does "not beg the question against democracy" and that makes "wise critical judgments possible" in public discourse.[53] This means that the kinds of experiences he will want to identify as religious are those that intensify and deepen our communion with the larger world of which we are a part. "An individual did not join a church," he says in *A Common Faith*. "He was born and reared in a community whose social unity, organization and traditions were symbolized and celebrated in the rites, cults and beliefs of a collective religion" (CF [LW9:41]).

DEMOCRATIC PIETY

Before Dewey turns to the issue of piety in chapter 1, "Religion Versus the Religious," he begins with a discussion of religious pluralism. This is part of Dewey's rejoinder to the definition of religion that he cites from the *Oxford English Dictionary*, which reads: "Recognition on the part of man of some unseen higher power as having control of his destiny and as being entitled to obedience, reverence and worship" (CF [LW9:4]).[54] The definition is important for putting in place several features to which we will return, including the character of the unseen, the meaning of having our destiny controlled, and the sense in which an object is entitled to obedience and reverence. After cataloguing a multitude of ways historic religions have defined the unseen he remarks: "There is no greater similarity in the ways in which obedience and reverence have been expressed" (CF [LW9:5]). If this is so, why believe that choice and diversity in matters regarding the object of people's piety and faith have ended (CF [LW9:6])? In highlighting the fact of pluralism, his point is not to reject the definition, but to reconstruct its content so that it can potentially be reflected throughout the various domains of life.

But Dewey's emphasis on pluralism does not intend for individuals to abandon, as some believe, specific religious institutions, beliefs, and rituals.[55] Instead, he focuses our attention on the absence of a *necessary* connection between specific beliefs and pious allegiance or faith. In every instance in which Dewey discusses institutions as being an encumbrance to religious experience, he is speaking of the configuration that imposes a necessary connection. Thus he writes: "I am not proposing a religion. . . . For the moment we have a religion, whether that of the Sioux Indian or of Judaism or of Christianity, that moment the ideal factors in experience that may be called religious take on a load that is not inherent in them" (CF [LW9:7]). For him, as he explains in the early part of that chapter, religion has, at least in the West, been historically understood "as a special body of beliefs and practices having some kind of institutional organization" (CF [LW9:8]). And again, "the adjective 'religious' denotes nothing in the way of a specifiable entity, either institutional or as a system of beliefs" (CF [LW9:8]).

Admittedly, all of this suggests that he wants us to rely as little as possible on the institutions of religion. But Dewey speaks in this categorical way because he does not want to confuse a specific stance or attitude that he is describing with a specific tradition, which might then lead to the conclusion that *one* religion exhausts the meaning of piety or faith. This is especially so given that in the West most traditional religions, in his view, often identify the unseen with a supernatural being (CF [LW9:19–20]). For Dewey, the result of this identification is that the description of what counts as religious experience falls to the level of unquestioned fact, cutting individuals off from the possibility that beliefs, institutions, objects, and the like that do not receive supernatural warrant may still invoke pious allegiance or faith. Indeed, this is one of the reasons he writes *A Common Faith*. His point is simply to say that there is a distinction between piety and faith as virtues, on the one hand, and the object to which they are attached, on the other. For him, we should not conflate the two, lest we find our common lives unnecessarily transformed into religious factions.[56]

To understand piety and faith as virtues means something very specific, which Dewey describes two years earlier in his *Ethics*. As before, he notes that the conditions of modernity prevent beliefs and frames of reference from sinking to the level of phenomenological fact. This much he says when speaking of the difference between *customary* and *reflective* morality, where the latter embodies the critical perspective of inquiry or epistemic self-reliance. The distinction between customary and reflective morality fits appropriately with an account of identity formation that was once exhausted by a relatively static set of specific commitments and institutions, but that now emerges across a wider and more contingent range of practices and obligations.

> In customary morality it is possible to draw up a list or catalogue of vices and virtues. For the latter reflect some definite existing custom, and the former some deviation from or violation of custom. The acts approved and disapproved have therefore the same definiteness and fixity as belong to the customs to which they refer. In reflective morality, a list of virtues has much more tentative status. Chastity, kindness, patriotism, modesty, toleration, bravery, etc., cannot be given a fixed meaning, because each expresses an interest in objects and institutions which are changing. In form, *as* interests, they may be permanent, since no community could endure in which there were not, say, fair dealing, public spirit, regard for life, faithfulness. But no two communities conceive the objects to which these qualities attach in quite identical ways. They can be defined, therefore, only on the basis of *qualities characteristic of interest*, not on the basis of permanent and uniform objects in which interest is taken. (E₃ [LW7:255–256] [original emphases])

As moral virtues, then, piety and faith can be understood only on the basis of the traits constitutive of the relevant interest, rather than on the permanent existence of some object in which the interest lies. In one sense, this makes formal any account offered of piety and faith. The critic will undoubtedly say that it is here Dewey empties the meaning out of these terms. But this formal description, in his view, can be accepted only under the qualification that faith and piety must always be embodied. In other words, individuals show pious allegiance to x and they have faith in y; filling out what x or y means will most certainly require more details and a narrative about the specific individuals and communities under question, but piety and faith in life would be incomplete without some articulation of the objects to which they refer. As he did in "Religion and Our Schools," Dewey intends in *A Common Faith* to warn us against inscribing the emblem of sacredness on existing beliefs, institutions, and traditions, because to do this undermines pluralism and critical revision, distorting the character of piety and faith under modern conditions. Once piety and faith are distorted in this way, we are not too far from antidemocratic politics.

In the context of what Dewey says in *A Common Faith* and in other works, such as "Religion and Our Schools" and *The Quest for Certainty*, where he takes up the term, "piety" serves an integrative function between self and world that deepens our sense of the actual. "Faith" extends that function to the very contours of identity, unifying the self in relation to an ideal. As we shall see in a moment, for Dewey faith is a belief that x should be in existence, a belief whose content is so inclusive as to harmonize the disparate features of the self and its context. This unification of the self, unlike the mere integration with the larger horizon that is made possible by the actual, is the result of the imaginative function of inference. Faith is not only a projection of possibilities, but more precisely a utopian vision that unifies the self psychologically and orients the self forward in action. This difference between piety and faith is one of degree. The latter is primarily where Dewey locates religious experience.

We should keep in mind then that the concern about piety, as Dewey understands, is a more general argument about the *past*, the ground upon which we stand as it has been built up by previous generations, in which institutions of religion are but one part. The concept "past" is another way of speaking of what Dewey refers to in another context as "the actual"; it has a temporal quality denoted by past experiences that are funneled directly into the present.[57] So to speak of the actuality of a tradition, relationship, belief, etc. is also implicitly to refer to its historical career. If this is so, surely the forward-looking quality of inquiry is bound to seem problematic. Those individuals who wish to give due homage to the past find themselves, according to a certain reading of Dewey's account of inquiry, robbed of this ability. This is particularly challenging in the context of religion. Individuals who feel this way are inclined to be troubled by the following formulation by Emerson: "No facts are to me sacred; none are profane; I simply experiment, an endless seeker with no Past at my back."[58]

But in Dewey's view, a past that infuses and aids one in negotiating the present is no past where that means historically antecedent and substantively irrelevant. So for him, a past that aids is what we call a living tradition or a habit. It means that the tradition though antecedent in its temporal formation is still substantively relevant in the present, and is thus actualized. This is what he means when he says that the logic of piety "compels us to inquire how much in religions now accepted are survivals from outgrown culture," where "outgrown" means that the "conception of the unseen powers and our relations to them" is not "consonant with the best achievements and aspirations of the present" (CF [MW9:6]).[59]

All of this helps us make good sense of the precise language Dewey's uses in defining piety. His account is almost identical to the one his fellow naturalist George Santayana offered some decades earlier in his work of religious naturalism, *The Life of Reason* (1905–1906). It is worth citing them both, beginning with Santayana:

> Piety . . . may be said to mean man's reverent attachment to the sources of his being and the steadying of his life by that attachment. . . . This consciousness that the human spirit is derived and responsible, that all its functions are heritages and trusts, involves a sentiment of gratitude and duty which we may call piety. The true objects of piety are, of course, those on which life and its interests really depend: parents first, then family, ancestors, and country; finally, humanity at large and the whole cosmos.[60]

> The fact that human destiny is so interwoven with forces beyond human control renders it unnecessary to suppose that dependence and the humility that accompanies it have to find the particular channel that is prescribed by traditional doctrines. . . . For our dependence is manifest in those relations to the environment that support our undertakings and aspirations as much as it is in the defeats inflicted upon us. . . . Natural piety is not of necessity either a fatalistic acquiescence in natural happenings or a romantic idealization of the world. It may rest upon a just sense of nature as the whole of which we are parts, while it also recognizes that we are parts that are marked by intelligence and purpose,

having the capacity to strive by their aid to bring conditions into greater conso-
nance with what is humanly desirable. (CF [MW9:18])

What both of these passages indicate is that a tradition or authority is often
a conversation across time that has at its core the following question: How
are we to understand this thing which partly makes us? Our reliance on it
helps us negotiate, manage, and cope—to fashion the kinds of people we wish
to become and the world we long to inhabit. It is a steadying of our life, as
Santayana says. Intelligence and purpose work in conjunction with nature,
or, as Dewey says in referring to its differentiated form, those relations to
the environment. Piety may thus have as its object an undifferentiated but
grand appreciation for nature, the whole of which we are but parts, or a more
sober differentiated reverence for specific relationships and institutions that
comprise nature.

In this context Dewey acknowledges that we are encumbered. Or to put
it in the form of a question: In his view, if these relationships did not exist,
could we render ourselves, not to mention our future, intelligible? He answers in the negative: "I do not for a moment suppose that the experiences
of the past, personal and social, are of no importance. For without them we
should not be able to frame any ideas whatever of the conditions under which
objects are enjoyed" (QC [LW4:217]). He says again in *A Common Faith*:
"The determining factor in the interpretation of the [religious] experience
is the particular doctrinal apparatus into which a person has been inducted"
(CF [LW9:10; cf. 6]).

In whatever garb it is wrapped, tradition provides a narrative of experience that controls our destiny by virtue of giving us resources to frame ideas
of what makes something an appropriate object of allegiance. The source of
control is the interpenetration between the background—that is, the narrative of experience—and the present, the nature of which illuminates the latter. This suggests, at least as Emerson, Dewey, and Santayana understand the
matter, that what we are to make of our inheritance is intimately bound up
with how it functions in living one's life. But when our past collides with the
inescapable present, when it no longer flows fluidly into the movement of life
signaled by the problems we confront, we must then ask the difficult but necessary question: Is such a past still a live option? The initiation of experimentation indicates that there is some *part* of our past that is no longer *living*. I
say "part" because Dewey is very clear that if the past "were wholly gone and
done with there would be only one reasonable attitude toward it. Let the dead
bury the dead" (DE [MW9:221]).

With this definition, Dewey infuses piety with the reflective and critical power of inquiry. Inquiry's functioning is therefore defined by the way in which piety orients individuals to the past. As Santayana says: "In honouring the sources of life, piety is retrospective."[61] Piety is thus the kind of moral virtue that is attentive to relationships of dependence. Here we are reminded of the importance of practical wisdom to inquiry, as discussed in the last chapter. The relationship between the two reveals that the agent is psychologically funded over time with resources (i.e., past experiences, previous obligations and commitments, etc.). When one displays wisdom, we imagine that that person has experienced much and learned how to use that experience in the service of life. Such a person lives with the past, but not in it; traditions aid her on her journey, but never wholly determine her destination point. Such individuals agree with "Emerson . . . that consistency should be thrown to the winds when it stands between us and the opportunities of present life" (HNC [MW14:72]). So Dewey is clear that authority in life is necessary, but it must also be answerable to life's demands.

The moment we make the objects of pious allegiance answerable, we can no longer see them through the lens of blind deference. In fact, he believes this is often the problem with traditional religions: "In the past men have sought many symbols which no longer serve, especially since men have been idolaters worshiping symbols as things" (HNC [MW14:226]). Here, the past becomes a burden, crippling the imagination and arresting action. In this context, Dewey explains, when individuals begin to question, they are seen as "sacrilegious and perverse" (ROS [MW4:173]; cf. CF [MW9:27]). Those who part company with Dewey would have to believe that blind deference is healthy. Such claims would need to prove that somehow a circumstance in which objects are entitled to pious allegiance without explanation regarding their place in the functioning of one's life aids rather than undermines the critical capacities needed to sustain our social and political lives. But if we are going to make arguments in favor of this point, Dewey contends, we will have to do so without lapsing into dogmatic fundamentalism or private estheticism.

Instead, piety involves an evaluative moment of attunement—a taking stock of resources in relation to one's life and fortune, a linking of the past to the present to extend the reception and meaningful content of the present. In other words, piety involves an appraisal of what is ready-at-hand. This is what Dewey means in the passage cited much earlier from *The Quest for Certainty* where he says of piety that "respect and esteem will be given to that which is the means of realization of possibilities" (QC [LW4:244]; cf. HNC

[MW14:19]). If faith "looks to the end toward which we move," remarks Santayana, "piety looks to the conditions and the sources of life."[62] This does not misdescribe the forward-looking dimension of inquiry, but claims that what gives texture to inquiry is its movement within the already flowing stream of an individual's life.

But if Dewey is attempting to recast the meaning of religion as he cites it from the *Oxford English Dictionary*, it is unclear what exactly the unseen can mean in his naturalistic account. He gives us a clear idea of what he means with the following remark: "The idea of invisible powers would take on the meaning of all the conditions of nature and human association that support and deepen the sense of values which carry on through periods of darkness and despair to such an extent that they lose their usual depressive character" (CF [MW9:11]). What allows the periods of darkness and despair to lose their depressive character are the experiences and resources that feed directly into and are continuous with those moments. Dewey refers to these experiences and resources as the unseen because they are undifferentiated. In being undifferentiated, they resist complete articulation. To say it differently, he is referring to funded experiences that infuse and underwrite identity, and from which we form a more complete self-description of ourselves as particular individuals or give language to the objects of piety. This is precisely why when he refers to *all conditions of nature and human association* in the passage above, he is careful to qualify and contextualize. The conditions of nature and human association are those by virtue of which we render our lives meaningful. Articulation of the values that carry on through darkness and despair, then, can only take place through self-description and the defining of specific objects of piety, even as we acknowledge that no one condition of nature or human association falls to the level of an unquestioned fact.

Dewey is drawing our attention to an important political conclusion—signaled in the prior section of this chapter—that he solidifies in the context of *A Common Faith*. This amplifies the emphasis on pluralism and extends the value of the relationship between inquiry and piety. To begin, how should we understand the use of religious commitments in public discourse to justify or undermine political proposals? On one reading, in public debate the practice of appealing to religious commitments in support of a set of political proposals implies pious allegiance. Those who would stand in opposition to existing proposals on the political table are considered as engaging in bad faith, subject to all kinds of retributions on the part of both the divine and individuals who share the commitments that inform those proposals. Dewey willingly concedes that this is logically coherent. As he says in his *Ethics* on this very point: "Individuals trespass, deviating from these established purposes, but they do so with the conviction that thereby social condemnation, reinforced by supernatural penalties inflicted by divine beings, ensues" (E_3 [LW7:184]). This remark has a parallel in the last chapter of *A Common Faith* where Dewey speaks of communities once strongly animated by belief in supernaturalism:

> In earlier times . . . supernaturalism was, therefore, a genuinely social religion as long as men's minds were attuned to the supernatural. It gave an "explanation" of extraordinary occurrences while it provided techniques for utilizing supernatural forces to secure advantages and to protect the members of the community against them when they were adverse. (CF [LW9:46])

The formulation of the passage is crucial: supernaturalism was a genuinely social religion, indicating general agreement regarding background commitments. His point, however, indicated by his earlier emphasis on pluralism, is that no such agreement exists in the context of modern democracy, and therefore cannot be taken for granted epistemically or as we engage each other in public discourse. "To most of us in the United States," he says earlier in that chapter, "such a situation is . . . a remote historic episode" precisely because religion no longer occupies the "social centre of gravity" vis-à-vis "associations . . . for educational, political, economic, philanthropic and scientific purposes" (CF [LW9:41, 42]).

How, then, are we to engage each other politically, especially in cases where theological communities still exist within a democratic framework? For Dewey, we need to acknowledge that why some set of policy proposals should be entitled to pious obedience needs to be discursively negotiated— that is, rhetorically crafted and therefore made explicit. This simultaneously acknowledges the absence of agreement on the underlying commitments.

In this regard, Dewey appears to be in agreement with John Rawls, especially in his "political, not metaphysical" mode.[63] But Dewey's position does not entail that one's religious commitments be excluded from public debate. The reason for this is that we would find it difficult to explain why some religiously inclined individuals have entered public debate when their reasons for doing so cannot be part of the debate itself. Those who wish to employ such reasons but are prohibited will undoubtedly view this as an infringement on the ethical content of their identity that is otherwise protected by freedom of religious expression. More important, Dewey is less interested in the source to which one appeals in advancing claims precisely because he understands one's narrative of experience to be an essential resource in filling out the content of inquiry. As such, he avoids the problems that afflict the rationalist core of Rawls' outlook—a position that, because of its emphasis on "public reason," finds itself specifying the source to which one must appeal in public argument and thus overdetermining political debate.[64]

From a Deweyan perspective, public reason is an obstacle to inquiry's functioning. For him, and in contrast to Rawls, the only claim an inquirer can advance is that where the reasons for advocating a position involve appeal to religious commitments, we must do so responsibly and prudently. As Stout remarks on just this point: "It means, for example, that in most contexts it will simply be imprudent, rhetorically speaking, to introduce explicitly theological premises into an argument intended to persuade a religiously diverse public audience."[65] But notice that this is an argument situated in the domain of politics, rather than an attempt to purify it through the stipulation of criteria because one lacks the courage political life demands.

One immediate retort is that Dewey's argument shuffles in an implicit connection between democratic fallibilism and religious commitments that is untenable. This is because it paints a political world likely to remain uninhabited by "True" believers of the "Faith." As Ian Shapiro writes (with a different target in mind), this view of discursive negotiation works only for those "fundamentalists who also count themselves as fallibilist democrats. That, I fear, is an empty class, destined to remain uninhabited."[66] Shapiro's target in this context is Amy Gutmann and Dennis Thompson's *Democracy and Disagreement*, but I believe the criticism, which presents itself as an empirical claim more realistically attuned to the political and religious landscape, can equally be extended to Dewey. If I am correct, how might he respond?

The problem that Shapiro raises is an important and difficult one that cannot be easily dispensed with, not even within Dewey's writings. Yet we should wonder if the problem itself is as clear as Shapiro states it. After all, when Shapiro uses fundamentalism, he seems to think that it necessarily entails a commitment to dogmatism. And this is how we tend to think of the term in our everyday discourse. In this view, any attempt to draw a connection between inquiry and piety will appear simply utopian at its best and unintelligible at its worst. If this is so, one would expect more extensive political and, indeed, violent sectarian conflicts in the United States. But given all of our political disagreements in the United States, both in Dewey's time and ours, religious conflicts have rarely captured the political imagination to the disadvantage of democracy (rather than a particular election). Indeed, even some Christian fundamentalists, for example, willingly concede the inherent fallibility of their reason and so inability to completely understand the claims of scripture, even though scripture remains *fundamental* to their engagement with the world. The reason for this, we might say, is precisely what

Dewey is identifying—namely, absent significant background agreement on religious commitments, coupled with humility regarding the limits of one's knowledge, religious accommodation and negotiation can have greater currency in political matters. Perhaps then the class of fallibilist democrats is not as uninhabited as Shapiro thinks.

Once again, Dewey's argument about modernity is not that religious commitments can no longer be deployed or that somehow they are presumptively irrational, but that a theological framework no longer serves as a unifying background from which we advance our claims. As such, this heightens the necessity of giving and asking for reasons in public discourse. This does not deny that conflicts, even religious ones, will occur, but it does suggest that such conflicts can exist within a democratic framework. As Dewey writes:

> Democracy is the belief that even when needs and ends or consequences are different for each individual, the habit of amicable cooperation—which may include, as in sport, rivalry and competition—is itself a priceless addition to life. To take as far as possible every conflict which arises—*and they are bound to arise*—out of the atmosphere and medium of force, of violence as a means of settlement into that of discussion and of intelligence is to treat those who disagree—even profoundly—with us as those from whom we may learn, and in so far, as friends. (CD [LW14:228] [emphasis added])

So we tend not, as Shapiro assumes, to collapse fundamentalism and dogmatism—a collapse that would most certainly weaken attempts to resolve conflicts through an exchange of reasons. For if we did, we would tend to see our opponents as enemies that we must resist at all costs lest our souls be damned, rather than see them, as Dewey suggests, as fellow citizens with whom we ought to negotiate. Since the former is not the case, then something of the latter must hold sway.

To be sure, conflicting claims emerge and need to be negotiated, but this does not happen in a linguistic and conceptual bubble. As indicated in both this and the last chapter, in Dewey's view, self-understanding emerges as part of a more complex and layered field. This means that uncontested terrain may be discovered to assess the merits of conflicting claims. We referred to this earlier as an implicit solidarity; Dewey uses the phrase "a more comprehensive point of view." This does not mean for him that we find epistemically neutral beliefs, since he concedes that these are also formed in the intersubjective, discursively redeemable context of practical action. His claim is that when inquiry is functioning, we will often find a set of commitments ancillary to the problematic context that need to be made explicit so as to provide points of entry into the issue in question. Incompatibility among beliefs does not mean incommensurability among worldviews, and it is the primacy of the former in modern times that renders the project of democracy not only intelligible but viable.

FAITH, IMAGINATION, AND THE IDEAL

Having considered at some length Dewey's views on piety, we are now prepared to examine the other feature of *A Common Faith*, namely, faith. When he takes up this topic he discusses two different things: first, its psychological function, and second, its moral dimension vis-à-vis the external environment. Regarding the first of these, Dewey remarks that its religious impact signifies:

> [C]hanges in ourselves in relation to the world in which we live that are much more inclusive and deep seated. They relate not to this and that want in relation to this and that condition of our surroundings, but pertain to our being in its entirety. . . . There is a composing and harmonizing of the various elements of our being such that . . . it is a change *of* will conceived as the organic plentitude of our being, rather than any special change *in* will. It is the claim of religions that they effect this generic and enduring change in attitude. I should like to turn the statement around and say that whenever this change takes place there is a definitely religious attitude. . . . The idea of a whole, whether of the whole personal being or of the world, is an imaginative, not a literal, idea. The limited world of our observation and reflection becomes the Universe only through imaginative extension. (CF [LW9:12–13, 14] [original emphases])

Precisely because agents are constituted amid the flux of existence, realizable through the unfolding of practical action, they remain psychologically incomplete. After all, to speak of the primacy of habits in the life of the self only signifies the self's relative stability over time, but this in no way constitutes, in Dewey's view, a unified or fixed identity. A unified self implies a comprehensive picture of the whole of reality and one's life therein, undistorted or unobscured. The "organic plentitude" of our being is an appropriate phrase in this instance; it implies that the teleological structure of action is continuous with the environment. "The self," he says, "is always directed toward something beyond itself and so its own unification depends upon the idea of the integration of the shifting scenes of the world into that imaginative totality we call the Universe" (CF [LW9:14]). Hence the last sentence speaks of the imagination as extending current observation and reflection—a form of expressive freedom, we might say—so as to project what the unknown might be were it present.

Dewey does not explain precisely how the imagination works in *A Common Faith*, and so we must look elsewhere. In his major work on aesthetics, *Art as Experience*, which he publishes during the same year as *A Common Faith*, he writes the following: "Art is thus prefigured in the very process of living" (AE$_2$ [LW10:30]). For him, we confront our lives in the way an artist confronts a canvas stained with color. There is a picture of life to complete, ends and purposes to be stipulated, sought after, and reached, that makes the life we live our own. The simple point is that the process of socialization does not exhaust identity formation. But the ends, as Dewey says, are "presented only imaginatively" (CF [LW9:14]). What exactly this means he suggests in his account of the conflict that the artist undergoes, although this claim is not confined to this example:

> One way of stating it concerns the opposition between inner and outer vision. There is a stage in which the inner vision seems much richer and finer than any outer manifestation. It has a vast and enticing aura of implications that are lacking in the object of external vision . . . the matter of the inner vision seems wraith-like compared with the solidity and energy of the presented scene. The object is felt to say something succinctly and forcibly that the inner vision reports vaguely, in diffuse feeling rather than organically. The artist is driven to submit himself in humility to the discipline of the objective vision. But the inner vision is not cast out. It remains as the organ by which the outer vision is controlled, and it takes on structure as the latter is absorbed within it. The interaction of the two modes of vision is imagination; as imagination takes form the work of art is born . . . [the artist] finds himself obliged to go back to objects if his speculations are to have body, weight, and perspective. (AE$_2$ [LW10:273])

Here he captures the dialectical relationship between vision and context, in which the end or ideal to be reached occurs through a transmutation and extension of experience. The imagination reconstructs and extends experience, thus giving a more complete representation of ends than is suggested by the environment in which we find ourselves. The reconstruction is not merely of discreet happenings—the present situation—but more dramatically, the funded nature of the present so that the end product of the imagination has a career both in the present and in what precedes it. As Dewey remarks: "For while the roots of every experience are found in the interaction of a live creature with its environment, that experience becomes conscious, a matter of perception, only when meanings enter it that are derived from prior experiences. Imagination is the only gateway through which these meanings find their way into [the] present" (AE₂ [LW10:276]; cf. CF [LW9:33–34]).⁶⁷ Through the use of the imagination, we are simultaneously acknowledging that the possibilities of identity and context are "unrealized in fact [but] come home to us [imaginatively] and have power to stir us [practically]" (CF [LW9:30]). "The experience enacted," he continues in *Art as Experience*, "is human and conscious only as that which is given here and now is extended by meanings and values drawn from what is absent in fact and present only imaginatively" (AE₂ [LW10:276]). This makes the suggested telos an object for testing. This much he says in his essay "What I Believe" of 1930: "Faith is a tendency toward action," and in being so, it "can be tried and tested only in action" (WIB [LW5:267, 278]).

As these passages indicate, Dewey applies the inferential dimension of inquiry discussed in the last chapter to the very psychological makeup of the self. The implication is that the existing contour of identity and context and its transmutation by the imagination vividly display departure and destination points that control action. "[I]maginative experience," he says, "is what happens when varied materials of sense, quality, emotion, and meaning come together in a union that marks a new birth in the world" (AE₂ [LW10:272]). This new birth is not the realization of the ideal end or whole self as such, but what results from pursuit of such ends.

But given what Dewey says about the self in the context of modern conditions, why make harmony, complete psychological integration, a goal at all? In answering this question we should keep in mind that religious faith functions to create adjustment between self and its context, and a pervasive imaginative harmony that affects the contours of identity and directs actions. This means that the particular ideals that Dewey has in mind which animate us are of such a nature that they render us harmonious and integrate us with the environment. "I should describe this faith," he says, "as the unification of the self through allegiance to inclusive ideal ends, which imagination presents to us and to which the human will responds as worthy of controlling our desires and choices" (CF [LW9:23]). So the formal account of faith that he offers conditions the objects to which it attaches in a very specific way. He amplifies the remark several pages later: "The unity signifies not a single Being, but the unity of loyalty and effort evoked by the fact that many ends are one in the power of their ideal, or imaginative, quality to stir and hold us" (CF [LW9:30]).

In the context of the question above, this means that the commitment to harmony flows from a vision of the self whose complete unfolding in time would settle the existential and practical demand of action. "The religious attitude signifies something that is bound through imagination to a *general* attitude. This comprehensive attitude, moreover, is much broader than anything indicated by 'moral' in its usual sense" precisely because it completes the demands of the moral life (CF [LW9:17] [original emphasis]). I say "completes" in this context for several reasons. First, the social world gives our actions moral import. The extent to which we are agents and patients implies a constant attempt to manage the world of practical action. Second, the religious attitude, as Dewey describes it, thus stipulates ideals, regulative to be sure, by virtue of which the moral life is fulfilled. In other words, the far-reaching character of the religious attitude outstrips the term "moral" in its usual sense, which, as I read Dewey, seeks to settle this or that specific problematic.

We can deepen this account by turning to the second of the two themes, namely, the moral dimension of religious faith.

> The intimate connection of imagination with the ideal elements in experience is generally recognized. Such is not the case with respect to its connection with faith. The latter has been regarded as a substitute for knowledge, for sight. It is defined, in the Christian religion, as *evidence* of things not seen. The implication is that faith is a kind of anticipatory vision of things that are now invisible because of the limitation of our finite and erring natures. (CF [LW9:14–15] [original emphasis])

From Dewey's perspective, however, faith is not, as traditionally conceived, about the immanence of an ideal whose realization is hampered by our natures. In that account, the ideal becomes reified and the meaning of faith is obscured. The ideal is reified in the sense that it cannot undergo revision in the light of the experiential dimension of self-formation. Questions about how an ideal conditions action, or why some ideal as opposed to another ought to guide conduct and belief, are cordoned off from the practice of giving and asking for reasons. It would follow from this view that the relationship Dewey envisions between inquiry's reason-giving character as discussed in the last chapter and faith is ruled out of hand.

Dewey's claim is that even as ideals are stipulated on which our faith hinges and as something toward which we strive, they are revisable by virtue of their impact on practical action. This is why our relationship to ideals need not be idolatrous.[68] Ideals have the character of being *ultimate ends,* to be sure, but not in the sense wherein that term implies unassailable knowledge of what human nature demands. They are "ultimate" in Dewey's view because they adequately serve to control and guide all secondary actions. But an appropriate stipulation of ideals never loses sight of the reflexive dimension of practical action—that is, in which secondary actions retrospectively inform commitment to ideals, disclosing the fallibilistic and experimental quality of the entire project of ideal formation. So even as ideals work to effect a transformation in action, the resulting change in experience becomes an evaluative moment to assess the viability of and warrant for those ideals as something that ought to guide life. It is this dynamism the gives the teleological character of life a flexible and internally differentiated character.

More significant, in the traditional view, the value of faith often hinges on the credit of its supernatural author. As Dewey explains: "Faith was once almost universally thought to be acceptance of a definite body of intellectual propositions, acceptance being based upon authority—preferably that of revelation from on high" (WIB [LW5:267]). So faith by this description at once becomes commitment to an ideal whose realization is blocked by our nature. But the ideal nonetheless demands intellectual assent because of its author. This is precisely why religious faith is traditionally embodied in assent to "a body of propositions [and] ... reasons" that enter to "demonstrate the reasonableness of giving such credit" to a supernatural author (CF [LW9:15]).[69] Here once again questions about its appropriateness are rule out of hand. But as with piety, Dewey rejects the necessary connection: "The actual religious quality in experience described is the *effect* produced, the better adjustment in life and its conditions, not the manner and cause of its production" (CF [LW9:11] [original emphasis]).[70]

Insofar as we understand these claims, they signal the radical nature of Dewey's experimentalism. This returns us to the discussion initiated in the last chapter regarding the various dimensions of inquiry. As I indicated there, given the formal description of inquiry, it would be necessary to return to the relationship between belief, evidence, and context in order to understand precisely inquiry's internal dynamism. The issue is particularly important since Hilary Putnam insists that Dewey is "less sensitive than [William] James to the limits of intelligence as a guide to life," where this means that commitment to a belief, theory, or ideal is not primarily about a sufficient or preponderance of the evidence we may have to support it.[71] Genuine experimentalism involves, in Putnam's view, both risk and courage—an existential imprimatur.

Putnam has in mind two different cases that we need to separate. On the one hand, he wants to say that Dewey's insistence on the importance of inquiry to action is not attentive to instances where two competing moral choices equally pull on us, thus requiring a leap of faith. On the other hand, Putnam's criticism is operative in cases where individuals are acting in the service of theories, the full reasons for which are still to be garnered in experience.[72] If I understand him correctly, in both cases the underlying issue to which Dewey seems less sensitive than James is simply this: reasons for choosing between two moral claims or belief in theory x is not wholly about evidence—and, if it were, it is unclear how a decision, not to mention progress, could ever take place in an uncertain world. For our purposes, I want to bracket the first case, coming back to this more explicitly in chapter 4.

The second case and the underlying problem present a formidable objection to Dewey's account of inquiry. But Putnam's reading seems to unnecessarily place James and Dewey at odds, the result of which when applied in the context of *A Common Faith* misdescribes altogether Dewey's understanding of the relationship between faith and inquiry. After all, the inferential dimension of inquiry requires, as emphasized in chapter 2, a leap into the unknown. Precisely because Dewey redefines the relationship between theory and practice, he is able to extend Aristotle's insight regarding contingency via Darwin to all domains of human action. Experience in toto thus constitutes an experimental domain. So while the warrant for the leap is grounded in an existing state-of-affairs and evidence, the reason for taking the leap is not exhausted by evidence presented for its accuracy. There is little doubt that this is what Dewey means:

> But belief or faith has also a moral and practical import. . . . Apart from any theological context, there is a difference between belief that is a conviction that some end should be supreme over conduct and belief that some object or being exists as a truth for the intellect. . . . Reflection, often long and arduous, may be involved in arriving at the conviction, but the import of thought is not exhausted in discovery of evidence that can justify intellectual assent. The authority of an ideal over choice and conduct is the authority of an ideal, not of a fact, of a truth guaranteed to intellect, not of the status of the one who propounds the truth. Such moral faith is not easy. . . . Moral faith has been bolstered by all sorts of arguments intended to prove that its object is not ideal and that its claim upon us is not primarily moral or practical, since the ideal in question is already embedded in the existent frame of things. . . . They have failed to see that in converting moral realities into matters of intellectual assent they have evinced lack of *moral* faith (CF [LW9:15–16] [original emphasis]).

In this passage he separates the claim that we have faith in an ideal because of evidence of its existence from the claim that our faith in an ideal should have command over our conduct and beliefs despite evidence needed to justify our devotion. To be sure, the existing state-of-affairs is important, for our faith is liable to become fantasy if not tempered by experience. This is precisely why reflection may be involved in arriving at ideals. But in making faith rely on evidence we obscure the work imagination effects, since the ideal longed for is not in existence. More critically, it undermines the courage that faith in the ideal demands, since in being realizable through imagination its specific impact on action is most uncertain.

What Dewey is drawing our attention to is that the traditional account merely begs the question which the test of an ideal in experience seeks to answer—namely, why this ideal ought to command our attention (cf. PD [MW11:41–49]). So, in his view, the weight we accord ideals, the authority they exercise over us, is not exhausted in discovery of evidence that may underwrite intellectual assent. This is simply to say that while ideals are emergent from experience via the imagination, their authoritative role in action *ultimately* runs ahead of evidentiary support or external authorization into "a world of surmise, of mystery, [and] of uncertainties" (AE$_2$ [LW10:41]).[73] As he says, the "imaginative presentation of ideals . . . has been the means of keeping alive the sense of purposes that outrun evidence and of meanings that transcend indurated habit" (AE$_2$ [LW10:350]). This is precisely what makes faith difficult and courage necessary.[74] Indeed, James says as much in his 1882 essay, "The Sentiment of Rationality": "[F]aith is the readiness to act in a cause the prosperous issue of which is not certified to us in advance. It is in fact the same moral quality which we call courage in practical affairs."[75] Contrary to Putnam's reading, Dewey and James are in agreement.

If we apply the foregoing discussion once more to the definition cited from the *Oxford English Dictionary*, we hit upon Dewey's reconstruction. We have already considered the way in which an ideal commands allegiance and guides our action. But we have said very little explicitly about his reconstruction of the unseen. He provides the description with his account of the ideal: "An unseen power controlling our destiny becomes the power of an ideal. . . . For all endeavor for the better is moved by faith in what is possible, not by adherence to the actual. The outcome, given our best endeavor, is not with us" (CF [LW9:17]). The controlling factor, unlike with piety, is not the past as such, but the uncertain future. This means we can only wait patiently, with humble expectations that, because our judgments have been fortified by critical reflection and the resources of the communities to which we belong, our effort will be rewarded in experience. But beyond this, the rest belongs to fate.

For present purposes I hope to have shown that Dewey's description of piety and faith—his religious naturalism—is part of a much larger conversation about what a democratic ethos demands. But if this account is correct, it is important to observe that his conception of inquiry, which has been operative throughout, provides a point of orientation that is contextually sensitive, imaginatively rich, and discursively open so that the ends of inquiry are subject to assessment and revision. The result of this last claim partly works to humble the agent of inquiry—a fact that is not usually associated with Dewey's philosophy, but which I have argued for both here and in the previous chapters. For him, such an orientation is necessary in the absence of epistemic certainty under conditions of pluralism.

What are the implications of this description for understanding the ways in which inquiry can navigate our ethical and democratic life? Within a horizon marked by the intellectual acceptance of pluralism, the intersubjective development of identity, and the necessity of articulating a vision of democracy that does not privilege experts in managing our collective lives, inquiry must become a strategy, as I believe Dewey intends, that specifies more clearly the normative content of a well-functioning political order attentive to the ethical well-being of its citizens. This raises a complicated set of issues that dovetail with concerns relating to conflict and democratic legitimacy, and also points directly to those scholars who would have us believe that Dewey has nothing insightful to say on these matters. As we shall see in the next two chapters, there is much in Dewey worth our attention.

The issue to which we turn immediately concerns our discussion in both this chapter and previous chapters. It relates to the normative resources within our self-understanding that serve as a compass in managing our moral lives. Here we come back to Hodge and Weber. If pluralism defines the modern horizon because there is no nonhuman objective or sacred background, does this not imply a crisis in normative evaluation? Dewey's discussions of the constraining and freeing aspects of practical action in chapter 2 and the meaning of democratic self-reliance in this chapter were all attempts to address this question. But in all instances the answer was embedded in other, more important matters pertaining to the place of contingency in Dewey's philosophy and his specific understanding of the religious dimension of experience in the context of democracy. Chapter 4 will allow us to respond directly to the matter by attending carefully to Dewey's attempt to describe the moral life as an emergent property of our social psychology. In doing so, he disentangles the pluralism issue from the supposed crisis in normative evaluation. He can thus say with James, "Whether a God exist, or whether no God exist, in yon blue heaven above us bent, we form at any rate an ethical republic here below."[76] I take John McDowell to assert the same point when he remarks that "the ethical is a domain of rational requirements, which are there in any case, whether or not we are responsive to them."[77] This is simply to say that human agency is *always already* normative. For him, the issue is not whether we will be moral agents, but rather with what skill we will exercise that agency and refine the reflective and perceptual capacities it includes.

WITHIN THE SPACE OF MORAL REFLECTION

Dewey's attempt to elucidate the importance of inquiry to moral and political action has always generated concern. The reason for this is a simple one: inquiry seemingly obscures the inescapable imprecision and messiness that moral and political life can present. When inquiry is connected to morality it seems too reductionist; it cannot address one of the central themes of modernity—namely, the crisis of normative evaluation. What is meant by this, as contemporary thinkers explain, is that we often confront both as a society and within the unfolding of our individual lives a conflict among competing visions of the Good, Right, and Virtue without a fixed rule for assessment (cf. TIM [LW5:279–89]; E$_3$ [LW7: pt. II]).[1] In this regard we are reminded of Charles Hodge's worry that in the wake of Darwin, we would lose those standards that prefigure the human, but are nonetheless essential to guiding our individual and social lives. This argument was echoed later by Max Weber, who identified the crisis in normative evaluation with the modern horizon itself. The issue for him was not the absence of values, but rather the plurality and diversity of values that emerge once an objective horizon disappears. In such a world how could normative evaluation be anything but mere whim or conviction?

The argument against Dewey's account of inquiry, with its aspirations to achieving synthetic harmony among conflicting claims, is that he distorts and fails to take seriously this aspect of the modern condition. As scholars argue, this is a relic of his much earlier commitment to Hegelian idealism—the ontological framework in which inquiry is located.[2] If Hodge and Weber are correct about the conditions of modern life and Dewey's critics are correct about his philosophy, we run into a twofold problem. The first is that he cannot provide us with resources to defend the proposition that the relationship between mind and world is thoroughly normative at the most basic epistemic level. Second, he seems unable to take seriously the irreducibility of moral conflict that develops after the eclipse of a unifying sacred foundation. The two problems are related; it is the absence of a normatively laden world to which we might appeal to guide our judgments that contributes to the rise of conflict.

The aim of this chapter is to explore the way the post-Darwinian development of Dewey's philosophy mitigates any presumptive belief in synthetic harmony. This much we see in four of his mature works—*Democracy and Education* (1916), *Human Nature and Conduct: An Introduction to Social Psychology* (1922), "Three Independent Factors of Morals" (1930), and *Ethics* (1932).[3] In these works, two dimensions emerge in Dewey's moral philosophy. The first stipulates ethical harmony as a goal of deliberation in the context of conflict, and the second nonetheless views deliberation as potentially deepening our apprehension of conflict, defying harmony.

These two dimensions, however, are embedded within the larger framework of Dewey's philosophy that we have considered throughout and that centers on the normative character of self-understanding. While he willingly acknowledges the absence of a determinant rule for settling moral conflicts, he does not believe this bespeaks some general crisis in normative evaluation. As I argue in the first section below, this is because for him the moral life is grounded in and coterminous with what I call *mutual responsiveness*—a kind of attentiveness to the claims of others that creates the framework necessary for thinking about moral situations from the outset. The moral life, to appropriate George Herbert Mead's language, is "in a genuine sense constituted within the social process of experience, by the communication and mutual adjustment of behavior among the individual organisms which are involved in the process and which carry it on."[4] For both Dewey and Mead, mutual responsiveness is part and parcel of our introduction into the social world and signals the immanence of normativity. This claim is part of Dewey's social psychology and serves as a counterpart to his philosophy of action and defense of democratic self-reliance.[5]

In proceeding this way, we can distinguish two different levels of analysis. The first relates to the generative character of the normative world and the reflective and perceptual capacities that it includes. The second concerns the place of conflict in the modern self-understanding and its specific character.[6] For Dewey, the need for moral deliberation emerges precisely at the point where the socially constituted value-sphere in which individuals are located fractures, implicating them in conflicting possibilities for a concrete situation. At this juncture the following practical question arises: What should I do? (E_3 [LW7:164]). The question invites a reconstructive and evaluative moment in our moral experience.

This reconstructive and evaluative moment is more fundamentally a way of seeing the landscape from within the space of moral reflection. But the essential point for Dewey is that because the social world is always already normative, we can only reflect from inside that space. In this regard I turn in the second section to elucidating the outlook of the deliberating agent— that is, the *best achievable state* that allows, in Dewey's view, individuals to track the salient features of the current moral situation in order to do justice to the competing factors.[7] We should read him, as I remarked at the conclusion of chapter 2, as attempting to engender an outlook toward the art of living that transforms the emotional and intellectual course one takes into any one particular issue in life. The point is to provide people who see themselves as moral agents with insight into how to make reflection more enlightened.[8]

What are the habits of character that render reflection more enlightened, that allow the self to see and hear clearly the call of competing claims? In short, what is the substantive content of the best achievable state? For Dewey, to be a practical actor engaged in deliberation in the context of a moral problem requires willingness to see one's judgments as revisable, ability to assess the place of general principles in particular situations, and, most important, a sense of "sympathy"—that is, the ability to imaginatively participate in the life of others (E_3 [LW7:249–251]).[9] When taken together, these elements help fill out and define the dramatic character of deliberation (HNC [MW14: chaps. 16–17]; E_3 [LW7:298–301]). As such, "best achievable state" denotes an *ideal perceptive condition*, whose aim is to track the deliverances from a person's character on the one hand and the larger environment on the other in the context of concrete conflicts.

The role of sympathy is especially important in this process. For Dewey, sympathy works through the imagination (i.e., the inferential dimension of inquiry) to foreground the complex and variegated landscape in which the agent is situated.[10] In other words, sympathy registers content from the world, and in so doing prepares the individual for the potential expansion of her provincial horizons—so that she may become, as Dewey says, an "impartial observer" (E_3 [LW7:251]; cf. AE_2 [LW10:338]).[11] This use of "observer" rather than "actor" is significant, for it captures the spectatorial role Dewey intends for the agent to assume. But the emphasis should not be placed on the image of the spectator as occupying a view from nowhere. Rather, Dewey imagines the spectator as that of a surveyor—one who sees and measures the texture and diversity of the moral landscape for decision-making. Through sympathy, contextual sensitivity becomes the key to an impartial or objective outlook.

In the last part of this chapter, "The Tragic Self: Deliberation and Conflict," I turn to the disjunction in Dewey's moral philosophy that scholars overlook. Here I mean the difference in his analysis of deliberation that informs *Human Nature and Conduct*, on the one hand, and "Three Independent Factors of Morals" and specific examples he offers in his *Ethics*, on the other. Precisely because deliberation proceeds from the domain of practical action, it has the potential to make the goal of synthetic harmony and our teleological psychologies problematic. Deliberation does not always resolve conflict by enlarging our thoughts and dramatically proposing a course of action that encompasses the conflicting factors. So "best achievable state" does not imply that if we sincerely engage in deliberation we will always dissolve conflict. In fact, deliberation for Dewey may potentially deepen our sense of conflict. We come to discover that the various factors of moral life are truly at "cross purposes and exercise divergent forces" in which choice becomes a question of what kind of person I want to be and what kind of world I long to inhabit (TIM [LW5:280]). We must forgo one if another is to be realized. Dewey's much earlier Hegelian commitment to ethical harmony is thus redescribed on Darwinian grounds: "[T]he Hegelian emphasis upon continuity and the function of conflict persisted on empirical grounds after my earlier confidence in dialectic had given way to skepticism."[12]

THE MORAL LIFE AND THE PLACE OF CONFLICT

In previous chapters we discussed the social character of action and self-understanding for Dewey, with its liberating and constraining aspects (chap. 2, third section). We considered the way our actions are explicable through a practice of reason-giving (chap. 2, last section), a kind of mutual responsiveness. This is a feature upon which democratic life is based and which attempts to support it (chap. 3, first section). Yet Dewey wants to make a stronger claim about mutual responsiveness—for him, it forms the generative core of moral life. That is, to inhabit a social world is to live within a normative one. He thus agrees with the Jamesian point cited at the conclusion of the last chapter: "Whether a God exist, or whether no God exist, in yon blue heaven above us bent, we form at any rate an ethical republic here below."[13] It cannot be denied that there will most certainly be conflicts within such a world about what the good life comprises or about which rights to uphold and defend. But this is a separate issue, *pace* Hodge and Weber, from the one that questions the existence of the world in which those conflicts emerge. We are awakened to the demands of the moral life by acquiring a kind of conceptual awareness that is slowly refined and honed through reflection and deliberation. This is part of what Dewey refers to as our "secondary and acquired" nature (HNC [MW14:63]). He would thus agree with John McDowell's recent description of the normative dimension of social existence—a description, I should add, that is framed specifically against the disenchantment thesis:

> When a decent upbringing initiates us into the relevant way of thinking, our eyes are opened to the very existence of this tract of the space of reasons. There-after our appreciation of its detailed layout is indefinitely subject to refinement, in reflective scrutiny of our ethical thinking. We can so much as understand, let alone seek to justify, the thought that reason makes these demands on us only at a standpoint within a system of concepts and conceptions that enables us to think about such demands, that is, only at a standpoint from which demands of this kind seem to be in view.[14]

To ask the question "Why be attentive to the demands of the moral life?," says Dewey, is like asking the question, "Why live?" And the only answer, he continues, "is that if one is going to live one must live a life of which these things form the substance" (HNC [MW14:58]). Of course, he can understand the crisis in normative evaluation, but he encourages us not to find the crisis gripping.

WITHIN THE SPACE OF MORAL LIFE

For Dewey, the emergence of moral life is coterminous with conditioning individuals for mutual responsiveness.[15] As with dancing, for example, mutual responsiveness is what allows us to follow the movements of our partners from the perspective of our own moves. Responsiveness thus means that moral life requires us to react appropriately to an experience of the world, its evidence, and objects that now call on our attention. We can begin to interpret this point if we turn to chapter 5 of *Human Nature and Conduct*, "Custom and Morality," where he investigates morality's authoritative force. In this context, he is aware of the age-old question: "Why be moral?" For him, all moral claims can be reduced to this question if we so choose. Yet Dewey seems to think that at the empirical level the answer is straightforward, suggesting that the question "Why be moral?" is often one of theoretical analysis rather than practical concern. And so the claim morality has on us, he answers dramatically, "is that of life" (HNC [MW14:57]).

But what does he mean when he invokes the term "life"? Before turning specifically to how he answers, let us consider for a moment the word itself. At first blush it isn't clear how the word can function authoritatively. What is its content and who is its author to which I am answerable? This way of approaching the term may obscure its more mundane function. After all, when the term "life" is invoked authoritatively it comes in common phrases such as "That's life" or "Such is life." Both phrases attempt to reconcile us to fate—the way things are. In doing so they generate a feeling of inevitability—the sense that things could not be otherwise. That Dewey invokes the term authoritatively in the context of the moral life equally aims to invoke this sense of inevitability. We are, for him, beings for whom it is natural to be moral creatures.

The suggestion for this reading comes in the final chapter of *Human Nature and Conduct*, entitled, "Morality Is Social," where Dewey begins to explain how he uses the term:

> When a child acts, those about him react. They shower encouragement upon him, visit him with approval, or they bestow frowns and rebuke. What others do to us when we act is as natural a consequence of our action as what the fire does to us when we plunge our hands in it. The social environment may be as artificial as you please. But its action in response to ours is natural not artificial. *In language and imagination we rehearse the response of others just as we dramatically enact other consequences. We foreknow how others will act, and the foreknowledge is the beginning of judgment passed on action.* (HNC [MW14:216] [emphasis added])

This is the first half of this all-important but compact passage. Here Dewey indicates that the internal process of "life" is the practice of taking the attitude of others, which I shall say more about in a moment. But at this juncture, he understands morality as a social function precisely because it generates by its very workings a kind of foreknowledge indexed to the attitude of others. Through a process of acculturation we come to experimentally, and therefore inferentially, adjust our linguistic and social behavior in advance as part of interacting with others. The adjustment is a reading, if you will, of the action of the other. Mead captures this point when he writes: "Just as in fencing the parry is an *interpretation* of the thrust, so, in the social act, the adjustive response of one organism to the gesture of another is the interpretation of that gesture by that organism—it is the meaning of that gesture."[16] If this were not the case we would permanently experience each others' actions as wholly foreign, indexed to something we know not (HNC [MW14:65–67]; DE [MW9:32–33]).

The previous point, along with the claim about the importance of acculturation, should not be understated. Dewey is drawing our attention to the importance of our "second nature" and the way it opens us up to the moral life. "For practical purposes," he says, "morals mean customs, folkways, established collective habits. . . . They are the pattern into which individual activity must weave itself" (HNC [MW14:54]). This theme also figures prominently in the ethical naturalism of McDowell and Sabina Lovibond, both of whom are concerned with showing the continuity between reason and nature and so revealing the immanence of normativity. For them, as well as for Dewey, acculturation involves the biological hardware that makes our first nature receptive to acquiring a second nature. This much he explains in his discussion of habits, keeping in mind that habits function as norms for action at both the basic and most complex levels of life:

> Habits as organized activities are secondary and acquired, not native and original. They are outgrowths of unlearned activities which are part of man's endowment at birth. . . . In the life of the individual, instinctive activity comes first. But an individual begins life as a baby, and babies are dependent beings. Their activities could continue at most for only a few hours were it not for the presence and aid of adults with their formed habits. And babies owe to adults more than procreation, more than the continued food and protection which preserve life. They owe to adults the opportunity to express their native activities in ways which have meaning. Even if by some miracle original activity could continue without assistance from the organized skill and art of adults, it would not amount to anything. It would be mere sound and fury. In short, the *meaning* of native activities is not native; it is acquired. It depends upon interaction with a matured social medium. (HNC [MW14:65] [original emphasis])

Notice that this formulation recalls our discussion of the liberating and constraining aspects of practical action, since acculturation limits what we can do even as it provides resources for transformation. In this context, however, Dewey's point is that our entrance and participation in social life gives rise to an acquired nature. We might say, as Dewey and Lovibond do, that it is akin to learning our first language (HNC [MW14:57]).[17] We would not call the acquired first language "natural" in the sense that we come already wired with it, but neither would we see it as unnatural to have acquired such a language. Similarly, we would not call our norms for action, which we can acquire only through participation in social life, "natural" at the biological level, although our biology participates in allowing us to acquire and develop them. For Dewey, we should appropriately understand our second nature as continuous and emergent from our first (QC [LW4:171–172]).

But observe how he describes the matter in the quoted passage. For him, the social medium provides the opportunity to express native capacities— which is simply to say there are native capacities for norm acquisition that are necessary for acquiring the specific norms that we do take in.[18] Our "second nature," then, refers not only to the specificity of collective habits, but also to the conceptual framework in which those habits are located. The former awakens us to the existence of the latter such that it becomes impossible for us to see ourselves otherwise. If this description is accurate, there should be no legitimate question about the very *idea* or *existence* of habits as norms for action, apart from those that we address in our encounters with specific habits.[19]

We may still worry about what Dewey is attempting to elucidate if we conclude that taking on the attitudes of others, for instance, which is essential to entering and managing social life, means mere imitation. Habit talk often carries this connotation. And imitation also seems to be implied by his earlier discussion of rehearsal. We may think that the category of the social as implied by acculturation looms too large and threatens to trap us within a narrow horizon. For all of their insight, there are unfortunately few social-psychological resources in McDowell and Lovibond to allow us to get at the dynamism of the process. Merely referring to our second nature does not yet elucidate the energetic process that acquiring a second nature implies. Yet Dewey's account, owing to his Darwinian commitments, is intended to be adaptive and more generative even as he insists on the relevance of the imitative dimension (HNC [MW14:49–50]; cf. HWT$_2$ [LW8:283–284]; DE [MW9:39]).[20]

We can make sense of this if we consider once again the case of language, to which Dewey often refers as a model for thinking about moral life. One's ability to respond to a question—that is, to give a reply that is intelligible to its recipient—implies an interpretation of what constitutes "responding." This could only be possible because the individual is at some point simultaneously acting as both questioner and responder—that is, the agent has internalized the differentiation of roles and responsibilities that questioning and responding embody. "The act," says Dewey, "must come before the thought, and a habit before an ability to evoke the thought at will" (HNC [MW14:25]; cf. EN [LW1:135]). Through my response, I see myself from the standpoint of the person I address so that I import something of their conduct—i.e., a way of feeling, thinking, and doing—into my own that makes my response intelligible. We have a moment of taking the attitude of the other (a kind of imitative process that fits with Dewey's language of rehearsal), but with a difference attributable to the asymmetry of the response needed to complete the process (EN [LW1:140–144]; cf. DE [MW9:40]).[21]

The example of language is important because it does substantive work for Dewey. Language, for him, is the paradigmatic example with which to think about social practices generally, but morality in particular, because language is the grounding mechanism for the emergence of common and shared inferences that underwrite any practice we label "social." Our coordination and interaction are at once funneled through the use of signs that orient us in a certain kind of way, which simultaneously gives those signs meaning for future appropriation.[22] As Mead explains, we rehearse the response of others (i.e., they represent symbols) just as we dramatically enact other consequences, so that we come not merely to respond in the same way (i.e., imitate others), but to respond *appropriately* (i.e., address the symbols because they elicit specific responses).[23] "Responding appropriately" must only mean that the meaning-content of the response is intelligible, not that the content comports with what the listener wishes to hear. Only through language, however, can I hold out the hope of getting my interlocutors to see things as I do, to change their minds such that they register an order other than their own thickly layered one. This process is what leads Dewey to the following claim: "When communication occurs all natural events are subject to reconsideration and revision; they are readapted to meet the requirements of conversation, whether it be public discourse or that *preliminary discourse termed thinking*" (EN [LW1:132] [emphasis added]).

Of course, for Dewey there are those instances in which behavioral expectations reach all the way down into meaning itself. We might consider a brief example of this. In baseball, when the batter hits the ball we immediately (all things considered) expect him to run to the appropriate base. Now walking would obviously satisfy getting the batter to the next base, but we would surely question his interest in getting "safe," and so potentially garnering points for the team, if he decided to walk rather than run. We would even wonder if he knows how the game is played. He has not responded to the event (i.e., the hitting of the ball and its movement through the air) in view of its place in an inclusive social practice (i.e., baseball). In other instances behavioral expectations and their meaning-content are not understood to be immediately indexed to each other. This may be either the result of the asymmetrical form of the relationship itself or simply the result of trying to reach some understanding of the subject matter or object to which we are oriented (E_3 [LW7:218–219]). But we cannot yet ascertain this prior to our immersion in a context that includes intentions and expectations. This is precisely why Dewey's aim is to articulate a more fundamental account in which the general composition of mutual responsiveness is explained.

Developmentally the practice of taking on the attitude of others is not always an outer conversation—as we often see between parent and child, teacher and student, coach and player—but rather becomes a truncated, inner conversation with oneself (HNC [MW14:217]; DE [MW9:32–35]; EN [LW1:134]). In the case of conduct, Dewey is saying that one becomes reflexively aware through a process of communication of the social significance of one's actions (they represent symbols to self and other and achieve independent status) and can continue an interaction given this awareness. This is only possible because, as he argues, a human form of consciousness emerges from a communicatively mediated process by which we take on the attitude of others—that is, are responsive to them and them to us. "Through speech," Dewey explains, "a person dramatically identifies himself with potential acts and deeds; he plays many roles . . . in a contemporaneously enacted drama. Thus mind emerges" (EN [LW1:135]).[24]

We finally come to the precise meaning of morality's authoritative force that Dewey intends to capture with the term "life." Let us turn to the second half of the passage quoted from the chapter "Morality Is Social" in *Human Nature and Conduct*, beginning with the last sentence from the passage above.

> We foreknow how others will act, and the foreknowledge is the beginning of judgment passed on action. We know *with* them; there is conscience. An assembly is formed within our breast which discusses and appraises proposed and performed acts. The community without becomes a forum and tribunal within, a judgment-seat of charges, assessments and exculpations. Our thoughts of our own actions are saturated with the ideas that others entertain about them, ideas which have been expressed not only in explicit instruction but still more effectively in reaction to our actions. (HNC [MW14:216–217] [original emphasis])

In this passage he describes a discursively formed practice that is internalized by the self through a process of socialization, what Mead refers to as "the generalized other." Mead explains it this way:

> In abstract thought the individual takes the attitude of the generalized other toward himself, without reference to its expression in any particular other individuals; and in concrete thought he takes that attitude in so far as it is expressed

in the attitudes toward his behavior of those other individuals with whom he is involved. . . . And only through the taking by individuals of the attitude or attitudes of the generalized other toward themselves is the existence of a universe of discourse, as that system of common or social meanings which thinking presupposes at its context, rendered possible.[25]

In both accounts there is an implicit normative claim that is entailed by the process itself. As Dewey says, we know not as them, but *with* them. Another way to capture the dual feature that "with" intends to register is to say that the process allows us to track each others' commitments, assess entitlement to our own, and chastise ourselves and others for "commitments undertaken irresponsibly."[26] This is the function that the "tribunal" imagery serves in Dewey's account.

As Dewey and Mead understand the matter, this normative claim becomes a feature of character formation as such. We assess and guide our own actions and hold others to account for theirs, which alone determines for all participants the meaning and significance of those actions and the objects to which they are directed from the outset. To recall Dewey's earlier remark: "The only answer is that if one is going to live one must live a life of which these things form the substance" (HNC [MW14:58]). Herein lies the sense of inevitability referred to earlier—we are the kind of organisms for which it is second nature to live within a normative world. As he says, the central question is not whether we will be moral agents—that is, whether or not we will engage in normative evaluation—but rather with what competency will we exercise that agency. "In short, the choice is not between a moral authority outside custom and one within it. It is between adopting more or less intelligent and significant customs" (HNC [MW14:58]). The point merely restates an observation made earlier about our second nature: there is no legitimate question about the very idea and existence of norms and the place they occupy in our lives, apart from investigation of specific norms.

At this juncture, we can begin to see Dewey's subtle understanding of the importance of our second nature specifically and its relationship to identity formation generally. For him, identity formation is not exhausted by the process of socialization that his account of mutual responsiveness implies. Nor does it imply a form of moral reflection that is undetermined by that process and whose imaginative resources are therefore detached from a narrative of experience. So when he speaks of an "assembly" being formed within "our breast which discusses and appraises proposed and performed acts," he means to capture the core of what makes moral life possible, independent of the specific content of that life. This is what allows Mead to say in agreement, "We must not forget this other capacity, that of replying to the community and insisting on the gesture of the community changing. We can reform the order of things; we can insist on making the community standards better standards."[27] This is because our actions and the commitments they express emerge from a general responsiveness that, although realized through a specific community, becomes necessary for one to be a competent moral agent in both that world and all future social worlds one inhabits. Comparing the moral life to language once more, Dewey speaks of it as having "transcendent importance" because "it creates demands which take effect [and] extends to the common life in communication, counsel and instruction" (HNC [MW14:57]). This simply means, to appropriate McDowell's language, that the moral life "stands over against all parties to communication in it, with a kind of independence of each of them that belongs with its meriting a kind of respect."[28]

But this picture of moral transcendence is not independent of one's socially constituted identity; rather, it moves in the same direction that mutual responsiveness already demands. And this direction is one in which, as McDowell explains, "we make ourselves answerable not just to the verdicts of our fellows but to the facts themselves."[29] Dewey makes the point with the following example:

> A traffic policeman holds up his hand or blows a whistle. His act operates as a signal to direct movements. But it is more than an episodic stimulus. It embodies a rule of social action. Its proximate meaning is its near-by consequences in coordination of movements of persons and vehicles; its ulterior and permanent meaning—essence—is its consequence in the way of security of social movements. Failure to observe the signal subjects a person to arrest, fine or imprisonment. . . . The essence embodied in the policeman's whistle is not an occult reality superimposed upon a sensuous or physical flux and imparting form to it; a mysterious subsistence somehow housed within a psychical event. Its essence is the rule, comprehensive and persisting, the standardized habit, of social interaction, and for the sake of which the whistle is used. . . . This meaning is independent of the psychical landscape, the sensations and imagery, of the policeman and others concerned. But it is not on that account a timeless spiritual ghost nor pale logical subsistence divorced from events. (EN [LW1:149]).

Dewey's talk of independence in this passage merely recalls the harmless view of transcendence expressed by him, McDowell, and Robert Brandom, as discussed in chapter 2. He is concerned to show that "meanings" have objective status, even though the objectivity of "meanings" is not independent of human practices. The meaning of a gesture, for instance, is determined by its connection to a more complete context of norms and practices. I correctly grasp the meaning of the officer's hand gesture when I respond appropriately according to that established meaning. Whether I succeed in discerning the correct meaning is a matter of consequence: Am I able to get along in this practice? The meaning is objective in the following senses. First, it is grounded in a socially shared habit that transcends the understanding of particular individuals. Second, correct interpretation is determined by responses and consequences. These are objective in the sense that they are publicly observable events in the world to which we are answerable whether we acknowledge it or not. I take Dewey to mean here what Charles S. Peirce maintained in a much earlier context: "Reality is independent, not necessarily of thought in general, but only of what you or I or any finite number of men may think about it."[30]

For Dewey, "answerable" does not mean, for instance, that we necessarily go along with the policeman's wishes, for we may think that the whistle has been used inappropriately (e.g., by attempting to stop a legitimate protest) or that there is some more effective use to achieve traffic management. So the use of the whistle may be out of step with what it claims to be about or its use may not be the best way of realizing its intended purpose. But notice that even in this context, the norm that governs the practice—what Dewey refers to as its meaning—has a kind of independence to which our reasons are directed, even if those reasons potentially expand and transform the norm itself.

This is not to deny, as James famously says, that "the trail of the human serpent is thus over everything."[31] But if we are to hold on to an intelligible account of the objectivity of norms, and properly understand what both James and Dewey mean, we should take seriously the definite article in James' remark that precedes his invocation of the word "human". That our norms are human-dependent simply means that they would neither emerge nor be intelligible to us if we were not beings for whom it is second nature to employ them as fundamental to our social practices. This is what Dewey means when he affirms the independence of meaning, but then cautions us not to interpret independence as a "timeless spiritual ghost" or "pale logical subsistence divorced from events." He wants to discourage us from reifying any particular norm, even as we acknowledge that norms *qua* norms are part and parcel of human social practices.

Another way to understand this harmless view of transcendence is to say that we participate in the practice of giving and asking for reasons that leave our perspective and its conceptual content susceptible to being constrained, improved, or expanded by the world we inhabit. This practice, says Dewey, "sets up a heightened emotional appreciation and provides a new motive for fidelities previously blind. It sets up an attitude of criticism, of inquiry, and makes men sensitive to the brutalities and extravagancies of customs" (HNC [MW14:55]). I take him to mean that if we are to remain committed to our norms, it will not simply be because our fellows give a nod. As he says in his *Logic* of 1938: "A proposition does not gain validity because of the number of persons who accept it" (L [LW12:484 n. 4]). Rather, our commitment to our norms will persist because they can withstand the challenge of reason, evidence, and argumentation.[32] Where such evidence exists but is nonetheless ignored by someone or when someone refuses to engage in the practice of reason-giving, the question is not what we will say to them, but what we will say about their epistemic position in the world. That is, what stands in the way of a reciprocal willingness to fully engage in discursive exchange? And are the obstacles of the kind that seek to keep in place some dubious and, perhaps, harmful set of practices?[33]

This leads us to an important observation. In forming moral judgments in a conflict situation, for instance, identities are open (whether we perceive the fact or not) to experiential and discursive testing, given the holistic and moving encounter between self, other, and environment. What Jürgen Habermas rightly says of Mead must also apply to Dewey: The "formation of moral judgments" is emergent from a process that "simultaneously *socializes* and *temporalizes* practical reason."[34] For them, "temporalizing" practical reason means making explicit the experimental and developmental quality mutual responsiveness implies in future moral evaluation. As we shall see, Dewey's account of moral deliberation is expressive of just this process. But before we move there, we need a characterization of the moral situation and conflict.

THE CHARACTER OF CONFLICT UNDER MODERN CONDITIONS

Dewey's description of the immanence of the normative world puts in place a framework in which to locate and think about conflict, even as it holds off the supposition that the emergence of conflict implies a crisis in normative evaluation. To separate these two issues is of crucial importance. It allows us to better understand how he thinks about the character of conflict under modern conditions while simultaneously separating out the reflective resources he believes are necessary to managing conflict. Once we understand this, we can then return to elucidating those reflective resources while holding off the suggestion that Dewey is insensitive to the irreducibility of conflict.

We should begin with his *Ethics*. In part 2 of that work, "Theory of the Moral Life," Dewey opens with a background description of the modern condition. Here the question at the heart of moral reflection comes into view precisely because of this specific background. After all, he writes his *Ethics* primarily as a college textbook, and so he principally seeks to orient the student to the moral life and the demands that emerge. Consider that all-important opening passage:

> The intellectual distinction between customary and reflective morality is clearly marked. The former places the standard and rules of conduct in ancestral habit; the latter appeals to conscience, reason, or to some principle which includes thought. The distinction is as important as it is definite, for it shifts the centre of gravity in morality. Nevertheless the distinction is relative rather than absolute. Some degree of reflective thought must have entered occasionally into systems which in the main were founded on social wont and use, while in contemporary morals, even when the need of critical judgment is most recognized, there is an immense amount of conduct that is merely accommodated to social usage. In what follows we shall, accordingly, emphasize the difference in *principle* between customary and reflective morals rather than try to describe different historic and social epochs. (E₃ [LW7:162] [original emphasis])

Dewey's distinction between *customary* and *reflective* morality is based on the now-familiar story—discussed in the last chapter—regarding the absence of a dominant ethical or theological framework to which all appeal. In post-traditional societies, there is more of a disjunction between the meaning and purpose of life and its relationship to institutional and symbolic structures; in the last chapter this was expressed as the absence of some dominant theological framework underwriting self and society. For this reason, Dewey set out to provide a post-traditional account of piety and faith that is sensitive to the fact of pluralism. In the context of the moral life, the distinction between customary and reflective also implies that there is no de facto normative position of "my station and its duties" to which the agent retreats in thinking about moral situations and which necessarily does justice to the particular details that characterize such situations.[35] "The necessity for judgment and choice," Dewey writes, "comes from the fact that one has to manage forces with no common denominator" (TIM [LW5:280]).

For him this is the determinant horizon from which moral reflection takes its point of departure in modern times. Dewey explains this several paragraphs later: "Moral theory cannot emerge when there is positive belief as to what is right and what is wrong, for then there is no occasion for reflection. It emerges when men are confronted with situations in which different desires promise opposed goods and in which incompatible courses of action seem to be morally justified" (E₃ [LW7:164]). This passage makes a number of claims, not the least of which is the centrality of conflict to his thinking. We shall come back to this point in a moment. There is, however, a more critical observation we ought to underscore: *The absence of a solution in the moral situation constitutes the problem; it sparks the practical question of what to do.*[36]

The next point to observe about the relationship between this background account and moral reflection is the following: *Philosophers of morality are in no more of a certain position about what to do regarding moral action in general than the agent who finds himself in a specific situation.* Because Dewey insists on drawing a distinction in principle between customary and reflective morality, he rejects exhibiting blind deference to existing norms in order to solve the moral predicament (E₃ [LW7:165]). Speaking once more to the student, he says that moral philosophy "does not offer a table of commandments in a catechism in which answers are as definite as are the questions which are asked. . . . [T]he student who expects more from moral theory will be disappointed" (E₃ [LW7:166]).

But what exactly does he mean by moral conflict? This question is central to appreciating the role he ascribes to moral theory vis-à-vis conflict and to understanding the function of individual reflection in the light of the same. To answer this question we need to turn briefly to an address Dewey delivered before the French Philosophical Society in 1930, namely, "Three Independent Factors of Morals." Unfortunately this address receives surprisingly little consideration from both admirers and critics.[37] And yet it remains the locus, in my view, for understanding how attentive Dewey is to both conflict and its irreducibility.

One purpose of this lecture, among others, is to address what Dewey takes to be the central outlook of most moral theories: "[A]ll postulate one single principle as an explanation of moral life" (TIM [MW5:280]; cf. RIP [MW12:172–173]). Here he distinguishes between two major theories. The first postulates the Good, understood as "happiness . . . pleasure, [or] self-realization," as the universal end by which all action is measured and presumed to be in the service of (TIM [MW5:281]; cf. RIP [MW12: chap. 7]; E₃ [LW7: chap. 11]). The other major theory makes the Right, "understood as the morality of law," central (TIM [MW5:281]). Unlike the postulate of the Good, the morality of law prescribes what is legitimate and obligatory, so that "moral good becomes that which is in agreement with juridical imperative, while the opposite is not true" (TIM [MW5:281]; cf. RIP [MW12: chap. 7]; E₃ [LW7: chap. 12]).

We do not need a substantive explication of these two traditions or their specific representatives; it seems sufficient to say that these descriptions cover much of the philosophical terrain in moral philosophy.[38] Notwithstanding this, however, in each case Dewey is very clear that both branches of thought elide conflict and the uncertainty that it presents. His point at this stage of the essay is to argue that once morality is reduced to a single principle, the genuineness of conflict no longer seems plausible.

To see how this is so, consider two problems that Dewey identifies. The first is that reliance by traditional moral theories on one principle of assessment is based on the quest for certainty (TIM [LW5:282–283]; cf. RIP [MW12:174–175]; QC [LW4: chap. 10]). As previously noted, the quest for certainty is understood largely as an epistemic affair, so that certain beliefs (either located deep in the self or found in nature) are then used as directives on the political and ethical level of existence. Such beliefs act through the guise of a covering-law universalism, so that justification has only one universally valid factor. Yet for him, the fact that the history of human action reveals a disjunction between being good and doing good, between norms for action and what the natural and social world will allow, indicates that moral action often places us in a position where we court adverse circumstances that cannot be subsumed under one normative category. The quest for certainty is seemingly inattentive to just this dimension of experience, and in so being distorts the psychology of expectation Dewey believes is so important to a modern outlook.

The second problem that emerges, which is connected to the first, is what Dewey characterizes as insensitivity to the uniqueness of the situations in which individuals find themselves (RIP [MW12:176]). After all, we may be able with some intellectual energy to explain *how* two duties and the actions to which they commit us can be in conflict, and yet be unable to see *why* those duties are at loggerheads. To answer the "why" question will often require a richer narrative about individuals and their relationship to the situation of concern. "The selective determination and relation of objects in thought"— that is, the choices that now recommend themselves to the agent—"is controlled by reference to a situation" (QT [LW5:246]). The situation calls out in the self diverse habits that give the entire encounter between self and situation a qualitative unity. Consider the following example he offers of moral conflict:

> Take . . . the case of a citizen of a nation which has just declared war on another
> country. He is deeply attached to his own State. He has formed habits of loyalty

and of abiding by its laws, and now one of its decrees is that he shall support war. He feels in addition gratitude and affection for the country which has sheltered and nurtured him. But he believes that this war is unjust, or perhaps he has a conviction that all war is a form of murder and hence wrong. One side of his nature, one set of convictions and habits, leads him to acquiesce in war; another deep part of his being protests. He is torn between two duties: he experiences a conflict between the incompatible values presented to him by his habits of citizenship and by his religious beliefs respectively. Up to this time, he has never experienced a struggle between the two; they have coincided and reinforced one another. Now he has to make a choice between competing moral loyalties and convictions. The struggle is not between a good which is clear to him and something else which attracts him but which he knows to be wrong. It is between values each of which is an undoubted good in its place but which now get in each other's way. (E$_3$ [LW7:165])

This is a revealing example of Dewey's thoughts at work because it shows us how the conflict arises out of the deeper features of one's character. This passage reveals the concern we have for and owe to the objects and/or persons to which the conflicting values point. There is a story we could tell that allows us to understand why the patriot's values were never previously in conflict. And there are reasons to be had, as James tells us, for why incompatible courses of action now appear from the outset of reflection as "living options."[39] Uniqueness is thus located in the texture of the narrative.

"Sometimes," Dewey says in his *Ethics*, "a juncture is so critical that a person, in deciding upon what course he will take, feels that his future, his very being, is at stake" (E$_3$ [LW7:171]). Now *why* one feels his very being to be at stake requires attentiveness to one's character and the stand that each of the choices takes in the life of the individual. As Dewey explains, the "failure to acknowledge the situation leaves, in the end, the logical force of objects and their relation inexplicable" (QT [LW5:246]). The primacy of insensitivity prevents us from seeing, inquiring into, and explaining just these dimensions of the morally problematic situation.

If insensitivity prevents these two traditional accounts from seeing the uniqueness of the situation, it also obscures the potential irreducibility of moral conflict. Obviously, the language of "irreducibility" is what critics of Dewey deny that he is capable of acknowledging. And so despite his emphasis on deliberation, they maintain, he nonetheless occludes this potentially tragic dimension of the moral life. We will return to this in the final section of this chapter, but for the moment two comments are in order.

1. As Dewey understands the matter, the intimate connection between self and context aids in explaining not only why the competing factors recommend themselves to the agent, but also, more important, why conflict may defy reconstructive analysis. "Because the environment," Dewey maintains, "is not all of one piece, man's house is divided within itself, and at times, against itself" (HNC [MW14:39]). This remark may seem vague, unless we understand that it occurs in a larger passage from *Human Nature and Conduct* regarding the objective status of multiple habits and commitments. These constitute one's moral horizon. But there is no presumptive belief that they are internally harmonized. Notwithstanding, Dewey is keen to highlight that "diversity does not of itself imply conflict" (HNC [MW14:38]). In other words, if a value-judgment is to serve a practical purpose then some state of affairs must obtain in *fact* that brings the otherwise divergent values into conflict. In such instances the "possibility of conflict" that diversity suggests "is realized in fact" (HNC [MW14:38]; cf. L [LW12:112]). This is the point the passage above conveys.

2. But in what sense might Dewey mean that moral conflict potentially defies reconstructive analysis? In answering this question, it would be a gross misreading of him to conclude that in recognizing value commitments that pull in different directions the goal is to order them such that we get out of the conflict. Isaac Levi has advanced this point in his essay "Conflict and Inquiry." As he writes against thinkers such as Bernard William, Martha Nussbaum, and Isaiah Berlin: "Following Dewey, I would say that when we find ourselves endorsing two value commitments which cannot be jointly satisfied, we ought first to extricate ourselves from inconsistency by modifying our value commitments so that we no longer regard ourselves under an obligation either to perform the act or to refrain from doing so."[40] But nowhere in the *Ethics* or *Human Nature and Conduct*, even when he speaks about reconstructing the moral situation, do we find this position. In fact, Dewey is much closer to these thinkers regarding value pluralism. He acknowledges the possibility of incommensurability just to the extent that he views mere modification of value commitments as obscuring the hold such commitments have on us.

Appreciating Dewey's careful response to the question above and the correction to Levi's reading that I am advancing requires us to accept the truth of two previous claims. First, he never abandons his interest in cultivating a more humble psychology of expectation. Second, cultivating that outlook is part of appropriately orienting students to the moral life. From these two positions follows a third tentative, yet implied, commitment. As Rosalind Hursthouse points out, insensitivity will often prevent us from understanding that the question at issue may not simply be: "Which is the morally right decision, to do x or to do y?," but more precisely, "Which is the morally right action (with no qualification about remainder, the good action about which the agent need feel regret), x or y?"[41] As with Dewey's example of the patriot above, notice that Hursthouse's formulation takes for granted that a choice will be made. This is not the issue. If the conflict is genuine, as Dewey's example intends to suggest, then even if we choose, we will not be shielded from a sense of loss or regret.[42]

These two questions are the same, but with a difference attributable to a kind of perceptive state that is more thoroughly bound up with and partly defines reflection. This is expressed in the second formulation. For Dewey, this sensitivity is part of what it means to see the situation as a conflict among competing values. His explicit acknowledgment of this comes out in "Three Independent Factors," where he cautions us from beginning with the claim that conflict is "specious and apparent" (TIM [LW5:280]).[43] It follows that his emphasis on the importance of being sensitive intends for agents to track not only those cases in which the first question is appropriately asked, but also those instances in which the answer is attentive to the substantive implications of the parenthetical in the second formulation. We need to be prepared to ask which we should choose, x or y, where the answer, following reflection, does not extinguish the possibility of feeling regret and loss because a plan of action and the value it registers go unrealized. To be sure, we move on and develop along that chosen path, but there remains a place in our memories where we dare not visit often, and when we do, we do so with a seriousness of mind and a somberness of voice.

Dewey's understanding of moral conflict comes into view against his rejection of the quest for certainty in the moral life on the one hand, and the insensitivity that follows on the other. Conflict refers to the incompatibility of ends within a particular situation, where the pull of those ends is realized at the intersection of subject and context. For him, conflict is between some portion of an agent's values (as in the example above), or between the agent's values and those of the other members of the situation of concern, or between some values expressed by a more generalized community (E_3 [LW7:324–325]). The immediate identification of conflict—that is, the recognition that these two values cannot be actualized concurrently—means that the agent (or agents, given the political bent of the latter) must engage in the process of reflection to find a resolution.

In contemporary parlance, his identification of these three kinds of conflict reveals that Dewey acknowledges both moral (i.e., the obligatory) and ethical (i.e., questions pertaining to the Good) conflicts as the subject matter of reflection. Indeed, to capture this point he stipulates the various moral properties that historically have come into conflict and may still do so. These properties are part of the topography of moral experience, as Dewey understands it. Thus he writes in "Three Independent Factors":

> I shall content myself with presenting the hypothesis that there are at least three independent variables in moral action. Each of these variables has a sound basis, but because each has a different origin and mode of operation, they can be at cross purposes. . . . Goods, I repeat, have to do with deliberation upon desires and purposes; the right and obligatory with demands that are socially authorized and backed; virtues with widespread approbation. (TIM [LW5:280, 286]; cf. E_3 [LW7: chaps. 11–13])

As the passage reveals, he is clear that his list may not be exhaustive, but his claim is that each of the features identified has an undeniable place within our moral experience. In saying "undeniable," I mean to suggest that for Dewey we can survey our social experiences and find factors that appeal to our desires and purposes given our narrative of experience but which have nothing to do with what is obligatory. And there are rights and duties just insofar as their claim on us is not exhausted by what we desire. As Dewey notes in a section of his *Ethics* entitled "The Idea of the Right," the Right denotes both phenomenologically and linguistically "*exaction, demand,*" a feature that is at once missing from the Good, but that is ready for discursive and experiential unpacking to bring the Good in harmony with it (E_3 [LW7:215]). This explains why, in the section entitled "The Justification of a Claim," Dewey argues that while "particular rights and duties may, then, be arbitrary there is nothing arbitrary or forced in the existence of right and obligation" (E_3 [LW7:228]). What undermines the arbitrary quality of a particular right and potentially brings freedom and law into harmony is the extent to which it is open to "examination and criticism" regarding its contribution "to a good in which the one from whom an act is demanded will *share*" (E_3 [LW7:229–230] [original emphasis]).[44]

As the passage on the independent factors makes clear, we can also identify expressions of praise and blame that serve as principles of action, but which are not reducible to the Right or the Good. To be sure, Dewey acknowledges that such expressions can "operate as reflex imputations of virtue and vice . . . as *sanctions* of right, and as an individual comes to prize the approving attitude of others as considerations to be taken into account in deliberating" (TIM [LW5:286] [original emphasis]). But he believes that virtues nonetheless seem capable of functioning in a way that has little to do with satisfying one's desires or making demands upon others. After all, saying that someone is heroic or courageous is often rendered intelligible precisely because their acts have little to do with their vision of the Good or with what they are obligated to do. That individuals may define their conception of the Good as involving heroic or courageous actions—as we see, for example, among some of Homer's characters or our own military and law enforcement units—does not negate the fact that such virtues may stand on their own. Indeed, to say that someone has "gone beyond the call of duty" is to capture precisely the semantic and substantive moment when Virtue is unhinged from the Right and the Good.

For Dewey, that we may find it difficult to hear the call of some of these independent factors does not yet deny their claim on us; rather, it helps us to define the elements constituting the sensitivity of moral agency. Given the social-psychological account provided earlier, "total deafness regarding the hold of these factors on us" would be an inaccurate descriptive characteristic of any agent we could recognize as moral. Consider the following example of *Antigone*, which Dewey does not use but I think is helpful for sharpening the point. Creon is not deaf to Antigone's claim to give her brother an appropriate burial—that is, Creon can recognize the claim. This is part of the moral repertoire of his community, even if the meaning-content of his response does not comport with what Antigone desires to hear. Similar to the moral theorist described above, Creon is insensitive to the pull of competing factors, and so he fails to acknowledge the legitimate place of Antigone's claim as a rival to his own position.

What is crucial to observe about Creon, however, is that he does not engage Antigone's discursive move because the cultural and institutional apparatus—which makes him king—blunts the need for him to be responsive to her claim. That this reading is consistent with Dewey's outlook is obvious when he argues that a failure to be answerable to the claims of others implies a

> defect in effective apprehension of the realities of human association. . . . This deficiency and perversion in apprehension indicates a defect in education—that is to say, in the operation of actual conditions, in the consequences upon desire and thought of existing interactions and interdependencies. . . . It is an endeavor [by existing institutions] to "rationalize" this defect. Like all rationalizations, it operates to divert attention from the real state of affairs. Thus it helps maintain the conditions which created it, standing in the way of effort to make our institutions more humane and equitable. (HNC [MW14:224–225])

Obviously for Dewey, a world of kings and subjects is very different from a world of representatives and citizens. Both, in his view, involve some element of mutual responsiveness (DE [MW9:89–90]), but it is clear that one of these worlds makes the practice and necessity of reason-giving more constitutive of how it conducts its ongoing affairs. This is, after all, the basis for his distinction between customary and reflective morality; in the latter the practice of reason-giving is more *consistently* invoked with the hopes of refining it in conduct.

In failing to do justice to the conflict, Creon finds himself implicated in a more terrible situation, which includes the death of his son.[45] As Creon's son makes clear before his death: *"Whoever thinks that he alone is wise, his eloquence, his mind, above the rest, come the unfolding, shows his emptiness."*[46] Dewey's belief in the political and moral importance of democracy follows precisely from this kind of outlook—that is, the extent to which democracy encourages each individual to understand that he or she has no special access to wisdom (see specifically DEA [LW11:215–225]). As we will see in chapter 5, the idea of having no special access to wisdom is what Dewey explicates as a normative element to curb an elitist vision of democracy; it points away from a vision of political decision-making based on deference to experts and toward a view of democratic legitimacy as expressed in the criteria of reciprocal and general acceptance among the governed. In short, democracy takes the reason-giving quality implicit in mutual responsiveness as the key for understanding political legitimacy.

This last statement reveals an important political dimension to Dewey's threefold distinction. He does not deny that there is an ethical character to our identities, but Dewey is concerned to retain that element alongside the legal-moral character our identities assume in the context of democracy. Here he touches two debates in contemporary moral and political philosophy. The first is over the relationship between the Right and Good under modern conditions of pluralism; it revisits some of the considerations of the last chapter. The second relates to the scope of the "we" that ought to comprise democratic decision-making. We may miss the political thrust of his distinctions if we do not offer comments at precisely this juncture—comments that clearly point to how Dewey understands what I want to call the "best achievable state" of moral agency.

For him, specific rights and duties achieve legitimacy insofar as they embody mutual responsiveness and generality for those who fall within their orbits (E_3 [LW7:225–231]). Otherwise, their authoritative quality will derive from arbitrary force, emptying "morality" generally and democracy specifically of much that we find appealing and rationally defensible in their function.[47] To link legitimacy to mutual responsiveness and general acceptance means that individuals can absorb the content of those rights into their conceptions of the Good[48]—that is, without good opposing argument. This is why he says that such rights and duties contribute to *a* good in which one can share, and this claim appears, you will recall, in his section of *Ethics* entitled "Justification of a Claim."

But what does this mean? Dewey does not tell us explicitly, but I believe we can offer a plausible inference. In concrete terms, rights that protect various forms of difference, for example, do not necessarily require an ethical commitment on my part to those forms of difference, but rather a moral obligation of respect—an obligation grounded in my own desire to be different and to freely practice that difference. We can therefore speak, as Dewey did above, of absorbing those rights into our specific vision of the Good. Rights, in this instance, are internally differentiated along the lines of ethical acceptance on the one hand and moral respect on the other. In order for claims respecting various differences to become enshrined in law there must be some overlap between the ethical and the moral, otherwise the emergence of the claims will be inexplicable. But from the perspective of the entire citizenry, overlap is not necessary for such rights to be legitimate, and, indeed, will often be impossible to achieve.

This means, for Dewey, that to have a vision of the Good under modern conditions is in fact to potentially confront its limitation as an answer for guiding the lives of others. We may simply fail to convince others that how we see the world creates a space in which they can find a home. But as with his discussion of religious beliefs, it does not follow from the fact of pluralism and the absence of a unifying ethical horizon that we are precluded from engaging in the practice of reason-giving. Unable to exchange reasons, we would never be able to bring about an overlap between the ethical and the moral. His account places a limit—to be hammered out within political life, to be sure—on the extent to which that "thickness" can be encoded into laws. To the extent that democracy makes public deliberation central to its account of justification conflict is not necessarily dissolved; rather, it "bring[s] . . . conflicts out into the open where their special claims can be seen and appraised," thus raising "social issues for moral decisions which did not exist for most men and women so long as government was autocratic and confined to a few" (LSA [LW11:56]).

We should observe that Dewey's contextualism potentially expands, if the problem so demands, beyond a determinant political community.[49] Here we touch the second issue identified above—an issue that replicates the way mutual responsiveness positions us to expand beyond our specific moral horizon. For him, because of the inherent instability of the space of political reflection—that is, no one has privileged access to knowledge and therefore authority—we need not feel impotent when trying to figure out its scope. If rights and laws are indexed on the one side to justification by mutual responsiveness and general acceptance and on the other side to the specificity of problems in which one's interests are at stake, then going beyond existing narratives of experience for Dewey can relate to a determinant political community (i.e., the nation-state) or to a community that denotes humanity as such. In other words, "problems," as used here, may refer to the internal dynamism of a political society or to interactions between political communities. But in both cases, the substantive content of these problems will point to the exhaustion of the existing value-sphere and the necessity of creative, but nonetheless situated, responses to alleviate or remove altogether the ways in which these problems are affecting specific communities or nations.

In this view, we cannot hold a presumptive commitment to democratic closure based on a determinant political community or a state-centric model. For Dewey, the "we" of decision-making is understood as an emergent property. This is because whether or not one is a citizen, the claim to having a say in collective decision-making in the context of a democracy is bound up with the extent to which one will be potentially impacted by the settled decisions (PP [LW2: chaps. 1–3]). As he explains in his *Ethics*, tracking the effects of decision-making—that is, being attentive to the complexity and depth of the landscape—potentially mitigates the extent to which we will be driven by narrow "nationalistic sentiments" in favor of "broader conceptions of human welfare" (E_3 [LW7:371]). Whether they are citizens or aliens (in the legalistic sense), we are poised to regard more appropriately, to use a title, the pain of others.

To be fair to any potential criticisms: Dewey is not clear on when problems register on the local, nation-state level rather than the more global, international level. However, he does gesture toward an answer: "There is no better evidence of a well formed moral character than knowledge of when to raise the moral issue and when not. It implies a sensitiveness to values which is the token of a balanced personality" (E_3 [LW7:170]). In short, he points us to the best achievable state of moral agency in which one struggles to hear and see the situation in its appropriate light. The above remarks, coming as they do in the context of a discussion of moral conflict, only distract us if we deny the political dimension to his threefold distinction. If, however, we take it seriously, as this discussion intends to do, then the best achievable state of moral agency will be understood as the backdrop of moral conflict as such, whether it is experienced by one individual, between individuals, or by an entire community.

THE EXPANDED SELF:
DELIBERATION, IMAGINATION, AND SYMPATHY

We have considered at some length Dewey's account of moral conflict, to which deliberation is oriented. This is part of his social-psychological account, which places mutual responsiveness at the core of moral life and conditions the rationality of its participants. As I have discussed, mutual responsiveness for Dewey has both a descriptive and normative component. His account is descriptive in that it simply tells us how human beings are, but it also outlines what is necessary for the display of moral agency. For Dewey, this is significant if, from the perspective of an elucidation of deliberation, we are to explain what outlook the self ought to assume in confronting conflict. There are several conclusions we must keep in mind. First, in emphasizing the importance of mutual responsiveness and taking on the attitude of others in his philosophy, we have already found the link to sympathy that Dewey will highlight in his understanding of deliberation. Second, this responsiveness makes the agent sensitive to the various factors that make demands in a moral conflict. Moreover, in those instances where such a conflict involves others, the agent is capable of imaginatively assuming their attitudes as a way to inform his own judgment. Third, these features are central, in Dewey's view, if the agent is to reconstruct moral experience in the service of developing an alternative option that can reconcile the factors that now conflict.

These considerations point us back to previous discussions (see, for example, the end of chapter 2). Dewey is clear that he does not want to overdetermine the content of deliberation. He does, however, seek to explain the best achievable state of the agents so that they are prepared to hear and see the situation appropriately. This is not a contradiction. After all, the starting point for responding to any problem hinges on our ability to appropriately describe the situation so as to propose an action plan. In attributing the language of "best achievable state" to Dewey, I mean that he seeks to describe an ideal perceptive condition, that is, a state in which the self is open to the deliverances from her character on the one hand and the environment on the other. As he says of judgment: "To every shade of imagined circumstances there is a vibrating response; and to every complex situation a sensitiveness as to its integrity, a feeling of whether it does justice to all facts, or overrides some to the advantage of others. Decision is reasonable when deliberation is so conducted" (HNC [MW14:135]). The aim is to mediate the conflict such that the choice absorbs the claims expressed by the two competing factors. In this section, then, we are after a view of the agent who sees widely and feels deeply. The points to be discussed in understanding this include his notion of dramatic rehearsal, the place of principles as cumulative wisdom, and the relationship between sympathy and imagination.

We might nonetheless think that the language of "best achievable state" and "ideal perceptive condition" is unhelpful. We might ask the following: How does this help us think about moral reflection and justification? Dewey scholars might ask more directly: Since Dewey does not use this language, in what way can such terms be attributed to him?[50] The first question gets at the theoretical worth of the idea for illuminating the practice of moral reflection, and the second question allows us to connect the answer given to the first to Dewey's self-understanding. As Matthew Festenstein remarks:

> Dewey's account of morality does not attempt to provide an external vindication of an "ultimate law." The thought that there exists such a Platonic vindication which it is the task of philosophy to articulate is part of the rejected conception of knowledge and philosophy. . . . However, the absence of such a vindication is not thought to entail skepticism about ethics *tout court*. Rather, what is attempted [by Dewey] is an internal elucidation of what it is to be a moral agent.[51]

Dewey's attempt to elucidate the content of moral agency provides the hook for understanding how "best achievable state" and "ideal perceptive condition" function. They are conceptual vehicles for understanding ourselves as living within a normative world, a world in which our judgments and actions are attentive to evidence and susceptible to justification. In Dewey's view, this requires us to abandon skepticism about being embedded within narratives of experience, having a character by that fact, and being able to trace the origin of that character to inform how we act and what we value. Indeed, these elements—narrative horizon, character, and its historically emergent process—make possible generalizable assessments that are explicable to those who exist within the space of moral reflection.

For Dewey, I am antecedently attentive to the moral life just insofar as I am a being that participates in social practices. The properties of the moral life that make a demand, constrain our actions, and implicate us in being responsive to others, and them to us, achieve their significance because without them our moral identity would be wholly vacant. If we accept this claim as a minimum feature of engaging the moral life, Dewey argues, our analysis can be redirected. For him, because our moral frameworks are the products of more or less intelligence, they are susceptible to better or worse ideal descriptions of how we ought to stand within them.[52]

DRAMATIC REHEARSAL AND IMAGINATION

What does Dewey mean by the term "dramatic rehearsal"? He gives us some clue when he writes the following: "We begin with a summary assertion that deliberation is a dramatic rehearsal (in imagination) of various competing possible lines of action" (HNC [MW14:132]). Each "conflicting habit," he says, "unrolls a picture of its future history, of the career it would have if it were given head" (HNC [MW14:133]). Here he moves too quickly, conflating dramatic rehearsal with deliberation as such. But we know that he intends for us to understand dramatic rehearsal as a feature within the overall deliberative process. As the language above makes clear, dramatic rehearsal encompasses the middle stages of deliberation or inquiry—that is, where possibilities are suggested and advanced as hypotheses to be tested (see chapter 2, pp. 95–97). This also constitutes the most reflexive moment of the process. Notwithstanding, the two formulations above point to several features that define his understanding of dramatic rehearsal: the narrative character of identity and the imaginative dimension of reflection.[53]

As noted in chapter 2, Dewey's account of character as a web of habits implies a narrative structure to our identity. Our habits are generated through an interaction with our social environment that is time sensitive. When pressed to explain why we have acted this or that way we can readily tell a story that draws not merely from the present, but treats our character as a historical treasure trove to be unloaded as part of the account we offer. In such moments we are recounting the drama that is our life. What habit-talk means for Dewey in a shorthand way is precisely what Alasdair MacIntyre says explicitly of the relationship between narrative and action: it is the "basic and essential genre for the characterization of human actions."[54]

Consider the following example of an individual who acts out of character. When one departs from what is expected, we say that somehow the person is not acting like him- or herself. Anyone who knows this person treats his or her actions as departures from the anticipated action, and so identifies those actions as violations of some truth about the person. Indeed, we draw on previous experiences as evidence, examine instances of their character, and even solicit reflections from friends and companions. All of these elements form the objective framework for understanding the person's action as a violation of what we know to be true of the person. We do not engage in this inquiry willy-nilly, for such an inquiry is not contingently connected to truth, justification, and verification. These elements comprise its essence; they are normative concepts that help guide the practice of mutual responsiveness. As such, there is something substantially present about the person that guides our reflection, a narrative of experience that embeds the person in various activities, events, and environments that render intelligible his or her character and to which we orient our investigation. Just insofar as something is substantially present we find ourselves within a practice of giving and asking for reasons.

But for Dewey, our characters, though stable enough to allow for the above account to take hold, do not reflect unalterable categorical desires corresponding to a harmonious field of commitments. To be sure, "an act must be the expression of a formed and stable character," but as he goes on to say, "stability of character is an affair of degrees, and is not to be taken absolutely" (E_3 [LW7:167]). This is because identity emerges for Dewey in a complex and layered set of social networks in which we play distinctive roles. These roles leave narrative lines that are expressive of, contribute to, and draw on different habits. Insofar as we find ourselves part of different social experiences, we may equally trace various narrative lines that contain their own web of subplots. Such lines point outward toward the world, but also reveal the inner recesses of the self. Character, says Dewey, is "the abiding unity" in which those roles and the acts they commit us to "leave their lasting traces" (E_3 [LW7:171; cf. 317]).

Yet given the two-directional structure of character, our identities never completely ossify. (Perhaps not even after death if the consequences of our actions are still felt.) In fact, this two-directional structure is at the core of those moments when we look on the early days of our lives and see ourselves as another person. We often say to our conversation partners, "I am not the person you once knew." To say this is simultaneously to make a claim about the narrative lines in which I have found myself since those early days of my life; the remark is thus susceptible to a more detailed articulation. This detailed articulation captures Dewey's earlier point that one's house is not simply divided *within* itself, but may potentially be divided *against* itself. All of this suggests agreement with MacIntyre's additional claim: "I can only answer the question 'What am I to do?' if I can answer the prior question 'Of what story or stories do I find myself a part?'"[55] As Charles Taylor remarks, this horizon provides us with an identity, "some sense of qualitative discrimination" that allows us to say some "actions, or feelings, or modes of life [are], in some way[s] morally higher or lower, noble or base, admirable or contemptible."[56] Part of what makes deliberation a dramatic rehearsal is just this narrative horizon that the self draws on to render explicable the choices which he now confronts, seeks to modify, or abandons.[57]

This emphasis on narrative and the way in which I have drawn a connection between Dewey on the one hand and MacIntyre and Taylor on the other may understate the difference of emphasis we find in their work on the teleological character of identity. In reflecting briefly on their differences, I will need to simplify the complex positions of MacIntyre and Taylor, which at times contain much ambivalence about the relationship between teleology and identity. Nonetheless, I do think there is a commitment in their writings that marks the difference between them and Dewey. This should allow me to clarify my earlier claim regarding my use of the Good in the context of Dewey's philosophy.

To begin, the language of the Good in contemporary parlance often gives the impression that what we need to recover in modern times but somehow have lost is a determinant vision of the Good that reflexively informs one's identity. In this view, the unfolding of one's narrative is seen as a way of orienting oneself retrospectively to a background Good and elucidating how it prospectively guides action. In this regard, we think of the Good as denoting what Weber calls *Weltanschauungen,* or worldviews.[58] And at times MacIntyre speaks this way when he says, the "unity of a human life is the unity of a narrative quest," whose defining feature is a "final *telos.*"[59] Despite his more careful understanding of modern identity, Taylor often writes in agreement, arguing that the ability to make qualitative discrimination in moral evaluation bespeaks a determinate account of "the good" which "has to be woven into my understanding of my life as an unfolding story."[60] This point is emphasized more forcefully when he speaks of the necessity of a "hypergood" to identity—that is, a Good that orders and allows us to rank lesser goods. As he says, "perhaps we will find that we cannot make sense of our moral life without something like *a* hypergood perspective, some notion of *a* good to which we can grow, and which then makes us see others differently."[61] For both Taylor and MacIntyre, at least when they speak this way, without such a determinant horizon our sense of agency is lost altogether. And so both seem to share the Weberian view of the self, which "entails a constant and intrinsic relation to certain ultimate 'values' or 'meanings' which are forged into purposes and thereby translate into rational-teleological action."[62]

The problem with this position is that it is typically framed in such a manner that it betrays the way the internal structure of our narratives is differentiated under modern conditions. In those moments, Dewey parts ways with Weber, Taylor, MacIntyre, and, indeed, much of contemporary discourse on the topic.[63] The various roles we play through work, school, religious organizations, civil society, and our more private and clandestine activities rarely refer to a harmonious set of values and beliefs. The meaningfulness of our modern lives simply does not hinge on a fixed and undifferentiated teleological quest. And Dewey is clear that if self-realization of such a quest is placed as the end-in-view, it will often blind us to the needs, details, and claims that the present situation places upon us, including elements of the situation that may otherwise register diverging features of our identity (E_3 [LW7:302]). Thus he writes: "Selfhood (except as it has encased itself in a shell of routine) is in a process of making and . . . any self is capable of including within itself a number of inconsistent selves, of unharmonized disposition" (HNC [MW14:96]).[64] Does this undermine our ability to engage in qualitative discrimination, which Taylor believes is so essential to moral agency? Of course not; it only claims that such discriminations are themselves flexible in the light of consequent experiences and are not beholden to an antecedently unitary framework.

So when the phrase "conception of the Good" is seen as having a place within Dewey's moral topography, it must be understood to reflect the unharmonized dynamism whose identification with the self does not exhaust the self's reflective capacity, which is central to the acquisition of a particular identity. To the extent that a conflict between these diverging features is brought out through some state of affairs under modern conditions, individuals are more sensitive to and capable of rethinking the larger narrative of their identity.[65] To appropriate Eric MacGilvray's words: "In particular, narratives provide a conceptual framework within which we become capable of doubting and revising our moral and ethical commitments, and a mode of discourse through which it becomes possible—though by no means assured—that we can make those commitments intelligible to others."[66] Otherwise, the give and take that Dewey describes between the Right and the Good cannot be thought possible in practice. On this reading, modern identities are neither wholly fragmented, unable to connect actions to each other, nor so organized as to suggest a bundle of harmonious and fixed values that we appropriate in our future orientations.

But if narrative helps us understand the layered character that informs the dramatic rehearsal, the imagination puts us in touch with its suspenseful and creative quality. We have already considered Dewey's discussion of the imagination in the light of his religious thought. Here, in his moral philosophy, the importance of the imagination returns, yet the relationship between imagination and moral judgment has often been seen as problematic. There is a strong belief that the imagination is often an impediment to acting in accord with duty. Imagination is seen as being too individualistic because it is caught in the emotional intensity of the moment that it paints.

Yet this account of the imagination trades on a mistake about its relationship to character and judgment. Perhaps an example is in order. While sitting in the living room of his home, Michael hears a crash in the adjacent room. It strikes him in an immediate way, to which he says to himself or another, "It sounds like someone broke the window." We should suspect that this is merely the beginning of his inquiry. For Dewey, a person experiences moral conflict in just this immediate way, and the moment of reflection seeks to work backward on asking whether we have appropriately identified the situation as a conflict. If the answer is affirmative, the agent works forward, reflecting on what the world would be like if he chooses between these two values and their corresponding actions, while simultaneously attempting to find a choice that sublimates the competing claims.

For Dewey, what we are imagining is the world and ourselves as we would be were we to adopt a course of action. But it is not simply future (i.e., other) selves that we are imagining but the future of the current self. This is what he means when he says in his *Ethics* that deliberation is "dramatic and active, not mathematical and impersonal; and hence it has the intuitive, the direct factor in it" (E_3 [LW7:275]). This remark is critical to understanding the constraining element of the imagination. If the intuitive and direct factor in deliberation is character itself, and we understand character to be expressive of a narrative horizon, then Dewey means that through the imagination we have access to and are able to focus on funded experiences for future possibilities. As he says in his *Ethics*, we need to make a distinction "between goods which, when they present themselves to imagination are approved by reflection after wide examination of their relations, and the goods which are such only because their wider connections are not looked into" (E_3 [LW7:203]). As this passage makes clear, he sees the imagination as providing concrete deliverances from the treasure trove that is our narrative—which, when considered, is partly necessary for making sense of our choice. In his view, ignoring the deliverances of the imagination potentially leaves choice inexplicable. That is, we cannot tie the perceived good of our choice to the larger horizon of our identity. When asked, "Why did you do x?," we find ourselves reduced to unintelligible utterances.

Deliberation, then, is not merely reflection on means to ends. As Dewey writes in his critique of utilitarianism's calculative understanding of deliberation: "It resembles the case in which a man has already made his final decision, say to take a walk, and deliberates only upon what walk to take. His end-in-view already exists; it is not questioned. The question is as to comparative advantages of this tramp or that" (HNC [MW14:149]). For him, the calculative approach undercuts the deliverances of the imagination, and in some instances simply ignores them altogether. In describing deliberation as fixed upon a perceived good, we will refuse to be moved by deliverances from our past that might suggest a different course of action. Indeed, the reason why a course of action unfolds imaginatively is so that we can see and feel the projected consequences and assess them before we engage in overt action (E$_3$ [LW7:275]). This implies that the assessment seeks to reflexively affect what we value, to strengthen its hold on us and enlarge its meaning or loosen its attachment. Dewey's point is not that referencing the deliverances of the imagination will necessarily clarify the potential fruits of the ends we seek or their apparent quality, but that we will be less well positioned to receive such enlightening information if ends and means are not fodder for the imaginative engine.

This general characterization provides us with a clear sense of the way in which deliberation is dramatic and a rehearsal. Let us now examine the two central steering mechanisms that fill out the reflective moment—namely, the place of principles as cumulative wisdom and the role of sympathy.

PRINCIPLES AS CUMULATIVE WISDOM

One way to think about the treasure trove that is our narrative which Dewey pursues is to explicate the place of principles in reflection. His contextualism, however, coupled with his aversion to a rule-based approach to moral judgment, may give the impression that he has little to say about the role of principles in reflection. And yet we would find it hard to make sense of a moral agent who did not bring general considerations in the form of principles to the table of deliberation. Dewey's aversion is not so much to principles as such, but to how they are thought to function within particular cases—that is, as rules that outstrip the complexity of specific cases and therefore are capable of settling the matter, rather than as cumulative wisdom that focuses and guides reflection. Based on this distinction between principles as cumulative wisdom and rules as fixed properties, Dewey seeks to defend, just as he did in his reflections on religion, a more modest position for the role of the past in guiding our judgments.

How does Dewey understand this distinction? He gives us an answer in his *Ethics*:

> Now a genuine principle differs from a rule in two ways: (a) A principle evolves in connection with the course of experience, being a generalized statement of what sort of consequences and values tend to be realized in certain kinds of situations; a rule is taken as something ready-made and fixed. (b) A principle is primarily intellectual, a method and scheme for judging, and is practical secondarily because of what it discloses; a rule is primarily practical. (E_3 [LW7:276]; cf. HNC [MW14: chap. 20])

As I read this passage, for Dewey generalized statements are nothing but a normative vocabulary that has emerged over time in an attempt to manage shared experiences—that is, they have become the product of reflective control, testing, and guidance. Principles thus apply to cases by virtue of some relevant properties. As he says, because situations have "like points, experience carries over from one to another, and experience is intellectually cumulative" (E_3 [LW7:275]). Rules, on the other hand, are especially insensitive to those points within experience that are not the same.

The service that principles provide is that they steer us to just those like points, so as to discern the importance of the situation. This much Dewey says:

> [W]hereas the object of moral principles is to supply standpoints and methods which will enable the individual to make for himself an analysis of the elements of good and evil in the particular situation in which he finds himself. No genuine moral principle prescribes a specific course of action; rules, like cooking recipes, may tell just what to do and how to do it. A moral principle, such as that of chastity, of justice, of the Golden Rule, gives the agent a basis for looking at and examining a particular question that comes up. It holds before him certain possible aspects of the act; it warns him against taking a short or partial view of the act. It economizes his thinking by supplying him with the main heads by reference to which to consider the bearings of his desires and purposes; it guides him in his thinking by suggesting to him the important consideration for which he should be on the lookout. (E_3 [LW7:280])

The functional power of principles is that when deployed they draw us to the salient elements within the situation—that is, the things that stand out and are ready to be cognitively digested. Understanding this salience is at once to see what one must consider in acting and what one may have reason to do or not to do. As Dewey says in *The Quest for Certainty* in a chapter appropriately entitled "The Construction of the Good": Without principles "we should not be able to frame any ideas whatever of the conditions under which objects are enjoyed nor any estimate of the consequences of esteeming and liking them" (QC [LW4:217]). In disclosing the salience of the situation to us, principles rein in our thinking by pointing us to what makes a difference in acting one way rather than another, but do not outstrip the descriptive and creative work that thinking must do.

This emphasis on principles is also a way of achieving continuity within our judgments and marking the moments of discontinuity that spark reflection. To be sure, for Dewey, if we were not equipped with any principles, we would be unable to unite our judgments across time. Indeed, we would find it difficult to identify and distinguish cases that are truly novel from those we have encountered before. Principles are important because in highlighting continuity, they equally mark the boundary of the previously experienced from the surprisingly new features that call for our attention (QC [LW4:217]).

SYMPATHY AND THE OTHER

Thus far we have been filling out the ideal perceptive condition by pointing to the narrative quality of judgment and the way it reveals how things matter to us, the role of imagination, and the place of principles in helping us to note the salience of the situation. The final element is the recurrence of mutual responsiveness. When Dewey comes back to mutual responsiveness, especially in thinking about deliberation, it appears through the concept of sympathy. The introduction of sympathy should be of special interest to interpreters of Dewey's ethical philosophy who underscore his importance in this regard.

Yet recent interpretations fail to explore sympathy's importance to Dewey's moral philosophy and in so doing narrow rather than expand (as they rightly intend) the richness of his moral philosophy.[67] Consider, however, the importance Dewey attributes to sympathy: "Sympathy is the animating mold of moral judgment not because its dictates take precedence in action over those of other impulses (which they do not do), but because it furnishes the most efficacious intellectual standpoint" (E₃ [LW1:270]). This efficacious standpoint, he goes on to say, is the ability to take stock, in the form of a broad imaginative survey of both the inner recesses of the self and the claims of others. Properly understood, sympathy makes us receptive to the texture of the landscape, and it is in that openness where objectivity lies for him.

Before addressing this point, Dewey is keen to distance his understanding of "intelligent sympathy" from an evaluative emotional intensity (E₃

[LW1:251]). For example, when we find ourselves torn between competing options that pull on us, and whose consequences will affect others, we engage in a dramatic rehearsal to see and feel the impact. In thinking about how we will be affected by our decision, we think about how future selves will also be in the light of our actions. We find ourselves drawn into vivid mental images, sometimes brought home to us by others communicating future pain and pleasure that will result from our consequences. They do not speak in the imprecise language of pain and pleasure, but paint vivid pictures that connect the particulars of their experiences with the potential consequences of our actions. In the midst of this emotional intensity, all other factors seem to fade into the background. We do not simply take stock of the impact of our actions on others as one factor among many, but we simultaneously and immediately take hold of that person's outlook as if it were our own. It saturates our outlook, leading others to caution us not to become "emotional." In a similar way, Dewey cautions: regard for the impact of consequences on others should not prompt us to immediately give way to "every sentiment of sympathy . . . which is experienced" (E_3 [LW1:251]). This kind of sentimentalism, whether it is oriented inward (a kind of self-pity) or outward toward others, "makes the immediate indulgence of a dominant emotion more important than results" (E_3 [LW1:251]). When he uses the language of "results" he is not reverting to a crass utilitarianism, but referring precisely to an understanding of results that is based upon a sense of having done justice to all factors at play.

Dewey's account of sympathy involves reconstructing the experiences of another, but without allowing a complete identification of that reconstructive moment with the evaluation the person attributes to those experiences (E_3 [LW1:250–251, 270–272]).[68] In this regard, sympathy is connected to the imagination. But how so? Answering this question is a matter of some delicacy. When Dewey distances intelligent sympathy from emotional absorption, this discussion comes in chapter 13 of his *Ethics*, "Approbation, the Standard, and Virtue," and so he identifies his account of sympathy as a virtue or excellence of character. Yet sympathy is not just that, because he wants to argue that it helps reflection engage in a broad survey both internally and externally. The upshot of this claim is discussed in that chapter, but it comes home most forcefully in chapter 14, "Moral Judgment and Knowledge," where he says that "an impartial sympathetic observer is the surest way to obtain objectivity of moral knowledge" (E_3 [LW7:270]).

Of what does the objectivity of moral knowledge consist? Here we need to examine more carefully the *internal* and *external* workings of sympathy and draw in more tightly the imagination. Let us go back for a moment. When

Dewey speaks of the dramatic element of deliberation and places particular emphasis on imagination, he introduces an important functional distinction between *actor* and *spectator*. As the different courses of action unfold along with the various potential consequences, our imagination creates a cognitive theater. He makes this point clear when he tells us what goes on when people deliberate: "Some people deliberate by dialogue. Others visualize certain results. Others rather take the motor imagery and imagine themselves doing a thing. Others imagine a thing done and then imagine someone else commenting upon it."[69] When understood as a complete rehearsal, however, these approaches collapse as part of one process of surveying the landscape. So the imagination at once places before us the unfolding of our habits and the actions to which they would potentially commit us, and in so doing simultaneously distances us from that unfolding.

We might say that the imagination allows us, as with the chorus in Greek tragedies, to be *in* the situation but not *of* it. As with the imagination, the chorus occupies a halfway position between the interested and committed characters who have only a partial view of the landscape, and the audience who sees the whole and the future anguish that will befall the characters, but who are nonetheless psychologically and practically protected. Notice that I am using the chorus rather than the audience as the key, since the latter stands outside the situation and so distorts the kind of independence Dewey is after. The chorus is a better model because it attempts to combine the deep interests and commitments of the characters with the audience's wide emotional and intelligent vision.

As I read Dewey, the dramatic rehearsal replicates these two distinct elements that we find in the Greek chorus. In the first instance, what comes before us in the dramatic rehearsal matters to us—where this means that the affective and intellectual dimensions of judgment are thoroughly collapsed—because we are the characters. In the second instance, reception of these deliverances through the imagination should be read as an attempt to see as widely as the audience. The process is an attempt to answer the following: Are we being attentive to all factors that come before us? But here we are surveying only the internal landscape of the self. This is precisely why Dewey says in an earlier remark that all relevant elements of the self have their say.

The process is not complete. The externalist claim, then, says that doing justice to all factors includes considering the impact such consequences will have on the lives of others. But just as we need to keep a distinction between actor and spectator to achieve impartiality in our judgment, so too must we safeguard ourselves during the reconstruction of others' experiences from completely identifying with the emotional content such reconstructions carry. As he says, intelligent sympathy "widens and deepens concern for consequences," it allows us to "put ourselves in the place of another, to see things from the standpoint of his aims and values," but without simultaneously making the evaluative judgment that often comes with that standpoint (E_3 [LW1:270]; cf. HNC [MW14:136]).

Intelligent sympathy thus refers to a more balanced perspective, situated between blind emotion and cold calculative and unaffected reason. It "[carries] thought out beyond the self and extends its scope . . . [and] saves considerations of consequences from degenerating into mere calculation, by rendering vivid the interests of others and urging us to give them weight" (E_3 [LW1:270]). He makes the point more dramatically only two years later in his *Art as Experience* (1934): "It is when the desires and aims, the interests and modes of response of another become an expansion of our own being that we understand him. We learn to see with his eyes, hear with his ears, and their results give true instruction" (AE_3 [LW10:338]). This, too, occurs in the context of a discussion regarding sympathy and the imagination. His point here is that sympathy urges us to give the experiences of others weight, and that in doing so it provides *true* instruction. This is not merely a reporting of and identification with psychological and emotional states, but a way of considering them so that they may inform rather than replace evaluation.

For Dewey, the aim of surveying both the internal recesses of the self and the external environment is the key to objectivity. In what is now a somewhat unfair characterization, Dewey attacks Kant for claiming that our duties are derived from the categorical imperative, where this is meant to be independent of any kind of sensitivity to the situation. Instead, he says in the 1908 edition of his *Ethics* that his approach "does not proceed (as Kant would have it) from a mere consideration of the moral law apart from a concrete end, *but from an end in so far as it persistently approves itself to reflection after an adequate survey of it in all its bearings*" (E_2 [MW5:284] [original emphasis]). Indeed, he argues (and I think more precisely) in the second edition of his *Ethics* that the *spirit* of the categorical imperative attempts to capture this point (E_3 [LW7:223]). But his phrase "in all its bearings" points us not away from particulars, but to their multiplicity and diversity both within and outside of the self as indexed to the details of the situation. This is precisely why Dewey believes that the impartial sympathetic observer provides access to objectivity in moral knowledge. So for him, objectivity consists not in distancing ourselves from the world, assuming a view from nowhere, but rather it emerges from a form of distance that obtains only because one seeks to be responsive to the specificity of the moment in all its bearings—that is, to see widely and feel deeply about the elements of the self that are at stake and the potential consequences that will follow externally when those elements are allowed to have their play.

THE TRAGIC SELF:
DELIBERATION AND CONFLICT

The argument here has advanced several important steps. Thus far, I have explicated Dewey understanding and defense of the immanence of normativity. As I argued, this provides a framework in which to situate his characterization of conflict under modern conditions. Proceeding this way, as I have suggested, allows us to take seriously moral conflict, but without interpreting conflict as resulting from some crisis in normative evaluation. And I filled out the contours of moral reflection or deliberation, which, in Dewey's estimation, is central to engaging and managing the moral life.

Nonetheless, his understanding of moral reflection is often understood as attempting much more than simply engaging and managing conflict. More precisely, it is usually read as denying the irreducibility of conflict. This simply means that implicit in his account of moral reflection is the belief that individuals who appropriately reflect will achieve harmony among conflicting claims. He seems unable to take seriously the sense of tragedy that can possibly come in the form of the irreducibility of conflict. This is what Robert Westbrook means when he says: "Dewey's ethics, at its worst, suggest that one could always find a synthetic resolution that harmonized competing values."[70] Although William Caspary highlights that for Dewey conflict is an "inescapable condition of democratic politics," he nonetheless concludes that, "Dewey neglects the tragic dimension in which characters are caught up in the anguish and dire consequences of irresolvable conflict," and so his views must be supplemented.[71] These reflections are crucial, coming as they do, from thoughtful Dewey interpreters. But we need to ask the following: What needs to be the case about his philosophy for this position to hold? In my reading, Westbrook and Caspary must mean that for Dewey inquiry does not simply *attempt* to harmonize competing values, but that Dewey believes that reconciliation of competing claims can always be achieved through inquiry. If my inference here is correct, this is not simply a claim about inquiry but about the social world in which it functions.

These thinkers are not alone. Hilary Putnam, as indicated in the last chapter, also advances this claim, contending that Dewey cannot do justice to individuals caught in moral dilemmas. As he explains: "While Dewey's social philosophy is overwhelmingly right, as far as it goes, his moral philosophy is less satisfactory when we try to apply it to individual existential choices."[72] He then refers specifically to an example provided by Jean-Paul Sartre's *Existentialism and Humanism* in which a young man finds himself caught between his commitment to going and aiding a resistance group and tending to his aging mother. The upshot of this example when used against Dewey is that he is unable to recognize the incommensurable quality of the conflict—that is, it defies reconstructive analysis, and so does not admit of a third way. Putnam then proceeds to appropriate James as a more useful guide.[73] Once again, implicit in this view is a claim not simply about the faith Dewey places in inquiry, but also an argument about the kind of social world Dewey believes we inhabit. Speaking positively of his position, Larry Hickman captures the point nicely: "But a part of [Dewey's] faith in the methods of science and democracy was his belief that even the most serious disagreements can be transcended if subjected to the proper tools."[74]

As we have seen in the last chapter, Putnam's approach wrongly drives a wedge between James and Dewey on this point. But one of Dewey's central claims about deliberation, as we have noticed, is the way it opens the self to the deliverances from one's character on the one hand and from the environment on the other. Unless he rejects the connection between practical reason and contingency articulated in chapter 2 (and I do not see why he would), he must acknowledge the extent to which reconstruction is not a necessary conclusion of deliberation. Indeed, the undercurrent of deliberation is that it may deepen our apprehension of conflict. For all of their insights, these thinkers are mistaken in their reading of Dewey on this point.

As I pointed out in the introduction, Dewey's post-Darwinian outlook mitigates any presumptive belief in synthetic harmony. And I argued in the first section of this chapter that he discourages us from beginning with the assumption that conflict is specious and apparent. To better understand the argument, we should go back to "Three Independent Factors" and its relationship to *Human Nature and Conduct* and the *Ethics*. In the two latter works, Dewey places specific emphasis on the reconstructive dimension of deliberation. In many ways, this approach makes a great deal of sense. We presume psychologically that if the competing factors have a hold on the agent in just the way he describes, then what that person will be after is a kind of proposal that does justice to the competing factors. The psychology of deliberation has an arc, if you will, that points toward doing justice to the competing claims. Just as diversity does not imply conflict, so too conflict does not imply incommensurability.

But Dewey is keen to highlight that this aim is itself a hypothesis that may be undercut by specific moral dilemmas. This is precisely why he says in the passage cited in the introduction that although the emphasis he places on continuity, a feature derived from his earlier idealism, continued throughout his philosophical career, it nonetheless had to proceed on empirical grounds. If empirical grounds track the relationship that obtains between practical action and contingency, as discussed in chapter 2, then the aim of synthetic harmony may potentially go unrealized. That is, we stand in a position of uncertainty regarding what we will discover about the nature of the conflict, and this may include discovering its irreducibility.

Consider the following. After he delivers his lecture "Three Independent Factors in Morals," it is pointed out during the question and answer session by the French pragmatist Emmanuel Leroux that in *Human Nature and Conduct* there is an emphasis placed on a "new state of equilibrium" that is brought about because of reflection. And yet in this lecture, Leroux continues, we find a "trinity . . . which [you] no longer want to reduce to a unity. Is there nevertheless an agreement between the two?" (TIM$_2$ [LW5:501]). Dewey responds that in *Human Nature and Conduct* he understood the "moral problem above . . . from the psychological point of view, while today [that is, in this lecture] he was concerned with action proper" (TIM$_2$ [LW5:502]). That is, he is concerned with those moments in which the psychological arc goes unrealized in the actual practice of moral deliberation because the substance of the conflict potentially embodies value incommensurability. The *Ethics*, then, stands as an all-encompassing text in relation to these other two works, and so holds out the possibility that deliberation may reveal the commensurability or incommensurability of values.

Armed with this analysis, let us go back once more. What is Dewey saying about deliberation in relation to moral conflict? In my view, he is making a two-pronged argument. For him, any decision made regarding moral conflicts must assume a reflective and experimental stance. We must be open to the possibility that our desires and vision of the world might change in the face of new evidence. This is a constitutive feature of deliberation. The self, as we know, is unfinished and is subject to change. In reflecting on the dilemma within the context of other agents and the concerns they raise, we might discover that it admits of a resolution. Our sympathetic outlook makes us ready to receive information, in the absence of which we might be inclined to misdescribe the situation or not see that a resolution potentially exists. That resolution, as we have noticed, sublimates the conflicting features. This simply means that we have found a way to do justice to the competing factors.

The second part of Dewey's argument, connected with the analysis of the texts above, is the following. We may discover through the process of deliberation itself that the dilemma is of the kind where choosing a path implicates us in feelings of loss or regret. I have discussed this in the context of an individual life, but this does not preclude us from speaking about a community internally torn in just this way. In this sense, deliberation sheds light on the residual impact of loss that will be produced when we act. Shedding light is precisely what the dramatic rehearsal seeks to do, and its results are readily captured in the anguish we experience when confronted with the prospect of choosing between two competing goods or making a decision that nonetheless leaves part of the community in a less-than-satisfied state. In order to avoid misunderstanding, we undoubtedly will go on with our lives and continue to develop and grow, but this does not undercut the feeling of disappointment and regret that we feel after acting. We regret not that we could have acted otherwise, but that there was no way of acting that could have produced a more satisfactory outcome.

But what exactly does this mean, and is there any textual evidence to support the contention? Here it is worth turning to a passage from chapter 15 of the *Ethics*, "The Moral Self." In this passage, Dewey is describing the end process of deliberation and its impact on the self:

> Now every choice sustains a double relation to the self. It reveals the existing self and it forms the future self. That which is chosen is that which is found congenial to the desires and habits of the self as it already exists. Deliberation has an important function in this process, because each different possibility as it is presented to the imagination appeals to a different element in the constitution of the self, thus giving all sides of character a chance to play their part in the final choice. The resulting choice also shapes the self, making it, in some degree, a new self. This fact is especially marked at critical junctures, but it marks every choice to some extent however slight. . . . But every choice is at the forking of the roads, and the path chosen shuts off certain opportunities and opens others. (E_3 [LW7:286–287])

What he is providing here is a descriptive account of how the decision following deliberation affects us. He observes that the decision made is congenial with the desires and habits of the self as it already exists. But we must be careful how we understand this point. A decision made in the case of a dilemma will undoubtedly appeal to different parts of our character—that is, the agent is receptive to each of the competing sides. Deliberation may very well deepen our apprehension of just this fact. Of course we know that a decision will be made, and it will be the case that one would be a different self, in some degree, had that decision not been made or made otherwise. At this juncture, Dewey does not specifically describe the end process of deliberation as one where the agent finds himself experiencing a sense of loss after a decision. Indeed, the image of anguish is missing. But this neutral presentation makes sense and therefore does not represent a deficit within his argument, as Caspary and Putnam contend. After all, he is offering a general descriptive account of how deliberation affects us, and it may very well be the case that we will reconstruct the situation such that no residual feeling of loss remains. Yet he adds an important caveat regarding choice, one which clearly suggests otherwise: "Every choice is at the forking of the roads, and the path chosen shuts off certain opportunities and opens others."

On one reading, it seems trivially true that to the extent that two options cannot be simultaneously realized we have to forgo one to realize the other. Yet such situations need not imply a sense of loss or regret. For this reading to hold, however, it must deny the kind of conflict Dewey is describing. For instance, I might like to purchase a house that had a large amount of rooms, but was also environmentally friendly. The fact that, as things stand regarding my financial situation, I must sacrifice one or the other of these attributes hardly seems tragic. Dewey's account can easily concede that this situation is not tragic, and he can do so under the rubric that it is trivially true that something has to be sacrificed. But this concession is necessary to cast into relief what he understands to be at stake in moral deliberation. For moral deliberation

> differs from other forms not as a process of forming a judgment and arriving at knowledge but in the kind of value which is thought about. The value is technical, professional, economic, etc., as long as one thinks of it as something which one can aim at and attain by way of having, possessing; as something to be got or to be missed. Precisely the same object will have a moral value when it is thought of as making a difference in the *self*, as determining what one will *be*, instead of merely what one will *have*. (E_3 [LW7:274] [original emphases])

This passage points to what my example above lacks. It is the importance of the values within any normal person's self-conception and larger vision of what gives their lives meaning that makes choosing tragic. Connecting choice to one's self-conception as Dewey does captures James' thought, *pace* Putnam, that the consequences of choosing are momentous. That there is no way to sublimate the conflicting claims in his view also fits with James' argument that the decision is between live options and therefore unavoidable.[75] Indeed, this is precisely the point that Sartre makes regarding a genuine inability to extricate oneself from the dilemma: "No rule of general morality can show you what you ought to do: no signs are vouchsafed in this world."[76] This fact will often be brought home to us, argues Dewey, by the very deliberative process we employ to find a third, satisfactory, option.

The claim that Dewey can accommodate tragic conflict will strike many as dubious. Indeed, the historical care provided by Westbrook in his elucidation of Dewey's philosophy and the philosophical acumen of Putnam's analysis may well seem to dwarf what I have provided here. But the fact that Dewey does not spend a great deal of time on tragic conflicts, I think, does not point to an unwillingness to acknowledge them or inattentiveness to the pluralism conflicts imply. I hope we can see that he does take this issue seriously. The more fair response is that he understands these moments to be *a* feature of our social and political world, rather than its *exclusive* feature. Our social and political engagements do not, on every occasion, constitute the high drama of Greek tragedy. Recall his earlier remark: "Sometimes a juncture is so critical that a person . . . feels that his future his very being, is at stake." But he continues on a Jamesian note, remarking that these cases are important for theoretical reflection because "some degree of what is conspicuous in these *momentous* cases is found in *every* voluntary decision" (E_3 [LW7:171] [added and original emphases, respectively]). What is conspicuous in these momentous cases that we find in every voluntary decision is simply that we must choose. But it is the difference between those choices that seem undisruptive and the ones that mark critical junctures in the understanding of an individual or community that potentially implicates the soul in feelings of loss. This leads us to a conclusion about Dewey's outlook that James crystallizes regarding his own position—namely, "the very 'seriousness' that we attribute to life mean[s] that ineluctable noes and losses form a part of it, that there are genuine sacrifices *somewhere* [but not everywhere], and that something permanently drastic and bitter always remains at the bottom of the cup."[77]

But if we are going to recognize such moments, it will be because we are struggling individually and collectively to see widely and feel deeply about the moral life. For when our judgments fail us, when we seem not to take seriously moral pluralism, it may often signal a deficit in our perceptual capacities. Dewey's argument regarding the best achievable state of the moral agent is not simply about what the end products will be once we occupy this position, although it profoundly shapes them, but more forcefully about how we ought to stand within the moral life. Properly understood, moral agency positions us to witness the miracle of human reflection, even as it awakens us to its limitations.

I have argued that Dewey's sensitivity to conflict should not obscure the larger framework in which his discussion is located. This allows us to separate the issue of the existence of a normative world from the conflicts that emerge therein. His account of conflict is thus framed by a more stable evaluative structure that steadies our inquiries and provides us with a way to expand our moral horizons in the context of specific conflicts. To be sure, in elucidating this point, his aim was not to overdetermine the process of deliberation, but rather to show how that evaluation looks from the inside. That is to say, what sort of beings must we be to engage in deliberation and what must this imply about our social psychology? What does this tell us about the resources within the world we inhabit for managing our moral lives?

The purpose of this chapter, then, was to provide an answer to these questions in order to better anchor the account of moral conflict. What has emerged is a vision of the moral life that is grounded more firmly in a kind of mutual responsiveness that, in Dewey's view, must be made explicit in future evaluative moments. Indeed, it is the extent to which we make this process explicit in our encounters with others that underscores its importance not only for the moral life, but for political justification as well. When examined closely, it provides us with a way to manage power in political life and avoid the looming threat of domination that emerges when decision-making is placed beyond the purview of public oversight. It is to this final issue that we must now turn.

CONSTRAINING ELITES AND MANAGING POWER

In chapter 2 I argued that for Dewey inquiry is a kind of practice whose legitimating quality draws from two different directions, the character of the individuals confronted with specific ruptures in experience and the larger environment. Legitimation is realized through a discursive medium of giving and asking for reasons for proposals, hypotheses, or plans of action—what I have referred to as a form of mutual responsiveness. This view, as seen in his reflections on both religion and morality in chapters 3 and 4, is bound up with a larger story about the absence of a common theological or ethical horizon and an increased recognition that our deeply held commitments are devoid of epistemic certainty. This need not lead us to a crisis of meaning or normative evaluation (à la Charles Hodge, Max Weber, and liberal Protestants), precisely because Dewey uncouples the value of our commitments from the visions of certainty to which they were previously linked. In other words, since inquiry develops out of fractures or problems in experience, the products of inquiry are judged as effective responses within that horizon. This opens our commitments to reflective evaluation and public contestability in the context of our ongoing social practices.

In one reading, however, Dewey's emphasis on inquiry seemingly, and somewhat ironically, leads away from expanding the domain of public contestability that is so central to democracy.[1] After all, it makes perfect sense to say that the emphasis on inquiry cannot help but signal the presence of a gradation in cognitive abilities. If what Walter Lippmann, Weber, and C. Wright Mills argue is true—that the complexity of modern democratic societies inevitably requires greater time in absorbing information and greater ca-

pacities for understanding that information—it is not clear how we can legitimately expand the domain of decision-making.[2] As Weber explains, when we
use modern science as a paradigm for decision-making the inevitable result
is that we find ourselves replacing the citizen with the expert. For some, the
situation in which expert agencies in conjunction with representative institutions are the exclusive site of decision-making is the only option—this is
Lippmann's basic claim in several works reflecting on the role of the public in
democracy. But for him, it is not that contestation on the part of the governed
is abandoned, but that from the perspective of policy formation, plans of action, etc., deliberation is confined to the expert few rather than those who will
be affected by the results of deliberation. The question that must be raised
then—one by Weber advanced in passing in chapter 1 but which we also find
in Mills—is how do we remain sensitive to the complexity of modern societies and the role that intellectual elites must necessarily play without rob-
bing democratic legitimacy of much that we find morally appealing?[3] How, in
other words, should we think about the relationship between the elites[4] and
the larger public?

This question is of critical importance here, since Dewey is accused not
only of being inattentive to the way his reliance on inquiry may in fact justify
a vanguard politics, albeit one guided by experts, but also of not sufficiently
dealing with the exercise of power that comes with such a model. Consider
Mills' formulation of the problem:

> The assimilation of problems of political power and of moral goods to a state-
> ment of thinking, of method, to a model of action and thought imputed to "sci-
> ence," occurred within the social context of a growing industrialization that
> was spreading across a physical continent and from a position of one in close,
> daily contact with the rising professional and skilled groups who were central
> in the implementation of this conquest of nature by machine. This model was
> highlighted by the many fingers pointing at the technological results of science
> and from the success of the professions implemented by them. But that model
> is generalized by Dewey into education and into the discussions of politics. In
> these contexts and particularly in the latter, "scientific method" becomes "the
> method of intelligence" and this method is equated with "liberal democracy."[5]

The generalization by Dewey, I take Mills to be signaling, leaves vacant the
nature of the political relationship, particularly as it relates to deliberation
and decision-making between those professional and skilled groups—i.e., experts—and the lay public. So if, as Mills says, the "scientific method" becomes
"the method of intelligence" that in turn is equated with liberal democracy,

why would the management of the latter not simply point toward exclusive reliance on experts, as Lippmann maintains? Hence Mills concludes that the connection Dewey draws between the scientific method and democracy "avoids a really definite recognition and statement of the problem of political power" that is implied by that relationship and so leaves us prey to the mercy of decision makers.[6] In short, we are left powerless. As Sheldon Wolin explains, Dewey cannot avoid this problem because he "never squarely associated democracy, local or otherwise, with participation in the exercise of power."[7] As he continues: "Questions of how problems become identified, who controls the communication of results, and who evaluates the consequences were all left indeterminate."[8]

If Weber, Mills, and Lippmann are right about the complexity of modern life, and Dewey's critics are correct about his philosophy, we run once more into a twofold problem. The first is that Dewey cannot provide a framework to help us think about the relationship between experts and the lay public that is so central to modern life. In not being able to provide an answer to the first question, Dewey seems inattentive to the workings of power that inform that relationship. How, then, do we retain the thought, which I have argued for throughout, that his position redirects us away from decision-making based on blind deference and toward a view of legitimacy as expressed in the criteria of reciprocal and general acceptance among the governed? Can reason-giving, which is central to inquiry, do the real political work we need it to do in modern times?

My aim in this chapter is to address these questions and in doing so to make good on my previous assertion that the importance Dewey accords mutual responsiveness is the result of him trying to block the use of power from becoming arbitrary. I do this against the backdrop of two contrasting pictures of democracy that highlight important features of modern life to which Dewey needs to be sensitive. My argument is that on a careful reading of his political and ethical writings he absorbs the worries of these two outlooks, without falling prey to the pessimism that informs them. The first picture of democracy makes elites central to governance, advances suspicion of the masses' cognitive abilities, worries about the anarchic possibilities that might follow if they are allowed to rule in any substantive sense, and emphasizes the complexities of modern society as an obstacle to broad-based inclusion.[9] The other view agrees with the first in terms of democracy's anarchic possibilities and also advances a view about the complexities of modern society, which undermine a robust conception of participation. This account of democracy, however, differs in that it rejects representation as a genuine substitute. Representation, stability, and order are thus ruses that conceal the fact that the people do not govern in any genuine sense. As such, democracy is most clearly at work and ought to be encouraged when, like a fugitive, it escapes the institutional form that otherwise acts as a restraint.[10] The first view includes thinkers such as Lippmann and Joseph Schumpeter, while the second is most clearly expressed in our time by Wolin.

Although the reason for engagement with Lippmann seems clear, readers may nonetheless worry about my selection of Wolin. But the selection is not as idiosyncratic as it may first appear. After all, he explicitly charges Dewey with not adequately understanding the function of modern democracy in terms of power dynamics and so represents a contemporary version of a standard criticism worth evaluating. But more importantly, I think, so much of Wolin's specific account of the disruptive nature of democracy in relation to settled practices and the suspicion it generates regarding the ossification of political institutions accords nicely with Dewey's own political outlook and anti-authoritarian impulse. The issue is how can we retain what is best in Wolin, and for that matter Lippmann as well, without taking on the problems that attend their respective positions. To engage both Lippmann and Wolin in order to tease out the complexity of Dewey's outlook is to confront the possibilities and limitations of democracy under modern conditions.

The chapter unfolds in three sections. In the first I provide a more thorough sketch of the two positions above. While Lippmann rightly challenges exaggerated notions of participatory democracy, his disenchantment with these claims leads him to overstate the role experts ought to play. By virtue of his criticism of an exaggerated notion of popular sovereignty, Lippmann nonetheless indicates a need for an epistemic division of labor to manage political life that we cannot simply ignore. Whereas Lippmann's criticism is against popular sovereignty, Wolin's attack is directed against institutional structures. Although he does not believe we can abandon political institutions, he seems unable to inspire faith in them. The irony of his position, however, is that insofar as representative government is expressive of authority, it always already stands in opposition to freedom. Notwithstanding this difficulty, Wolin's analysis does point us to the necessity of thinking about democracy as being always incomplete—an orientation, if taken seriously, that guards against the extent to which we would allow our institutions to ossify in the face of an ever-demanding public.

I turn in the second and third sections to Dewey's account of democracy. His commitment to democracy flows from the belief that it provides the widest arena for applying inquiry to the problems of collective organization. As such, it stands to reason that those most affected ought to serve as the beginning and terminal points for developing and testing solutions. As indicated in both chapters 3 and 4, this is coupled with the belief that in post-traditional societies all proposals, no matter where they emanate from, are potentially contestable. For Dewey, however, citizens do not merely authorize the use of power and so legitimize political action, but are genuinely authoritative. Among their contributions, citizens contextualize and give purpose to expertise; otherwise such expertise would be meaningless. This view is premised on yet another claim, namely, that in matters of politics there can be no political expertise independent from the wisdom of the public. A democratic understanding of collective problem-solving thus envisions deliberation as emerging from the relationship among experts, political representatives, and the larger public. This ensures, he believes, that justification of one's actions is not uncoupled from being accountable to the public.

Many scholars have observed the connection Dewey draws between inquiry and democracy, and the presumption of broad-based inclusion it implies.[11] Yet they have not made *explicit* how his understanding of democracy can be recast as a preoccupation with power and domination. Robert Westbrook rightly notes, for example, that for Dewey: "The planned society left the choice of ends to the powerful who used 'physical and psychological force' to secure conformity and left the choice of means to technicians who asked how but not why."[12] But Dewey worries about this, I argue, not simply because reflective self-governance is central to human growth, but, more importantly, because without all participants having a say, power may easily be used to dominate. As contemporary pragmatists and republicans alike argue, without my having a say in forming and guiding the ends to which power will be put, I leave my development and the community to which I belong open to arbitrary rather than directed control.[13] This makes my freedom uncertain precisely because the potential for input does not exist. It is Dewey's profound quest to make room for self-actualization that underscores his commitment to and defense of freedom as nondomination.

In the final part of this chapter, I reflect on Dewey's understanding of the public to anchor his commitment to nondomination. The aim is not merely to articulate a guiding principle of assessment such as freedom as nondomination, but an orientation toward power and its embodiment in representative institutions so that the principle itself is not lost from view. Our appreciation for those institutions, Dewey maintains, must be grounded in a broader understanding of democracy and the importance of the public. His account of the public, I shall argue, helps to bring into focus this broader description, in which democracy is seen from the outset as always in the process of *becoming*. In this regard, the public represents a permanent space of contingency—that is, there can be temporary closure to the public, delimited by specific problems in which claims are made and from which institutions and goods emerge, but not permanent closure. To make the practice of reason-giving central to legitimacy, and as a result fundamental to the functioning of the public, is to see democracy as an orientation that provides the resources for overcoming the ossification that will inevitably display itself in institutional structures. This captures the sense in which Dewey understands democracy as a "task before us" (CD [LW:14:224–230]). In reading the public in this way, Dewey encourages us to see democracy as permanently unsettled and always open to contestation and the possibility for improvement.

THE DANGER OF POLITICAL PESSIMISM:
BETWEEN LIPPMANN AND WOLIN

The relationship between democracy and elites poses theoretical and practical difficulties. This is not surprising. As Wolin notes, democracy was born in revolt—emerging from a bundle of "transgressive acts" in which "the demos could not participate in power without shattering the class, status, and value systems by which it was excluded" previously.[14] In the American context, we have always had problems deferring to our betters not because of an aversion to differences of intellectual abilities, as Alexis de Tocqueville argued,[15] but because such differences usually become justifications for suppressing the process of contestation and deliberation that should otherwise define the space of political reflection. Historically, we have often naturalized those differences and constructed institutions and rights to support them. But once power becomes a private monopoly, once the use of power fails to track the interests of those it affects, domination will inevitably follow. This leaves us in a condition that is far from democracy.

In this section I take up two attempts to understand the relationship between democracy and elites that can be found in the writings of Lippmann and Wolin. While there is much in their respective positions to which Dewey's vision of democracy needs to be sensitive, each position nonetheless suffers from deficiencies owing to the premises upon which it is based. The aim, then, is to get at the limitations and possibilities of each view. This will position us to see how Dewey at once overcomes these limitations while retaining what is beneficial in both.

LIPPMANN AND THE ILLUSIONS OF DEMOCRACY

Walter Lippmann's writings on democracy in both *Public Opinion* and *The Phantom Public* are part of a much larger discourse during the 1920s that challenged the viability of popular sovereignty—that is, the vision that the public informs and authorizes political action.[16] This much Lippmann explains when, in the latter work, he remarks:

> My sympathies are with [the citizen], for I believe that he has been saddled with an impossible task and that he is asked to practice an unattainable ideal. I find it so myself for, although public business is my main interest and I give most of my time to watching it, I cannot find time to do what is expected of me in the theory of democracy; that is, to know what is going on and to have an opinion worth expressing on every question which confronts a self-governing community.[17]

This passage contains the crux of Lippmann's sociological critique of the democratic ideal. In his view, given the complexities of modern democratic societies, conflicts develop between the vast technical nature of political issues that emerge and the time citizens have available to address and understand those issues. This tension points to yet another claim having to do with the importance and value that citizens accord participation. As Lippmann remarks, chiding classical democratic theorists for having a narrow understanding of human nature: "Mankind was interested in all kinds of other things, in order, in its rights, in prosperity, in sights and sounds and in not being bored. In so far as spontaneous democracy does not satisfy their other interests, it seems to most men most of the time to be an empty thing."[18] His point is that democracy does not exhaust the realm of what people find meaningful. As such, it seems mistaken, Lippmann maintains, to argue that people are most authentically human when civically engaged.

Lippmann advances a more profound criticism that is in keeping with much of the psychological literature of the time. His argument on this point comes in two steps, the first relating to what he calls stereotypes, and the second regarding the manipulation to which the symbolic content of those stereotypes is potentially subject. Stereotypes are value-laden conjectures about the world that arrange experience. They are part of a wider social network in which individuals exists and do not depend for their functioning on perpetual cognitive awareness. As he says: "The subtlest and most pervasive of all influences are those which create and maintain the repertory of stereotypes. We are told about the world before we see it. . . . And those preconceptions, unless education has made us acutely aware, govern deeply the whole process of perception."[19] This is particularly so in industrial societies precisely because people are asked to reflect on issues of which they can have no first-hand experience.

While stereotypes serve several key functions, the most important of these involves security. Lippmann thus refers to stereotypes as the "fortress of our tradition" because they stave off challenges from contrary forms of life or ways of being that appear menacing.[20] Although he occasionally speaks as if there is a one-to-one correspondence between stereotypes and the phenomena of the natural and social world, more often he argues that the cultural resources that feed into and comprise stereotypes create a "pseudo-environment."[21] Stereotypes seem to economize our thinking just to the extent that they help us reconstruct the complex environment on "a simpler model before we can manage it."[22] These simpler patterns of understanding "determine a very great part of men's political behavior."[23]

Given the importance he accords stereotypes not merely for individual identity, but also for political behavior, he worries about the extent to which they are manipulated in the context of public life. Not only do stereotypes work to "censor out much that needs to be taken into account" about complex political phenomena,[24] but they are uniquely susceptible to control given their already existentially charged content. "The stereotypes," Lippmann explains, "are loaded with preference, suffused with affection or dislike, attached to fears, lusts, strong wishes, pride, hope."[25] Most individuals, he says earlier, employ stereotypes with a level of "gullibility" that prevents them from seeing the partiality of their position.[26] Individuals seeking to win political power use symbols that are indexed to the passions that infuse stereotypes. And they do so either to cultivate solidarity among large segments of the population or to exploit the power such symbols represent for their own distinct ends. "He who captures the symbols," says Lippmann, "by which public feeling is for the moment contained, controls by that much the approaches of public policy. . . . A leader or an interest that can make itself master of current symbols is a master of the current situation."[27]

The picture that emerges is one in which citizens have little time or desire to participate. But more strikingly, even if citizens did possess the requisite time and interest, Lippmann maintains that they are inherently resistant to information that would call into question their deeply held beliefs. My use of "inherently" is intended to be a loaded term and carries profound implications for understanding Lippmann's position. To be clear, he shares with Dewey a similar understanding of belief-formation and the role of mutual responsiveness therein. However, he doubts that we remain "curious and open-minded" such that we are ready to rethink our beliefs if good reasons emerge.[28] The fact that we do not remain curious and open-minded is, for him, bound up with the process of socialization by which we come to acquire the stereotypes that we do: "No wonder, then, that any disturbance of the stereotypes seems like an attack upon the foundations of the universe. It is an attack upon the foundations of *our* universe, and, where big things are at stake, we do not readily admit that there is any distinction between our universe and the universe."[29]

Notice that Lippmann's argument is that for most of us our beliefs fall to the level of ontological fact. The result is that we place our beliefs beyond the reach of inquiry. Given this description, it is no wonder that he prefaces *Public Opinion* with an extended passage from book 7 of Plato's *Republic*, presumably not only to draw an analogy between the shadows on the cave wall that are believed to be real and the way stereotypes function, but also to highlight the danger that comes when those images are threatened.[30] As he says: "The public must be put in its place . . . so that each of us may live free of the trampling and the roar of a bewildered herd."[31]

It is against this background that Lippmann begins to articulate his alternative—elitist—vision of democracy. Prefiguring Schumpeter's view that democracy means "only that the people have the opportunity of accepting or refusing the men who are to rule them," Lippmann argues more pointedly that the "public does not select the candidate, write the platform, outline the policy any more than it builds the automobile or acts the play. It aligns itself for or against somebody who has offered himself."[32] Indeed, both arguments are continuous with James Madison in linking democracy to representative government, and defining the latter as the "total exclusion of the people in their collective capacity."[33]

Lippmann, however, holds an additional view that diverges from both Madison's position and that of later democratic realists.[34] Let us recall his previous remark: "I find it so myself for, although public business is my main interest and I give most of my time to watching it, I cannot find time to do what is expected of me in the theory of democracy." To do what is expected means not merely paying attention to political issues, but having the requisite knowledge to understand those issues. But Lippmann goes further in his argument, since here too he believes political decisions by elected representatives are also in need of prior supplementation and clarification. It is worth turning to two passages from *Public Opinion*, one from chapter 16 relating to Lippmann's views on Congress, and the second from chapter 1 relating to representative government proper:

The congress of representatives is essentially a group of blind men in a vast, unknown world. Since the real effects of most laws are subtle and hidden, they cannot be understood by filtering local experiences through local states. They can be known only by controlled reporting and objective analysis. And just as the head of a large factory cannot know how efficient it is by talking to the fore- man, but must examine cost sheets and data that only an accountant can dig out for him, so the lawmaker does not arrive at a true picture of the state of the union by putting together a mosaic of local pictures.[35]

[As such] representative government, either in what is ordinarily called politics, or in industry, cannot be worked successfully, no matter what the basis of elec- tion, unless there is an independent, expert organization for making the unseen facts intelligible to those who have to make the decisions. I attempt, therefore, to argue that the serious acceptance of the principle that personal representa- tion must be supplemented by representation of the unseen facts would alone permit a satisfactory decentralization, and allow us to escape from the intoler- able and unworkable fiction that each of us must acquire a competent opinion about all public affairs.[36]

As I read Lippmann, insofar as representatives seek to track various per- spectives among their constituents to create a better picture of political real- ity, they will be misguided. Given the way he understands stereotypes and their hold on us, he believes that partial perspectives will either cancel each other out if they diverge or reinforce each other. In either case, the net re- sult is an incomplete picture that corrupts decision-making. The alternative that Lippmann recommends is one in which the unseen facts are "managed only by a specialized class" of social-scientific experts who are distinct from the "men of action."[37] Presumably, locating decision-making with the elected representatives, and therefore outside the purview of experts, obstructs the extent to which they may employ their knowledge for ends that reach be- yond public oversight. Their role, he explains, is to examine and report on the unseen political phenomena that are blocked from view by our stereotypes. They direct their results to political officials, rather than the public, and take their point of direction from these same individuals.

Yet Lippmann's language in the first passage suggests much more than mere reporting, indicative of his example of the factory owner and his rela- tionship to the foreman and the accountant. The accountant provides not only facts, but an interpretation of the current financial condition of the com- pany, its short- and long-term problems given current operations. If we reason from this example to his understanding of the role of experts in politics, it is not an exaggeration to say that for Lippmann experts give shape to the problems that are only dimly perceived by both citizens and political officials. The cognitive authority he attaches to experts thus slides into a kind of political power that shapes the landscape in which political officials and the citizenry function from the outset.

LIMITATIONS AND POSSIBILITIES OF LIPPMANN'S ANALYSIS

This is a bare sketch of Lippmann's argument, and, as Dewey indicates in his reviews (RPO [MW13:337–345]; RPP [LW2:213–220]) of both books, there is much to recommend within it. He agrees with Lippmann's discussion of stereotypes and the poverty of the public's knowledge in decision-making. He, too, is unconvinced by a view of democracy that envisions citizens as omni-competent. Yet Dewey takes issue with both the emphasis Lippmann places on educating "officials and directors" over and against the public, and his corollary belief that experts do not need to be informed by or receive input from the public (RPO [MW13:343]).

These disagreements point to a slippage in Lippmann's argument that Dewey signals. His rejection of what he considers the classical description of democratic citizens wrongly slides into an attack on their deliberative capacities. In doing so, he obscures alternative ways of understanding the public, especially the extent to which citizens ought to serve as the beginning and ending points for understanding problems and assessing potential proposals. This slippage is largely based on Lippmann's assertion that most of us are simply dogmatic and irrational when it comes to our beliefs.[38] But there is no reason to posit this as fundamental to human psychology and human socialization, precisely because citizens invariably do move away from or rethink the beliefs they hold.[39] This is not to deny that resistance to changing one's beliefs is real; rather, the simple point for Dewey is that we cannot assume that citizens will take a dogmatic stance independent from a specific deliberative context. Lippmann's failure on this point leads him to set up a false distinction between the objective outlook of the experts and the subjective and narrow perspective of citizens, and to identify the former as the appropriate guardians of democracy.

For Dewey, Lippmann's position fails to acknowledge a view that has achieved normative and empirical currency within Western modernity, one which understands knowledge as being formed through the historical specificity of our social practices. Knowledge is the fruit of our transactions with the natural and social world. How we perceive political problems, as well as formulate the content of policy proposals, is constitutive of and constituted by the contexts in which we are located. In other words, how we come to understand political problems and respond implies a kind of local knowledge and communal vision that is beyond the purview of experts. As Dewey says on just this point, Lippmann's approach "ignores [the] forces which have to be composed and resolved before technical and specialized action can come into play" (PP [LW2:313]). Indeed, while experts may be able to provide technical knowledge, they have no way of judging the "bearing of [that] knowledge" (PP [LW2:365]).[40] For him, expert knowledge lacks purpose and may be subject to any number of blindnesses unless it is placed within the wider horizon of values and concerns that animate the public. That is, expertise is connected to some narrow domain, however important it may be, rather than being expertise of political affairs. Dewey's aim, then, is to offer a vision of democracy that, in keeping with Lippmann, acknowledges the need for an epistemic division of labor, but one that does not allow inequalities in information to undermine the necessity of deliberation, as is the case in Lippmann's account.

To be fair, Lippmann does believe that experts should be checked by a periodic plebiscite, an up-or-down vote on their performance, and that the public can serve in this role.[41] This is precisely why it still makes sense to speak of him as offering an account of democracy even in its attenuated form. But it is more often than not that expertise alone is not sufficient for responding to political problems—that is, expertise needs to be contextualized by a much larger set of political imperatives and this indicates that the resources for managing political affairs cannot simply be reduced to a technical affair. This points to the need for a more robust account of deliberation and a principle of normative assessment than Lippmann can provide, even as we concede the importance of experts to modern democracies. So deference to experts cannot be the de facto position of democratic legitimacy. Even if we say, then, that the dispute, properly speaking, is between plebiscitary and deliberative democracy rather than between democracy and technocracy, the original concern remains. We need to find an approach that accommodates both elites and the demos in the service of collective problem-solving.

WOLIN AND FUGITIVE DEMOCRACY

In a series of essays and books, Sheldon Wolin defends a radical notion of democracy against the constraining effects of institutions. There are affinities between Dewey's description of democracy and Wolin's political vision, especially when the latter speaks of democracy as a "mode of being" that is "concerned with the political potentialities of ordinary citizens, that is, with their possibilities for becoming political beings through the self-discovery of common concerns and of modes of action for realizing them."[42] Despite the importance he attaches to community and his emphasis on inclusion and deliberation, there is a fundamental tension inherent in Wolin's political vision that is missing from Dewey's account. This tension emerges at the very moment in which democracy allies itself with institutional form, a union that, for Wolin, necessarily undermines the notion of popular sovereignty: "Democracy does not complete its task by establishing a form and thus being fitted into it. A political constitution is not the fulfillment of democracy but its transfiguration into a 'regime' and hence a stultified and partial reification."[43] To understand this tension and therefore see where Wolin goes wrong, we need to examine more carefully the content of his description of democracy and his understanding of constitutionalism.

Wolin provides us with his account of democracy in three central essays: "Norm and Form: The Constitutionalizing of Democracy," "Fugitive Democracy," and "Transgression, Equality, and Voice." All three revolve around a vision of democracy as anarchic and transgressive. But it is in the second of the three essays where the description is most clearly articulated:

> Democracy is not about where the political is located but about how it is experienced. Revolutions activate the demos and destroy boundaries that bar access to political experience. Individuals from the excluded social strata take on responsibilities, deliberate about goals and choices, and share in decision that have broad consequences and affect unknown and distant others. This revolutionary transgression is the means by which the demos makes itself political. It is by *stasis*, not *physis*, that the demos acquires a civic nature.[44]

What we should first observe about this passage is the distinction that is at work between revolutionary and normal modes of managing collective affairs. Wolin discusses this explicitly at the outset of the essay when he defines "the political" as a moment of collective problem-solving that is forged and managed through public deliberation to preserve the collective's well-being. He distinguishes this from what he refers to as "politics"—that is, a bitter negotiation over access to and distribution of resources among "unequal social powers."[45] In his view, democracy is an expression of the former precisely because it destabilizes what Wolin takes to be the natural state of politics. Its anarchic quality inheres in the fact that it constitutes a threat to "politics as

usual," which functions to the disadvantage of the powerless. Jacques Rancière provides a description of the demos that is in keeping with Wolin's view
and helps explain why the latter identifies democracy with the powerless:
"Before being the name of a community, *demos* is the name of a part of the
community: namely, the poor. The 'poor,' . . . simply designates the category
of peoples who do not count, those who have no qualifications to part-take in
arche, no qualification for being taken into account."[46]

Democracy, then, is both functionally and conceptually bound up with
revolution. Of course, this description has largely been the cause for suspicion—a view that was no less present in Lippmann's image of the "bewildered
herd." For Wolin, however, this is the source of admiration: "I propose accepting the familiar charges that democracy is inherently unstable, inclined
toward anarchy, and identified with revolution and using these traits as the
basis for a different, *a*constitutional conception of democracy."[47] His language here is a bit deceptive. Although he speaks of providing a "different"
conception of democracy, given what he goes on to say it seems unlikely that
he would countenance any other account. His view, then, is not advanced as a
competing understanding of democracy, but the only authentic description.

In terms much akin to Rancière, Wolin tells us that "the demos is created
from a shared realization that powerlessness comes from being shut out of
the councils where power's authority is located."[48] Individuals thus converge
around a common experience of exclusion from the political process, and this
provides both the beginnings of their deliberation and the ending points for
their responses. Throughout much of his writings, Wolin often invokes the
image of the Athenian citizen to elucidate his understanding of democracy,
but it is also the case that the link between democracy and revolution that he
draws finds contemporary embodiment in the social movements of the 1960s
and '70s. In the American context in particular, these extraordinary periods
witnessed the consolidation of civic power outside of the normal processes
of electoral politics, constraining both those processes and the larger constitutional structure in which they were located. The aim was to deepen the
purchase on freedom for wider segments of the population and restructure
the very constitution that was the source of exclusion from the outset. With
the seductive memory of these social movements in the background, it is no
wonder Wolin describes democracy as a form of "collective action that gath-
ers its power from outside the system."[49]

Wolin's description of politics (what I have referred to as the normal mode
of social organization for him) is embodied in the process of constitutionalism; it stands in opposition to his description of the political and democracy.[50]

Read in this light, constitutional democracy is not an attempt to formalize popular governance. Rather, it is both a strategic and clandestine attempt to put the demos in its place and contain its passion. "Constitutionalism," writes Wolin, "might be defined as the theory of how best to restrain the politics of democracy while ensuring the predominance of the social groups and classes represented by the 'best men.'"[51] He writes more dramatically in his condemnation of theorists from Plato to Tocqueville:

> It is no exaggeration to say that one of the, if not the, main projects of ancient constitutional theorists, such as Plato (*The Laws*), Aristotle, Polybius, and Cicero, as well as of modern constitutionalists, such as the authors of *The Federalist* and Tocqueville, was to dampen, frustrate, sublimate, and defeat the demotic passions. The main devices were: the rule of law and especially the idea of a sacrosanct "fundamental law" or constitution safeguarded from the "gust of popular passions"; the idea of checks and balances; separation of powers with its attempt to quarantine the "people" by confining its direct representation to one branch of the legislature; the "refining" process of indirect elections; and the suffrage restrictions. The aim was not simply to check democracy but to discourage it by making it difficult for those who, historically, had almost no leisure time for politics, to achieve political goals.[52]

Implicit in this passage is the classical distinction between democracy on the one side and oligarchy/aristocracy on the other, with the understanding that the selection of magistrates or representatives is an exclusive principle of the latter. But if this is right, as Wolin seems to think, then constitutionalism cannot help but be disingenuous when it speaks about the importance of popular participation. For democracy's conversion into constitutional form must necessarily come about by severely constraining the involvement of the people so as to serve ends not particularly hospitable to the demos. To say that modern constitutionalism is disingenuous means that for Wolin "power to achieve a desired result [is being used] without being accountable to the system that is being influenced."[53]

To be sure, traditional republican regimes often explicitly reserved tasks for the general populace and the aristocracy, involving both in a share of power as a way to manage conflict and avoid corruption. This was largely because society reflected these distinct classes more clearly. But for Wolin it was perhaps to the credit of the American system to devise a structure sensitive to the blurring of social classes, but which did not compromise the constraints that both classical thinkers and the American Framers thought necessary for a stable regime.[54] Modern representative government, Wolin contends, did not find a better way to express the collective power of the populace. Instead, it transferred that power to public agents and agencies, and in so doing transmuted how the populace viewed the *proper* expression of that power. The problem of modern democracy, he argues, "is that any conception of democracy centered on the citizen-as-actor and politics-as-episodic-activity is incompatible with the modern choice of the state as the fixed center of political life and the corollary conception of politics as organizational activity aimed at a single, dominating objective, control of state apparatus."[55] For the modern state, and its institutional appendages, has its origins in a desire to secure the privileged position of elites—whether their privilege is based on wealth, birth, or intellectual abilities—over and against popular participation.[56]

POSSIBILITIES AND LIMITATIONS OF WOLIN'S ANALYSIS

Wolin's argument is far more complicated than I have presented here, and addressing all of its details is beyond the scope of this chapter. For our purposes, it is enough to point out the inescapable tension in the argument, which distorts how we orient ourselves to the political landscape. This distortion takes place first at the level of how we understand representative democracy, and second at the level of how we conceive of freedom. To begin, Wolin describes the normal state of society as an oligarchy, and posits that representative government works to underwrite and protect the maintenance of that oligarchy. While he concedes in a number of different places that the complexities of modern society make representative democracy necessary, it is unclear how he is able to inspire faith in the system, given how he understands its origins. In fact, he is not encouraging a healthy sense of suspicion of representative institutions, but rather a corrosive contempt. "[A] few tokens," he says, "supposedly representing the remarkable diversity of American society are not synonymous with democracy but a parody of equalitarianism."[57] He says elsewhere that the "Presidency . . . is the cruelest symbol of the impotence of the demos."[58] Wolin's language does not advance suspicion against a particular person who may occupy the presidency, but rather against the very thought of executive authority.

The problem with his argument then is that he reifies his story of the origins of constitutionalism, placing it and democracy in an inevitable battle that defies intentionality and historical development. After all, modern liberal democrats, such as Benjamin Constant, Thomas Jefferson, and Dewey, do not glorify representative institutions, but they nonetheless understand the importance of such institutions given the size and, in Dewey's case, the diversity of the population. To be sure, this criticism against Wolin does not imply that reliance on the institutions of representative government is the only, or even the most significant, avenue to express and deepen democracy. It only means that such institutions are not necessarily inimical to those efforts.

The second problem that emerges relates to his understanding of freedom, especially as it is bound up with self-governance. If my first worry is accurate, then we can advance the additional inference that when the normal operations of government are active, we are somehow not free: "The true question is not whether democracy can govern in the traditional sense, but why it would want to. Governing means manning and accommodating to bureaucratized institutions that, *ipso facto*, are hierarchical in structure and elitist, permanent rather than fugitive—in short, anti-democratic."[59] Precisely because Wolin draws a fundamental connection between freedom and insurgency, it follows that the normal operations of government, which include the presence of bureaucracy and hierarchy, function in an inverse relationship to freedom itself. In making this argument, he places institutional authority and freedom in opposition in a way that cannot be reconciled.

Yet it is not clear in his writings why the presence of bureaucracy and hierarchy is necessarily anti-democratic and hostile to freedom. Of course they may become so insofar as their purpose comes unhinged from accountability to the public, and Wolin is helpful in reminding us that we need to keep our eyes open for when this happens. But to assume this as the starting point precludes us from employing such institutions to manage and negotiate the complexities of the modern world. Indeed, Wolin's tragic understanding of modern politics reduces freedom to a fleeting experience, suggesting that we must resign ourselves to a state of affairs in which we suffer under the weight of inevitable domination. As George Kateb keenly observes, for Wolin, "fugitive democracy is a sudden eruption of democracy that is doomed to subside and to leave the prevailing structures, nominally but not truly democratic, intact."[60]

Precisely because he holds on to this tension between freedom and authority, he ironically eviscerates hope and misdescribes the nature of political struggle. So although his argument for democracy is inspired by social movements, it is doubtful Wolin could inspire the emergence of such movements, given the bleak picture he paints. This is because those movements (at least the ones Wolin has in mind) were not anti-authority. Rather, they sought to redescribe the foundation from which authority emerged. They envisioned a time in which their pleas would be given full weight through policy and thus condition the ongoing affairs of political life.[61]

There is an important point here that we should observe. To understand, for example, the substantive results of social movements along the lines of incorporation need not preclude us from retaining, as Wolin intends, an open-ended view of democracy—that is, to see it as an unsettled political order. Here Wolin's contribution cannot be denied; at a practical level he orients us to the uses of power and warns us about the extent to which such power can become reified. This open-ended view potentially guards against interpreting, for example, existing inequalities and injustices as conditions to which we must resign ourselves rather than trying to overcome them. Yet for Dewey, to describe democracy as always in the process of becoming implies only a possible rather than a necessary tension between democracy's future and the current state of political life.

The foregoing discussion leaves us with a number of different questions as we shift to Dewey's writings. Is it possible for him to offer a view of democracy that advances a healthy suspicion of the institutional structures of the state but which nonetheless views such institutions as important to democracy? Can he also capture precisely the transgressive quality that Wolin attaches to democracy without it exhausting how we understand the meaning of that term? The answer to the first question, I believe, takes us to Dewey's concerns about power—a position that is a piece of his response to Lippmann. His answer to the second question allows us to explore the complexity and dynamism that inhere in the public. It is to these issues that we must now turn.

EMPLOYING AND LEGITIMIZING POWER

We have considered at some length the way that both Lippmann's and Wolin's understanding of democracy is plagued by a kind of political pessimism that either misdescribes the role of experts in decision-making or reduces democracy to fleeting moments of revolution that place political authority and freedom in perpetual opposition. The issue to which we must now turn is the precise way Dewey's account is able to provide a more balanced perspective than either of these two positions. In doing so, I argue, we can distill from his description of democracy a concern to manage power over those on whom it will be exercised so that its use does not become arbitrary. This comes out by first attending to why he believes citizens do not merely authorize power but are authoritative in decision-making. Second, his emphasis on the communal nature of knowledge formation, which the previous point suggests, shapes how he understands the legitimacy of political power and the kind of conditions that must exist if power is to enable freedom. We are free, in

Dewey's view, not simply by virtue of the control we have over our community (an argument about *exercising a capacity*), but because such control does not leave us vulnerable to the arbitrary uses of power (an argument about the *conditions under which we live in political society*). This secondary claim is a defense of freedom understood as nondomination.

DEMOCRATIC INQUIRY AND EXPERTISE

In *The Public and Its Problems* of 1927, Dewey acknowledges the technical dimensions of problems facing modern citizens. For him, the various innovations in communication and transportation, the global scale of warfare, and the ongoing developments of the economy made reliance on experts unavoidable. To be sure, he recognizes that we rely not merely on specific experts trained, for example, in the areas of law and engineering, but also on the very social and material world they help construct. This latter understanding refers to what Anthony Giddens calls "expert systems." Giddens describes a complex relationship in which the lay public passively trusts various corporate and social institutions based on the functional importance they accord those institutions and in the context of the relative security they enjoy when relying on those institutions.[62] Short of some breakdown, there is no reason to rethink the way these various elements hang together. In the context of democratic decision-making, however, what is important for Dewey is that we understand that how and why we rely on experts is itself a public judgment that makes inquiry genuinely cooperative.

This claim emerges when he describes the relationship between experts and the citizenry. He takes this up most clearly when, revisiting some of the thoughts expressed in his reviews of Lippmann's work, he writes:

> The final obstacle in the way of any aristocratic rule is that in the absence of an articulate voice on the part of the masses, the best do not and cannot remain the best, the wise cease to be wise. It is impossible for highbrows to secure a monopoly of such knowledge as must be used for the regulation of common affairs. . . . The man who wears the shoes knows best that it pinches and where it pinches, even if the expert shoemaker is the best judge of how the trouble is to be remedied. (PP [LW2:364]; cf. E$_3$ [LW7:251]; DEA [LW11:219])

This all-important passage is located in chapter 6, where he discusses the problem of method. Among the many arguments Dewey makes in that chapter, one of the chief claims he advances is that the hypotheses we form for responding to problems are only as good as the methods we employ—that is, the extent to which the methods make us receptive to data from various sectors of the environment. But problems themselves, as he understands, frame and guide our inquiry; they imply the existence of a complex horizon of value and meaning that is now fractured and in need of creative valuation to restore continuity. When we take this into consideration, his point in the passage above is not simply that without the input from the wearer of shoes the shoemaker will respond in such a way that would not address the existing pinch. Rather, without input from the individual experiencing the pinch, the expert shoemaker will not have the subject matter to initiate or guide his inquiry.

Unlike Lippmann, who elevates the role of experts—suggesting that they give shape to problems that need to be addressed—Dewey views their position as ancillary to that of citizens. As he says of experts: "[T]heir expertness is not shown in framing and executing policies, but in discovering and making known the facts upon which the [inquiry] depends" (PP [LW1:365]). Dewey is making two critical points here that are not easily discernible because of the brevity of the sentence. The first point is that expertise, properly understood, is always indexed to a more "technical" field of investigation. In this view, experts come to gain cognitive authority and so become bearers of knowledge because of the audience with which they engage and interact. Citizens are thus authorities just to the extent that it is their problems that create the framework in which expertise functions. And the complexity and texture of those problems, Dewey maintains, come into view through a discursive exchange among citizens that draws out existing and emerging concerns and worries (which are themselves not necessarily in harmony). All of this helps them determine what they will make of the information provided (SSSC [LW6:64–67]), but it also means that there will rarely be complete agreement on who the experts are and this will cut against any argument for blind deference.

The second point of the sentence is to indicate that if something like "expertise" of political affairs exists, it will have to emerge from the public. In other words, how citizens understand information is an issue about the ends to which they are moving as a political community, and this can emerge only through deliberation and not externally to that process. Central to this process are questions not merely about how we understand the problem from the outset (e.g., who are the subjects of this problem? what may be the long-term results if the problem is allowed to persist?), but about the implication of various proposals suggested to alleviate the problem (e.g., what are the value or economic trade-offs in choosing this or that proposal?). As he explains:

"Anything that may be called knowledge . . . marks a question answered, a difficulty disposed of, a confusion cleared up" (QC [LW4:181]). So for Dewey then, answering these questions—that is, arriving at knowledge—implies a kind of collective artisanship to social inquiry that draws on the specific experiences of individuals, facts about the problem in question, and potential risks of action. Hence he explains that policy experts cannot "secure a monopoly of such knowledge as must be used for the regulation of common affairs. In the degree in which they become a specialized class they are shut off from knowledge of the needs which they are supposed to serve" (PP [LW2:364]). Since citizens are uniquely situated to offer knowledge of their own experiences, their role in the design and implementation of policies is unavoidable (and rightfully so) if we are to address the problem at hand. "For the tools of social inquiry," Dewey explains, "will be clumsy as long as they are forged in places and under conditions remote from contemporary events" (PP [LW2:347]).

The significance Dewey accords deliberation among citizens yields two points. First, as he explains in *Liberalism and Social Action* of 1935, deliberation works to bring "conflicts [among citizens] out into the open where their special claims can be seen and appraised" in understanding the depth and complexity of political problems and policy proposals (LSA [LW11:55]). "The very heart of political democracy," he says elsewhere, "is adjudication of social difference by an exchange of views" (CLT [LW15:273]).[63] To say that deliberation brings conflict out into the open is not to deny that one result of this process may be a deepening of dissonance. As I argued in chapter 4, Dewey is clear that after abandoning Hegelian idealism, his interest in harmonizing the disparate features of social life remained, but it had to proceed on "empirical grounds."[64] Given how he understands the relationship between contingency and experience discussed in chapter 2, his use of the term "empirical grounds" implies that cooperative inquiry may reveal to us that the ends we seek are at odds with what the social and natural world will allow. Although in this context we engage in deliberation with the hope of constructing policy proposals that both respond to the problem and in doing so sublimate values that otherwise conflict, we must not lose sight of the fact that for Dewey this is itself a hypothesis that may go unrealized.[65] As he says: "Differences of opinion in the sense of differences of judgment as to the course which it is best to follow, the policy which it is best to try out, will still exist" (PP [LW2:362]). But he continues, indicating how he views the centrality of deliberation: "But opinion in the sense of beliefs formed and held in the absence of evidence will be reduced in quantity and importance. No longer will views generated in view of special situations be frozen into absolute standards and masquerade as eternal truths" (PP [LW2:362]). Second, deliberation functions to give shape to the very purpose of expertise in precisely the way described above.

Coextensive with democratic decision-making are both the transformative role that underwrites how we come to understand political problems in their various dimensions and that contributes to the possibility of forging shared values for action, and the informational purposes of communication in contextualizing expert knowledge.[66] These two elements suggest that lay and expert knowledge gains whatever vitality it has from being forged through a deliberative process that makes each responsive to the other.[67] This connection, Dewey argues, generates legitimate authority—that is, decisions that are permissible and binding. This is what Hilary Putnam rightly calls Dewey's "epistemological defense of democracy," for it means that "without the participation of the public in the formation of . . . policy, it could not reflect the common needs and interests of the society because those needs and interests were known only to the public."[68] Without the participation of citizens—understood by Dewey as substantive input—justification of one's actions would come uncoupled from being accountable to the public. So his point is that unlike other political ideals, democracy makes the practice of reason-giving constitutive to how it handles and legitimizes its ongoing affairs, the result of which is the "full application of intelligence to the solution of social problems"[69]

There is a practical upshot to this reading of Dewey. For example, where decision-making is based less on the continuous input from public hearings, town hall meetings, advisory councils, and other deliberative bodies there is greater reason to be concerned about the ends to which those decisions aim and the background interests from which they proceed. Moreover, there is reason to be equally suspicious of bureaucratic processes that are adverse to expanding decision-making power by taking a bottom-up approach.[70] Of course there may be good reasons not to take such an approach, as for example when we think about the obstacles that limited resources and time pose for political decision-making. Here Lippmann's point about the obstacles to broad-based inclusion is inescapable. But it follows from Dewey's argument that the burden of proof must rest with those who seek less rather than more inclusive arrangements.[71]

We should notice in this regard that Dewey's argument concedes that experts possess information that citizens facing a particular problem do not. He says, for instance, that "it is not necessary that the many should have the knowledge and skill to carry on the needed investigations" (PP [LW2:365]). It follows from this that understanding the intricacies of political problems and the kinds of emerging solutions bespeaks an inequality in both information and skill sets. Instances in which scientists make the public aware of the adverse effects of their current industrial activity on the environment clearly imply special knowledge and skills that do not exist in large measure throughout the population.

Yet, and in contrast to Lippmann, recognizing the epistemic limitations of citizens need not require us to abdicate or substantially diminish the role they ought to serve. Dewey's argument is that policy for what to do, what trade-offs will be made, and where to invest economic and educational resources is an issue that falls to the public precisely because the consequences of those decisions extend beyond the realm of experts. This is precisely why he says in that passage quoted earlier that the wise cease to be wise when they assume authority because the kind of knowledge needed for managing political affairs is a fundamental property of the public. Dewey means this in two senses. The first refers to those cases where local knowledge is needed to contextualize and certify expertise. But he also intends to include those instances in which experts give shape to the problems that are of public concern, but where the response nonetheless falls to the relevant citizenry because to do otherwise would leave them at the mercy of others. This follows from his previous claim that experts removed from common concern will undoubtedly be animated by private interests. To the extent that experts guide political power without taking direction from the public in the form of deliberation, the entire decision-making process loses in legitimacy what it gains in suspicion.

DEMOCRACY AS MANAGING POWER

The considerations above are part of how Dewey understands the historical emergence of modern liberal democracy as a way of broadening the use of political power.[72] In a number of works, for example, he consistently emphasizes the fortuitous emergence of political democracy (PP [LW2: chap. 3]; DEA [LW11:217–225]). By political democracy he means "a mode of government, a specified practice in selecting officials and regulating their conduct as officials" through universal suffrage, that emphasizes the transparency of decision-making (PP [LW2:286]; cf. ED [EW1:227–249]). Despite its contingent emergence, democracy's development nonetheless represents an "effort in the first place to counteract the forces that have so largely determined the possession of rule by accidental and irrelevant factors, and in the second place an effort to counteract the tendency to *employ political power to serve private instead of public ends*" (PP [LW2:287] [emphasis added]; cf. DEA [LW11:224–225]).

Although Dewey does not provide us with a definition of political power, we can nevertheless distill one from his writings. To be clear, in saying that Dewey's account of democracy implies a description of power, I do not mean to suggest that he provides us with a theoretical framework that is currently missing from the literature on power. I therefore do not seek to engage the theoretical complexities that inform the multiple faces of power.[73] Rather, my purpose is to indicate that Dewey's concern with political power helps us understand how he thinks about democracy and how we ought to orient ourselves to its use if it is to be employed legitimately.

In his 1936 address, "Authority and Social Change," at the Harvard Tercentenary Conference of Arts and Sciences, Dewey discusses the relationship between freedom and authority that informed the historical development of liberal democracy. In keeping with his discussions in *The Public and Its Problems* and *Liberalism and Social Action*, he sees liberal democracy emerging in an attempt to block political power from being exercised arbitrarily: "I would not minimize the advance scored in substitution of methods of discussion and conference for the method of arbitrary rule" (LSA [LW11:50]). The use of "arbitrary" functions for him in precisely the way it did in the previous chapter, where we examined his understanding of how specific rights and duties achieve legitimacy. Political power is arbitrary when it cannot be substantively informed by those over whom it will be exercised. This much he explains:

> [Liberal democracy] was also a struggle between groups and classes of individuals—between those who were enjoying the advantages that spring from possession of power to which authoritative right accrues, and individuals who found themselves excluded from the powers and enjoyments to which they felt themselves entitled. The [individualistic] philosophy which transforms this historic and relative struggle into an inherent and fixed conflict between the principle of authority and the principle of freedom tends, when accepted and acted upon, to present authority as purely restrictive power and to leave the exercise of freedom without direction. (ASC [LW11:133]; cf. LSA [LW11: chap. 1])

I shall come back in a moment to precisely how power, for Dewey, implies a corresponding account of freedom. At this juncture, however, we can say that for him political power is not merely restrictive—that is, it does not merely constrain freedom—but more significantly, it makes freedom possible. To be sure, the early rise of liberal democracy did worry about governmental intrusion on freedom, but this, Dewey maintains, was mistakenly interpreted as a "natural antagonism between ruler and ruled" when in fact the true target was abuse of political power (LSA [LW11:8]). Shifting our aim more accurately to this target, this means that authority, insofar as it is bound up with institutional structures that track the concerns of citizens, is not necessarily inimical to freedom. Political power thus refers to both the policing apparatus of communities and the way in which managing collective affairs is coextensive with enabling citizens to determine the area of potential action. Political power is also expressive of both the role individuals play in "forming and directing the activities" of the community to which they belong, and also the possibility that is open to them for "participating according to need in the values" that their community sustains (PP [LW2:328]). As he says above, this is the central advantage that emerges from the "possession of power to which authoritative right accrues."

This emphasis on power means that for Dewey the standard in assessing democracy is not whether it produces consensus or if it meets some distributional criteria regarding goods. Rather, democracy is assessed according to whether it does a better job than other ways of managing collective affairs in preventing power from becoming arbitrary.[74] This comparative approach makes sense from the perspective of Dewey's larger reliance on reason-giving. Alternative reasons must be offered for why democracy is less effective than other regimes for managing power. But we are likely to miss the importance of democracy if it is understood outside the context of "its historic[al] background" (PP [LW2:287]). Indeed, he continues, that when "men . . . damn democratic government absolutely" they usually do so "without comparing it with alternative polities" (PP [LW2:287]). The result is that they implicitly deny that all-important component of social criticism—namely, that "all intelligent political criticism . . . deals not with all-or-none situations, but with practical alternatives; an absolutistic indiscriminate attitude, whether in praise or blame, testifies to the heat of feeling rather than the light of thought" (PP [LW2:304]).

As Dewey describes it, democracy configures the political landscape differently, so as to keep in view the problem of arbitrary power. It defines membership not simply by virtue of the actual participation with which we engage in determining social possibilities, but also by the potential participation that remains open to us if need so arises. He makes this point in "Democracy and Educational Administration" of 1937 when he remarks that the "democratic faith in equality is the faith that each individual shall have a chance and opportunity to contribute" (DEA [LW11:220]). The operative thought here is that to the extent that power functions to determine social possibilities, those possibilities cannot be of such a nature that they preclude the future contestability and development of how power functions. Hence the following remark: "The strongest point to be made in behalf of even such rudimentary political forms as democracy has already attained, popular voting, majority rule and so on, is that to some extent they involve a consultation and discussion which uncover social needs and troubles" (PP [LW2:364]). This means that "policies and proposals for social action [must] be treated as working hypotheses, not as programs to be rigidly adhered to and executed" (PP [LW2:362]). That we hold in reserve the power to contest—that is, to initiate the practice of mutual responsiveness—indicates that the legitimacy of decision-making hinges on the extent to which citizens do not feel permanently bound by those decisions in the face of new and different political changes. Of course Lippmann would not deny this, but he is unable to flesh out a meaningful view of contestation that relies on the necessary input of the public.

From this follow two implications about how Dewey understands democratic governance. The first is an acknowledgment that insofar as power is social we will rarely escape from being subjected to how it functions. There is a habitual dimension to the functioning of social life that does not require our active involvement at every moment (PP [LW2:334–336]; cf. HNC [MW14: chaps. 4–5]). I take him to mean that power will often work on and through us for purposes of efficiency and productivity, leaving us to direct our cognitive interventions elsewhere. "Thus man," he says, "is not merely *de facto* associated, but he *becomes* a social animal in the make-up of his ideas, sentiments and deliberate behavior. *What* he believes, hopes for and aims at is the outcome of association and intercourse" (PP [LW2:251] [original emphases]).

The formulation is intentionally broad. Dewey is sensitive to the fact that society's functioning will often require us to be habituated for its stability. This may include, in contrast to Wolin's view, reliance on hierarchical relationships such as we see, for example, in the management of schools and government agencies. As scholars of social capital underscore, political institutions must involve a level of trust among participants if those institutions are to function without perpetual oversight.[75] As an earlier contributor to the social capital debates, Dewey understands that trust and habituation are the invisible institutions of society that make social coordination possible.[76] But that society may include hierarchies does not mean we are left to the mercy of how they function. That is, our trust is never completely passive, precisely because it implies an active reflexive interaction with those institutional arrangements. The fact that power exists in society does not necessarily imply that its use is illegitimate.

The second point says that to the extent that the first holds, the possibility must exist for sharing in and regulating the uses to which power will be put. Having no way to express grievances, for instance, against one's parents, bureaucratic policies, or state action implies not merely the incorrect working of power but relationships of domination. This point is of critical importance because it addresses John Patrick Diggins' criticism of Dewey specifically and democracy more generally. As he argues: "Democracy offers no guarantee that power will not become alienated from its legitimate source."[77] The quest for certainty implicit in this statement is far too strong for Dewey. No such guarantee can be provided. But taking a comparative approach, however, we might say that democracy offers better safeguards than other political ideals. As Dewey explains, the "two facts that each one is influenced in what he does and enjoys and in what he becomes by the institutions under which he lives, and that therefore he shall have, in a democracy, a voice in shaping them, are the passive and active sides of the same fact" (DEA [LW11:218]). To say that one shall have a voice—earlier he used the term "opportunity"—is to fracture participation itself into active and passive elements. The first refers to when individuals are literally vocal and participate in the use of power, while the other denotes a background condition in which the possibility for voice informs our orientation to political power from the outset even as we are being shaped by that power. The latter is a security mechanism to ensure that political power does not degenerate into a system that places us at the arbitrary will of another. (As I will argue in the final section below, it is the latter feature that is central to Dewey's description of the public.)

There is a stronger point here, I think, to be inferred from Dewey's position. His account prevents us, as Henry Richardson rightly worries, from "putting the day-to-day routines of administrators on par with the habits of autonomous individuals."[78] To do this may blind us to the fact that we have simply been "socialized to go on" with the way things are. To be sure, Dewey's language of habituation may potentially contribute to this worry.[79] Or the language of habituation may conceal the fact that Dewey simply shifts the burden to the role of mutual trust in sustaining the relationship between the lay public and experts, political officials, or bureaucratic structures. But as James Bohman highlights, "while trust is involved . . . it cannot bear the primary explanatory burden of explaining how the democratic and experimental cognitive division of labor is possible."[80] In my reading, Dewey does not need to rely heavily on mutual trust; in fact, to do so is to idealize a feature of modern democracy that, while important, simply cannot do all of the work that is necessary for sustaining political life. By making the management of political power central to his outlook, however, we can simultaneously absorb two important features of modern societies without any obvious cost to democracy and address both Richardson's and Bohman's worries. The first feature is the epistemic division of labor, which can be advantageous from the perspective of forming public policy, and the second is the presence of hierarchically organized relationships that can have gains in terms of efficiency and productivity.

On this reading, it follows from Dewey's argument that any gains we could potentially receive from the specific functioning of experts or the presence of specific hierarchical relationships must always be assessed, both before and after, based on whether such gains potentially leave us open to the abuse of power. Seeking to limit precisely the extent to which the routines of administrators and legislators are taken for granted, Dewey says the following in *Freedom and Culture* of 1939: "Tradition may result in habits that obstruct observation of what is actually going on; a mirage may be created in which republican institutions are seen as if they were in full vigor after they have gone into decline" (FC [LW13:102]). I take Dewey to mean that we must not rely simply on an ex post inquiry of specific abuses of power. In fact, it may often be the case that because we take the proper functioning of our institutions or the political goodwill of our legislators, experts, or bureaucratic agencies for granted, we become inattentive to corruption and misuse of power. His argument thus commits us to invoke ex ante the principle of avoiding such abuses as we structure and revise our institutions. The ex ante invocation forces us to focus on the extent to which such institutions or reforms do not emerge from a process that meaningfully involves those who will be affected in precisely the way Dewey indicated above.[81]

Tying the practice of reason-giving to Dewey's larger concern with managing and participating in the use of power entails that we look beyond the extent to which citizens are committed to, and institutional structures embody, the epistemic virtues of democracy. Both here and elsewhere his argument for the importance of inquiry has focused on its epistemic benefits to problem-solving—benefits that include a commitment to fallibilism, openness, testing consequences against expectations, and sensitivity to evidence and the texture of the landscape in which one acts. All of these elements are about how one cognitively orients oneself to problem-solving. And the virtues of inquiry, as indicated in previous chapters, provide resources for criticizing those who seem unwilling to engage in a deliberative process that is reciprocal. For Dewey, in such instances the issue, as I have said throughout, is not what you will say to those individuals but what you will say about them. Contemporary pragmatists such as Cheryl Misak, Jeffrey Stout, and Robert Talisse have picked up on the benefits of this point from an epistemic perspective.[82] Unfortunately, we need to say more if we are concerned about contemporary politics, since the absence of epistemic virtues does not relieve us from having to deal with such people or rely on institutions of which they are a part that affect our life chances. The account of reason-giving these thinkers above offer and which they share with deliberative democrats says very little regarding what Archon Fung refers to as the "decidedly nonideal circumstances that characterize contemporary politics."[83]

Given Dewey's concern to diminish the use of arbitrary power as I have construed it, we are not only positioned to focus on the fact that individuals fail to deploy the epistemic virtues of inquiry, but we can also highlight why they refuse. From his perspective this will not always relate to epistemic vices, but will also point more directly to material, social, and institutional incentives that discourage one from engaging in deliberation and genuine problem-solving. Such conditions highlight the extent to which power has become concentrated in the hands of a few to the disadvantage of broad-based inclusion and allow us to recognize, at the very least, when we have exhausted the quest to transform our institutions from within and must now stand in a more oppositional relationship to them. It may very well be the case that various incentives undermine the necessity of mutual responsiveness and block the road of collective inquiry. The result is that citizens will need to create, through protest or violence, a new space where inquiry may once again thrive in the service of collective problem-solving. Dewey's argument on this point relates more to his description of the public properly speaking, but it is important to flag it at this stage since it helps us see the kind of normative work his concern with managing power does and how it potentially enables radical transformation in practice.

FREEDOM AS NONDOMINATION

At several junctures I have invoked the language of freedom in discussing Dewey's attentiveness to power. I argued that he is concerned with a vision of freedom that points to nonarbitrary power and thus to nondomination. If this is correct, then freedom itself, when realized, implies an account of power on the part of agents. Let me clarify this view more carefully and so tie the realization of freedom more tightly to nondomination before turning to Dewey's account of the public.

When Dewey discusses freedom he often emphasizes its positive dimension. For example, in his *Ethics* of 1932 he argues that "freedom in its practical and moral sense is connected with possibility of growth, learning, and modification of character, just as is responsibility" (E₃ [LW7:305]; cf. HNC [MW14: chap. 25]). Here freedom is understood as reflective self-control— that is, the ability to engage in evaluation of one's actions, proposals, and life projects to assess their feasibility. As we have seen in previous chapters, reflective self-control implies a perceptual sensitivity not merely to the inner workings of one's character and the life experiences it suggests, but to one's larger social horizon. Freedom is measured, Dewey says in *Human Nature and Conduct* of 1922, in the ability to "foresee future objective alternatives and ... by deliberation to choose one of them and thereby weight its chances in the struggle for future existence" (HNC [MW14:214]). So understood, "positive freedom is not a native gift or endowment but is acquired" (E₃ [LW7:306]). In being acquired, he says, it requires "freedom of mind and whatever degree of freedom of action and experience is necessary to produce freedom of intelligence" (DEA [LW11:220]).

When Dewey's conception of freedom, particularly this positive character, is discussed what is usually emphasized is the connection between reflective self-control and human growth. The tendency is to then investigate what he means by human growth, its content, and to ask if it can it be rendered intelligible when shorn of a thick ethical notion of the good. But as I have argued in previous chapters, he is more than capable of discussing freedom without such a thick vision of the good. Indeed, he is suspicious of such a unitary notion.

More importantly, however, this way of engaging his positive notion of freedom often obscures the feature of democracy that he believes makes reflective self-control possible in the first instance. The aim is not to diminish this positive character, but to understand the larger horizon in which it is framed. Here I mean the very orientation that we are capable of assuming in relation to political institutions. When he discusses, for example, the relationship between freedom and organizational structures in *Human Nature and Conduct* he signals this point: "Organization tends ... to become rigid and to limit freedom. In addition to security and energy in action, novelty, risk and change are ingredients of the freedom which men desire" (HNC [MW14:212]). The possibility for changing the ways in which the organizational structures of the state are managed marks the difference, he contends, between "the free and the enslaved" (HNC [MW14:212]; cf. POF [LW3:92–114]). Dewey invokes this contrast most clearly in 1908 when he writes:

> *The Two Senses of Freedom.*—In its external aspect, freedom is negative and formal. It signifies freedom *from* subjection to the will and control of others; exemption from bondage; release from servitude; capacity to act without being exposed to direct obstructions or interferences from others. It means a clear road, cleared of impediments, for action. It contrasts with the limitations of prisoner, slave, and serf, who have to carry out the will of others. (E$_2$ [MW5:392])

Connecting the distinction between the free and the enslaved to the possibility of change means that where we do not have the opportunity to redescribe the boundaries of such organizations, we are not free. To be enslaved, then, does not imply a diminution in choices and the ability to act on those choices. This is not a question of exercising one's freedom understood as reflective self-control that is somehow now obstructed by the actions of some person or institutions. Dewey's point is more expansive. To be enslaved denotes a prior and more general condition in which the choices we make are framed from the outset by institutions or practices that preclude the possibility of *genuine* change. Indeed, it is his profound interest in human growth that prompts this deeper elucidation of what can potentially undercut its realization.

What exactly does this mean? What does "genuine," as I have used it above, explain about Dewey's position? The best way to elucidate his point is to think about the institution of slavery that he invokes in the passage above. And notice in the quoted passage that he slides from understanding negative freedom as actual interference to understanding negative freedom as being subjected to the will and control of others. We can clarify this latter description and so the invocations of slavery with a brief appeal to Philip Pettit's work on domination. As Pettit explains, although slavery is a terrible institution it can exist without actual interference:

> I may be the slave of another—for example, to go to the extreme case—without actually being interfered with in any of my choices. It may just happen that my master is of a kindly and non-interfering disposition. Or it may just happen that I am cunning or fawning enough to be able to get away with doing whatever I like. I suffer domination to the extent that I have a master.[84]

"Master" in this instance denotes a person or institution that has the capacity to *arbitrarily* exercise power over me. Where a master exists there will always already be a limit on the extent to which I can engage in novelty, risk, and change of the political practices and institutions to which I belong. These limits are beyond my power to influence, and indeed may reveal themselves at any unspecified moment. This is simply to say that the possibility of change is chimerical and so not genuine.

To enjoy freedom as nondomination means, for both Dewey and Pettit, that I am not subjected to the will of another under *this* specific temporal order or *any* future temporal order. For both, this "futural" dimension of nondomination is what makes novelty, risk, and change of political practices and institutions a genuine possibility. Consider Pettit's words once more:

> To enjoy . . . non-interference with the security of non-domination is to satisfy that condition plus a further modal condition: it is also not to be interfered with in those possible worlds where the attitudes of powerful agents vary, or my in-gratiating capacities are lessened, or my native cunning is not what it was, and so on. It is to remain resiliently possessed of non-interference across this range of possible worlds, as well as in the worlds originally considered.[85]

Perhaps we can give more texture to the point I am making here with specific reference to Dewey's understanding of freedom. Consider Dewey's 1937 essay "Freedom":

> The immediate result of the condition under which the people of the United States won their independence was, then, to identify freedom for the most part with political freedom, and to think of even this form of freedom largely in a negative way. Its positive expression was confined pretty much to the right to vote, to choose public officials, and thereby share indirectly in the formation of public policies, and perchance to be elected to office oneself. The ballot became the glorified symbol of freedom and every Fourth of July speech conjured up the spectacle of the procession of freemen wending their way to the polls to exercise the priceless gift of freedom. Meantime, the conditions under which citizens exercised the right of suffrage, conditions which in larger measure so circumscribed and controlled the right as to reduce it for many, perhaps for the masses, to something like an empty formality, were neglected. Corruption became rife; bosses and factional political machines managed from behind the scenes by bosses grew and flourished. . . . But the present political situation as well as the historic past should convince us that exclusive identification of freedom with political freedom means in the end the loss of even political freedom. (F [LW11:248]; cf. PP [LW2:298–299])

Dewey's worry in this passage, which has parallels elsewhere in his writings, is nicely indexed to the importance he accords change in understanding freedom, what I have referred to earlier as the ability to contest and influence the development of how power functions. Having the late nineteenth and early twentieth century of America as his background, he speaks of the reification of conditions that "circumscribed and controlled" the right of suffrage and made its purpose empty. Both control and circumspection, he maintains, resulted from the emergence of "bosses and factional political machines" whose distinct interests framed the ends to which political democracy was put. Here he is describing a situation in which the interests of the state and its institutional structures came unhinged from the demos as such (PP [LW2:255]). In this instance, to appropriate Pettit's language, power is exercised in a way that "tracks . . . the power-holder's personal welfare or world-view . . . rather than the welfare and world-view of the public."[86] For this reason, Dewey cautions us not to completely identify the protection of freedom with the institutional elements of democracy. If freedom understood as reflective self-control is going to be as robust as we often intend, it must imply the prospect of giving shape to the area of social possibilities. And when this does not exist, "political democracy is insecure" (DEA [LW11:225]). To be able to shape the area of social possibilities means that the space of political reflection in which citizens work is neither controlled nor circumscribed by the intentions of bosses, whether we describe those bosses based on their economic status or their intellectual abilities.

Negatively, this means we must always be cautious about how we orient ourselves to our political institutions. As Dewey says of the state, it is "something to be scrutinized, investigated, [and] searched for. Almost as soon as its form is stabilized, it needs to be re-made" (PP [LW2:255]). We must be careful how we understand this claim, lest we describe the relationship between the demos and the state from the outset as oppositional. As we have seen in Wolin's case, this can only erode any faith we might otherwise place in the government.

But there is a more realistic and moderate position we can assume. In saying that the state will need to be remade Dewey does not intend for us to abandon the institutions wholesale. Rather, his claim is that those institutions must be receptive to revision and expansion. They must be receptive in this way not simply because political problems are always about us, but also because, as Ian Shapiro explains, "power need not be abused, but it often is, and it is wise for democrats to guard against that possibility."[87] From a Deweyan perspective, the proviso "need not be" is what prevents us from describing the state and the demos in oppositional terms, even as it encourages us to "get rid of the ideas that lead us to believe that democratic conditions automatically maintain themselves, or that they can be identified with fulfillment of prescriptions laid down in a constitution" (FC [LW13:87]).

This statement from Dewey's *Freedom and Culture* is the closest he gets to Wolin's more contemporary position without falling prey to its problems, and is advanced, somewhat ironically, in the context of a discussion about the relationship between totalitarianism and democracy. His point in this context is to immediately disrupt, as we have seen in Wolin's own work, our congratulatory attitude toward democratic institutions. Dewey specifically rejects the claim that totalitarian regimes emerge in countries where a scientific spirit never existed, since some form of mutual responsiveness is essential to political governance (FC [LW13:87–88]). However, drawing a sharp divide between totalitarian and democratic regimes, with the former representing the absence of the scientific spirit and the latter embodying this spirit, blocks us from evaluating "what it is that commends, at least for a time, totalitarian conditions to persons otherwise intelligent and honorable" (FC [LW13:88]). But it also, and perhaps more significantly for Dewey, obscures the fact that our own institutions, even when formed in the name of democracy, may conspire against our best ideals:

> Beliefs of this sort[—namely, that democratic institutions maintain themselves automatically—]merely divert attention from what is going on, just as the patter of the prestidigitator enables him to do things that are not noticed by those whom he is engaged in fooling. For what is actually going on may be the formation of conditions that are hostile to any kind of democratic liberties. This would be too trite to repeat were it not that so many persons in the high places of business talk as if they believed or could get others to believe that the observance of formulae that have become ritualistic are effective safeguards of our democratic heritage. (FC [LW13:87])

His point, consistent with his earlier reflections in *The Public and Its Problems* and *Liberalism and Social Action*, is not that such ritualistic activities or the institutions associated with them are necessarily hostile to freedom and so will become a source of domination. After all, just as belief for him must be justified, so too must doubt. His claim is that even the best institutions may themselves become the locus of abuse precisely because their proper functioning does not require an unmediated use of power by ordinary citizens. Our faith in those institutions, then, must never run so deep that it prevents us from seeing the extent to which they degenerate into something antidemocratic.

THE PERMANENCE OF CONTINGENCY:
ON THE PRECARIOUS AND STABLE PUBLIC

Thus far I have argued that for Dewey the relationship between experts and citizens is grounded in a relationship of mutual responsiveness in order for them to understand political problems and frame policy proposals. I have maintained that the emphasis he attaches to mutual responsiveness is fundamentally a concern about preventing the use of power from becoming arbitrary. I have also elucidated his concern with both the actual involvement we have in managing power and the future possibilities that are open to us in managing the uses to which power will be put. The latter is bound up with a specific view of freedom as nondomination. Keeping this account of freedom in view allows us to do two things simultaneously: we can attach practical and normative weight to political democracy, in contrast to Wolin's position, even while we hold at bay the desire to completely identify the security of freedom with the institutions of political democracy.

This moderate position that Dewey carves out is most clearly embodied in how he understands the function of the public and its relationship to the state. His account envisions the public, I argue, as the permanent space of contingency in the sense that there can be no a priori delimitation, except as it emerges from individuals and groups that coalesce in the service of problem-solving and that therefore require the administrative power of the state to address their concerns. This description of the public envisions it as standing in a directive and supportive relationship to the state and its representative and administrative institutions. But insofar as the state is resistant to transformation because of ossification, the public then functions in a more oppositional role that builds its power external to the state. It is to this final issue that we must now turn.

CONTINUITY BETWEEN THE PUBLIC AND THE STATE

The obvious place to begin is with Dewey's understanding of the public as evidenced in chapter 1 of *The Public and Its Problems*. "The public," says Dewey, "consists of all those who are affected by the indirect consequences of transactions to such an extent that it is deemed necessary to have those consequences systematically cared for" (PP [LW2:245–246]). The emergence of the public is prompted by a set of transactions within society whose impact on a group of individuals is of such a nature that it requires focused action beyond what they themselves can provide. This need not imply that the association of individuals that comes to comprise the public was in existence prior to the problem; it will often be the case that the indirect consequences of transactions now perceived as problematic determine the members that make up the public.

This should not be confusing if we insert a distinction to clarify the description. For Dewey, society is an arrangement of individuals who simultaneously belong to distinct and overlapping associations, what he refers to in his 1908 edition of *Ethics* as "civil society." Civil society, he explains there, "represents those forms of associated life which are orderly and authorized, because constituted by individuals in the exercise of their rights, together with those special forms which protect and insure them" (E$_2$ [MW5:404]). In civil society, information and pressures get communicated across those associations. In such pluralistic conditions, problems and conflicts are bound to emerge, some of which may very well come from the functioning of governmental regulation or activities of the market economy. The result of such problems is that groups within civil society are politicized and so become a public. To say they become politicized only means that indirect consequences have affected individuals to such an extent that a distinct apparatus is needed to address their concerns. The associated group that emerges may already be in existence, albeit in a nonpolitical mode (e.g., religious organizations, professional associations, or cultural organizations), in civil society. Or it may be the case that the public is comprised of multiple associations that were already in existence, having no discernible relationship to each other until the problem emerged. The problem helps focus what is shared and provides the point of departure for collective problem-solving. If Dewey is to remain consistent with his general account of inquiry, it must follow that a shared problem does not yet imply agreement on a particular resolution or what to do. This would have to emerge from a deliberative process. If this seems to be ambiguous, as Matthew Festenstein argues,[88] I am inclined to say that for Dewey it inheres in the nature of democratic politics. For Dewey, we cannot determine prior to deliberation either what the response should be or the trade-offs that may potentially be involved.

A concern may nonetheless emerge at precisely this juncture regarding Dewey's account of the public. On the one hand, he speaks of "the public." Yet he seems quite clear that multiple groups and associations of individuals advance claims requiring systematic care. The former suggests a homogenous domain in which the whole of society is directed through a deliberative mechanism, while the latter points to a site that is internally plural in which deliberation is context-specific. As Westbrook observes, the ambiguity is something Dewey never addresses. But as he explains, and here I agree, this issue can be clarified in a way that is consistent with Dewey's description of the public: "*The* Public was, at most, a collective noun designating plural publics that concerned themselves with the indirect consequences of particular forms of associated activity."[89] We can go a bit further than Westbrook's already helpful point. Using a collective noun, Dewey is articulating a politicized domain between civil society and the government in which claims regarding the need for systematic care are mutually acknowledged among citizens who consolidate their identity for that reason. Because for Dewey there is no privileged access to mutually recognized concerns or solutions—that is, they are built up discursively—all members stand on equal footing. Here we can do justice to his earlier claim that citizens must have a voice in shaping institutions under which they live or the decisions by which they will be bound. "The public" becomes a politicized sphere in which citizens seek to translate the claims and grievances of specific publics into state power.

In explaining the meaning of systematic care, Dewey invokes the image of the state precisely to institutionalize claims built up from *the* public sphere that consolidate into *a* public. He writes the following: "[T]he state is the organization of the public effected through officials for the protection of the interests shared by its members" (PP [LW2:256]). So the translation of claims and grievances into state power requires officers and administrators who are charged as trustees of a public, holding fiduciary power: "Officials are those who look out for and take care of the interests thus affected" (PP [LW2:246]). In his understanding of the public sphere, the state does not necessarily need to find its organization through national officials. That is, we need to allow for the formation of both a particular public whose interests and concerns extend no further than a small town and one that extends across multiple boundaries and territories. In either case, Dewey imagines, as Jürgen Habermas does much later, that publics cannot rule by themselves, but must be articulated through a distinct administrative apparatus in which power is physically located, what he refers to as the officials and representatives. As Habermas writes on precisely this point: "The power available to the administration alters its aggregate condition as long as it remains tied in with a democratic opinion- and will-formation that does not just monitor the exercise of political power ex post facto but more or less programs it as well."[90] For Dewey, this means that publics, whether on the local or national level, do not just supervise how that power functions, but in many respects determine and influence the ends to which it will be put: "A public articulated and operating through representative officers is the state; there is no state without a government, but also there is none without the public" (PP [LW2:277]). Hence the state, from his perspective, is a "secondary form of association" (PP [LW2:279]). In other words, although the activity of political institutions—that is, the formation of laws, statutes, and binding regulations, or the establishment of administrative agencies, for example—will often be the result of those officials and representatives, this only comes about for Dewey and Habermas because the direction and purpose of these institutions is determined elsewhere. Although functioning at the fringes of the state, the public sphere is nonetheless configured as the site from which opinion- and will-formation originate and which is institutionalized via the state.

Dewey's account of the relationship between publics and the state specifically rejects the notion of a unified deliberative public that makes claims in the name of "the people." This is yet another reason for thinking that "the public," in his view, refers to a collective noun of unity and difference. He agrees in this regard with Iris Marion Young's claim that "processes of deliberation in complex mass society must be understood as subjectless . . . decentered" and so indeterminate.[91] This much Dewey explains when he says that scholars have looked for the state in the wrong place:

> They have sought for the key to the nature of the state in the field of agencies, in that of doers of deeds, or in some will or purpose back of deeds. They have sought to explain the state in terms of authorship. Ultimately all deliberate choices proceed from somebody in particular; acts are performed by somebody, and all arrangements and plans are made by somebody in the most concrete sense of somebody. Some John Doe and Richard Roe figure in every transaction. . . . The quality presented is not authorship but authority, the authority of recognized consequences to control the behavior which generates and averts extensive and enduring results of weal and woe. (PP [LW2:247])

His point here is that indexing the state *as* state to particular authors who comprise a public undercuts the extent to which the public sphere itself can function as a sensory network to register emerging problems that can then be managed by state institutions. Focusing on authorship for understanding the state fixes the character of the latter and imputes to the public sphere a substantively unified identity that in Dewey's own account is simply out of step with a pluralistic society. But if we understand the public as a "subjectless" sphere, then we are better able to see publics as the expression of "recognized consequences" among its members to "control the behavior which generates and averts extensive and enduring results of weal and woe."

So for Dewey there can be no permanent closure of the public sphere itself with a fixed identity from which the state can be inferred, even though there will be specific delimitations of particular publics. The latter—delimitations of particular publics—implies that state institutions and the substantive decisions that follow from those institutions (at both national and local levels of governance) will very well come into existence in response to the specific claims of *a* public, as for instance, those arguing for health-care reform (national), more equitable distribution of monies for public education (national and local), or better safeguards on businesses whose waste by-products are contaminating a local reservoir (local). The former point, that which relates to the public sphere as such, means that insofar as the claims of a particular public are instantiated in the state, they cannot exclude the possibility of addressing developing needs that require systematic care. To be sure, all developing needs may not be legitimate in this regard, but the first step in assessing their legitimacy will have to rest with the extent to which addressing those needs might potentially implicate us in relationships of domination. But insofar as reason-giving is central to how democracy conducts its ongoing affairs and is employed to potentially avoid the arbitrary uses of power, Dewey's point is that the public sphere is that site in which the democratic state attempts to see widely and feel deeply in order to make informed judgments.[92]

Dewey concedes, in this regard, that his account of the state is vague (PP [LW2:274]). "There is," he explains, "no sharp and clear line which draws itself . . . like the line left by a receding high tide, just where a public comes into existence which has interests so significant that they must be looked after and administered by special agencies, or governmental officers" (PP [LW2:275]). As he says, "there is often room for dispute. The line of demarcation between actions left to private initiative and management and those regulated by the state has to be discovered experimentally" (PP [LW2:275]; cf. PPI [LW2:375–376]). That is, the scope of the state understood in this sense "is something to be critically and experimentally determined" (PP [LW2:281]).

But here once again the openness of the state itself is required if we are not to court domination or become inattentive to enduring consequences affecting people that require action beyond what they can provide. An "experimentally determined state" means that its identity is always evolving and changing via the demands of multiple publics. And it may be necessary that we create institutional mechanisms (e.g., courts and bodies of arbitration) to partly assess and decide when the intervention of the state is necessary. Such institutions, as Shapiro points out, will simultaneously involve assessing and managing "conflicting claims about how pertinent interests are affected."[93] But all of this indicates that for Dewey, a democratic public sphere and by that fact a democratic state is radically inclusive, even though such inclusiveness means the emergence of distinct and exclusive publics.

Understanding the democratic public sphere and the state as undetermined is not based on a principle to which Dewey independently subscribes. It is important to see that this conclusion follows directly from the emphasis he places on reason-giving as being central to democratic legitimacy. Recall that democracy's comparative advantage is that it rejects the presumptive belief that citizens ought to defer to individuals or institutions that seemingly occupy some privileged position of authority. This is because from the perspective of knowledge formation, there can be no such privileged position. As a result, no one is exempt from having to participate in the practice of giving and asking for reasons. The upshot is that the very act of using political power and what the exercise of power becomes (e.g., institutions and/or laws) is coextensive with and based upon the principle of conditionality. The necessity of inclusiveness and openness follows directly from this principle and makes the "who" of the public sphere and state contingent, despite the relative stability that comes from distinct publics. Dewey's argument, as I understand it, is premised on what Claude Lefort identifies as "two apparently contradictory principles: on the one hand, power emanates from the people; on the other, it is the power of nobody [in particular]. And democracy thrives on this contradiction. Whenever the latter risks being resolved or is resolved, democracy is either close to destruction or already destroyed."[94]

Notwithstanding, what should be observed about Dewey's discussion of the public is the seamless continuity he draws between it and the state. As indicated earlier, when he says the state must be experimentally discovered he does not mean, for instance, that the United States, as the site of coercive power and from which legally binding decisions for society come, must be restructured. His point is more practical and centers on the substantive developments that need to take place within the state in order to respond to the public. "The public," he explains, "as far as organized by means of officials and material agencies to care for the extensive and enduring indirect consequences of transactions between persons is the *Populus*" (PP [LW2:246]). And when the "public . . . is involved in making social arrangements like passing laws, enforcing a contract, conferring a franchise, it still acts through concrete persons. The persons are now officers, representatives of a public" (PP [LW2:247]). He is not denying that the state is already in existence and functioning according to a number of preexisting imperatives—imperatives relating to economic stability, foreign relations, and domestic welfare—that are themselves the result of publics. We cannot deny, he writes, that "actual states exhibit traits which perform the function that has been stated and which serve as marks of anything to be called a state" (PP [LW2:260]). His point, however, is that such preexisting imperatives must be sufficiently flexible to absorb and address the demands of emerging publics. This is precisely why the emergence of publics should be interpreted as providing guidance for institutional transformation, but not as ultimately fixing the nature of those institutions. As Westbrook explains: "Consequently, *the* State was also a plural phenomenon, a collection of publics organized into representative institutions (though presumably one institution or collection of officials might serve several publics)."[95] Such a description allows for Dewey to envision, at least ideally, a fluid connection between the public and the state.

DISCONTINUITY BETWEEN THE PUBLIC AND THE STATE

In many ways Dewey's discussion of the public as laid out above has as its goal an inclusive state apparatus. This fits with his position more generally that their can be no *de facto* opposition to the institutions of the state. Experimentally determining the nature and scope of the state means we are attempting to envision supplemental appendages that need to be added to address the concerns of a particular public. But we are also implicitly testing the extent to which preexisting institutions are amenable to transformation. Insofar as such institutions are not, Dewey envisions the public sphere as standing in a more oppositional rather than supportive and guiding relationship to the state. In this instance, the claims of specific publics may ultimately point to the entrenched resistance and limitation of state institutions. As he explains of political development, "progress is not steady and continuous. Retrogression is as periodic as advance" (PP [LW2:254]).

In this context, the public sphere potentially stands in an uneasy relationship to the state, especially in its attempts to democratize the functioning of the state. Dewey captures this point where he worries about the extent to which state institutions ossify around a set of interests and so become unresponsive to new and emerging publics, the result of which generates a revolutionary impulse.

> These changes [relating to associated relationships] are extrinsic to political forms which, once established, persist of their own momentum. The new public which is generated remains long inchoate, unorganized, because it cannot use inherited political agencies. The latter, if elaborate and well institutionalized, obstruct the organization of the new public. They prevent that development of new forms of the state which might grow up rapidly were social life more fluid, less precipitated into set political legal molds. To form itself, the public has to break existing political forms. This is hard to do because these forms are

themselves the regular means of instituting change. The public which generated political forms is passing away, but the power and lust of possession remains in the hands of the officers and agencies which the dying public instituted. This is why the change of the form of states is *so often effected only by revolution.* (PP [LW2:254–255] [emphasis added])

We should not understate the importance of this passage in *The Public and Its Problems* precisely because it points to the radical character of Dewey's outlook. His claim is not simply that emerging publics cannot use existing state institutions because they are insufficient to address developing needs. Rather, existing institutions may be inimical to those new needs. Here, we might think, for example, of the legally instantiated power of white males in the American context—power that formed in direct resistance to the demands of women and black Americans seeking more equitable distribution and equal access. We can diversify our examples to include other rebellious groups: labor unions on behalf of workers, environmental organizations, and framers, just to name a few. To be sure, these movements exist on a scale that slides from being reform movements aimed at transformation of legal or institutional norms (e.g., trade unions and green organizations) to radical associations looking to redescribe the value system upon which institutional structures are based (e.g., civil rights movement and women's rights movement). But in all situations, Dewey argues, the claims of the public cannot flow fluidly into the administrative power of the state. Instead, publics must seek to build power externally, the result of which functions as a counterweight to public(s) that are entrenched via the state and wield arbitrary power. I take Nancy Fraser to mean precisely this when she remarks: "These *subaltern counterpublics* . . . are parallel discursive arenas where members of subordinated social groups invent and circulate counterdiscourses, which in turn permit them to formulate oppositional interpretations of their identities, interests, and needs."[96]

Given his larger account, Dewey's point is that the public sphere is always already internally differentiated. That is, the term incorporates both the substantively smooth incorporation of publics into the state, and the possibility of insurgent publics whose character is determined by virtue of state resistance and illegitimate acts of political authority. And they emerge not simply to offer oppositional interpretations of their needs, as Fraser describes, but to see a transformation in the state that substantively addresses those needs. This is precisely why Dewey says in that last sentence that when the power of the state ossifies, transformation often comes about through revolution.

Dewey is clear that much of the transformation in the democratic state will not come from the fluid relationship between the public sphere and state, although he envisions this as a genuine possibility and so sounds strikingly different from Wolin. Nonetheless, radical transformation comes about, he argues—and here he is in agreement with Wolin—from these more insurgent moments. He advances this point in an essay written in 1939, entitled "I Believe," where he specifically discusses the politicized function of civil society and so signals a relationship between these claims and his remarks from *The Public and Its Problems*: "For if history teaches anything it is that judgments regarding the future have been predicated upon the basis of the tendencies that are most conspicuous at the time, while in fact the great social changes which have produced new social institutions have been the cumulative effect of flank movements that were not obvious at the time of their origin" (IB [LW14:96]). The example Dewey offers to illustrate this is of a medieval lord who does not imagine that "the future of society was with the forces that were represented by the humble trader who set up his post under the walls of his castle" (IB [LW14:96]). The picture Dewey is painting is one in which the status of both lord and his seat of power in the castle is radically transformed by a power external to it.

When he uses the language of flank movements and indicates the necessity of disrupting ossified state power from without, I encourage us to read him as describing what we have today come to identify as social movements. Such movements are distinctive precisely because they represent unmediated experiences of power that potentially tilt public discourse in new directions, that envision alternative policy ideas aimed at alleviating specific problems, or that legitimize new forms of collective action that threaten the stability of the state.[97] That Dewey does not say much more about flank movements or these counterpublics than I can elucidate here, or legitimately infer from, should not diminish the fact that they easily find a home in his vision of democracy. More significant, the fact that these counterforces also, for him, emanate from the public sphere means that the state and its institutions are always a fiduciary power, the source of which lies elsewhere and is always in ready position to reclaim power if necessary.

The interpretation of Dewey's view of democracy advanced here derives from his desire to manage power and prevent its use from becoming arbitrary. As I have suggested, this complements and frames his understanding of the relationship between experts and citizens. For Dewey, power may often function without our explicit involvement or control. Nonetheless, the ends to which power will be put cannot be of such a nature that they block the future contestability of how that power functions. Managing political power is not, as he sees it, merely about the range of choices that may exist at any given moment for human beings, but more significantly the ability to initiate change to expand the area in which choice is made possible. To the extent that this possibility is open, freedom remains secure. And to the extent that such possibilities are closed to us, the state apparatus invites a more oppositional relationship between itself and the public sphere from which it otherwise receives its directives. This implies caution about how our institutions function, but not perpetual doubt. The first of these is healthy for a democracy because it guards against our natural tendency to see our political order as settled—a position that will seduce us into believing that existing inequalities and injustices are conditions not to be overcome but rather to which we must resign ourselves. Yet, the second of these—perpetual doubt—can only have a corrosive effect on how we see our political institutions.

Still, it might be said that Dewey's formulations are terribly imprecise. After all, he says nothing about institutions in concrete terms nor does he provide us with a blueprint for managing power relations as such. This worry, I think, misses its mark by wrongly assuming that the only way to speak meaningfully about democracy is through institutions, never realizing that such an approach often preempts precisely the kind of work that democratic citizens are suppose to do for themselves. It also loses sight, as Dewey reminds us, of the reality that there can be no final description of institutional arrangements that will be permanently responsive to problems that plague publics. The moment we believe otherwise, we will have ironically undermined the inclusiveness that ought properly to be the hallmark of democracy.

A more reasonable approach, the one taken here, says the following: By making power and the contestability of how power functions central to democracy, we have found a standard for assessing the construction of new institutions and the revision of institutions already in existence. This is not to say that power exhausts the field of inquiry when it comes to understanding democracy. But as Dewey well knows, many of democracy's problems emanate from situations in which individuals feel that they no longer have control over the forces that govern their lives. Another way to say this is that they feel that they are at the mercy of another's will, whether that is a large corporation, an impersonal school board, or their local politicians. To the extent that government institutions are complicit in this process of political alienation and domination, citizens are well within their rights to rethink the purpose and boundaries of those institutions. Whether or not citizens will do that is entirely another matter and cannot be answered in the abstract. For at the end of the day, it requires courage and the willingness to court danger.

But that democracy makes the practice of reason-giving central to the very essence of problem-solving and legitimacy means that whatever danger we court, it need not necessarily cripple us. In fact, the danger itself points to the openness of democracy—that is, the nonsovereign character of human action that is central to it and which is the hallmark of genuine freedom—and democracy's redemptive possibilities. For Dewey, this is the source of enduring allegiance and political hope. Such hope is what makes democracy under modern conditions of pluralism and complexity at once difficult and necessary if we are to realize a world better than the one we were given. As Dewey says: "The democratic road is the hard one to take. It is the road which places the greatest burden of responsibility on the greatest number of human beings. Backsets and deviations occur and will continue to occur. But that which is its weakness at particular times is its strength in the long course of human history" (FC [LW13:154]).

EPILOGUE

Works of interpretation such as this gain intellectual weight (if they do at all) because they enable us to see ourselves in a different light. They provide us with a picture of a self and a world that we may well want to inhabit. In those moments when we walk the path that a project such as this has laid before us, we may learn something not only about Dewey and what he envisioned for his fellow Americans, but about what may still be possible for us today. In these few concluding pages, let me try to recapitulate the major claim of this project and provide an answer to the following question: Why is Dewey's philosophy still important?

The argument that has developed over the preceding pages is that Dewey's philosophy represents a careful and measured attempt to defend a belief in human agency in a world shorn of ultimate foundations. By human agency I mean that which allows us to make sense of and legitimate our commitments to each other. Dewey's specific efforts develop out of the crisis of religious certainty in late-nineteenth-century America and its impact on perceptions of human agency. His approach, as argued in chapters 1 and 2, sets him apart from thinkers like Charles Hodge, who rejected Darwin out of hand, and the liberal Protestants, whose reformulation of evolution led to a reluctant experimentalism. With Dewey, the meaning of human agency takes on a different look. It emerges from our consequent management of the natural and social world, rather than from an appeal and adherence to antecedent phenomena.

This account of agency, as argued most explicitly in chapter 2, centralizes human inquiry, casting into relief its subtleties. These subtleties make us sensitive to the complexities of the horizon in which inquiry functions.

This is because contingency frames human action and signals the nonsovereign character of human intervention—that is, the belief that we are not wholly masters of our fate. This not only gives a new character to Dewey's philosophy, but places him in a category with thinkers as diverse as Machiavelli and Hannah Arendt, both of whom identify contingency as a fruitful ground for understanding the limits and possibilities of freedom. Dewey, in particular, severs the freedom that human agency implies from mastery and connects it instead to an empirical claim regarding uncertainty. This gives inquiry both its radical bent and a sober quality, revealing its continuity with the eighteenth-century Enlightenment, to be sure, but extending beyond it by cultivating a strong sense of humility. He retains the Promethean emphasis on human intervention—but in an account that is inescapably bound by contingency.

Dewey's approach then attempts to articulate the psychological disposition of an agent standing at the intersection of what we might call modernity and postmodernity. On the one hand, we are beings thoroughly aware of our creative powers with respect to institutions and values and so recognize the historicity of our own existence. On the other hand, we view our institutions as more than the results of evanescent desires and believe in values that do not dissolve into ethical nihilism. At this juncture the latter, postmodern, position parts company with the irony of Rortian subjectivity; it demands, in Dewey's view, that, despite the constructivist nature of our world and by dint of our embeddedness and psychological propensities, we be more responsible in our decision-making and engagement with others. Creation and socialization are mutually implicated; they prevent the dissolution of the self by enabling processes that reproduce and transform the world. While such processes are not independent of human perspective as such, they will often be independent of the perspective of any one individual. Reference to our own perspective will undoubtedly be necessary in explaining and providing reasons for action, but it cannot by that fact alone be sufficient for such explications.

Although this account of inquiry courts danger, it does not lead to the kind of spiritual malaise regarding the meaningfulness of the objects of inquiry that we find in Hodge or Max Weber. This is because, with the aid of Darwin, Dewey is able to articulate and defend a psychological orientation in which the epistemic status of our norms and values is no longer bound up with the quest for incorrigible foundations. Our norms and values can now be understood as emerging at the intersection between individuals confronting specific ruptures or problems in experience that need attention and the larger social and natural environment in which they are located. On the one hand, this view of inquiry reinvigorates Aristotle's notion of *phronēsis* because it places particular emphasis on the imprecision of human inquiry despite the methodological benefits it offers. Yet Dewey also expands *phronēsis* beyond the ethical and political domains in which it was exclusively located. Moreover, inquiry is best understood as a practice of giving and asking for reasons for proposals, hypotheses, or plans of action.

That reason-giving becomes central to the process of imparting legitimacy partly follows from Dewey's claim that in a post-Darwinian world it becomes increasingly difficult to argue from the standpoint of some privileged access to reality as a way to guide our religious, moral, and political lives. This means that negotiating our social and natural environments must depend on a process of reflective contestability if we are going to describe the ongoing management of our social practices as legitimate among those who participate in them. But if this is correct, then there can be no fundamental difference at the epistemic level for how we justify our religious commitments, moral choices, or political decisions. Indeed, all require one and the same process of inquiry, which implies one and the same practice of reason-giving and testing the consequences of proposals in the flowing stream of experience.

Of what use, however, is this outlook in the twenty-first century? What does it reveal and what work does it allow us to do? In answering this question, we might begin in the reverse order, taking Dewey's democratic theory first. His reflections on democracy keep in view an important consideration that both hovers over political philosophy and often stimulates a return to his work. I am referring to pragmatism's criterion of assessment, which, in its broadest scope, searches for the emancipatory potential within critical reflections on society. By this I mean the ability to speak to the institutional and natural processes and fissures that limit or preclude freedom and justice, or somehow dehumanize us by making human transformation through those processes impossible. Although this criterion most clearly takes on its political bent in Dewey's philosophy, it was already present in the philosophies of Charles S. Peirce and William James. In its political bent, however, it is precisely this explicit effort to articulate an emancipatory politics that orients and unites philosophies as diverse as the left Hegelians (such as Max Horkheimer, Theodor Adorno, Jürgen Habermas, and Seyla Benhabib), neo-Kantians (John Rawls), neo-republicans (Quentin Skinner and Philip Pettit), and neo-pragmatists (Richard Rorty, Cornel West, Jeffrey Stout, Ian Shapiro, and Eddie Glaude). All are seeking to liberate us by means of a more fair and inclusive set of political arrangements. What Glaude says of pragmatists might well be said of all these thinkers: "Pragmatists express a profound faith in the capacity of everyday, ordinary people to transform their world. There are certainly constraints, but it is through our various practical transactions that we work to make a substantive difference in our conditions of living."[1]

Given the presence of such an emancipatory bent, we should immediately turn back to my discussion of Dewey's account of the public. If we say that "the public" denotes not merely the actual activity of citizens, but more significantly an arena in which citizens hold in reserve the power to direct institutions, we find ourselves with a very dynamic understanding of the public sphere as such. In other words, if we think along the lines of social theory, the distinction between potentially and actually having input in understanding political problems and framing policy decisions leads inexorably to the dual picture described in chapter 5. The first of these points to a modest conception of participation. After all, as Dewey describes it, the necessity of participation is indexed to an internally differentiated social sphere along the lines of emergent political problems that generate the need for systematic care. The extent of the area of participation, then, is coextensive with determining the nature of political problems. This elastic area of participation relies on and gives meaning to the administrative institutions of the state.

The second view points to the uncertainty that the public sphere represents. Here the concern is not with the local resonance of political problems, but with the way in which they achieve broader currency. In this regard, the public sphere functions for Dewey in much the same way that it does for Habermas. It is a sensory network that responds to various pressures that may be of concern to the citizenry at large.[2] But Dewey is very clear that both the communication of those pressures and the ability to act to alleviate them may need to be distinguished from the regulatory controls of the government. This account, which picks up on the elastic feature emphasized in the first point above, highlights the internal indeterminacy of the public sphere. It implies that reliance on the state should never be purchased at the expense of being able to realize substantive democratic goods.

This point is of critical importance. As John Dryzek rightly points out, if the interests of a particular public do not relate to existing state imperatives, it will often be the case that "inclusion means being co-opted or bought off cheaply" with symbolic rewards.[3] But symbolic rewards—as Dewey might easily acknowledge given his focus on problem-solving—"are correspondingly indefensible if they are offered as promissory notes for more tangible goods, but turn out to be substitutes for these goods."[4] This is precisely why Dewey's own account of the public sphere always retains a utopian impulse that is distinct from reliance on the state—thereby embracing, I think, precisely the transgressive quality Sheldon Wolin prefers but without the pessimism that is otherwise bound up with his view of fugitive democracy.

The implications of this for democracy are twofold. In the first instance, we should resist the desire to articulate a determinate social grouping that can and should legitimately occupy the space of political reflection. The public sphere is defined by contingency in the sense that the determination of *what* counts as a problem and *who* counts as the subject of that problem is an emergent property that guides inquiry, resists prior stipulation, but always already has a claim on us. By "claim on us," I mean the right to initiate the practice of giving and asking for reasons, with the genuine possibility of bringing about change. As Ian Shapiro explains: "Unless people can challenge prevailing norms and rules with the realistic hope of altering them, the requirement that the inherited past not bind us inalterably would be empty."[5]

In the second instance, the public sphere is that space in which the democratic ideal acquires legitimacy. In other words, it guards against complete identification between democracy and the current state of political affairs. In this context the public may assume an oppositional stance to the state as such. Although the public may function with and through the administrative institutions of the state in order to bring about political change, the effects of that relationship, Dewey suggests, should be such that they do not block the potential operation of the public in this more confrontational sense—if power is not to lapse into domination. The possibility of this second description allows for the public in the first instance to present itself as legitimate. It refers less to the actualities of participation and more to a condition in which transformative political activism can emerge if the need so arises. So understood, democracy not only makes mutual responsiveness central to legitimizing decision-making, but in doing so, it underscores the perpetual contestability and conditionality of power that always already point to the possibility of political transformation.

When we consider the positive contribution of Dewey's moral philosophy to current reflections, we should be drawn to the way in which he understands identity as such. In this regard there emerges a fundamental difference in the language of the Good and the Right among contemporary communitarians such as Alasdair MacIntyre and Michael Sandel on the one hand, and Dewey on the other. The former accept, as indicated in chapter 4, Max Weber's classic claim that under the conditions of modernity, inquiry confronts a kind of pluralism that is differentiated among various *Weltanschaungen* (worldviews) rather than the more modest account of the Good that Dewey provides.[6]

But there is a problem with this claim. To begin, Weber is clear that such worldviews are ultimate, where this means that they provide direction in life and, presumably, are at the core of psychological repose. Indeed, this vision lends itself to Carl Schmitt's more dangerous division of the political sphere into friends and enemies.[7] Yet, this is in tension with Weber's own analysis (and contemporary sociologists) that modernity is partly defined by a weakening of just this sense of the ultimate given the transformations within the economic and social spheres of the West and the corresponding division of labor such changes imply. Precisely because of this weakening of the sacred, our worldviews tend to be more internally differentiated, much like a web, so that challenges or revisions to various sides need not destroy the web as such. If this is so, as I believe it is, pluralism still exists in modern times but it is not mapped to the sacred in the way that Weber's language of the ultimate suggests. Instead, pluralism is indexed, as Dewey argues, to a diversity of goods rather than some more comprehensive understanding that accords with worldviews. Of course this means that the quest for "moral coherence and socio-political integration" that Hegel and Tocqueville described and that Taylor and Sandel hope for must be abandoned.[8] And while one critical result is the emergence of conflict, as Dewey understands the matter, the character of conflict will rarely rise to the level that Weber describes and Schmitt seems to desire. Another important point here, however, is that moral conflicts should be distinguished from the evaluative structure of mutual responsiveness in which they are located. The existence of moral conflict should not, as Dewey argues, be understood as referring to some deeper crisis in normative evaluation. If we take this account seriously, we shall not find ourselves worrying about the extent to which the Right and the Good can be made to coexist. But more important, we shall not find ourselves implicitly subscribing to the friend/enemy distinction that would inevitably undermine deliberation before it begins.

If we are encouraged to acknowledge the reflective contestability of our commitments, and do not read the conflicts between us and our fellow citizens as based on some darker ontological distinction, it is unclear to me why we must presume Dewey asks us to forgo religious commitments. As I have argued, Dewey's aversion to religion, when it reveals itself, is no different from his distaste for philosophical or scientific dogmatism. If we keep this in mind, we see that he shows us how to be pious without lapsing into blind deference and so threatening democracy. And he shows us how to have faith, without that faith being placed beyond the purview of reflection. Perhaps it is the advantage of modern fragmentation that it requires this kind of reflective and practical agility—an agility Dewey seeks to make explicit.

It is, of course, this understanding of piety and faith described in chapter 3 that should ring important in these uncertain times. For piety and faith, unhinged from reflection, will often be the language behind which a lust for tribalism hides. This will inspire action while abandoning intelligence, and seduce the public into believing that loyalty and allegiance are only genuine when the voices of reason and dissent are silent. But when that happens, deliberation is emptied of its transformative intent and we find ourselves living at the mercy of others without the possibility for redress. The space of power will be occupied and democracy, as Claude Lefort remarks, will be "close to destruction or already destroyed."[9]

To embrace Dewey's philosophy, however, is to hold at bay this possibility. It requires us to demand that all claims, even those based on religious commitments, be defended before the public if the occasion arises. This does not imply that through mutual responsiveness we will be saved from error or some darker fate. But it does imply that when we are no longer responsive to each other and the world about us we can be sure that error will most likely follow. Dewey's philosophy struggles against the impulse of our age to be unresponsive. It is not an alternative to how we conduct ourselves and manage our social affairs, but rather a quest to make explicit and defend that fundamental element from which our social practices derive their legitimacy and emancipatory potential. In the words of Dewey: "And when the emotional force, the mystic force one might say, of communication, of the miracle of shared life and shared experience is spontaneously felt, the hardness and crudeness of contemporary life will be bathed in the light that never was on land or sea" (RIP [MW12:201]).

NOTES

INTRODUCTION

1. Robert Westbrook, *John Dewey and American Democracy* (Ithaca: Cornell University Press, 1991), xv, 317–318, 433–454; see also Alfonso Damico, *Individuality and Community: The Social and Political Thought of John Dewey* (Gainesville: University Press of Florida, 1979), chap. 5; Alan Ryan, *John Dewey and the High Tide of Liberalism* (New York: Norton, 1995).

2. See, for example, Richard Bernstein, *Philosophical Profiles: Essays in a Pragmatic Mode* (Philadelphia: University of Pennsylvania Press, 1986); Hilary Putnam, "A Reconsideration of Deweyan Democracy," in *Pragmatism in Law and Society*, ed. Michael Brint and William Weaver (Boulder: Westview Press, 1991), 217–243; Robert Westbrook, *Democratic Hope: Pragmatism and the Politics of Truth* (Ithaca: Cornell University Press, 2005), chaps. 1, 3–4; Matthew Festenstein, *Pragmatism and Political Theory* (Chicago: University of Chicago Press, 1997); Axel Honneth, "Democracy as Reflexive Cooperation: John Dewey and the Theory of Democracy Today," *Political Theory* 26.6 (1998): 763–783; James Kloppenberg, *The Virtues of Liberalism* (New York: Oxford University Press, 1998), chap. 6; James Bohman, "Democracy as Inquiry, Inquiry as Democratic: Pragmatism, Social Science, and the Cognitive Division of Labor," *American Journal of Political Science* 43.2 (1999): 590–607; William Caspary, *Dewey on Democracy* (Ithaca: Cornell University Press, 2001); Eric MacGilvray, *Reconstructing Public Reason* (Cambridge, MA: Harvard University Press, 2004).

3. Walter Lippmann, *Public Opinion* (1922; New York: Free Press, 1965); Lippmann, *The Phantom Public* (1927; New Brunswick, NJ: Transaction Publishers, 2004);

Joseph Schumpeter, *Capitalism, Socialism, and Democracy* (New York: Harper and Row, 1942), pt. 4; Robert Dahl, *A Preface to Democratic Theory* (Chicago: University of Chicago Press, 1963); Dahl, "Hierarchy, Democracy, and Bargaining in Politics and Economics," in *Political Behavior*, ed. H. Eulau et al. (New York: Random House, 1956), 66–89; Giovanni Sartori, *Democratic Theory* (Detroit: Wayne State University Press, 1962); Adam Przeworski, "Minimalist Conception of Democracy: A Defense," in *Democracy's Value*, ed. Ian Shapiro and Casiano Hacker-Cordón (New York: Cambridge University Press, 1999), 23–55.

4. See generally John Dryzek, *Discursive Democracy: Politics, Policy, and Political Science* (New York: Cambridge University Press, 1990); Amy Gutmann and Dennis Thompson, *Democracy and Disagreement* (Cambridge, MA: Harvard University Press, 1996); Seyla Benhabib, "Toward a Deliberative Model of Democratic Legitimacy," in *Democracy and Difference: Contesting the Boundaries of the Political*, ed. Seyla Benhabib (Princeton: Princeton University Press, 1996), 67–94; Joshua Cohen, "Procedure and Substance in Deliberative Democracy," in the same volume, 95–119; Cohen, "Deliberation and Democratic Legitimacy," in *Deliberative Democracy: Essays on Reason and Politics*, ed. James Bohman and William Rehg (Cambridge, MA: MIT Press, 1997), 67–93; James Bohman, "Survey Article: The Coming of Age of Deliberative Democracy," *Journal of Political Philosophy* 6.4 (1998): 400–425.

5. Bertrand Russell, *Philosophical Essays* (New York: Longmans, Green, and Co., 1910), 110.

6. John Patrick Diggins, *The Promise of Pragmatism* (Chicago: University of Chicago Press, 1994), 304.

7. Ibid., 224.

8. Patrick Deneen, *Democratic Faith* (Princeton: Princeton University Press, 2005), chaps. 1–2, 6. See also Cornel West, *The American Evasion of Philosophy: A Genealogy of Pragmatism* (Madison: University of Wisconsin Press, 1989), chap. 3; Reinhold Niebuhr, *Moral Man and Immoral Society* (1932; New York: Scribner's, 1960); Niebuhr, "The Pathos of Liberalism," *The Nation* 141 (1935): 303–304; Christopher Lasch, *The True and Only Heaven: Progress and Its Critics* (New York: Norton, 1991).

9. Putnam, "A Reconsideration of Deweyan Democracy," 235–238. See also Raymond Boisvert, "The Nemesis of Necessity: Tragedy's Challenge to Deweyan Pragmatism," in *Dewey Reconfigured: Essays on Deweyan Pragmatism*, ed. Casey Haskins and David I. Seiple (Albany: State University of New York Press, 1999), 151–168; Westbrook, *Democratic Hope*, 112–113.

10. MacGilvray, *Reconstructing Public Reason*, 136. See also Timothy Kaufman-Osborn, "John Dewey and the Liberal Science of Community," *Journal of Politics* 46.4

(1984): 1152; Dorothy Ross, *The Origins of American Social Science* (New York: Cambridge University Press, 1991), 163–169.

11. C. Wright Mills, *Sociology and Pragmatism: The Higher Learning in America* (New York: Oxford University Press, 1969), 418–419; Christopher Lasch, *The New Radicalism in America* (New York: Vintage Press, 1965). See also Waher Feinberg, "The Conflict Between Intelligence and Community in Dewey's Educational Philosophy," *Educational Theory* 19.3 (1969): 234–248; Joseph G. Metz, "Democracy and the Scientific Method in the Philosophy of John Dewey," *Review of Politics* 31.2 (1969): 242–262; Clarence Karier, "Making the World Safe for Democracy: An Historical Critique of John Dewey's Philosophy of the Warfare State," *Educational Theory* 27.1 (1977): 12–47.

12. Judith Green, *Deep Democracy: Community, Diversity, and Transformation* (Lanham, MD: Rowman and Littlefield, 1999), 19, 31–33; see also Sheldon Wolin, *Politics and Visions*, expanded ed. (Princeton: Princeton University Press, 2004), 516–517.

13. As far as my argument goes, nothing hangs on the linguistic difference between "ontology" and "metaphysics" and so I shall use them interchangeably. Depending on how one pursues the matter, the study of Being can be understood as yielding concepts or categories that unite all of natural philosophy (understood, more or less, as "science" in our time) and as serving as the final place for epistemic justification. "Metaphysics" may in fact refer to something beyond the sensible that is inferred from existence or it may appeal to something materially ascertainable by the senses. There are reasons one might want to distinguish between the metaphysician's quest to ascertain what is beyond the sensible but that cuts across natural philosophy, and the scientist's desire to find what is materially ascertainable. The scientist may then be seen as having a materialist ontology but being silent on metaphysical claims. Nonetheless, historically there is, in my view, too much of a preoccupation with outlining the boundaries of existence and reality in both accounts, and attempting to secure certain knowledge within to allow for this distinction. For assistance on this point see Barry Smith, "Ontology," in *A Companion to Metaphysics*, ed. Jaegwon Kim and Ernest Sosa (Malden, MA: Blackwell, 1995), 373–374; Peter Simons, "Metaphysics," in the same volume, 310–312; also W. H. Walsh, "Nature of Metaphysics," in *The Encyclopedia of Philosophy*, ed. Paul Edwards, vol. 5 (New York: MacMillian, 1972), 300–306.

14. MacGilvray, *Reconstructing Public Reason*, 130. See also Deneen, *Democratic Faith*, 51.

15. I will elucidate this point more carefully below with reference to textual evidence. My only intention here is to indicate that at certain moments the criticisms they

advance against Dewey carry implications about his understanding of reality that often fit with the description above.

16. Ralph Ketcham, *The Idea of Democracy in the Modern Era* (Lawrence: University Press of Kansas, 2004), chap. 6; Hilary Putnam, *Enlightenment and Pragmatism* (Amsterdam: Koninklijke Van Gorcum, 2001).

17. Jonathan Israel, *Enlightenment Contested: Philosophy, Modernity, and the Emancipation of Man, 1670–1752* (New York: Oxford University Press, 2006), 218. See also Jerrold Seigel, *The Idea of the Self: Thought and Experience in Western Europe Since the Seventeenth Century* (New York: Cambridge University Press, 2005), chap. 2; Henry F. May, *The Enlightenment in America* (New York: Oxford University Press, 1976).

18. Further historical evidence of this earlier continuity can be found in Mark A. Noll, *America's God: From Jonathan Edwards to Abraham Lincoln* (New York: Oxford University Press, 2002), chap. 6.

19. Paul Jerome Croce, "Probabilistic Darwinism: Louis Agassiz vs. Asa Gray on Science, Religion, and Certainty," *Journal of Religious History* 22.1 (1998): 40; see also Ralph Bates, *Scientific Societies in the United States*, 2nd ed. (New York: Columbia University Press, 1958), 28–84; E. Brooks Holifield, *Theology in America: Christian Thought from the Age of the Puritans to the Civil War* (New Haven: Yale University Press, 2003), pt. 2.

20. See on this point the excellent four-volume edition Frank X. Ryan, ed., *Darwinism and Theology in America: 1850–1930* (Bristol, England: Thoemmes, 2002).

21. See Mark A. Noll and David N. Livingston, "Introduction: Charles Hodge and the Definition of 'Darwinism,'" in Charles Hodge, *What Is Darwinism? and Other Writings on Science and Religion*, ed. Mark A. Noll and David N. Livingston (1874; Grand Rapids: Baker Books, 1994), 18; see also W. Andrew Hoffecker, *Piety and the Princeton Theologians: Archibald Alexander, Charles Hodge, and Benjamin Warfield* (Phillipsburg, NJ: Presbyterian and Reformed Publishing Co., 1981), 55–81; Bruce Kuklick, "The Place of Charles Hodge in the History of Ideas in America," in *Charles Hodge Revisited: A Critical Appraisal of His Life and Work*, ed. John W. Stewart and James H. Moorhead (Grand Rapids: Eerdmans, 2002), 63–101.

22. James Kloppenberg, *Uncertain Victory: Social Democracy and Progressivism in European and American Thought, 1870–1920* (New York: Oxford University Press, 1986), 23. See also Louis Menand, *The Metaphysical Club: A Story of Ideas in America* (New York: Farrar, Strauss, Giroux, 2001), chap. 6.

23. These thinkers are of particular consequence because of their explicit confrontation with Darwin and theories of evolution that are consistent with the account here sketched. This does not, however, exhaust other articulations of liberal theology. In many respects I have left out the most important figures among liberal

theologians, such as Horace Bushnell and Walter Rauschenbusch. In this regard, I do not mean to understate their importance, but rather to draw attention to the individuals whose effort to reconcile science and religion are wrought by complexity owing to their encounter with Darwinian evolution.

24. Dewey's understanding of the matter is overdrawn here. On this point see Kloppenberg, *Uncertain Victory*.

25. D. H. Meyer, "American Intellectuals and the Victorian Crisis of Faith," in *Victorian America*, ed. Daniel Walter Howe (Philadelphia: University of Pennsylvania Press, 1976), 69. See also George Cotkin, *Reluctant Modernism: American Thought and Culture, 1880–1900* (New York: Twayne, 1992), intro., chap. 1.

26. Max Weber, "Science as a Vocation," in *From Max Weber: Essays in Sociology*, trans. H. H. Gerth and C. Wright Mills (1919; New York: Oxford University Press, 1946), 129–156; Weber, "The Social Psychology of the World Religions," in the same volume, 267–301.

27. Bert James Loewenberg, "Darwinism Comes to America, 1859–1900," *Mississippi Valley Historical Review* 28.3 (1941): 341; Richard Hofstadter, *Social Darwinism in American Thought*, rev. ed. (1944; Boston: Beacon, 1955), chap. 1; James Turner, *Without God, Without Creed: The Origins of Unbelief in America* (Baltimore: Johns Hopkins University Press, 1983), chaps. 3–6; James R. Moore, *The Post-Darwinian Controversies* (New York: Cambridge University Press, 1979), pts. II–III.

28. William James, *Pragmatism* (1907; Cambridge, MA: Harvard University Press, 1996), 31.

29. James' concerns are captured in Paul Jerome Croce, *Science and Religion in the Era of William James: Eclipse of Certainty, 1820–1880* (Chapel Hill: University of North Carolina Press, 1995); Menand, *Metaphysical Club*, pt. 2.

30. Weber, "Science as a Vocation," 139.

31. Stephen White, *Sustaining Affirmations: The Strengths of Weak Ontology in Political Theory* (Princeton: Princeton University Press, 2000), 6–7.

32. Ibid., 8.

33. Ibid., 4.

34. Charles Peirce, "Notes on Scientific Philosophy," *Collected Papers of Charles S. Peirce*, vol. 1, ed. Charles Hartshorne, Paul Weiss, and Arthur W. Burks (1905; Cambridge, MA: Harvard University Press, 1931), 52.

35. Steven C. Rockefeller, *John Dewey: Religious Faith and Democratic Humanism* (New York: Columbia University Press, 1991), 488, but see also chaps. 3–6.

36. Ibid., 296–297.

37. See also Richard J. Bernstein, *Beyond Objectivism and Relativism: Science, Hermeneutics, and Praxis* (Philadelphia: University of Pennsylvania Press, 1983), 69.

38. See also Thomas M. Alexander, *John Dewey's Theory of Art, Experience, and Nature: The Horizons of Feeling* (Albany: State University of New York Press, 1987), chap. 5; Hans Joas, *The Creativity of Action*, trans. Jeremy Gains and Paul Keast (Chicago: University of Chicago Press, 1996); Steven Fesmire, *John Dewey and Moral Imagination: Pragmatism in Ethics* (Bloomington: Indiana University Press, 2003), chap. 4. I am sympathetic to the insights expressed by these thinkers regarding the aesthetic dimension to action, but I develop these insights in a different way.

39. I will not take up Rorty's specific worries over Dewey's use of scientific inquiry and method, which are quite distinct from the concerns above. For responses to Rorty's challenge see Ian Shapiro, *Political Criticism* (Berkeley: University of California Press, 1990), 19–54; Richard J. Bernstein, *The New Constellation: Ethical-Political Horizons of Modernity/Postmodernity* (Cambridge, MA: MIT Press, 1992), 258–292; Westbrook, *John Dewey*, 539–542; *Democratic Hope*, 5–11, chap. 6; Richard Shusterman, "Pragmatism and Liberalism: Between Dewey and Rorty," *Political Theory* 22.3 (1994): 391–413; James Kloppenberg, "Pragmatism: An Old Name for Some New Ways of Thinking?," in *The Revival of Pragmatism: New Essays on Social Thought, Law, and Culture*, ed. Morris Dickstein (Durham: Duke University Press, 1998), 83–127.

40. Raymond Boisvert, *Dewey's Metaphysics* (New York: Fordham University Press, 1988), chap. 2; James Campbell, *Understanding John Dewey: Nature and Cooperative Intelligence* (Chicago: Open Court, 1995), chap. 2.

41. Boisvert, "Nemesis of Necessity," 151–168.

42. John Rawls, *Political Liberalism* (New York: Columbia University Press, 1996).

43. Michael Eldridge, *Transforming Experience: John Dewey's Cultural Instrumentalism* (Nashville: Vanderbilt University Press, 1998), 10; see chaps. 5–6.

44. Jeffrey Stout, *Democracy and Tradition* (Princeton: Princeton University Press, 2004), 97.

45. For ambivalence see Westbrook, *Democratic Hope*, 112; Caspary, *Dewey on Democracy*, 3, 129. For denial see Putnam, "Reconsideration of Deweyan Democracy," 230–234; MacGilvray, *Reconstructing Public Reason*, chap. 5.

46. Of course, Sidney Hook advances this argument about pragmatism (*Pragmatism and the Tragic Sense of Life* [New York: Basic Books, 1974], chap. 1), but he fails to textually substantiate his claims. My account here, which picks up on some of my earlier reflections, has the closest affinity to Eddie Glaude's argument (Melvin L. Rogers, "John Dewey and the Theory of Democratic Deliberation" [M.Phil. diss., Cambridge University, 2000], chap. 3; see also Glaude, *In a Shade of Blue: Pragmatism and the Politics of Black America* [Chicago: University of Chicago Press, 2007], chap. 1).

47. This position is similar to the one articulated by Shapiro and MacGilvray. The latter, however, treats this argument in a separate chapter from the one where he discusses Dewey's view of democracy. See Ian Shapiro, *Democratic Justice* (New Haven: Yale University Press, 1999), chaps. 1–2; MacGilvray, *Reconstructing Public Reason*, chaps. 4–5.

48. Sheldon Wolin, *The Presence of the Past: Essays on the State and the Constitution* (Baltimore: Johns Hopkins University Press, 1989); "Norm and Form: The Constitutionalizing of Democracy," in *Athenian Political Thought and the Reconstruction of American Democracy*, ed. J. Peter Euben, John R. Wallach, and Josiah Ober (Ithaca: Cornell University Press, 1994), 30–58; "Fugitive Democracy," in *Democracy and Difference: Contesting the Boundaries of the Political*, ed. Seyla Benhabib (Princeton: Princeton University Press, 1996), 31–45; "Transgression, Equality, Voice," in *Dēmokratia*, ed. Josiah Ober and Charles Hedrick (Princeton: Princeton University Press, 1996), 63–90; *Politics and Visions*, 600–606.

1. PROTESTANT SELF-ASSERTION AND SPIRITUAL SICKNESS

1. See George Dykhuizen, *The Life and Mind of John Dewey* (Carbondale: Southern Illinois University Press, 1973), chaps. 7–8; cf. Robert Westbrook, *John Dewey and American Democracy* (Ithaca: Cornell University Press, 1991), chaps. 3–6; Jay Martin, *The Education of John Dewey: A Biography* (New York: Columbia University Press, 2002), bk. 2; James E. Block, *A Nation of Agents: The American Path to a Modern Self and Society* (Cambridge, MA: Harvard University Press, 2002), chap. 13.

2. Steven C. Rockefeller, *John Dewey: Religious Faith and Democratic Humanism* (New York: Columbia University Press, 1991).

3. Hans Joas, *The Genesis of Values*, trans. Gregory Moore (1997; Chicago: University of Chicago Press, 2000), 121, and 122–123.

4. Block, *Nation of Agents*, 534. See also Patrick J. Deneen, *Democratic Faith* (Princeton: Princeton University Press, 2005), 75–77, 174–178.

5. Willian James, *The Varieties of Religious Experience* (1902; New York: Modern Library, 1999), 151; cf. "The Will to Believe" (1897), in *The Will to Believe and Other Essays in Popular Philosophy* (New York: Dover, 1956), 40–41.

6. James, "Will to Believe," 1–32.

7. See the example of Leo Tolstoy in James, *Varieties*, 167–184; cf. Paul Jerome Croce, *Science and Religion in the Era of William James: Eclipse of Certainty, 1820–1880*, vol. 1 (Chapel Hill: University of North Carolina Press, 1995), intro. and concl.

8. For accounts that substantiate these claims in greater historical detail see D. H. Meyer, "American Intellectuals and the Victorian Crisis of Faith," in *Victorian*

America, ed. Daniel Walter Howe (Philadelphia: University of Pennsylvania Press, 1976), 59–77; George Cotkin, *Reluctant Modernism: American Thought and Culture, 1880–1900* (New York: Twayne, 1992), chap. 1; James Turner, *Without God, Without Creed: The Origins of Unbelief in America* (Baltimore: Johns Hopkins University Press, 1983), chaps. 3–6; Gary Scott Smith, *The Seeds of Secularization: Calvinism, Culture, and Pluralism in America, 1870–1915* (Grand Rapids: Christian University Press, 1985), chaps. 6–7; T. J. Jackson Lears, *No Place of Grace: Antimodernism and the Transformation of American Culture, 1880–1920* (Chicago: University of Chicago Press, 1984), chap. 1.

9. James, *Varieties*, 535–538.

10. In emphasizing this alternative, I do not mean to suggest that this was the only option of the day. There are the earlier movements of transcendentalism and idealism, both of which precede the impact of Darwinism. My point in focusing on this approach is to underscore the importance of its encounter with Darwin. Transcendentalism and idealism are not preoccupied with Darwinism in any significant sense largely because natural selection challenges cognitivist rather than "experiential-expressive" approaches to theology. On this distinction see George A. Lindbeck, *The Nature of Doctrine: Religion and Theology in a Postliberal Age* (Philadelphia: Westminster Press, 1984), 16–17.

11. Although I have relied on Hans Blumenberg's account of self-assertion at certain points, the concept as I use it here is not completely consistent with his. The reason for this is that much of what Blumenberg says in *The Legitimacy of the Modern Age* on the topic of self-assertion rejects the Platonic feature that I want to retain (Blumenberg, *The Legitimacy of the Modern Age*, trans. Robert M. Wallace [Cambridge, MA: MIT Press, 1983], pt. 2, chap. 5; cf. Plato's discussion of the creator God in his *Timaeus*, trans. Donald J. Zeyl, in *Plato: Complete Works*, ed. John M. Cooper and D. S. Hutchinson [Indianapolis: Hackett, 1997], 1234–1242; Luciano Floridi, "Two Approaches to the Philosophy of Information," *Mind and Machine* 13.4 [2003]: 464). So although there is some continuity between this conception and mine, we should not confuse the two. For an insightful discussion of Blumenberg on which I have relied see Robert B. Pippin, *Idealism as Modernism: Hegelian Variations* (New York: Cambridge University Press, 1997), chaps. 10–11. Nor should my use of the Promethean image be confused with that description employed by David E. Cooper's *The Measure of Things: Humanism, Humility, and Mystery* (New York: Oxford University Press, 2002). The reason for this is that we can, *pace* Cooper, hold on to the Promethean outlook without simultaneously believing that human will wholly constitutes the world of meaning and value. Believing that one has greater room to *shape* the world is different from believing that one has *constituted* it *ex nihilo*.

12. T. J. Jackson Lears nicely captures the sense of emotional and psychological emptiness that secularism wrought and that prompted a turn toward "mental hygienists" (Lears, *No Place of Grace*, 55, see also chap. 4; cf. James, *Varieties*, 110–143).

13. Westbrook, *John Dewey*, chap. 3.

14. Herbert Hovenkamp, *Science and Religion in America, 1800–1860* (Philadelphia: University of Pennsylvania Press, 1978), chap. 2; cf. Robert V. Bruce, *The Launching of Modern American Science: 1846–1876* (Ithaca: Cornell University Press, 1987).

15. Charles Darwin, *The Origin of Species* (1859; New York: Modern Library of America, 1936), and in the same volume *The Descent of Man* (1871).

16. For a good analysis of earlier evolutionary doctrine see Moore, *Post-Darwinian Controversies*, pt. 2; Robert M. Young, *Darwin's Metaphor: Nature's Place in Victorian Culture* (New York: Cambridge University Press, 1985), chaps. 2 and 4.

17. Keith Ward, *Religion and Human Nature* (New York: Oxford University Press, 1998), 129.

18. Darwin, *Origins*, 373.

19. Another reason to believe that the previous passage cited from Darwin is a dubious example of his belief in human perfectibility is that he really means this to refer to incredible adaptations of specific organs within living creatures and not creatures in their totality. For more on this point see Derek Freeman, "The Evolutionary Theories of Charles Darwin and Herbert Spencer," in *Herbert Spencer: Critical Assessments*, ed. John Offer (1974; New York: Routledge: 2000), 2:19–20; cf. Darwin, *Origins*, 133–135.

20. Darwin, *Origins*, 149; cf. 129.

21. Max Weber, "Science as a Vocation," in *From Max Weber: Essays in Sociology*, ed. H. H. Gerth and C. Wright Mills (1919; New York: Oxford University Press, 1946), 152–153.

22. This is not particularly new even in a pre-Darwinian world. We need think only of Job.

23. John Henry, *The Scientific Revolution and the Origins of Modern Science* (New York: St. Martin's, 1997), chap. 2.

24. Stephen Toulmin, *Cosmopolis: The Hidden Agenda of Modernity* (Chicago: University of Chicago Press, 1990), 70 (original emphasis).

25. For some helpful characterizations of modernity on which I have relied, see Henry F. May, *The Enlightenment in America* (New York: Oxford University Press, 1976); Toulmin, *Cosmopolis*, chap. 2; *Return to Reason* (Cambridge, MA: Harvard University Press, 2001), chaps. 1–5; David Carrithers, "The Enlightenment Science of Society," in *Inventing Human Science: Eighteenth-Century Domains*, ed. Christopher Fox, Roy Porter, and Robert Wokler (Berkeley: University of Califor-

nia Press, 1995), 236–247; Henry, *Scientific Revolution*, chaps. 5 and 7; Jonathan Israel, *Enlightenment Contested: Philosophy, Modernity, and the Emancipation of Man, 1670–1752* (New York: Oxford University Press, 2006); Jerrold Seigel, *The Idea of the Self: Thought and Experience in Western Europe Since the Seventeenth Century* (New York: Cambridge University Press, 2005).

26. Israel, *Enlightenment Contested*, 10, see also chaps. 3–4, 8; cf. Seigel, *Idea of the Self*, chaps. 2–3.

27. Charles Hodge, *Systematic Theology* (1872–1873; Grand Rapids: Eerdmans, 1981), 1:16.

28. Ibid., 1:16.

29. Mark A. Noll and David N. Livingston, "Introduction: Charles Hodge and the Definition of 'Darwinism,'" in Charles Hodge, *What Is Darwinism? and Other Writings on Science and Religion*, ed. Mark A. Noll and David N. Livingston (1874; Grand Rapids: Baker Books, 1994), 18. See also Mark A. Noll, *America's God: From Jonathan Edwards to Abraham Lincoln* (New York: Oxford University Press, 2002), 317–319; W. Andrew Hoffecker, *Piety and the Princeton Theologians: Archibald Alexander, Charles Hodge, and Benjamin Warfield* (Phillipsburg, NJ: Presbyterian and Reformed Publishing Co., 1981), 55–81; E. Brooks Holifield, *Theology in America: Christian Thought from the Age of the Puritans to the Civil War* (New Haven: Yale University Press, 2003), chap. 18.

30. Hodge, *What Is Darwinism?*, 156. See also John T. Duffield, "Evolutionism Respecting Man, and the Bible," *Princeton Review* 54 (1878): 150–177; Robert Dabney, *Syllabus and Notes of the Course of Systematic and Polemic Theology* (Richmond: Presbyterian Committee of Publication, 1890).

31. Hodge, *Systematic Theology*, 1:10.

32. Ibid., 1:13.

33. See Hodge, *What Is Darwinism?*, 89–124; cf. *Systematic Theology*, 2:12–30.

34. Theodore D. Bozeman, *Protestants in an Age of Science: The Baconian Ideal and Antebellum American Religious Thought* (Chapel Hill: University of North Carolina Press, 1977), chaps. 1 and 5; Hovenkamp, *Science and Religion in America*; Curt J. Ducasse, "Francis Bacon's Philosophy of Science," in *Theories of Scientific Method: The Renaissance Through the Nineteenth Century*, ed. Ralph M. Blake et al. (New York: Gordon and Breach, 1989), 50–74.

35. Hodge, *What Is Darwinianism?*, 130. On Darwin's naturalism and the novelty of his methodology see John Green, *Darwin and the Modern World View* (Baton Rouge: Louisiana State University Press, 1961).

36. Thomas Reid, *Inquiry and Essays*, ed. Ronald E. Beanblossom and Keith Lehrer (1785; Indianapolis: Hackett, 1983).

37. Bozeman, *Protestants in an Age of Science*, 13.

38. Hodge, *Systematic Theology*, 3:266; see also 1:237–240.

39. Ibid., 1:57.

40. Ibid., 1:171.

41. Ibid. (emphasis added). Of course, for Hodge and others there is much in Darwin that indicates the remoteness of his evidence and the strong conjectural character of his proofs that leaves him open to attack. See Croce, "Probabilistic Darwinism: Louis Agassiz vs. Asa Gray on Science, Religion, and Certainty," *Journal of Religious History* 22.1 (1998): 43; cf. Michael T. Ghiselin, *The Triumph of the Darwinian Method* (Berkeley: University of California Press, 1969), 55; David L. Hull, *Darwin and His Critics: The Reception of Darwin's Theory of Evolution by the Scientific Community* (Chicago: University of Chicago Press, 1973), 16–36; Moore, *Post-Darwinian Controversies*, 194–196.

42. For a very helpful analysis of Descartes and Newton respectively see Seigel, *Idea of the Self*, pt. I; Israel, *Enlightenment Contested*, chap. 8; Betty Jo Teeter Dobbs and Margaret C. Jacob, *Newton and the Culture of Newtonianism* (New York: Humanity Books, 1998).

43. Hodge, *Systematic Theology*, 1:9.

44. Bert James Loewenberg, "Darwinism Comes to America, 1859–1900," *Mississippi Valley Historical Review* 28.3 (1941): 341; Richard Hofstadter, *Social Darwinism in American Thought*, rev. ed. (1944; Boston: Beacon, 1955), chap. 1.

45. Weber, "Science as a Vocation," 129–156.

46. Lawrence A. Scaff, "Weber on the Cultural Situation of the Modern Age," in *The Cambridge Companion to Weber*, ed. Stephen Turner (New York: Cambridge University Press, 2000), 105.

47. Weber, "The Social Psychology of the World Religions," in *From Max Weber*, 293; see also *Economy and Society*, ed. Buenther Roth and Claus Wittich (1922; Berkeley: University of California Press, 1978), vol. 2, chap. 11, pp. 1001–1002.

48. Jürgen Habermas, *The Theory of Communicative Action*, vols. 1 and 2, trans. Thomas McCarthy (Boston: Beacon Press, 1984), 1.II–III, 2.V; John McDowell, *Mind and World* (Cambridge, MA: Harvard University Press, 1994).

49. James, "*Lectures and Essays* and *Seeing and Thinking*, by William K. Clifford" (1879), in *Essays, Comments, and Reviews* (Cambridge, MA: Harvard University Press, 1987), 357.

50. Hodge, *Systematic Theology*, 1:235–240, at 235; cf. 1:339–346.

51. Ibid., 1:172–178.

52. Theodore T. Munger, *The Freedom of Faith* (Boston: Houghton, Mifflin, and Company, 1883), 6.

53. Matthew Arnold, "Stanzas from the Grande Chartreuse" (1855), in *The Portable Matthew Arnold*, ed. Lionel Trilling (New York: Viking, 1949), 151.

54. Arnold, "Dover Beach" (1867), in *Portable Arnold*, 166.

55. Weber, "Science as a Vocation," 139.

56. Hodge, *Systematic Theology*, 1:172.

57. Weber, "Science as a Vocation," 155.

58. Eyal Chowers, *The Modern Self in the Labyrinth: Politics and the Entrapment Imagination* (Cambridge, MA: Harvard University Press, 2004), 69.

59. Hodge, *What Is Darwinism?*, 87. On Hodge's precise formulation of what our moral and religious natures consist in see *Systematic Theology*, 1:341–344.

60. Interestingly enough, James offered a similar claim that is worth mentioning here. In his 1891 essay, "The Moral Philosopher and the Moral Life," James argues in contrast to the position of Hodge that independent of God, life is an ethical universe by virtue of the presence of human beings. Yet toward the end of the essay James seems to say that something else is needed if that ethical universe is to appear as more than mere subjective preference—as having depth and levels of value: "This is why in a solitary thinker this [strenuous] mood might slumber on forever without waking. His various ideals, known to him to be mere preferences of his own, are too nearly of the same denominational value: he can play fast or loose with them at will. This too is why, in a merely human world without a God, the appeal to our moral energy falls short of its maximal stimulating power. Life, to be sure, is even in such a world a genuinely ethical symphony; but it is played in the compass of a couple of poor octaves, and the infinite scale of values fails to open up. . . . When, however, we believe that a God is there, and that he is one of the claimants, the infinite perspective opens out. The scale of the symphony is incalculably prolonged" (James, "The Moral Philosophy and the Moral Life," in *Will to Believe*, 212).

61. Thus: "In these laws are included some which have no direct application to the natural sciences. Such, for example, as the essential distinction between right and wrong; that nothing contrary to virtue can be enjoined by God; that it cannot be right to do evil that good may come . . . and other similar first truths, which God has implanted in the constitution of all moral beings" (Hodge, *Systematic Theology*, 1:10).

62. Ibid., 3:260; cf. 3:348–360.

63. Of course, religious belief does not simply go out the window with the appearance of *Origins of Species*. Nor are individuals at a lost for how they ought to conduct themselves vis-à-vis each other. There are, however, other forces at work, including the rise of the historical and hermeneutical criticism of the Bible, as well as anthropological investigations into the origin of extant and extinct religions (see Maurice Mandelbaum, *History, Man, and Reason: A Study in Nineteenth-Century Thought* [Baltimore: Johns Hopkins University Press, 1971], 28–41).

64. Munger, *Freedom of Faith*, 6.

65. James, *Varieties*, 90–144, at 144.

66. Henry Ward Beecher, "Progress of Thought in the Church," *North American Review* 135.309 (1882): 106. See also John Fiske, *The Destiny of Man Viewed in the Light of His Origin* (Boston: Houghton, Mifflin, and Company, 1884); Munger, *Freedom of Faith*; James McCosh, *The Religious Aspect of Evolution* (1890), in *Darwinism and Theology in America: 1850–1930*, ed. Frank X. Ryan (Bristol, England: Thoemmes, 2002), 2:1–49; Lyman Abbott, *The Evolution of Christianity* (New York: Outlook Company, 1892); Abbott, *The Theology of an Evolutionist* (New York: Houghton, Mifflin, and Company, 1897); George Harris, *Moral Evolution* (New York: Houghton, Mifflin, and Company, 1896).

67. Fiske, *Through Nature to God* (Boston: Houghton, Mifflin, and Company, 1899), 128.

68. Henry Ward Beecher, "The Study of Human Nature" (1872), in *American Protestant Thought: The Liberal Era*, ed. William R. Hutchison (New York: Harper and Row, 1968), 42.

69. Beecher, *Evolution and Religion, Part I and 2* (New York: Fords, Howard, and Hulbert, 1885), 1:26.

70. Ibid., 1:26; cf. Abbott, *Theology of an Evolutionist*, 41–42.

71. This formulation already betrays Darwin and seems to be a throwback to the Lamarckian idea that there exists an inherent progressive element living within nature (compare, in this regard, Moore's analysis of Lamarckian theory with my discussion: *Post-Darwinian Controversies*, 142–146). But as Young points out of Darwin, Robert Chambers, Charles Lyell, Herbert Spencer, and others: "All of these theorists confused metaphysical, methodological, and scientific levels of analysis, but as they retreated from specific scientific explanations, there remained the influence of their work as contributions to the mainstream of nineteenth-century naturalism [and theological naturalism], leading to a growing acceptance of the philosophical principle of the uniformity of nature, a principle which could be harmlessly identified with the intentions and the nature of the Deity" (Young, *Darwin's Metaphor*, 90). So for Young it makes sense that we find interpretations of evolution that are reconciled with religion, even though John Dewey faults such accounts for excluding the central claim upon which Darwin's account of evolution is based—namely, chance and contingency—in order to retain a metaphysical belief in progress.

72. Beecher, "Progress of Thought," 113.

73. Ibid., 113. See also Munger, *Freedom of Faith*, 13–25.

74. Beecher, *Evolution and Religion*, 1:34–37.

75. Ibid., 1:139. See also H. Shelton Smith, *Changing Conceptions of Original Sin: A Study in American Theology Since 1750* (New York: Scribner, 1955), specifically chaps. 7–8.

76. Christ is consistently invoked in these works, but the lesson to learn is that he is a teacher of moral character, rather than a redeemer of humanity proper (see, for example, the invocation of Christ in Beecher, *Evolution and Religion*, 2: chap. 1; Abbott, *Theology of an Evolutionist*, chap. 5; Munger, *Freedom of Faith*, chaps. 4–6). To suggest that this is indicative of a secular turn obscures the tradition in Christian thought in which the power of God is seen as working within history, revealing itself in the temporal horizon as a way to guide humanity. The line between the infinite sacred and the finite secular blurs. On this see William Dean, "Pragmatism, History, and Theology," in *Pragmatism and Religion: Classical Sources and Original Essays*, ed. Stuart Rosenbaum (Champaign: University of Illinois Press, 2003), 153–175.

77. Abbott, *Theology of Evolutionist*, 42.

78. Beecher, "Human Nature," 43. See also "Progress of Thought in Church," 113.

79. Beecher, *Evolution and Religion*, 1:18.

80. Beecher, "Human Nature," 43. See also "Progress of Though in Church," 113.

81. Beecher, *Evolution and Religion*, 1:80 (emphasis added).

82. McCosh, "Natural Selection and the Origin of Man" (1871), in *Darwinism and Theology in America*, ed. Ryan, 2:70.

83. Charles Taylor, *Varieties of Religion Today: William James Revisited* (Cambridge, MA: Harvard University Press, 2002), 39–40.

84. William Clebsch, *American Religious Thought: A History* (Chicago: University of Chicago Press, 1973), 8. See also Weber, *The Protestant Ethic and the Spirit of Capitalism*, trans. Talcott Parsons (1930; New York: Routledge, 1992), chap. 5.

85. See also Charles S. Peirce: "We cannot begin with complete doubt. We must begin with all the prejudices which we actually have when we enter upon the study of philosophy. These prejudices are not to be dispelled by a maxim, for they are things which it does not occur to us can be questioned. Hence this initial skepticism will be a mere self-deception, and not real doubt; and no one who follows the Cartesian method will ever be satisfied until he has formally recovered all those beliefs which in form he has taken up. . . . A person may, it is true, in the course of his studies, find reason to doubt what he began by believing; but in that case he doubts because he has a positive reason for it, and not on account of the Cartesian maxim. Let us not pretend to doubt in philosophy what we do not doubt in our hearts" (Charles S. Peirce, "Some Consequences of Four Incapacities" [1868], in *The Essential Peirce: Selected Philosophical Writings*, ed. Nathan Houser and Christian Kloesel [Bloomington: Indiana University Press, 1992], 1:28–29).

86. Weber, "Science as a Vocation," 152.

87. James, *Pragmatism* (1907; Cambridge, MA: Harvard University Press, 1996), 37.

88. For analysis of this see John R. Shook, *Dewey's Empirical Theory of Knowledge and Reality* (Nashville: Vanderbilt University Press, 2000), chap. 6.

89. Richard Rorty, *Contingency, Irony, and Solidarity* (New York: Cambridge University Press, 1989), xiv.

90. Ibid.

91. Ibid., 75.

92. Charles Taylor, *Sources of the Self: The Making of the Modern Identity* (Cambridge, MA: Harvard University Press, 1989), pt. 1 and chaps. 24–25.

93. Connolly describes this as a kind of "compensatory" ontology which, in my narrative, is therapeutic reedification. But the implication is the same, that is, they are compensations for the "modern 'loss'" which then secure themselves by denying the threat from the outset; see William Connolly, *The Ethos of Pluralization* (Minneapolis: University of Minnesota Press, 1995), chap. 1, at 24.

94. Hilary Putnam, *Pragmatism: An Open Question* (Malden, MA: Blackwell, 1995), 21 (original emphasis).

95. Cheryl Misak, *Truth, Politics, Morality: Pragmatism and Deliberation* (New York: Routledge, 2000), 52. See Robert Brandom, *Making It Explicit: Reasoning, Representing, and Discursive Commitment* (Cambridge, MA: Harvard University Press, 1994), chap. 8, §§IV, VI; John McDowell, *Mind and World* (Cambridge, MA: Harvard University Press, 1994); McDowell, "Towards Rehabilitating Objectivity," in *Rorty and His Critics*, ed. Robert Brandom (Malden, MA: Blackwell, 2000), 109–123; Sabina Lovibond, *Ethical Formation* (Cambridge, MA: Harvard University Press, 2002); Jeffrey Stout, *Democracy and Tradition*, chaps. 9–11; Stout, "On Our Interests in Getting Things Right: Pragmatism Without Narcissism," in *New Pragmatists*, ed. Cheryl Misak (New York: Oxford University Press, 2007), 7–31.

96. Friedrich Nietzsche, *Thus Spoke Zarathustra: A Book for None and All*, trans. Walter Kaufmann (1883–1885; New York: Penguin, 1978), "Zarathustra's Prologue"; cf. *Beyond Good and Evil: Prelude to a Philosophy of the Future*, trans. Walter Kaufmann (1886; New York: Vintage, 1989), pt. 3, esp. aphorism 56.

97. See also George Santayana, *The Life of Reason* (1905–1906; New York: Prometheus Books, 1998), 258; Stout, *Democracy and Tradition*, chap. 1.

98. For contemporary iterations of this point see Connolly, *Ethos of Pluralization*, chap. 1; Stephen K. White, *Sustaining Affirmation: The Strengths of Weak Ontology in Political Theory* (Princeton: Princeton University Press, 2000), chap. 1; Jane Bennett, *The Enchantment of Modern Life: Attachments, Crossings, and Ethics* (Princeton: Princeton University Press, 2001), chap. 8.

99. Cited in Douglass R. Anderson, "Theology as Healing: A Meditation on *A Common Faith*," in *Dewey Reconfigured*, 86; cf. Dewey, EKV (LW14:79–80).

100. Thus, when Dewey remarks in his autobiographical reflections four years before *A Common Faith* that he has "not been able to attach much importance to religion as a philosophic problem; for the effect of that attachment seems to be in the end subornation of . . . thinking to the alleged but factitious needs of some special set of convictions," he means this for a specific rather than a general account of religion, one which undermines inquiry and distorts the meaning of piety and faith (AE$_1$ [LW5:153]; see also Richard Bernstein, *John Dewey* [New York: Washington Square Press, 1967], 161–165).

2. AGENCY AND INQUIRY AFTER DARWIN

1. By philosophy of action, I do not mean the view prevalent among analytic philosophers that begins with the premise that when we say "action" we mean it to denote an isolated event that proceeds from an independent psychological state. Dewey's "transactionalism" mentioned in the last chapter immediately bars this premise.

2. There is a substantial body of literature on Dewey that explicates his account of inquiry rather than his philosophy of action, of which it is a part. See in this regard J. E. Tiles, *Dewey* (New York: Routledge, 1988); Michael Eldridge, *Transforming Experience: John Dewey's Cultural Instrumentalism* (Nashville: Vanderbilt University Press, 1997); Robert Westbrook, *John Dewey and American Democracy* (Ithaca: Cornell University Press, 1991); James Campbell, *Understanding John Dewey: Nature and Cooperative Intelligence* (Chicago: Open Court, 1995); Matthew Festenstein, *Pragmatism and Political Theory: From Dewey to Rorty* (Chicago: University of Chicago Press, 1997); William R. Caspary, *Dewey on Democracy* (Ithaca: Cornell University Press, 2000); John R. Shook, *Dewey's Empirical Theory of Knowledge and Reality* (Nashville: Vanderbilt University Press, 2000). The exceptions are Richard Bernstein, *Praxis and Action: Contemporary Philosophies of Human Activity* (Philadelphia: University of Pennsylvania Press, 1971), chap. 3; Hans Joas, *The Creativity of Action*, trans. Jeremy Gains and Paul Keast (Chicago: University of Chicago Press, 1996), chaps. 2–3.

3. The exceptions here include Ralph W. Sleeper, *The Necessity of Pragmatism: John Dewey's Conception of Philosophy* (New Haven: Yale University Press, 1986); Raymond D. Boisvert, *Dewey's Metaphysics* (New York: Fordham University Press, 1988).

4. For contemporary revisionists reading of Aristotle that would take issue with this account see Richard G. Mulgan, *Aristotle's Political Theory: An Introduction for Students of Political Theory* (New York: Oxford University Press, 1977), chap. 7;

Martha Nussbaum, *The Fragility of Goodness: Luck and Ethics in Greek Tragedy and Philosophy* (New York: Cambridge University Press, 1986), chap. 10; Stephen Salkever, *Finding the Mean: Theory and Practice in Aristotelian Political Philosophy* (Princeton: Princeton University Press, 1990), chap. 1; Jill Frank, *A Democracy of Distinction: Aristotle and the Work of Politics* (Chicago: University of Chicago Press, 2005), intro.–chap. 1.

5. Aristotle, *Nicomachean Ethics* [hereafter *Ethics*], bk. 6, trans. W. D. Ross, in *The Basic Works of Aristotle*, ed. Richard McKeon (New York: Random House, 1941); see also bk. 10.7–9. All references will be to the *Basic Works* unless otherwise noted.

For helpful works on which I partly rely in elucidating these distinctions see Nicholas Lobkowicz, *Theory and Practice: History of a Concept from Aristotle to Marx* (Notre Dame: University of Notre Dame Press, 1967), chaps. 1–4; Joseph Dunne, *Back to the Rough Ground: "Phronesis" and "Techne" in Modern Philosophy and in Aristotle* (Notre Dame: University of Notre Dame Press, 1993), pt. 2; Julia Annas, *The Morality of Happiness* (New York: Oxford University Press, 1993), 73–91; Christopher P. Long, "The Ontological Reappropriation of Phronēsis," *Continental Philosophy Review* 35.1 (2002): 35–60; Amélie Oksenberg Rorty, "The Place of Contemplation in Aristotle's *Nicomachean Ethics*," in *Essays on Aristotle's Ethics*, ed. Rorty (Berkeley: University of California Press, 1980), 377–395; Nussbaum, *Fragility*, chap. 10, and 373–378; John McDowell, *Mind, Value, and Reality* (Cambridge, MA: Harvard University Press, 1998), pt. 1. I use the word "partly" because there are revisionist aspects to some of these readings of Aristotle that I have not endorsed in the context of my reading. My argument here is about Dewey, not Aristotle.

6. Hannah Arendt, *The Human Condition* (Chicago: University of Chicago Press, 1958); Hans-Georg Gadamer, *Truth and Method*, 2nd ed. rev., trans. Joel Weinsheimer and Donald G. Marshall (1960; New York: Continuum, 1989); Hans-Georg Gadamer, *Reason in the Age of Science*, trans. Frederick G. Lawrence (Cambridge, MA: MIT Press, 1981), 21–38, 69–88, 151–171; Leo Strauss, *Natural Right and History* (1953; Chicago: University of Chicago Press, 1970).

7. Aristotle, *Ethics*, bk. 6; cf. bk. 10.7–9.

8. Ibid., bk. 6.3 [1139^a]–6.5; cf. *Politics*, trans. Benjamin Jowett in *Basic Works of Aristotle*, ed. McKeon, bk. 1.4 [1254].

9. Aristotle, *Politics*, bk. 1.3.

10. Aristotle, *Ethics*, bk. 6.7 [1141^{a}20–b9], 10.7–9. To be fair, Aristotle recognizes composite practices that involve both *phronēsis* and *technē* and so muddle the distinction. Nonetheless, he seems especially concerned to see these elements as distinct when discussing ethical and political practices. In other words, he does not

allow the composite practices to destabilize his commitment to firm ontological distinctions.

11. This claim is compatible with contingency, for if one was constantly subject to bad fortune, it would allow us to construct predictive models of failure. Part of what makes contingency unsettling is our inability to construct predictive models in just this way. As such, we ought to believe that the person's problem is that they lack practical wisdom.

12. Only rarely do we attribute wisdom to judgments that do not have fruitful results, and this is usually in cases where the realization of the judgment's content is beyond our control. Here Dewey uses the example of the surgeon, so that we "would not say that the act of a surgeon is necessarily to be condemned because an operation results in the death of a patient . . . morally his act was beneficent, although unsuccessful from causes which he could not control" (E_3 [LW7:173–174]). Notwithstanding, Dewey's point nonetheless rejects Aristotle's contention that "in the variable are included both things made and things done; making and acting are different (for their nature we treat even the discussions outside our school as reliable); so that the *reasoned state of capacity to act is different from the reasoned state of capacity to make*" (Aristotle, *Ethics* 6.3 [1140ᵃ] [emphasis added]).

13. Robert B. Brandom, "The Pragmatist Enlightenment (and Its Problematic Semantics)," *European Journal of Philosophy* 12.1 (2004): 2; see also Ralph Ketcham, *The Idea of Democracy in the Modern Era* (Lawrence: University of Kansas Press, 2004), chaps. 4–6; John P. Anton, "John Dewey and Ancient Philosophies," *Philosophy and Phenomenological Research* 25.4 (1965): 497; Bernstein, *Praxis and Action*, 213–219. On the importance and rise of probability and statistics in late-nineteenth-century America see Paul Jerome Croce, *Science and Religion in the Era of William James: Eclipse of Certainty, 1820–1880*, vol. 1 (Chapel Hill: University of North Carolina Press, 1995), intro. I recognize that the origin of this experimental approach predates Darwin. For Dewey, however, experimentalism in the context of Darwin's biological paradigm solidifies an important way of understanding inquiry.

14. For more on these two competing dimensions within modernity see Stephen Toulmin, *Return to Reason* (Cambridge, MA: Harvard University Press, 2001); Stephen Eric Bronner, *Reclaiming the Enlightenment* (New York: Columbia University Press, 2004), chap. 2.

15. Thus he says: "Were we to define science not in the usual technical way, but as a knowledge that accrues when methods are employed which deal competently with problems that present themselves, the physician, engineer, artist, craftsman, lay claim to scientific knowing" (QC [LW4:159]).

16. The term is appropriated from Anthony Giddens, although I do not depart significantly from what he means; see Giddens, *Modernity and Self-Identity: Self and*

Society in the Late Modern Age (Palo Alto: Stanford University Press, 1991), 36–47, at 36–37.

17. A good example of this is suggested by David Hume, *A Treatise of Human Nature*, ed. P. H. Nidditch (1740; New York: Oxford University Press, 1978), 87.

18. To be sure, Dewey offers more careful investigations of these thinkers elsewhere (RIP [MW12: chaps. 1 and 2]; QC [LW4:47–53]; PWHS [MW3:193–202]). And it can scarcely be denied that there is some interpretative violence being done, for those "interested in philosophy may object that the criticisms passed are directed . . . at a man of straw," Dewey observes (QC [LW4:23]). But it is important to understand that Dewey's treatment of these thinkers and the traditions to which they belong does not seek accuracy of their thought in toto. His approach is that of the historian of ideas, wherein he searches after the development of ideas and their impact through succeeding generations. For ideas, as he explains, "have an empirical origin and status" (QC [LW4:91]). That is, they are "plans of operations to be performed" and therefore are "integral factors in actions," orienting us one way rather than another. He is thus after the ways in which these ideas of knowledge, experience, and science orient us to and make specific claims about the world (QC [LW4:111]). Dewey does not deny the translatable quality of ideas across generations of thinkers, and indeed believes that this possibility builds up a history of philosophy. He accepts in this regard that such ideas are funneled through problems generated in specific contexts, but he believes that those problems can come to be described in one way rather than another owing to the philosophical baggage we carry.

19. With Jonathan Israel's recent study there is good reason to believe that Dewey's argument is of genuine historical worth; see Israel, *Enlightenment Contested: Philosophy, Modernity, and the Emancipation of Man, 1670–1752* (New York: Oxford University Press, 2006).

20. Immanuel Kant, *Critique of Practical Reason*, trans. Lewis White Beck, 3rd ed. (1788; Upper Saddle River, NJ: Prentice Hall, 1993), 31; *Critique of Pure Reason*, trans. Norman Kemp Smith (1787; Boston: Bedford Press, 1965), chap. 3; cf. Dewey QC (LW4:47–50).

21. This term is not meant to carry any special meaning or to indicate a deep connection with the ethic of care movement in moral philosophy.

22. Dana Villa, *Arendt and Heidegger: The Fate of the Political* (Princeton: Princeton University Press, 1996), 51; cf. Dewey, LJP (MW8: §§III–IV, at 39).

23. Isaiah Berlin, *Four Essays on Liberty* (New York: Oxford University Press, 1969), 131.

24. In emphasizing the importance of Darwin, my account is consistent with John Shook's insistence on the priority of Hegel to Dewey's philosophy precisely because I am not trying to explain "the transformation of his absolute idealism into in-

strumentalist empiricism" or to answer the question, "When did Dewey stop being an idealist and become a pragmatist?" (Shook, *Dewey's Empirical Theory*, chaps. 1 and 5, at 202 and 210). The settlement of this issue is to be found in a remark by John Herman Randall: "John Dewey is a cardinal illustration of the fact that Darwin seemed to bring biological, that is, 'scientific' support to an essential Hegelian 'mode of thinking'. Darwin forced Dewey to reconstruct many of the Hegelian ideas, to be sure: he compelled a basic pluralizing of Hegel, and a putting of his thought upon an experimental basis" (Randall, "The Changing Impact of Darwin on Philosophy," *Journal of the History of Ideas* 22.4 [1961]: 450). Unfortunately, Hegel did not have an understanding of the naturalistic mechanics of evolution.

25. Eric MacGilvray, *Reconstructing Public Reason* (Cambridge, MA: Harvard University Press, 2004), 109. See also James Bohman, "Realizing Deliberative Democracy as a Mode of Inquiry: Pragmatism, Social Facts, and Normative Theory," *Journal of Speculative Philosophy* 18.1 (2004): 23–43.

26. Cornel West, *The American Evasion of Philosophy: A Genealogy of Pragmatism* (Madison: University of Wisconsin Press, 1989), 226, and cf. chap. 3; *Keeping Faith: Philosophy and Race in America* (New York: Routledge, 1993), 107–118.

27. Raymond D. Boisvert, "The Nemesis of Necessity: Tragedy's Challenge to Deweyan Pragmatism," in *Dewey Reconfigured: Essays on Deweyan Pragmatism*, ed. Casey Haskins and David I. Seiple (Albany: State University of New York Press, 1999), 158. See also Patrick J. Deneen, *Democratic Faith* (Princeton: Princeton University Press, 2005), 77–75, 176–180, 182–185.

28. That Boisvert would say this of Dewey in the first instance is very strange, since he writes elsewhere: "Unlike the philosophers he criticizes, Dewey does not begin with a prior commitment to achieve absolute certainty. Human knowing is provisional, incomplete, and probabilistic. We rarely act with the absolute security that our choices are the absolute appropriate ones" (Boisvert, *John Dewey: Rethinking Our Time* [Albany: State University of New York Press, 1998], 16; cf. 25). In the essay of his to which I referred in note 27, Boisvert often speaks of Dewey incorporating "elements central to the tragic," but he then concludes that "whereas the tragedian realizes that mind will always be in some ways blind to the multifarious working of necessity, Dewey's reformist faith leads him to lean in the opposite direction. For him mind can come to dominant necessity" (Boisvert, "Nemesis of Necessity," 163). That mind can come to dominant necessity does not mean it will. This claim seems to me completely consistent with acknowledging the fact that we are blind to the multifarious workings of necessity, which may intervene to our disadvantage.

29. West, *American Evasion*, 100–102; Boisvert, "Nemesis of Necessity," 151–168.

30. Boisvert, "Nemesis of Necessity," 158.

31. Arendt, *Human Condition*, 222. For helpful analysis of this in Arendt see Villa, *Arendt and Heidegger*, 82–89; cf. Patchen Markell, *Bound by Recognition* (Princeton: Princeton University Press, 2003), chap. 3, at 64.

32. John Patrick Diggins, *The Promise of Pragmatism* (Chicago: University of Chicago Press), 304. See also James E. Block, *A Nation of Agents: The American Path to a Modern Self and Society* (Cambridge, MA: Harvard University Press, 2002), chap. 13; Deneen, *Democratic Faith*, 75–77, 174–178.

33. William James, *Psychology: Briefer Course* (1892; Cambridge, MA: Harvard University Press, 1984), chap. 10; George Herbert Mead, *Mind, Self, and Society*, ed. Charles W. Morris (1934; Chicago: University of Chicago Press, 1967), pts. 3–4.

34. See Alasdair MacIntyre, *After Virtue* (Notre Dame: University of Notre Dame Press, 1981); Hayden White, "The Value of Narrativity in the Representation of Reality," in *On Narrative*, ed. W. J. T. Mitchell (Chicago: University of Chicago Press, 1981), 1–23; Owen Flanagan, *Varieties of Moral Personality: Ethics and Psychological Realism* (Cambridge, MA: Harvard University Press, 1991), 148–158; Mark Johnson, *Moral Imagination: Implications of Cognitive Science for Ethics* (Chicago: University of Chicago Press, 1994), chap. 7; Seyla Benhabib, *The Claims of Culture* (Princeton: Princeton University Press, 2002), 15–22.

35. John McDowell, *Mind and World* (Cambridge, MA: Harvard University Press, 1994), 78–86. See also Aristotle, *Ethics*, bk. 2; Sabine Lovibond, *Ethical Formation* (Cambridge, MA: Harvard University Press, 2002), 25.

36. Robert B. Brandom, "Freedom and Constraint by Norms," in *Hermeneutics and Praxis*, ed. Robert Hollinger (Notre Dame: University of Notre Dame Press, 1985), 182 (original emphasis). See also McDowell, *Mind and World*, 82.

37. John McDowell, "Towards Rehabilitating Objectivity," in *Rorty and His Critics*, ed. Robert B. Brandom (Malden, MA: Blackwell, 2000), 118.

38. Herbert W. Schneider, *A History of American Philosophy* (New York: Columbia University Press, 1946), 556.

39. McDowell, *Mind and World*, 78.

40. Obviously Dewey's remarks overlap with Arendt's much later reflections on action, in particular the concept of "natality." For Arendt, this constitutes our second birth, and is coextensive with the emergence of our distinctiveness as individuals. But some confusion seems to emerge at precisely this point. For our insertion into the world, on Arendt's view, "is not forced upon us by necessity, like labor, and it is not prompted by utility, like work. It may be stimulated by the presence of others whose company we may wish to join, but it is never conditioned by them" (Arendt, *Human Condition*, 176–177). Yet insertion seems to be bound up with "beginning something new on our own initiative" (ibid., 177). What needs now to be explained by Arendt is why individuals feel the need to begin something new. What prompts

initiative? Her answer cannot simply be the *fact* that one has speech and can act, because individuals may simply be speaking the language of their community, engaging in the acts of those with whom they are associated. Note, she says in the example of joining a group, that one is stimulated to do so. But wherein lies the source of stimulation? Speaking and acting, Dewey would say, comprise the *potential* source of beginnings, but the very existence of agents does not yet constitute a beginning—that is, as understood by Arendt. In short, something must precede initiative. This will often, in Dewey's view, be prompted by necessity or utility, although I think what those terms mean for him will be far more expansive than what we find in Arendt.

41. Brandom, "Freedom and Constraint"; McDowell, *Mind and World*, lecture I.

42. Brandom, "Freedom and Constraint, " 185 (original emphasis). See also McDowell, *Mind and World*, lecture IV.

43. Dewey to James, cited in Ralph Barton Perry, *The Thought and Character of William James* (Boston: Little, Brown, and Company, 1935), 2:522–523.

44. See also William James, *Essays in Radical Empiricism* (1912; New York: Longman, Green, and Company, 1922), 10.

45. We should note that Dewey is referring to those moments in which experience is distinguished from nature proper. This requires a cognitive operation, the emergence of which is a self-contained process, causally aimed at meaning. Here the distinction between mind and world is necessary in his account, but it is a functional distinction. On this reading, then, his criticism of traditional philosophy relates to the fact not that this distinction holds, but that it is allowed to ossify in a specific way that rejects from the outset the original union and so undermines a basic naturalism. In such instances, the response consists in trying to find the appropriate bridging operation—a move that Dewey does not need to pursue.

46. McDowell formulates the same point as such: "The conceptual capacities drawn into play in experience belong to a network of capacities for active thought, a network that rationally governs comprehension-seeking responses to the impacts of the world on sensibility. And part of the point of the idea that the understanding is a faculty of spontaneity—that conceptual capacities are capacities whose exercise is in the domain of responsible freedom—is that the network, as an individual thinker finds it governing her thinking, is not sacrosanct. Active empirical thinking takes place under a standing obligation to reflect about the credentials of the putatively rational linkages that govern it. There must be standing willingness to refashion concepts and conceptions if that is what reflection recommends" (McDowell, *Mind and World*, 12–13).

47. Arendt, *Human Condition*, 236.

48. Ibid., 236.

49. Indeed, as he says later on in that work: "Men who devote themselves to thinking are likely to be unusually unthinking in some respects, as for example in immediate personal relationships. A man to whom exact scholarship is an absorbing pursuit may be more than ordinarily vague in ordinary matters. Humility and impartiality may be shown in a specialized field, and pettiness and arrogance in dealing with other persons" (HNC [MW14:137]).

50. Markell, *Bound by Recognition*, 79. That he attributes this to Aristotle does not seem problematic given the argument Dewey advances against Aristotle, since Markell is discussing this issue in the context of moral and political matters and not human action in toto.

51. Jean-Pierre Vernant and Pierre Vidal-Naquet, *Tragedy and Myth in Ancient Greece*, trans. J. Lloyd (Atlantic Highlands, NJ: Humanities Press, 1981), 20.

52. Thomas Alexander, "Dewey and the Metaphysical Imagination," *Transactions of the Charles S. Peirce Society* 28.2 (1992): 212; Alexander, "The Art of Life: Dewey's Aesthetics," in *Reading Dewey: Interpretations for a Postmodern Generation*, ed. Larry A. Hickman (Bloomington: Indiana University Press, 1998), 8; cf. James Campbell, *The Community Reconstructs* (Evanston: University of Illinois Press, 1992), 91–110.

53. Richard Bernstein, "Introduction," in *Dewey: On Experience, Nature, and Freedom*, ed. Richard Bernstein (New York: Liberal Arts Press, 1960), xviii. There is a long-standing debate between those who read Dewey as offering a metaphysics of existence and those who see him as offering a metaphysics of experience. See Sleeper, *Necessity of Pragmatism*; Thomas Alexander, *John Dewey's Theory of Art, Experience, and Nature: The Horizons of Feeling* (Albany: State University of New York Press, 1987), chap. 3; John Stuhr, "Dewey's Reconstruction of Metaphysics," *Transactions of the Charles S. Peirce Society* 28.2 (1992): 161–176; Stuhr, *Genealogical Pragmatism: Philosophy, Experience, and Community* (Albany: State University of New York Press, 1997), 126–130; Raymond Boisvert, "Dewey's Metaphysics: Ground-Map of the Prototypically Real," in *Reading Dewey: Interpretations for a Postmodern Generation*, ed. Larry A. Hickman (Bloomington: Indiana University Press, 1998), 149–165.

54. Aristotle, *Ethics*, bk. 6.4 [1140^{b}20]; 6.10 [1143^{a}8–15].

55. Aristotle, *Ethics*, bk. 3.3 [1112^{a}30–^{b}13] (emphasis added); cf. 6.5 [1140^{a}30–35].

56. Aristotle, *Ethics*, bk. 6.5 [1140^{a}25]; 6.7 [1141^{b}15]; 6.8 [1142^{a}12]; 6.11 [1143^{a}29–34].

57. Once again, the revisionist account of Aristotle would want to take issue with this reading. On this see Mulgan, *Aristotle's Political Theory*, chap. 7; Nussbaum, *Fragility*, chap. 10; Salkever, *Finding the Mean*, chap. 1; Frank, *Democracy of Distinction*, intro.–chap. 1.

58. In this case the situation would be cognitively inaccessible.

59. Brandom, "Freedom and Constraint," 180.

60. McDowell, *Mind, Value, and Reality*, 51. See also Lovibond, *Ethical Formation*, pt. 1. It is important to note that although sympathy is used in this context to denote what appears to be solitary reflection, it would be a mistake to conclude this. Dewey intends for sympathy to function during dialogical exchanges, making us receptive to the other and their perspective. I explore this issue in chapter 4.

61. Robert Brandom, *Making It Explicit: Reasoning, Representing, and Discursive Commitment* (Cambridge, MA: Harvard University Press, 1994); Jeffrey Stout, *Democracy and Tradition* (Princeton: Princeton University Press, 2004); Jürgen Habermas, *The Theory of Communicative Action*, trans. Thomas McCarthy (Boston: Beacon Press, 1987), vol. 2, chap. 5; Habermas, *Moral Consciousness and Communicative Action*, trans. Christian Lenhardt and Shierry Weber Nicholsen (Cambridge: Polity, 1990); cf. Cheryl Misak, *Truth, Politics, Morality: Pragmatism and Deliberation* (Malden, MA: Routledge, 2000).

62. See also Brandom, *Making It Explicit*, xiv, 245–255; Stout, *Democracy and Tradition*, 231–237; Habermas, "Moral Consciousness and Communicative Action," in *Moral Consciousness and Communicative Action*, 43–115; Misak, *Truth, Politics, Morality*, 94–106.

63. This reading borrows from Lovibond, especially when she writes: "Such evaluative distinctions suggest the further thought that there is such a thing as a *best possible* condition of the individual deliberator with respect to the appreciation of objective reasons" (Lovibond, *Ethical Formation*, 8).

64. Cited in Norwood Russell Hanson, *Patterns of Discovery: An Inquiry Into the Conceptual Foundations of Science* (New York: Cambridge University Press, 1958), 85.

65. Ibid. (original emphasis).

66. We should note in this regard that Dewey is not particularly interested in whether individuals denote the ends of inference as hypotheses, ideas, conjectures, guesses, suggestions, theories, or beliefs. Let the domain determine the appropriate idiom.

67. As Joas nicely writes of the pragmatists: "Hypotheses are put forward: suppositions about new ways of creating bridges between the impulses to action and the given circumstances of a situation. Not all such bridges are viable" (Joas, *Creativity of Action*, 133).

68. I take this to be a Peircean insight that Dewey never abandons. For this reading of Peirce see Misak, *Truth, Politics, Morality*; Robert Talisse, *A Pragmatist Philosophy of Democracy* (New York: Routledge, 2007), chap. 3; see also Dewey, L (LW12:17 n.1; cf. 343 n. 6).

69. I say "expansion" because Annas is clear that she needs to go beyond Aristotle at this juncture of her argument; see Annas, *Morality of Happiness*, 67–73.

70. Ibid., 71.

71. Ibid.

72. Ibid., 71–72.

73. Richard Rorty, "Dewey's Metaphysics," in *The Consequences of Pragmatism* (Minneapolis: University of Minnesota Press, 1982), 72–90.

74. See n. 53.

75. Stephen White, *Sustaining Affirmation: The Strengths of Weak Ontology in Political Theory* (Princeton: Princeton University Press, 2000), 8.

76. West, *American Evasion*, 101.

3. FAITH AND DEMOCRATIC PIETY

1. For a more historical account on the debate surrounding *A Common Faith* see Steven C. Rockefeller, *John Dewey: Religious Faith and Democratic Humanism* (New York: Columbia University Press, 1991), 512–540.

2. For views that deemphasize the importance of religion to Dewey see Michael Eldridge, *Transforming Experience: John Dewey's Cultural Instrumentalism* (Nashville: Vanderbilt University Press, 1997), 168; Jerome Paul Soneson, *Pragmatism and Pluralism: John Dewey's Significance for Theology* (Minneapolis: Fortress Press, 1993), 127; cf. Horace Friess, "Dewey's Philosophy of Religion," in *Guide to the Works of John Dewey*, ed. Jo Ann Boydston (Carbondale: Southern Illinois University Press, 1970), 202.

3. Dewey is very clear that William James seems to abandon his critical eye when "theological notions are under consideration" (WPP [MW4:109]). For a helpful text on James' religious thought see Henry S. Levinson, *The Religious Investigations of William James* (Chapel Hill: University of North Carolina Press, 1981). Charles S. Peirce seems to work from a standard design argument in matters of religion; see Peirce, "A Neglected Argument for the Reality of God" (1908), in *The Essential Peirce: Selected Philosophical Writings*, ed. Nathan Houser and Christian Kloesel (Bloomington: Indiana University Press, 1998), 434–450.

4. Here I am drawing on language from Rainer Forst in *Contexts of Justice: Political Philosophy Beyond Liberalism and Communitarianism*, trans. John M.M. Farrell (Berkeley: University of California Press, 2002), chap. 3, at 88.

5. Jeffrey Stout, *Democracy and Tradition* (Princeton: Princeton University Press, 2004), 20. See also Beth Eddy, *The Rites of Identity: The Religious Naturalism and Cultural Criticism of Kenneth Burke and Ralph Ellison* (Princeton: Princeton University Press, 2003), chap. 1; Dewey, CF (LW9:18).

6. Ralph Waldo Emerson, "The Divinity School Address" (1838), in *Emerson: Essays and Lectures / Nature: Addresses and Lectures / Essays: First and Second Series*

/ *Representative Men* / *English Traits* / *The Conduct of Life*, ed. Joel Porte (New York: Library of America, 1983), 91. All citations of Emerson's essays will come from this collection, unless otherwise noted. Compare Walt Whitman's remark in "Democratic Vistas" when he says: "Our fundamental want to-day in the United States, with closest, amplest reference to present conditions, and to the future, is of a class, and the clear idea of a class, of native authors, literatuses, far different, far higher in grade than any yet known, sacerdotal, modern, fit to cope with our occasions, taste, belief, breathing into it a new breath of life, giving it decision, affecting politics far more than popular superficial suffrage" ("Democratic Vistas" [1882], in *Specimen Days and Collect* [New York: Dover, 1995], 203–257, at 205–206).

7. Cf. Thomas M. Alexander, *John Dewey's Theory of Art, Experience, and Nature: The Horizons of Feeling* (Albany: State University of New York Press, 1987), 260–266; James Campbell, *Understanding John Dewey: Nature and Cooperative Intelligence* (Chicago: Open Court, 1995), 152–155.

8. John Dewey to Max Otto, January 14, 1935, in *The Correspondence of John Dewey*, ed. Larry Hickman, Barbara Levine, Anne Sharpe, and Harriet Furst Simon (Intelex Past Masters, electronic edition, 2004).

9. Emerson, "Self-Reliance" (1841), 275; cf. "The American Scholar" (1837), 53–71. Dewey himself invokes the term in precisely this way in several contexts (E_2 [MW5:422]; CC [LW5:139]; E_3 [LW7:327, 377]).

10. Alexis de Tocqueville, *Democracy in America*, trans. Harvey C. Mansfield and Delba Winthrop (1835/1840; Chicago: University of Chicago Press, 2000), bk. 1, pt. 2, chap. 9, 282.

11. The parenthetical insertions are my own, and are meant to clarify the distinctions that will be explained in greater detail below.

12. Hans Joas, *The Genesis of Values*, trans. Gregory Moore (Chicago: University of Chicago Press, 2000), 123.

13. Alan Ryan, *John Dewey and the High Tide of American Liberalism* (New York: Norton, 1995), 219–220.

14. See especially Bernard Yack's comments on this distinction in *The Problems of a Political Animal: Community, Justice, and Conflict in Aristotelian Political Thought* (Berkeley: University of California Press, 1993), 13–15, 30–32; cf. Stout, *Democracy*, 278–283; cf. Campbell, *Understanding John Dewey*, 173–174; James Campbell, "Community Without Fusion: Dewey, Mead, Tufts," in *Pragmatism: From Progressivism to Postmodernism*, ed. Robert Hollinger and David Depew (Westport, CT: Praeger, 1995), 56–71.

15. Here I am appropriating Ian Shapiro's language, but amending the imagery of democracy as a subordinate foundational good; see Shapiro, *Democratic Justice* (New Haven: Yale University Press, 1999), 21–24, at 21; "Revisiting *Democratic Justice*: A Response to Critics" *The Good Society* 11.2 (2002): 92.

16. I have no doubt that in his self-description, democracy would be Dewey's religious faith—that is, it is the source of his pious allegiance and unifies him in imagination (see also Robert B. Westbrook, "An Uncommon Faith: Pragmatism and Religious Experience," in *Pragmatism and Religion: Classical Sources and Original Essays*, ed. Stuart Rosenbaum [Champaign: University of Illinois Press, 2003], 190–205). This is clear from his life as a social reformer. But a psychoanalytic interpretation of Dewey must be careful not to read this as the point of *A Common Faith* as such, for it is simply inconsistent with his claim that the term "religious" can be a property of any feature of experience (DR [LW9:218–219]).

17. Cf. Whitman, "Democratic Vistas," 208; Stout, *Democracy*, 27; Thomas M. Alexander, "John Dewey and the Roots of Democratic Imagination," in *Recovering Pragmatism's Voice: The Classical Tradition, Rorty, and the Philosophy of Communication*, ed. Lenore Langsdorf and Andrew R. Smith (Albany: State University of New York Press, 1995), 131–154.

18. Emerson, "Man the Reformer" (1841), 137–138.

19. Emerson, *Nature* (1836), 10.

20. Ibid., 8.

21. Ibid.

22. Whitman says in agreement: "We shall, it is true, quickly and continually find the origin-idea of the singleness of man, individualism, asserting itself, and cropping forth, even from the opposite ideas. But the mass, or lump character, for imperative reasons, is to be ever carefully weigh'd, borne in mind, and provided for. Only from it, and from its proper regulation and potency, comes the other, comes the chance of individualism" (Whitman, "Democratic Vistas," 213; cf. 228).

23. For this criticism see Quentin Anderson, *The Imperial Self* (New York: Knopf, 1971); Sacvan Bercovitch, "Emerson, Individualism, and the Ambiguities of Dissent," in *Ralph Waldo Emerson: A Collection of Critical Essays*, ed. Lawrence Buell (Englewood Cliffs, NJ: Prentice Hall, 1993), 101–129; Christopher Newfield, *The Emerson Effect: Individualism and Submission in America* (Chicago: University of Chicago Press, 1996). We also see this in Cornel West, although he does gesture toward the social quality in Emerson's philosophy (*The American Evasion of Philosophy: A Genealogy of Pragmatism* [Madison: University of Wisconsin Press, 1989], 12–13, 19, 36).

24. Stout, *Democracy*, 31.

25. Emerson, "Man the Reformer," 135; cf. "The American Scholar," 63.

26. Thus Dewey writes of liberalism: "Born in revolt against established forms of government and the state, the events which finally culminated in democratic political forms were deeply tinged by fear of government, and were actuated by a desire to reduce it to a minimum so as to limit the evil it could do. Since established political forms were tied up with other institutions, especially ecclesiastical, and with a solid

body of tradition and inherited belief, the revolt also extended to the latter. Thus it happened that the intellectual terms in which the movement expressed itself had a negative import even when they seemed to be positive. Freedom presented itself as an end in itself, though it signified in fact liberation from oppression and tradition. . . . Thus 'individualism' was born, a theory which endowed singular persons in isolation from any associations, except those which they deliberately formed for their own ends" (PP [LW2:288–289]).

27. That it is an ambivalent conception of selfhood means that liberalism's notion of freedom need not be understood in such narrowly negative terms. Indeed, we find in thinkers like John Locke, J.S. Mill, and Thomas Green (thinkers with whom Dewey was obviously familiar) and in more contemporary thinkers like John Rawls a view that reconciles freedom and authority. So convinced that, once historicized, he can expand the normative dimension of liberalism's account of freedom, Dewey describes himself as working within that tradition. But if this view is right, then the revival of republicanism (à la Quentin Skinner and Philip Pettit), which distinguishes itself from liberalism, should be cautiously embraced. See Philip Pettit, *Republicanism: A Theory of Freedom and Government* (New York: Oxford University Press, 1997); cf. Quentin Skinner, *Liberty Before Liberalism* (New York: Cambridge University Press, 1998). For my specific worries about neo-republicanism see Melvin L. Rogers, "Republican Confusion and Liberal Clarification," *Philosophy and Social Criticism* 34.8 (2008).

28. Cf. George Kateb, *Emerson and Self-Reliance* (Thousand Oaks, CA: Sage, 1995), 171; Emerson, "Self-Reliance," 273.

29. Michael Sandel, *Liberalism and the Limits of Justice* (Cambridge, MA: Harvard University Press, 1982), chap. 1, especially at 58–62; cf. chap. 4.

30. Sandel, *Liberalism*, 150.

31. In fairness to Sandel, he does want to distinguish between a "situated" and "radically situated subject," but without giving us an account of why revision is and may be possible, it is unclear how he can sustain this distinction (Sandel, *Liberalism*, 20–21; see also 179–183). Moreover, because the identity of the subject (not resources for identity formation, as pointed out in the last chapter) is so thoroughly dependent on the community's self-understanding, Sandel appears to have made the claims of the community vis-à-vis its members both antecedent and therefore absolute. The tension is obvious when Sandel says that individuals do not "choose" their identity, they "find" it, which betrays his claim that individuals "participate" in the constitution of their identity (Sandel, *Liberalism*, 153; see also 179–180). For a similar critique see Forst, *Contexts*, chap. 1.

32. Reinhold Niebuhr, "The Pathos of Liberalism," *The Nation* 141 (September 11, 1935): 303.

33. Reinhold Niebuhr, *The Nature and Destiny of Man: Human Nature* (1941; New York: Scribners, 1964), 1:111.

34. Niebuhr, *Moral Man and Immoral Society* (1932; New York: Scribners, 1960), chaps. 1 and 10; *Nature and Destiny of Man*, chaps. 7–9; *The Children of Light and the Children of Darkness* (New York: Scribners, 1944), chap. 1. For an excellent biography, which details Niebuhr's political activism, see Richard Fox, *Reinhold Niebuhr: A Biography* (New York: Pantheon, 1985).

35. Eldridge, *Transforming Experience*, 61.

36. Niebuhr to Morton White, New York, 17 May 1956, in *Remembering Reinhold Niebuhr: Letters of Reinhold and Ursula Niebuhr*, ed. Ursula Niebuhr (San Francisco: Harper, 1991), 378–379; cf. Robin W. Lovin, *Reinhold Niebuhr and Christian Realism* (New York: Cambridge University Press, 1995), 46–56.

37. In saying this, I am unconvinced that the mythical character Niebuhr attributes to the divine is proof that he parts company from the standard Christian outlook.

38. Niebuhr, *Children of Light*, 16–17; cf. *Nature and Destiny of Man*, chap. 7.

39. Niebuhr, *Moral Man*, 19; cf. *Nature and Destiny of Man*, 178–179. For the all-important reception of *Moral Man* see Fox, *Reinhold Niebuhr*, 132–150.

40. Niebuhr, *Nature and Destiny of Man*, 100–103.

41. Niebuhr, *Children of Light*, 80–85, at 84; cf. 70–71. It is no surprise then to find Niebuhr saying that, "I stand in the William James tradition. He was both an empiricist and a religious man, and his faith was both the consequence and the presupposition of his pragmatism" (quoted in Jane Bingham, *Courage to Change: An Introduction to the Life and Thought of Reinhold Niebuhr* [New York: University Press of America, 1993], 224). For an interesting set of reflections on Niebuhr's Jamesian moment see West, *American Evasion*, 150–164; cf. Stanley Hauerwas, *With the Grain of the Universe: The Church's Witness and Natural Theology* (Grand Rapids: Brazos Press, 2001), chap. 4, at 96–105; Fox, *Reinhold Niebuhr*, 84.

42. I borrow the phrase from Judith Shklar's essay, "Emerson and the Inhibitions of Democracy," in *Redeeming American Political Thought*, ed. Stanley Hoffmann and Dennis F. Thompson (Chicago: University of Chicago Press, 1998), 49–65.

43. As he says later on: "Those contemporary theologians who are interested in social change and who at the same time depreciate human intelligence and effort in behalf of the supernatural, are riding two horses that are going in opposite directions" (CF [MW9:52]).

44. Fox, *Reinhold Niebuhr*, 146.

45. Against this Niebuhr seems to argue that sin is produced, as if to indicate its historical character (Niebuhr, *Nature and Destiny*, 251–260). The paradox, however, is that this is the result of our freedom, which is why he says all achievement is tainted by pride. But if freedom is a fundamental feature of being human that *al-*

ways leads us to sin, then the historical analysis is read back into an ontological contention about human nature as such. Cornel West seems to think otherwise, believing that even after Niebuhr "turned to the Pauline and Augustinian traditions he remained a liberal Christian ... [unwilling] to decenter human creative powers" (West, *American Evasion*, 155). While I believe his political activism may suggest this, I do not believe it can flow coherently or consistently from his theological position.

46. Emerson, *Conduct of Life* (1860), 945.

47. Compare Dewey's self-description in the 1930s after confronting his own disappointments as a reformer. It carries more than a hint of caution: "Forty years spent wandering in a wilderness like that of the present is not a sad fate unless one attempts to make himself believe that the wilderness is after all itself the promised land" (Dewey, AE [LW5:160]). As Robert Westbrook rightly notes in this regard: "Dewey never believed that American democracy was out of the woods" (*John Dewey and American Democracy* [Ithaca: Cornell University Press, 1991], 462; cf. Ryan, *John Dewey*, chaps. 7 and 8). Stanley Cavell thus misses the Emersonian voice in Dewey, reducing his understanding of inquiry to scientism (*Conditions Handsome and Unhandsome: The Constitution of Emersonian Perfectionism* [Chicago: University of Chicago Press, 1991], intro.). For several good responses to Cavell with which I agree, see Richard Shusterman, *Practicing Philosophy: Pragmatism and the Philosophic Life* (New York: Routledge, 1997); Philip W. Jackson, *John Dewey and the Philosopher's Task* (New York: Teachers College Press, 2002), chap. 5; Vincent Colapietro, "The Question of Voice and the Limits of Pragmatism: Emerson, Dewey, and Cavell," in *The Range of Pragmatism and the Limits of Philosophy*, ed. Richard Shusterman (Malden, MA: Blackwell, 2004), 174–196.

48. Emerson, "The Conservative" (1841), 177 (emphasis added); cf. Dewey, AE$_2$ (LW10:34).

49. For a more generous comparison between Niebuhr and Dewey specifically see Daniel Rice, *Reinhold Niebuhr and John Dewey: An American Odyssey* (Albany: State University of New York Press, 1993).

50. Santayana offers similar reflections that have a somewhat different inflection, but parallel and deepen the themes found in Emerson and Dewey: "Now man is part of nature and her organization may be regarded as the foundation of his own; the word nature is therefore less equivocal than it seems, for every nature is Nature herself in one of her more specific and better articulated forms. Man therefore represents the universe that sustains him; his existence is a proof that the cosmic equilibrium that fostered his life is a natural equilibrium, capable of being long maintained. . . . But even if this equilibrium, by which the stars are kept in their courses and human progress is allowed to proceed, is fundamentally unstable, it

shows what relative stabilities nature may attain. Could this balance be preserved indefinitely, no one knows what wonderful adaptations might occur within it, and to what excellence human nature in particular might advance.... I am not sure that a humanity such as we know, were it destined to exist forever, would offer a more exhilarating prospect that a humanity having indefinite elasticity together with a precarious tenure of life. Morality has its compensations: one is that evils are transitory, another that better times may come" (George Santayana, *The Life of Reason* [1905–1906; New York: Prometheus Press, 1998], 84–85).

51. On this distinction see John Smith, *Purpose and Thought: The Meaning of Pragmatism* (New Haven: Yale University Press, 1978), 224–225, n. 86; cf. P. Eddy Wilson, "Emerson and Dewey on Natural Piety," *Journal of Religion* 75.3 (1995): 336.

52. The claims articulated thus far depart from both Patrick Deneen's criticism of Emerson and Dewey and his cautious praise of Niebuhr in his recent book (see *Democratic Faith* [Princeton: Princeton University Press, 2005], chaps. 1, 2, and 9, at 246–260). The fundamental problem at the core of his reading has to do with the implicit or explicit meaning of "transformation" for both Emerson and Dewey. But unlike the conception of transformation we find in Rousseau, Emerson and Dewey do not mean a species-wide change, a fact that Deneen seems not to recognize (Deneen, *Democratic Faith*, intro., chap. 5). To say it differently: Emerson's and Dewey's conception of transformation is not located at the ontological level, and so is able to account for the recalcitrant features of human nature that cut against democratic governance and our natural sociality. As I have argued, Niebuhr seems unable to serve as a potential corrective to the emergence of "mean egotism" without making an ontological claim about humans as fallen creatures. This ontological (specifically theological) argument undermines any belief that human intervention may potentially bring about change in the world. Contra Deneen, both Emerson and Dewey are capable of showing us how to be humble—of understanding the potential limitations of being human and engaging the natural world that may undermine democratic possibilities—without making a theological claim.

53. Stout, *Democracy*, 28.

54. The phrase "unseen higher" should actually be "higher unseen" (see the substantive variants in quotations, MW9:519).

55. For this claim see Edward L. Schaub, "Dewey's Interpretation of Religion," in *The Philosophy of John Dewey*, ed. Paul Arthur Schilpp (Evanston, IL: Northwestern University Press, 1939), 398–399; cf. Friess, "Dewey's Philosophy of Religion," 209–210; John Herman Randall Jr., "The Religion of Shared Experience," in *Philosophy After Darwin: Chapters for the Career of Philosophy, Volume III, and Other Essays*, ed. Beth J. Singer (New York: Columbia University Press, 1977), 261; Wil-

lard E. Arnett, "Critique of Dewey's Anticlerical Religious Philosophy," *Journal of Religion* 34.4 (1954): 256–266.

56. Thus Dewey is clear that even the symbols and rites of religions that "have so often claimed to be realities and which have imposed themselves as dogmas and intolerances" often carry "some trace of a vital and enduring reality, that of a community of life in which continuities of existences are consummated" (HNC [MW14:226]).

57. See passage cited from Dewey on page 124 of this chapter.

58. Emerson, "Circles" (1841), 412; cf. Dewey, CF [MW9:27].

59. This theme figures prominently in Eddie Glaude's skillful application of pragmatism to the contemporary problems of black politics; see Glaude, *In a Shade of Blue: Pragmatism and the Politics of Black America* (Chicago: University of Chicago Press, 2007), esp. chap. 3.

60. Santayana, *Life of Reason*, 258.

61. Ibid., 264.

62. Ibid.

63. This phrase is understood by Rawls in the context of an "overlapping consensus" on principles that "persist over generations" and which "gain a sizable body of adherents in a more or less just constitutional regime, a regime in which the criterion of justice is that political conception itself" (John Rawls, *Political Liberalism* [New York: Columbia University Press, 1993], 13–15, at 15; cf. 133–172).

64. Ibid., 251–255.

65. Stout, *Democracy*, 98. In many ways, I read Stout as providing us with an updated version of what Dewey was up to. Yet he reads *A Common Faith* as being "too militant, too sure of its ability to debunk traditional forms of faith as irrational, to play the role Dewey wanted it to play in his public philosophy" (Stout, *Democracy*, 32). As he says earlier: "The question is whether his denial of supernaturalism can be an essential component of the *common* faith he proposes for democratic citizens" (Stout, *Democracy*, 23–24). But I do not believe it is right to read Dewey's political project as expressing an aversion to supernaturalism as such. He is concerned, in precisely the way Stout is, about it disqualifying public claims that do not proceed from the same starting point. One basic reading of Stout's argument is that he is providing us with an answer to the following question: If a theological perspective is no longer the assumed starting point of public dialogue, how then are we to proceed? If what I have been saying is accurate, then surely we can read Dewey as his ally, as agreeing with him that "the mark of secularization . . . is . . . that participants in a given discursive practice are not in a position to take for granted that their interlocutors are making the same religious assumptions they are" (Stout, *Democracy*, 97).

66. Ian Shapiro, *The State of Democratic Theory* (Princeton: Princeton University Press, 2003), 26.

67. Cf. "When a man desires ardently to know the truth, his first effort will be to imagine what the truth can be. He cannot prosecute his pursuit long without finding that imagination unbridled is sure to carry him off the track. . . . He can stare stupidly at phenomena; but in the absence of imagination they will not connect themselves together in any rational way" (Charles S. Peirce, "Lessons from the History of Science" (1896), in *Collected Papers of Charles Sanders Peirce*, ed. Charles Hartshorne and Paul Weiss [Cambridge, MA: Harvard University Press, 1931], 1:20).

68. Cf. "To put the issue in theological terms, a faith that excludes critical examination is a form of idolatry" (Richard J. Bernstein, "Pragmatism's Common Faith," in Richard J. Bernstein, *Pragmatism and Religion: Classical and Original Essays*, ed. Stuart Rosenbaum [Champaign: University of Illinois Press, 2003], 135).

69. Here Dewey has in mind Locke's claim that: "*Faith* . . . is the Assent to any Proposition, not thus made out by the Deductions of Reason; but upon the Credit of the Proposer, as coming from GOD, in some extraordinary way of Communication. This way of discovering Truths to Men, we call *Revelation*." And then again: "*Reason* is natural *Revelation*, whereby the eternal Faith of Light and Fountain of all Knowledge communicates to Mankind that portion of Truth, which he has laid within the reach of their natural Faculties: *Revelation* is natural *Reason* enlarged by a new set of Discoveries communicated by GOD immediately, which *Reason* vouches the Truth of, by the Testimony and Proofs it gives, that they come from GOD" (Locke, *An Essay Concerning Human Understanding*, ed. Peter H. Nidditch [1690; New York: Oxford University Press, 1979], bk. 4, chap. 18, ¶2; cf. bk. 4, chap. 19, ¶4 [original emphases]).

70. He provides us with a helpful example: "[Sherwood Eddy] says: 'I broke down from overwork and soon came to the verge of nervous prostration. One morning after a long and sleepless night . . . I resolved to stop drawing upon myself so continuously and begin drawing upon God. I determined to set apart a quiet time every day in which I could relate my life to its ultimate source, regain the consciousness that in God I live, move and have my being. That was thirty years ago. Since then I have had literally not one hour of darkness or despair.' This is an impressive record. I do not doubt its authenticity nor that of the experience. But it illustrates also the use of that quality to carry a superimposed load of a particular religion" (CF [LW9:9]). The example and commentary nicely capture the picture Dewey wishes to paint when he simultaneously says that the specificity of the experience indicates the religious aspect, but that this aspect receives a superimposed load because of the particular religion through which the experience is mediated. "Superimposed" suggests that somehow the experience as religious can be had without it. But that would not make sense given how he thinks of the social constitution of the self. Dewey must mean that the effect should not be reduced to the specificity of the meditated experience, since the tendency will then be to say

that to achieve results of this kind requires situations of this character or objects of this kind.

71. Hilary Putnam, "A Reconsideration of Deweyan Democracy," in *Pragmatism in Law and Society*, ed. Michael Brint and William Weaver (Boulder: Westview Press, 1991), 235–238; cf. James, "The Will to Believe" (1897), in *The Will to Believe and Other Essays in Popular Philosophy* (New York: Dover, 1956), 1–32.

72. Putnam, "Reconsideration of Deweyan Democracy," 233–237.

73. Cf. James, "Will to Believe," 24–25. Eric MacGilvray nicely explicates this position in the context of James' provocative essay. Unlike Putnam, he believes that Dewey is in agreement with James (MacGilvray, *Reconstructing Public Reason* [Cambridge, MA: Harvard University Press, 2004], chap. 2, at 67–68). But the central focus of MacGilvray's chapter is James' famous essay, and substantive references to Dewey's work are too few in number to do justice to the identification.

74. For a problematic interpretation with which I disagree see Victor Kestenbaum, *The Grace and the Severity of the Ideal: John Dewey and the Transcendent* (Chicago: University of Chicago Press, 2002), 183–184. In brief, Kestenbaum reads in Dewey a radical distinction between the kind of faith that underwrites ideal formation on the one hand, and belief formation on the other. But this misses the importance of inquiry to both.

75. James, "The Sentiment of Rationality" (1880) in *The Will to Believe*, 90.

76. James, "The Moral Philosopher and Moral Life" (1891), in *The Will to Believe*, 198. As mentioned before, however, James takes a more theological turn at the end of that essay.

77. John McDowell, *Mind and World* (Cambridge, MA: Harvard University Press, 1994), 82.

4. WITHIN THE SPACE OF MORAL REFLECTION

1. Note that I shall use capitals "G," "R", and "V" when discussing the good, right, and virtue in expansive terms. I shall revert to lower case when discussing specific goods, rights, and duties, or virtues and their relationship to action. For contemporary debates regarding which of these is more fundamental to moral life see the following: John Rawls, *A Theory of Justice* (Cambridge, MA: Harvard University Press, 1971), §18, §23, §68; Jürgen Habermas, "Moral Consciousness and Communicative Action" (1983), in *Moral Consciousness and Communicative Action*, trans. Christian Lenhardt and Shierry Weber Nicholsen (Cambridge: Polity, 1992), 116–195; Michael Sandel, *Liberalism and the Limits of Justice* (New York: Cambridge University Press, 1982); Alasdair MacIntyre, *After Virtue: A Study in Moral Theory* (Notre Dame: Notre Dame University Press, 1981); Bernard Williams,

Ethics and the Limits of Philosophy (Cambridge, MA: Harvard University Press, 1985); G. E. M. Anscombe, "Modern Moral Philosophy" (1958), in *Virtue Ethics*, ed. Roger Crisp and Michael Slote (New York: Oxford University Press, 1997), 26–45; Michael Stocker, "The Schizophrenia of Modern Ethical Theories" (1976), in the same volume, 66–78.

2. See Hilary Putnam, "A Reconsideration of Deweyan Democracy," in *Pragmatism in Law and Society*, ed. Michael Brint and William Weaver (Boulder: Westview Press, 1991), 217–243; Eric MacGilvray, *Reconstructing Public Reason* (Cambridge, MA: Harvard University Press, 2004), 135–136; Henry S. Levinson, "Stuck Between Debility and Demand: Religion and Enlightenment Traditions Among the Pragmatists," in *Knowledge and Belief in America: Enlightenment Traditions and Modern Religious Thought*, ed. William M. Shea and Peter A. Huff (New York: Cambridge University Press, 1995), 270–298. For a positive assessment of this argument that is then used against theorists of moral conflict see Isaac Levi, "Conflict and Inquiry," *Ethics* 102.4 (1992): 814–834. William Caspary is unique among these thinkers in recognizing the importance of conflict, but he nonetheless believes that Dewey's position needs to be supplemented (see Caspary, *Dewey on Democracy* [Ithaca: Cornell University Press, 2000], 3, 129).

3. The *Ethics* of 1932 with which I am concerned differs in a number of respects from the much earlier version of it that was published in 1908. Both versions were written in conjunction with James Hayden Tufts. The work is divided into three parts, "The Beginnings and Growth of Morality," "Theory of the Moral Life," and "The World of Action." The second, and more theoretical, section of the work bears the ink of Dewey's pen. Although attentive to the claims of sections 1 and 3, I shall rely primarily on the second section. For a more historical discussion of Dewey's *Ethics*, including the revisions between the 1908 and 1932 versions, see Abraham Edel and Elizabeth Flower, "Introduction," to *Ethics* (LW7:vii–xxxv); Abraham Edel, *Ethical Theory and Social Change: The Evolution of John Dewey's Ethics, 1908–1932* (New Brunswick, NJ: Transaction Publishers, 2001).

4. George Herbert Mead, *Mind, Self, and Society*, ed. Charles W. Morris (1934; Chicago: University of Chicago Press, 1967), 78. See also "The Social Self" (1913), in *Selected Writings*, ed. Andrew J. Reck (Chicago: University of Chicago Press, 1964), 142–149.

5. The importance of Mead to Dewey's self-understanding cannot be ignored. As his daughter recounts in a biographical piece she edited with materials provided by him, Dewey did not attempt a full-blown social psychology but rather "took [elements] over from Mead and made them a part of his subsequent philosophy, so that, from the nineties on, the influence of Mead ranked with that of James" ("Biography of John Dewey," ed. Jane Dewey, in *The Philosophy of John Dewey*, ed.

Paul A. Schilpp and Lewis Edwin Hahn [Evanston, IL: Northwestern University Press, 1939], 26). Speaking directly to this issue at Mead's memorial service in 1931, Dewey candidly remarks: "One would have to go far to find a teacher of our own day who started in others so many fruitful lines of thought; I *dislike* to think what my own thinking might have been were it not for the seminal ideas which I derived from him" (GHM [LW6:24] [original emphasis]). For helpful commentary on this relationship see Hans Joas, *G.H. Mead: A Contemporary Re-examination of His Thought*, trans. Raymond Meyer (Cambridge: Polity, 1980), 60–61; Gary A. Cook, *George Herbert Mead: The Making of a Social Pragmatist* (Urbana: University of Chicago Press, 1993), chaps. 4–5.

6. I take Putnam as intending something like this distinction when he says of pragmatism: "Pragmatism anticipated an idea that has become a commonplace in contemporary moral philosophy, the idea that disagreement in individual conceptions of the good need not make it impossible to approximate (even if we never finally arrive at) agreement on just procedures and even agreement on such abstract and formal values as respect for one another's autonomy, non-instrumentalization of other persons" (Hilary Putnam, "Pragmatism and Moral Objectivity," in *Words and Life*, ed. James Conant [Cambridge, MA: Harvard University Press, 1994], 155).

7. Here I am borrowing from, although not remaining completely consistent with, Sabina Lovibond's outlook in *Ethical Formation* (Cambridge, MA: Harvard University Press, 2002), 8.

8. Cf. Aristotle, *Nicomachean Ethics*, bk. 1.3, trans. W. D. Ross, in *The Basic Works of Aristotle*, ed. Richard McKeon (New York: Random House, 1941); Williams, *Ethics and the Limits of Philosophy*, 26–27; Jonathan Lear, *Aristotle: The Desire to Understand* (New York: Cambridge University Press, 1988), chap. 5.

9. Cf. Steven C. Rockefeller, *John Dewey: Religious Faith and Democratic Humanism* (New York: Columbia University Press, 1991), 414–416; Steven Fesmire, *John Dewey and Moral Imagination: Pragmatism in Ethics* (Bloomington: Indiana University Press, 2003), chaps. 3–4; Donald Morris, *Dewey and the Behavioristic Context of Ethics* (Bethesda, MD: International Scholars Publication, 1996), 87–89; Thomas Alexander, "John Dewey and the Roots of Democratic Imagination," in *Recovering Pragmatism's Voice: The Classical Tradition, Rorty, and the Philosophy of Communication*, ed. Lenore Langsdorf and Andrew R. Smith (Albany: State University of New York Press, 1995), 133.

10. Cf. Alexander, "John Dewey and the Roots of Democratic Imagination," 131–154; Fesmire, *John Dewey and Moral Imagination*, pt. 2.

11. In using this language, Dewey is obviously indebted to Adam Smith, but to what extent he differs from Smith or David Hume in that matter I do not pursue. See generally Hume, *A Treatise of Human Nature*, 2nd ed., ed. L. A. Selby-Gigge, rev.

P. H. Nidditch (1739–1740; New York: Oxford University Press, 1978); Smith, *The Theory of Moral Sentiments* (1759; New York: Prometheus Books, 2000).

12. Quoted in Jane Dewey, "Biography of John Dewey," 18. For a similar set of considerations see Sidney Hook, *Pragmatism and the Tragic Sense of Life* (New York: Basic Books, 1974), chap. 1; Eddie S. Glaude, *In a Shade of Blue: Pragmatism and the Politics of Black America* (Chicago: University of Chicago Press, 2007), chap. 2.

13. William James, "The Moral Philosopher and Moral Life" (1891), in *The Will to Believe and Other Essays in Popular Philosophy* (New York: Dover, 1956), 198.

14. John McDowell, *Mind and World* (Cambridge, MA: Harvard University Press, 1994), 82. Cf. Lovibond, *Ethical Formation*, pt. 1.

15. The most recent explication of this within the tradition of pragmatism is found in Jeffrey Stout, *Democracy and Tradition* (Princeton: Princeton University Press, 2004), chap. 12.

16. Mead, *Mind, Self, and Society*, 78 (emphasis added). Cf. HNC (MW14:41); EN (LW1:140).

17. Lovibond makes a similar claim when she says: "Human beings are a species to whom it is natural—at the level of 'first,' or biological, nature—to undergo initiation into a culture; this initiation may or may not have an official, legally regulated aspect, but in any case depends upon learning to talk and to take part in a variety of social *activities*, as envisaged by Wittgenstein under the head of 'language-games.' Over time, our participation in these activities . . . gives rise to a 'second,' or acquired, nature. This second nature is manifested in behavior which, though learned, is largely unreflective (like the speaking of a first language); and which, if we do make it into an object of reflection, usually produces in us a sense of inevitability" (Lovibond, *Ethical Formation*, 25 [original emphasis]); cf. McDowell, *Mind and World*, 94–96.

18. Although Dewey's language is different and he would want to emphasize the ongoing process of habituation, he nonetheless agrees with Aristotle's remark that: "[I]ntellectual virtue in the main owes both its birth and its growth to teaching (for which reason it requires experience and time), while moral virtue comes about as a result of habit, whence also its name *ethike* is one that is formed by a slight variation from the world *ethos* (habit). . . . Neither by nature, then, nor contrary to nature do the virtues arise in us; rather we are adapted by nature to receive them, and are made perfect by habit" (Aristotle, *Ethics*, bk. 2.1).

19. This is a deliberate play on McDowell's claim that if we take our second nature seriously, we are left with "no genuine questions about norms, apart from those that we address in reflective thinking about specific norms" (McDowell, *Mind and World*, 95).

20. While I agree with David Bakhurst that McDowell's account of *Bildung* is austere, I think it is a mistake to conclude that there are "few resources in Dewey's treatment of habits" for us to understand the dynamism of what it means to be initiated into the moral point of view (Bakhurst, "Pragmatism and Ethical Particularism," in *New Pragmatists*, ed. Cheryl Misak [New York: Oxford University Press, 2007], 134–136).

21. Cf. Mead, *Mind, Self, and Society*, 148–164.

22. This description captures Dewey's way of seeing a sign as a "fence" (a way of abstracting and detaching meaning among diversity), as a "label" (a way of retaining and storing meaning), and as a "vehicle" (a way to transport meanings to other areas of experience to achieve comprehension) (HWT$_2$ [LW8:303–305]; Alexander, "John Dewey and the Roots of Democratic Imagination," 143–147).

23. Mead, *Mind, Self, and Society*, 60.

24. The importance of problem-solving that we have considered throughout this work undoubtedly emerges in some rudimentary form to move language's development. There is a connection between this and Dewey's philosophy of action. When he uses social acts as the beginning point for thinking about action, he does so to emphasize the importance of socialization for the emergence of self-understanding. "Thus man," he writes, "is not merely *de facto* associated, but he *becomes* a social animal in the make-up of his ideas, sentiments and deliberate behavior. *What* he believes, hopes for, and aims at is the outcome of association and intercourse" (PP [LW2:251] [original emphases]). Dewey does not begin, as Habermas argues, with an "isolated actor's instrumental dealings with things and events" (Habermas, "Individuation Through Socialization: On George Herbert Mead's Theory of Subjectivity," in *Postmetaphysical Thinking: Philosophical Essays*, trans. William Mark Hohengarten [Cambridge, MA: MIT Press, 1996], 174). Thus language becomes the paradigmatic case from which he examines the organizing principles of conduct—i.e., morality. Stephen White is on to something when, drawing from pragmatism, he says: "Communicative rationality has to be understood finally as a practice of *coping with* the emergence of *problems within a context of intersubjectivity*" ("The Very Idea of a Critical Social Science," in *The Cambridge Companion to Critical Theory*, ed. Fred Rush [New York: Cambridge University Press, 2004], 319 [original emphases]). In this regard, Mead never needed, as Habermas encourages us to believe, to free himself from "Dewey's model of an isolated actor's . . . dealings" because this was never Dewey's beginning point. For a similar argument, although in response to James Hoopes, see Robert Westbrook, *Democratic Hope: Pragmatism and the Politics of Truth* (Ithaca: Cornell University Press, 2005), 42–45.

25. Mead, *Mind, Self, and Society*, 155–156.

26. Stout, *Democracy*, 270. Hence Dewey says: "Because of converse, social give and take, various organic attitudes become an assemblage of persons engaged in converse, conferring with one another, exchanging distinctive experiences, listening to one another, over-hearing unwelcome remarks, accusing and excusing" (EN [LW1:135]).

27. Mead, *Mind, Self, and Society*, 168.

28. McDowell, *Mind and World*, 184. It should be noted that although McDowell is speaking about language in this instance, he does so to indicate the extent to which the moral life is constitutively tied to language use.

29. John McDowell, "Towards Rehabilitating Objectivity," in *Rorty and His Critics*, ed. Robert Brandom (Malden, MA: Blackwell, 2000), 119. I take this also to be Habermas' point when he says: "By no means do these universal pragmatic presuppositions of communicative action suggest the objectivistic fallacy according to which we could take up the extramundane standpoint of a subject removed from the world, help ourselves to an ideal language that is context-free and appears in the singular, and thereby make infallible, exhaustive, and thus definitive statements which, having neither the capacity nor the need for a commentary, would pull the plug on their own effective history. From the possibility of reaching understanding linguistically, *we can read off a concept of situated reason that is given voice in validity claims that are both context-dependent and transcendent*" (Habermas, "The Unity of Reason in the Diversity of Its Voices," in *Postmetaphysical Thinking*, 138–139 [emphasis added]).

30. Charles S. Peirce, "How to Make Our Ideas Clear" (1878), in *The Essential Peirce: Selected Philosophical Writings*, ed. Nathan Houser and Christian Kloesel (Bloomington: Indiana University Press, 1992), 1:139.

31. William James, *Pragmatism* (1907; Cambridge, MA: Harvard University Press, 1996), 37; cf. Stout, *Democracy*, chap. 12.

32. Although Richard Rorty has been criticized for denying this point, I think he was far more careful than his critics acknowledge. As he says in *Philosophy and the Mirror of Nature* against problematic notions of Truth: "The aim of all such explanations is to make truth something more than what Dewey called 'warranted assertability': more than what our peers will, *ceteris paribus*, let us get away with saying" (Rorty, *Philosophy and the Mirror of Nature* [Malden, MA: Blackwell, 1980], 176). I understand two points to follow from this statement. First, peers need not be confined to a specific community. Second, the term *ceteris paribus* (all other things being equal) implies that reason, evidence, and argumentation have not revealed factors that may call the norm into question.

33. This raises an important question. How are we to proceed under conditions that are unfavorable to the practice of reason-giving? The conditions I have in mind in-

clude economic inequality that leads to asymmetrical power positions or a simple unwillingness on the part of individuals or a group to engage in reason-giving because various institutional arrangements insulate them from having to take part in deliberation. I will come back to this issue in the next chapter.

34. Habermas, "Individuation Through Socialization," 184 (original emphasis). See also Habermas, "Reconciliation Through the Public Use of Reason: Remarks on John Rawls's Political Liberalism," *Journal of Philosophy* 92.3 (1995): 117–118.

35. F. H. Bradley, "My Station and Its Duties" (1876), in *Ethical Studies*, 2nd ed. (New York: Oxford University Press, 1927), 160–214.

36. This account does not rule out situations that require moral action, but which are not dependent on reflection. What to do when you see a person who is about to be hit by a car and you are in a position that enables you to push her to safety requires little thought. That situation is not a moral problem in the way Dewey describes. However, the decision to push an individual from harm's way in a situation in which your own security is in jeopardy will no doubt constitute a problem in Dewey's sense. That one may have only a split second to think does not undermine the genuineness of the problem (cf. Michael Festenstein, *Pragmatism and Political Theory: From Dewey to Rorty* [Chicago: University of Chicago Press, 1997], 54).

37. The exception in this regard is Edel, *Ethical Theory and Social Change*.

38. For the primacy of these two traditions in contemporary moral philosophy see Robert B. Louden, *Morality and Moral Theory: A Reappraisal and Reaffirmation* (New York: Oxford University Press, 1992), 27.

39. James, "The Will to Believe" (1897), in *The Will to Believe*, 3.

40. Levi, "Conflict and Inquiry," 822.

41. Rosalind Hursthouse, *On Virtue Ethics* (New York: Oxford University Press, 1999), 47.

42. Cf. James, "The Moral Philosopher and the Moral Life" (1891), 184–215; Isaiah Berlin, "Two Concepts of Liberty" (1958), in *Four Essays on Liberty* (New York: Oxford University Press, 1969), 118–172; Bernard Williams, "Conflict of Values," in *Moral Luck: Philosophical Papers, 1973–1980* (New York: Cambridge University Press, 1981), 71–83; Martha Nussbaum, *Fragility of Goodness: Luck and Ethics in Greek Tragedy and Philosophy* (New York: Cambridge University Press, 1986), chaps. 1–2; Cheryl Misak, *Truth, Politics, Morality: Pragmatism and Deliberation* (New York: Routledge, 2000), 141–144; Hook, *Pragmatism and the Tragic Sense*, chap. 1; Glaude, *In a Shade of Blue*, chap. 2.

43. In doing so, he rejects two presumptive beliefs about the self that underwrite these two traditional ways of reasoning conflict away. The first is a belief that conflict emerges from a cognitive deficiency; the self is viewed from the outset as not being able to see the situation in its appropriate light. The second belief is that conflict

emerges from a weakness of will to follow what obviously seems to be the right course of action.

44. Implicit in this account is a distinction between the Right as an ideal and specific conceptions of it. As James Campbell points out, in Dewey's view the former is "never fully specifiable. The closest we come to specifiability is in the various conceptions of the term, conceptions that are subject to dispute" (*Understanding John Dewey: Nature and Cooperative Intelligence* [Chicago: Open Court, 1995], 153). Insofar as examination and criticism are absent, our various conceptions about what the Right embodies "have a tendency over time to usurp the place of [the] more abstract ideal" (ibid., 155).

45. Sophocles, *Antigone*, trans. Elizabeth Wyckoff, ed. David Grene and Richmond Lattimore (Chicago: University of Chicago Press, 1954), ll. 1170–1173.

46. Ibid., ll. 700–710 (emphasis added).

47. This is precisely why we do not generally see the law as an affront to our freedom, because for Dewey, like neo-republicans, "being unfree consists . . . in being subject to arbitrary sway," rather than merely "being restrained" (Philip Pettit, *Republicanism: A Theory of Freedom and Government* [New York: Oxford University Press, 1997], 5; see also Quentin Skinner, *Liberty Before Liberalism* [New York: Cambridge University Press, 1998], chap. 1). As we observed in the previous chapter, for Dewey, placing restraint as the key element in understanding freedom and its absence is based on a misguided atomistic ontology that underwrites social life.

48. I shall leave to the side the internal homogeneity implied by contemporary understanding, especially among liberals and communitarians, of the Good, which I am here conflating with Dewey's account. I shall qualify Dewey's position in the next section. For a helpful survey on the liberal-communitarian debate, which captures this, see Stephen Mulhall and Adam Swift, *Liberals and Communitarians*, 2nd ed. (Oxford: Blackwell, 1996).

49. My thinking about Dewey on this score is owed to a number of works: Sheldon Wolin, *Politics and Vision: Continuity and Innovation in Western Political Thought*, exp. ed. (Princeton: Princeton University Press, 2004), 511–513; Ian Shapiro, *The State of Democracy Theory* (Princeton: Princeton University Press, 2003); Seyla Benhabib, *The Rights of Others: Aliens, Residents, and Citizens* (New York: Cambridge University Press, 2004).

50. Among all Dewey scholars, I think Thomas Alexander is very much aware of the importance of this perceptive condition, although he does not examine it in the context of Dewey's moral philosophy; see Alexander, "The Art of Life: Dewey's Aesthetics," in *Reading Dewey: Interpretations for a Postmodern Generation*, ed. Larry A. Hickman (Bloomington: Indiana University Press, 1998), 12–13.

51. Festenstein, *Pragmatism and Political Theory*, 46.

52. Cf. Lovibond, *Ethical Formation*, 36.

53. Cf. Caspary, *Dewey on Democracy*, chap. 4.

54. MacIntyre, *After Virtue*, 208. Cf. Charles Taylor, *Sources of the Self: The Making of Modern Identity* (Cambridge, MA: Harvard University Press, 1989), 52.

55. MacIntyre, *After Virtue*, 215–216.

56. Taylor, *Sources*, 47. See also "The Diversity of Goods," in *Philosophy and the Human Sciences: Philosophical Papers 2* (New York: Cambridge University Press, 1985), 234.

57. Eric MacGilvray pursues similar themes, although with very different intentions; MacGilvray, *Reconstructing*, chap. 3.

58. Max Weber, "Science as a Vocation" (1919), in *From Max Weber: Essays in Sociology*, trans. H. H. Gerth and C. Wright Mills (New York: Oxford University Press, 1946), 129–158.

59. MacIntyre, *After Virtue*, 219; cf. *Whose Justice? Which Rationality?* (Notre Dame: University of Notre Dame Press, 1988), 92–93, 165–166. At other times MacIntyre sounds more like Dewey; see *After Virtue*, 187–190, 222.

60. Taylor, *Sources*, 47.

61. Taylor, *Sources*, 71 (emphasis added).

62. Weber, *Roscher and Knies: The Logical Problems of Historical Economics*, trans. Guy Oakes (1905; New York: Free Press, 1975), 192. Cf. Eyal Chowers, *The Modern Self in the Labyrinth: Politics and the Entrapment Imagination* (Cambridge, MA: Harvard University Press, 2004), 70.

63. Daniel M. Savage gives an interesting, although more generous, reading of the connection between Dewey and thinkers like Taylor and MacIntyre; see Savage, *John Dewey's Liberalism: Individual, Community, and Self-Development* (Carbondale: Southern Illinois University Press, 2002).

64. David Miller articulates a similar although much later claim when he remarks that modern identity is "a matter of the radical experience of equally real, but mutually exclusive aspects of the self. Personal identity cannot seem to be fixed. . . . The person experiences himself as many selves, each of which is felt to have . . . a life its own, coming and going without regard to the centered will of a single ego," but one that is, as he says earlier, "surprisingly . . . not sensed as pathology" (Miller, *The New Polytheism* [New York: Harper and Row, 1974], 193, 78; cf. Kenneth J. Gergen, *The Saturated Self: Dilemmas of Identity in Contemporary Life* [New York: Basic Books, 1991]).

65. Obviously this reliance on narrative to understand identity and character need not imply a radical political position. The transformative possibilities that attend inquiry in Dewey's view here depart from the more conservative position we find in MacIntyre.

66. MacGilvray, *Reconstructing*, 73.

67. Here I am referring to what are otherwise good works on Dewey's ethical philosophy: Jennifer Welchman, *Dewey's Ethical Thought* (Ithaca: Cornell University Press, 1995); Gregory Fernando Pappas, "Dewey's Moral Theory: Experience as Method," *Transactions of the Charles S. Peirce Society* 33.3 (1997): 520–556; Gregory Fernando Pappas, "To Be or to Do: John Dewey and the Great Divide in Ethics," *History of Philosophy Quarterly* 14.4 (1997): 447–472; Edel, *Ethical Theory and Social Change*; Todd Lekan, *Making Morality: Pragmatist Reconstruction in Ethical Theory* (Nashville: Vanderbilt University Press, 2003).

68. This marks an important advancement over Dewey's much earlier treatment of sympathy in his *Psychology* of 1887, in which it literally meant "feeling someone else's feelings" and thereby obscured the difference of evaluation one might offer about those feelings (cited in Morris, *Dewey and Behavioristic Context of Ethics*, 89). Donald Morris takes up this earlier treatment of sympathy as well as the later use of the concept, but does not point us to this crucial shift.

69. Dewey, "Psychology of Ethics," Lecture XXIX, March 18, 1901, in *Lectures on Ethics: 1900–1901*, ed. Donald F. Koch (Carbondale: Southern Illinois University Press, 1991), 241–245, at 245.

70. Westbrook, *Democratic Hope*, 112.

71. Caspary, *Dewey on Democracy*, 3, 129.

72. Putnam, "Reconsideration of Deweyan Democracy," 233.

73. Ibid., 234.

74. Larry Hickman, "Dewey: Pragmatic Technology and Community Life," in *Classical American Philosophy: Its Contemporary Vitality*, ed. Sandra Rosenthal, Carl Hausman, and Douglas Anderson (Champaign: University of Illinois Press, 1999), 107.

75. William James, "The Will to Believe" (1897), in *The Will to Believe and Other Essays*.

76. Jean-Paul Sartre, *Existentialism and Humanism*, trans. Philip Mairet (New York: Haskell House, 1948), 38.

77. James, *Pragmatism*, 141 (emphasis added).

5. CONSTRAINING ELITES AND MANAGING POWER

1. Christopher Lasch, *The New Radicalism in America* (New York: Vintage Press, 1965); see also Waher Feinberg, "The Conflict Between Intelligence and Community in Dewey's Educational Philosophy," *Educational Theory* 19.3 (1969): 234–248; Joseph G. Metz, "Democracy and the Scientific Method in the Philosophy of John Dewey," *Review of Politics* 31.2 (1969): 242–262; Clarence Karier, "Making

the World Safe for Democracy: An Historical Critique of John Dewey's Philosophy of the Warfare State," *Educational Theory* 27.1 (1977): 12–47.

2. Max Weber, *Economy and Society*, ed. Buenther Roth and Claus Wittich (1922; Berkeley: University of California Press, 1978), vol. 2, chap. 11; Walter Lippmann, *Public Opinion* (1922; New York: Free Press, 1965); *The Phantom Public* (1925; New Jersey: Transaction Publishers, 2004); C. Wright Mills, *The Power Elite* (New York: Oxford University Press, 1956), chaps. 1–3, 11–13.

3. By this phrase I mean nothing more than the belief that individuals ought to be able to participate in the construction of the laws by which they are governed and that this is something we have come to find important in political life and which must find a home in any theoretical or practical reflection on democracy.

4. By "elites," I mean nothing more complicated than experts or political officials who occupy or can come to occupy a privileged decision-making position because of their presumed knowledge and/or skills of governance.

5. C. Wright Mills, *Sociology and Pragmatism: The Higher Learning in America* (New York: Oxford University Press, 1969), 418–419.

6. Ibid., 423.

7. Sheldon Wolin, *Politics and Vision: Continuity and Innovation in Western Political Thought*, exp. ed. (Princeton: Princeton University Press, 2004), 517. See also John Patrick Diggins, *The Promise of Pragmatism* (Chicago: University of Chicago Press, 1994), chap. 7; Judith M. Green, *Deep Democracy: Community, Diversity, and Transformation* (Lanham, MD: Rowman and Littlefield, 1999), 31–32; John Stuhr, *Pragmatism, Postmodernism, and the Future of Philosophy* (New York: Routledge, 2003), chap. 8; Stephen K. White, "The Very Idea of a Critical Social Science: A Pragmatist Turn," in *The Cambridge Companion to Critical Theoryy*, ed. Fred Rush (New York: Cambridge University Press, 2004), 314.

8. Wolin, *Politics and Vision*, 517.

9. See generally, Lippmann, *Public Opinion*; Lippmann, *Phantom Public*; Joseph A. Schumpeter, *Capitalism, Socialism, and Democracy*, 3rd ed. (1942; New York: Harper and Row, 1950); cf. Robert Dahl, *Who Governs? Democracy and Power in an American City* (New Haven: Yale University Press, 1961); Dahl, *A Preface to Democratic Theory* (Chicago: University of Chicago Press, 1963); Adam Przeworski, "Minimalist Conception of Democracy: A Defense," in *Democracy's Value*, ed. Ian Shapiro and Casiano Hacker-Cordón (New York: Cambridge University Press, 1999), 23–55; Richard A. Posner, *Law, Pragmatism, and Democracy* (Cambridge, MA: Harvard University Press, 2002), chaps. 4–5. Although Dahl seemingly rejects rule by elites, his understanding of the political strata looks very much akin to Lippmann's class of experts (see Dahl, *Who Governs?*, 90–91; cf. Lippmann, *Public Opinion*, 194–195). For helpful summaries and criticisms of

this tradition see Carole Pateman, *Participation and Democratic Theory* (New York: Cambridge University Press, 1970), specifically chap. 1; Quentin Skinner, "The Empirical Theorists of Democracy and Their Critics," *Political Theory* 1 (1973): 287–305.

10. Sheldon Wolin, "Norm and Form: The Constitutionalizing of Democracy," in *Athenian Political Thought and the Reconstruction of American Democracy*, ed. J. Peter Euben, John R. Wallach, and Josiah Ober (Ithaca: Cornell University Press, 1994), 30–58. Wolin, however, is not alone in understanding democracy's relationship to regime construction in this way; see also Cornelius Castoriadis, "The Greek Polis and the Creation of Democracy," *Graduate Faculty Philosophy Journal* 9.2 (1983): 79–115; Ernesto Laclau and Chantel Mouffe, *Hegemony and Socialist Strategy* (London: Verso, 1985); Claude Lefort, *The Political Forms of Modern Society: Bureaucracy, Democracy, Totalitarianism* (Oxford: Polity Press, 1986); Lefort, *Democracy and Political Theory* (Minneapolis: University of Minnesota Press, 1988); Chantel Mouffe, *On the Political* (New York: Routledge, 2005); Jacques Rancière, *Disagreement: Politics and Philosophy*, trans. Julie Rose (Minneapolis: University of Minnesota Press, 1999); Rancière, "Ten Theses on Politics," *Theory and Event* 5.3 (2001): http://muse.jhu.edu/journals/theory_and_event/toc/archive.html#5.3.

11. For some representative texts see the following: Richard Bernstein, *Philosophical Profiles: Essays in a Pragmatic Mode* (Philadelphia: University of Pennsylvania Press, 1986); Hilary Putnam, "A Reconsideration of Deweyan Democracy," in *Pragmatism in Law and Society*, ed. Michael Brint and William Weaver (Boulder: Westview, 1991), 217–247; Robert B. Westbrook, *Democratic Hope: Pragmatism and the Politics of Truth* (Ithaca: Cornell University Press, 2005), chaps. 1, 3–4; Matthew Festenstein, *Pragmatism and Political Theory: From Dewey to Rorty* (Chicago: University of Chicago Press, 1997); Axel Honneth, "Democracy as Reflexive Cooperation: John Dewey and the Theory of Democracy Today," *Political Theory* 26.6 (1998): 763–783; James Kloppenberg, *The Virtue of Liberalism* (New York: Oxford University Press, 1998), chap. 6; James Bohman, "Democracy as Inquiry, Inquiry as Democratic: Pragmatism, Social Science, and the Cognitive Division of Labor," *American Journal of Political Science* 43.2 (1999): 590–607; William Caspary, *Dewey on Democracy* (Ithaca: Cornell University Press, 2001); Eric MacGilvray, *Reconstructing Public Reason* (Cambridge, MA: Harvard University Press, 2004).

12. Robert B. Westbrook, *John Dewey and American Democracy* (Ithaca: Cornell University Press, 1991), 456.

13. Philip Pettit, *Republicanism: A Theory of Freedom and Government* (New York: Oxford University Press, 1997); Ian Shapiro, *Democratic Justice* (New Haven: Yale University Press, 1999); Shapiro, *The State of Democratic Theory* (Princeton:

Princeton University Press, 2003); Henry S. Richardson, *Democratic Autonomy: Public Reasoning About the Ends of Policy* (New York: Oxford University Press, 2002), pt. 1; MacGilvray, *Reconstructing*, pt. 2; Cornel West, *Democracy Matters: Winning the Fight Against Imperialism* (New York: Penguin, 2004). I have said in several other instances that this view has affinities with the neo-republican conception of freedom as nondomination, which I shall explicitly invoke in this chapter (see chap. 3, n. 27; chap. 4, n. 47). Although neo-republicans such as Pettit and Quentin Skinner defend this notion as an alternative to liberalism, I am skeptical of whether this is the best way to understand the distinctiveness of republicanism in relation to liberalism. After all, Dewey is a liberal who concerns himself with expanding liberalism's conceptual and practical vocabulary for understanding freedom. As far as my argument here goes, nothing hangs on identifying Dewey with this tradition, although I shall indicate the use of domination in understanding what he is after.

14. Wolin, "Fugitive Democracy," in *Democracy and Difference: Contesting the Boundaries of the Political*, ed. Seyla Benhabib (Princeton: Princeton University Press, 1996), 37. Cf. Dewey (FC [LW13:136]).

15. Alexis de Tocqueville, *Democracy in America*, trans. Harvey C. Mansfield and Delba Winthrop (1835–1840; Chicago: University of Chicago Press, 2000), bk. I, pt. II, chap. 5.

16. My understanding of Lippmann in these passages is owed to Charles Wellborn, *Twentieth-Century Pilgrimage: Walter Lippmann and the Public Philosophy* (Baton Rouge: Louisiana State University Press, 1969), chap. 2; Ronald Steel, *Walter Lippmann and the American Century* (Boston: Little, Brown, 1980), chaps. 13–17; Barry D. Riccio, *Walter Lippmann—Odyssey of a Liberal* (New Brunswick, NJ: Transaction Publishers, 1994), chaps. 3, 5; Westbrook, *John Dewey*, 294–300.

17. Lippmann, *Phantom Public*, 10.

18. Ibid., 196; cf. Lippmann, *Public Opinion*, chap. 10.

19. Lippmann, *Public Opinion*, 59.

20. Ibid., 64.

21. Ibid., 10.

22. Ibid., 11.

23. Ibid., 13.

24. Ibid., 64.

25. Ibid., 74.

26. Ibid., 60.

27. Ibid., 133.

28. Ibid., 66.

29. Ibid., 63.

30. Ibid., vii.

31. Lippmann, *Phantom Public*, 145. Indeed, precisely because of his suspicion of public opinion he is unconvinced that universal suffrage will improve the quality of democracy: "If the voter cannot grasp the details of the problems of the day because he has not the time, the interest or the knowledge, he will not have a better public opinion because he is asked to express his opinion more often" (Lippmann, *Phantom Public*, 26–27).

32. Schumpeter, *Capitalism, Socialism, and Democracy*, 284–285; Lippmann, *Phantom Public*, 47.

33. Alexander Hamilton, James Madison, and John Jay, *The Federalist*, ed. Jacob E. Cooke (1787–1788: Middletown, CT: Wesleyan University Press, 1961), no. 63:428; cf. "Had every Athenian citizen been a Socrates every Athenian assembly would still have been a mob," no. 55:374.

34. There seems to be a difference between the early democratic realists, such as Lippmann, Harold Lasswell, and Charles Merriam, and later thinkers, such as Schumpeter, Dahl, Downs, and Przeworski. The groups appear to be in agreement about the societal obstacles to participation, they diverge slightly in their emphasis regarding the cognitive challenges, and they agree that the procedures under which the elected are made responsive to the electorate should be emphasized more consistently than they have been in earlier accounts of democracy. The fundamental difference, however, revolves around the quality of decision-making. The earlier thinkers seem much more interested in isolating how political decision-making can be made more "intelligent," less driven by bias. They have a greater preoccupation with political objectivity then the latter set of thinkers. For some help in thinking about this see Edward A. Purcell Jr., *The Crisis of Democratic Theory: Scientific Naturalism and the Problem of Value* (Lexington: University Press of Kentucky, 1973), chaps. 6, 10–11, 13.

35. Lippmann, *Public Opinion*, 182.

36. Ibid., 19.

37. Ibid., 195, 236.

38. Lippmann amplifies this view much later when he suggests that the habits necessary to engaging in experimental intelligence can be obtained by only a few—a position he expands upon in his later work (see, for instance, Lippmann, *Essays in the Public Philosophy* [New York: Mentor, 1955], bk. 2). This claim sets Lippmann off from the more traditional pragmatists of both his time and ours.

39. James Fishkin, *The Voice of the People: Public Opinion and Democracy* (New Haven: Yale University Press, 1997); *The Deliberative Democracy Handbook: Strategies for Effective Civic Engagement in the Twenty-First Century*, ed. John Gastil and Peter Levine (San Francisco: Jossey-Bass, 2005); Diana C. Muntz, *Hearing the*

Other Side: Deliberative Versus Participatory Democracy (New York: Cambridge University Press, 2006).

40. This is not to say that there will be no trade-offs between the local and the communal perspectives, but such trade-offs (and here I am getting ahead of myself) are measured by the extent to which they do not block the future contestability of their own consequences.

41. Lippmann, *Phantom Public*, chap. 4.

42. Wolin, "Fugitive Democracy," 43, 31.

43. Wolin, "Norm and Form," 55.

44. Wolin, "Fugitive Democracy," 38. Cf. *Politics and Vision*, chap. 17, §§12–14.

45. Wolin, "Fugitive Democracy," 31.

46. Rancière, "Ten Theses on Politics" (original emphasis).

47. Wolin, "Norm and Form," 37 (original emphasis).

48. Wolin, "Transgression, Equality, and Voice," in *Dēmokratia: A Conversation on Democracies, Ancient and Modern*, ed. Josiah Ober and Charles Hedrick (Princeton: Princeton University Press, 1996), 64.

49. Ibid. Although Wolin does not discuss Lefort's account of democracy, there seem to be strong affinities between the two, especially when the latter writes: "And the fact that [society] is organized as *one* despite (or because of) its multiple divisions and that it is organized as *the same* in all its multiple dimensions implies a reference to a place from which it can be seen, read and named. Even before we examine it in its empirical determinations, this symbolic pole proves to be power; it manifests society's self-externality, and ensures that society can achieve a quasi-representation of itself. . . . It would be more accurate to say that power makes a gesture towards something *outside*, and that it defines itself in terms of that outside" (Lefort, *Democracy and Political Theory*, 225 [original emphasis]).

50. It is worth noting that in Wolin's view these distinctions between normal and revolutionary moments of collective organization, politics and the political, constitutionalism and democracy find their respective embodiments at the moment of the American founding in the federalists and anti-federalists. On this point see Wolin, *The Presence of the Past: Essays on the State and the Constitution* (Baltimore: Johns Hopkins University Press, 1989), chap. 5.

51. Wolin, "Norm and Form," 35; cf. "Fugitive Democracy," 34.

52. Wolin, "Democracy: Electoral and Athenian," *PS: Political Science and Politics* 26.3 (1993): 476; cf. "Norm and Form," 32.

53. Wolin, *Politics and Vision*, 600.

54. Wolin, *Presence of the Past*, chaps. 1, 3, 5, and 10.

55. Wolin, "Norm and Form," 39.

56. Indeed, this seems to be the sole purpose, at least as he understand it, for which constitutions were constructed. "Greek theorists," he explains, "developed a cri-

tique of democracy and then constructed a conception of a constitution as a means of demonstrating how democracy might be domesticated, rendered stable, orderly, and just" (Wolin, "Norm and Form," 35).

57. Wolin, *Presence of the Past*, 4.

58. Wolin, "Fugitive Democracy," 34.

59. Wolin, *Politics and Vision*, 602–603.

60. George Kateb, "Wolin as a Critic of Democracy," in *Democracy and Vision: Sheldon Wolin and the Vicissitudes of the Political*, ed. Aryeh Botwinick and William E. Connolly (Princeton: Princeton University Press, 2001), 39.

61. See generally Sidney Tarrow, *Power in Movement: Social Movements, Collective Action, and Politics* (New York: Cambridge University Press, 1994), chaps. 1, 5–6, 10–11; John Markoff, *Waves of Democracy: Social Movements and Political Change* (Thousand Oaks, CA: Pine Forge Press, 1996), chap. 2; Charles Tilly, *Social Movements, 1768–2004* (Boulder: Paradigm, 2004), chaps. 1–2, 5–6.

62. Anthony Giddens, *The Consequences of Modernity* (Stanford: Stanford University Press, 1990), 27.

63. On the centrality of conflict to decision-making in Dewey's political thought see Caspary, *Dewey on Democracy*, chaps. 1 and 4.

64. "Biography of John Dewey," ed. Jane M. Dewey, in *The Philosophy of John Dewey*, ed. Paul A. Schilpp and Lewis Edwin Hahn (Chicago: Northwestern University Press, 1939), 18.

65. To be sure, in his early writings Dewey often suggests that social conflict results from what MacGilvray identifies as "self-defeating ignorance or blindness" (MacGilvray, *Reconstructing*, 135–136). But to recall the argument of the last chapter, Dewey is very clear in his mature writings that while these *may be* the cause of social conflict, we should not begin our inquiry with the thought that conflict is "specious and apparent" (TIM [LW5:280]). In fact, in the context of politics he begins with an adversarial notion of politics, albeit one that encourages us not to see our opponent as the enemy (CD [LW14:228]).

66. Obviously this point has clear affinities with deliberative democracy. For some representative texts, see John Dryzek, *Discursive Democracy: Politics, Policy, and Political Science* (New York: Cambridge University Press, 1990); Amy Gutmann and Dennis Thompson, *Democracy and Disagreement* (Cambridge, MA: Harvard University Press, 1996); Seyla Benhabib, "Toward a Deliberative Model of Democratic Legitimacy," in *Democracy and Difference: Contesting the Boundaries of the Political*, ed. Benhabib (Princeton: Princeton University Press, 1996), 67–94; Joshua Cohen, "Procedure and Substance in Deliberative Democracy," in the same volume, 95–119; Cohen, "Deliberation and Democratic Legitimacy," in *Deliberative Democracy: Essays on Reason and Politics*, ed. James Bohman and William Rehg (Cambridge, MA: MIT Press, 1997), 67–93; James Bohman, "Survey Article:

The Coming of Age of Deliberative Democracy," *Journal of Political Philosophy* 6.4 (1998): 400–425.

67. For interpretative and translation difficulties between the lay and the expert public that are in need of remedy see Bohman, "Democracy as Inquiry," 598–599; Frank Fischer, *Citizens, Experts, and the Environment: The Politics of Local Knowledge* (Durham: Duke University Press, 2000), pts. 2–3. Dewey himself was well aware of this issue; see PP (LW2:347–348).

68. Putnam, *Enlightenment and Pragmatism* (Amsterdam: Koninklijke Van Gorcum, 2001), 24. Cf. "A Reconsideration of Deweyan Democracy," 217–243; Putnam and Ruth Anna Putnam, "Dewey's Logic: Epistemology as Hypothesis," in *Words and Life*, ed. James Conant (Cambridge, MA: Harvard University Press, 1994), 215–218.

69. Putnam, "A Reconsideration of Deweyan Democracy," 217.

70. Dewey himself did not work out what either of these would look like from an institutional perspective, although he provides norms for guidance that I am here fleshing out. For a Deweyan-inspired approach that focuses on institutional reforms see Archon Fung and Erik Olin Wright, "Introduction," in *Deepening Democracy: Institutional Innovations in Empowered Participatory Governance* (New York: Verso, 2003); Fung, "Deliberative Democracy, Chicago Style: Grass-Roots Governance in Policing and Public Education," in the same volume, 111–143; Gianpaola Baiocchi, "Participation, Activism, and Politics: The Porto Alegre," in the same volume, 45–76; Fung, *Empowered Participation: Reinventing Urban Democracy* (Princeton: Princeton University Press, 2004).

71. For more on this point see MacGilvray, *Reconstructing*, chap. 4.

72. As Dewey says: "Something that bears the name democracy existed in Athens but it had little in common with the democratic movement of modern times" (LFW [LW14:316]).

73. For the various faces of power see: Robert Dahl, "The Concept of Power," *Behavioral Science* 2 (1957): 201–215; Nelson Polsby, *Community Power and Political Theory* (New Haven: Yale University Press, 1963), 202–210; Peter Bachrach and Morton S. Baratz, *Power and Poverty: Theory and Practice* (New York: Oxford University Press, 1970); Steven Lukes, *Power: A Radical View* (New York: Macmillan, 1974). For helpful surveys of the power debate see John Gaventa, *Power and Powerlessness: Quiescence and Rebellion in an Appalachian Valley* (Chicago: University of Illinois Press, 1980), 3–32; Clarissa Rile Hayward, *De-Facing Power* (New York: Cambridge University Press, 2000).

74. The most recent explication of this, on which I rely, is in Philip Pettit and Ian Shapiro; see Pettit, *Republicanism*, chaps. 1–3; Shapiro, *State of Democratic Theory*, chaps. 1–2; Shapiro, *Democratic Justice*, chaps. 1–3.

75. Claus Offe, "How Can We Trust Our Fellow Citizens?" in *Democracy and Trust*, ed. Mark E. Warren (New York: Cambridge University Press, 1999), 42–88; Eric M. Uslaner, "Democracy and Social Capital," in the same volume, 121–151.

76. James Farr, "Social Capital: A Conceptual History," *Political Theory* 32.1 (2004): 6–33.

77. Diggins, *Promise of Pragmatism*, 304.

78. Richardson, *Democratic Autonomy*, 71.

79. Ibid.

80. Bohman, "Democracy as Inquiry," 595–596.

81. If this reading of Dewey is accurate, he could easily say with MacGilvray that "to the extent that a case is made against this ideal [of inclusion], it is made not by criticizing the norm of inclusion itself but rather by drawing attention to the practical constraints . . . that stand in the way of its realization. Thus to be engaged as a pragmatist in normative political inquiry is to be concerned with the problem of bringing the experimental intelligence of all citizens to bear in public life to the fullest extent possible" (MacGilvray, *Reconstructing*, 111).

82. See generally Cheryl Misak, *Truth, Politics, Morality: Pragmatism and Deliberation* (New York: Routledge, 2000); Jeffrey Stout, *Democracy and Tradition* (Princeton: Princeton University Press, 2004); Robert Talisse, *A Pragmatist Philosophy of Democracy* (New York: Routledge, 2007).

83. Fung, "Deliberation Before the Revolution: Toward an Ethics of Deliberative Democracy in an Unjust World," *Political Theory* 33.3 (2005): 399.

84. Pettit, *Republicanism*, 22. Cf. Shapiro, *Democratic Justice*, chaps. 1–3.

85. Pettit, *Republicanism*, 69–70 n. 6.

86. Ibid., 56.

87. Shapiro, *Democratic Justice*, 42.

88. Festenstein, *Pragmatism and Political Theory*, 86.

89. Westbrook, *John Dewey*, 305.

90. Jürgen Habermas, *Between Facts and Norms: Contributions to a Discourse Theory of Law and Democracy*, trans. William Rehg (Cambridge: Polity, 1997), 300.

91. Iris Marion Young, *Inclusion and Democracy* (New York: Oxford University Press, 2000), 167.

92. Dewey worries about the extent to which democratic institutions can effectively absorb what is essential to their maintenance under conditions of complexity, namely, "a scattered, mobile and manifold public" (PP [LW2:327]). This, for him, was primarily an intellectual problem to which he did not provide an answer. Tentatively, I am inclined to say that the Internet may serve as the structural analogue to face-to-face communication through which discursive claims can be built up and around which people consolidate. For more on this possibility as a solution to

the problem Dewey specifically poses see James Bohman, *Democracy Across Borders* (Cambridge, MA: MIT Press, 2007), 74–83.

93. Shapiro, *State of Democratic Theory*, 54.

94. Lefort, *Political Forms of Modern Society*, 279.

95. Westbrook, *John Dewey*, 305 (original emphasis).

96. Nancy Fraser, *Justice Interruptus: Critical Reflections on the "PostSocialist" Condition* (New York: Routledge, 1997), 81 (original emphasis).

97. Here I am drawing generally from the following texts: Tarrow, *Power in Movement*, chaps. 10–11; Markoff, *Waves of Democracy*, chap. 2; Tilly, *Social Movements*, chaps. 5–6; Dryzek, *Deliberative Democracy and Beyond: Liberals, Critics, Contestations* (New York: Oxford University Press, 2000), chap. 4; Young, *Inclusion and Democracy*, chap. 5.

EPILOGUE

1. Eddie S. Glaude, *In a Shade of Blue: Pragmatism and the Politics of Black America* (Chicago: University of Chicago Press, 2007), 7.

2. Jürgen Habermas, *Between Facts and Norms: Contributions to a Discourse Theory of Law and Democracy*, trans. William Rehg (Oxford: Polity Press, 1998), chap. 8.

3. John S. Dryzek, *Deliberative Democracy and Beyond: Liberals, Critics, Contestations* (New York: Oxford University Press, 2000), 96.

4. Ibid., 97.

5. Ian Shapiro, *Democratic Justice* (New Haven: Yale University Press, 1999), 39.

6. Max Weber, "Science as a Vocation" (1919), in *From Max Weber: Essays in Sociology*, trans. H.H. Gerth and C. Wright Mills (New York: Oxford University Press, 1946), 129–158.

7. Carl Schmitt, *The Concept of the Political*, trans. George Schwab (1932; Chicago: University of Chicago, 1996), §§2–3.

8. Dana Villa, "Hegel, Tocqueville, and 'Individualism,'" *Review of Politics* 67.4 (2005): 684.

9. Claude Lefort, *The Political Forms of Modern Society* (Oxford: Polity Press, 1986), 279.

BIBLIOGRAPHY

Abbott, Lyman. *Christianity and Social Problems*. New York: Houghton, Mifflin, and Company, 1896.

——. *The Evolution of Christianity*. New York: The Outlook Company, 1892.

——. *The Theology of An Evolutionist*. New York: The Outlook Company, 1897.

Alexander, Thomas M. "The Art of Life: Dewey's Aesthetics." In *Reading Dewey: Interpretations for a Postmodern Generation*, ed. Larry A. Hickman, 1–22. Bloomington: Indiana University Press, 1998.

——. "Dewey and the Metaphysical Imagination." *Transactions of the Charles S. Peirce Society* 28, no. 2 (1992): 203–215.

——. "John Dewey and the Roots of Democratic Imagination." In *Recovering Pragmatism's Voice: The Classical Tradition, Rorty, and the Philosophy of Communication*, ed. Lenore Langsdorf and Andrew R. Smith, 131–154. Albany: State University of New York Press, 1995.

——. *John Dewey's Theory of Art, Experience, and Nature: The Horizons of Feeling*. Albany: State University of New York Press, 1987.

Anderson, Douglass R. "Theology as Healing: A Meditation on 'A Common Faith.'" In *Dewey Reconfigured: Essays on Deweyan Pragmatism*, ed. Casey Haskins and David I. Seiple, 85–95. New York: State University of New York Press, 1999.

Anderson, Quentin. *The Imperial Self*. New York: Knopf, 1971.

Annas, Julia. *The Morality of Happiness*. New York: Oxford University Press, 1993.

Anscombe, G. E. M. "Modern Moral Philosophy" (1958). In *Virtue Ethics*, ed. Roger Crisp and Michael Slote, 26–45. New York: Oxford University Press, 1997.

Anton, John P. "John Dewey and Ancient Philosophies." In *Philosophy and Phenomenological Research* 25, no. 4 (1965): 477–499.

Arendt, Hannah. *The Human Condition*. Chicago: University of Chicago Press, 1958.

Aristotle. *Nicomachean Ethics*. Trans. W. D. Ross. In *The Basic Works of Aristotle*, ed. Richard McKeon. New York: Random House, 1941.

——. *Politics*. Trans. Benjamin Jowett. In *The Basic Works of Aristotle*, ed. Richard McKeon. New York: Random House, 1941.

Arnett, Willard E. "Critique of Dewey's Anticlerical Religious Philosophy." *Journal of Religion* 34, no. 4 (1954): 256–266.

Arnold, Matthew. "Dover Beach" (1867). In *The Portable Matthew Arnold*, ed. Lionel Trilling, 165–167. New York: Viking, 1959.

——. "Stanzas from the Grande Chartreuse" (1855). In *The Portable Matthew Arnold*, ed. Lionel Trilling, 148–155. New York: Viking, 1949.

Bachrach, Peter, and Morton S. Baratz. *Power and Poverty: Theory and Practice*. New York: Oxford University Press, 1970.

Baiocchi, Gianpaolo. "Participation, Activism, and Politics: The Porto Alegre." In *Deepening Democracy: Institutional Innovations in Empowered Participatory Governance*, ed. Archon Fung and Erik Olin Wright, 45–76. New York: Verso, 2003.

Bakhurst, David. "Pragmatism and Ethical Particularism." In *New Pragmatists*, ed. Cheryl Misak, 122–141. New York: Oxford University Press, 2007.

Bates, Ralph. *Scientific Societies in the United States*. 2nd ed. New York: Columbia University Press, 1958.

Beecher, Henry Ward. *Evolution and Religion, Part 1 and 2*. New York: Fords, Howard, and Hulbert, 1885.

——. "Progress of Thought in the Church." *North American Review* 135, no. 309 (1882): 99–118.

——. "The Study of Human Nature" (1872). In *American Protestant Thought: The Liberal Era*, ed. William R. Hutchison, 37–45. New York: Harper and Row, 1968.

Benhabib, Seyla. *The Claims of Culture*. Princeton: Princeton University Press, 2002.

——. *The Rights of Others: Aliens, Residents, and Citizens*. New York: Cambridge University Press, 2004.

——. *Situating the Self: Gender, Community, and Postmodernism in Contemporary Ethic*. New York: Routledge, 1992.

——. "Toward a Deliberative Model of Democratic Legitimacy." In *Democracy and Difference: Contesting the Boundaries of the Political*, ed. Seyla Benhabib, 67–94. Princeton: Princeton University Press, 1996.

Bennett, Jane. *The Enchantment of Modern Life: Attachments, Crossings, and Ethics*. Princeton: Princeton University Press, 2001.

Bercovitch, Sacvan. "Emerson, Individualism, and the Ambiguities of Dissent." In *Ralph Waldo Emerson: A Collection of Critical Essays*, ed. Lawrence Buell, 101–129. Englewood Cliffs, NJ: Prentice Hall, 1993.

Berlin, Isaiah. *Four Essays on Liberty.* New York: Oxford University Press, 1969.

Bernstein, Richard J. *Beyond Objectivism and Relativism: Science, Hermeneutics, and Praxis.* Philadelphia: University of Pennsylvania Press, 1983.

——. "Community in the Pragmatic Tradition." In *The Revival of Pragmatism: New Essays on Social Thought, Law, and Culture*, ed. Morris Dickstein, 141–156. Durham: Duke University Press, 1998.

——. "Introduction." In *Dewey: On Experience, Nature, and Freedom*, ix–xlvii. New York: Liberal Arts Press, 1960.

——. *John Dewey.* New York: Washington Square Press, 1967.

——. *The New Constellation: Ethical-Political Horizons of Modernity/Postmodernity.* Cambridge, MA: MIT Press, 1992.

——. *Philosophical Profiles: Essays in a Pragmatic Mode.* Philadelphia: University of Pennsylvania Press, 1986.

——. "Pragmatism's Common Faith." In *Pragmatism and Religion: Classical and Original Essays*, ed. Stuart Rosenbaum, 129–141. Champaign: University of Illinois Press, 2003.

——. *Praxis and Action: Contemporary Philosophies of Human Activity.* Philadelphia: University of Pennsylvania Press, 1971.

Bingham, Jane. *Courage to Change: An Introduction to the Life and Thought of Reinhold Niebuhr.* New York: University Press of America, 1993.

Block, James E. *A Nation of Agents: The American Path to a Modern Self and Society.* Cambridge, MA: Harvard University Press, 2002.

Blumenberg, Hans. *The Legitimacy of the Modern Age.* Trans. Robert M. Wallace. Cambridge, MA: MIT Press, 1983.

Bohman, James. *Democracy Across Borders.* Cambridge, MA: MIT Press, 2007.

——. "Democracy as Inquiry, Inquiry as Democratic: Pragmatism, Social Science, and the Cognitive Division of Labor." *American Journal of Political Science* 43, no. 2 (1999): 590–607.

——. "Realizing Deliberative Democracy as a Mode of Inquiry: Pragmatism, Social Facts, and Normative Theory." *Journal of Speculative Philosophy* 18, no. 1 (2004): 23–43.

——. "Survey Article: The Coming of Age of Deliberative Democracy." *Journal of Political Philosophy* 6, no. 4 (1999): 400–425.

Boisvert, Raymond. *Dewey's Metaphysics.* New York: Fordham University Press, 1988.

——. "Dewey's Metaphysics: Ground-Map of the Prototypically Real." In *Reading Dewey: Interpretations for a Postmodern Generation*, ed. Larry Hickman, 149–165. Bloomington: Indiana University Press, 1998.

——. *John Dewey: Rethinking Our Time.* Albany: State University of New York Press, 1998.

——. "The Nemesis of Necessity: Tragedy's Challenge to Deweyan Pragmatism." In *Dewey Reconfigured: Essays on Deweyan Pragmatism*, ed. Casey Haskins and David I. Seiple, 151–168. Albany: State University of New York Press, 1999.

Bowen, Francis. *The Principles of Metaphysical and Ethical Science Applied to the Evidences of Religion*. Boston: Brewer and Tileston, 1855.

Bozeman, Theodore D. *Protestants in an Age of Science: The Baconian Ideal and Antebellum American Religious Thought*. Chapel Hill: University of North Carolina Press, 1977.

Bradley, F. H. *Ethical Studies*. 1876. 2nd ed., New York: Oxford University Press, 1927.

Brandom, Robert. "Freedom and Constraint by Norms." In *Hermeneutics and Praxis*, ed. Robert Hollinger, 173–189. Notre Dame: University of Notre Dame Press, 1985.

——. *Making It Explicit: Reasoning, Representing, and Discursive Commitment*. Cambridge, MA: Harvard University Press, 1994.

——. "The Pragmatist Enlightenment (and Its Problematic Semantics)." *European Journal of Philosophy* 12, no. 1 (2004): 1–16.

Bronner, Stephen Eric. *Reclaiming the Enlightenment*. New York: Columbia University Press, 2004.

Bruce, Robert. *The Launching of Modern American Science, 1846–1876*. New York: Cornell University Press, 1987.

Campbell, James. *The Community Reconstructs: The Meaning of Pragmatic Social Thought*. Urbana: University of Illinois Press, 1992.

——. "Community Without Fusion: Dewey, Mead, Tufts." In *Pragmatism: From Progressivism to Postmodernism*, ed. Robert Hollinger and David Depew, 56–71. Westport, CT: Praeger, 1995.

——. *Understanding John Dewey: Nature and Cooperative Intelligence*. Chicago: Open Court, 1995.

Carrithers, David. "The Enlightenment Science of Society." In *Inventing Human Science: Eighteenth-Century Domains*, ed. Christopher Fox, Roy Porter, and Robert Wokler, 236–247. Berkeley: University of California Press, 1995.

Caspary, William R. *Dewey on Democracy*. Ithaca: Cornell University Press, 2000.

Castoriadis, Cornelius. "The Greek Polis and the Creation of Democracy." *Graduate Faculty Philosophy Journal* 9, no. 2 (1983): 79–115.

Cauthen, Kenneth. *The Impact of American Religious Liberalism*. New York: Harper and Row, 1962.

Cavell, Stanley. *Conditions Handsome and Unhandsome: The Constitutions of Emersonian Perfectionism*. Chicago: University of Chicago Press, 1990.

Chowers, Eyal. *The Modern Self in the Labyrinth: Politics and the Entrapment Imagination*. Cambridge, MA: Harvard University Press, 2004.

Clebsch, William A. *American Religious Thought: A History*. Chicago: University of Chicago Press, 1973.

Cohen, Joshua. "Deliberation and Democratic Legitimacy." In *Deliberative Democracy: Essays on Reason and Politics*, ed. James Bohman and William Rehg, 67–93. Cambridge, MA: MIT Press, 1997.

——. "Procedure and Substance in Deliberative Democracy." In *Democracy and Difference: Contesting the Boundaries of the Political*, ed. Seyla Benhabib, 95–119. Princeton: Princeton University Press, 1996.

Colapietro, Vincent. "The Question of Voice and the Limits of Pragmatism: Emerson, Dewey, and Cavell." In *The Range of Pragmatism and the Limits of Philosophy*, ed. Richard Shusterman, 174–196. Malden, MA: Blackwell, 2004.

Connolly, William E. *The Ethos of Pluralization*. Minneapolis: University of Minnesota Press, 1995.

Cook, Gary A. *George Herbert Mead: The Making of a Social Pragmatist*. Urbana: University of Illinois Press, 1993.

Cooke, Maeve. *Re-Presenting the Good Society*. Cambridge, MA: MIT Press, 2006.

Cooper, David E. *The Measure of Things: Humanism, Humility, and Mystery*. New York: Oxford University Press, 2002.

Cotkin, George. *Reluctant Modernism: American Thought and Culture, 1880–1900*. New York: Twayne, 1992.

Coughlan, Neil. *Young John Dewey*. Chicago: University of Chicago Press, 1975.

Croce, Paul Jerome. "Probabilistic Darwinism: Louis Agassiz vs. Asa Gray on Science, Religion, and Certainty." *Journal of Religious History* 22, no. 1 (1998): 35–58.

——. *Science and Religion in the Era of William James: Eclipse of Certainty, 1820–1880*. Chapel Hill: University of North Carolina Press, 1995.

Dabney, Robert. *Syllabus and Notes of the Course of Systematic and Polemic Theology*. Richmond: Presbyterian Committee of Publications, 1890.

Dahl, Robert. "The Concept of Power." *Behavioral Science* 2 (1957): 201–215.

——. "Hierarchy, Democracy, and Bargaining in Politics and Economics." In *Political Behavior*, ed. H. Eulau et al., 66–89. New York: Random House, 1956.

——. *A Preface to Democratic Theory*. Chicago: University of Chicago Press, 1963.

——. *Who Governs? Democracy and Power in an American City*. New Haven: Yale University Press, 1961.

Damico, Alfonso. *Individuality and Community: The Social and Political Thought of John Dewey*. Gainesville: University Presses of Florida, 1978.

Darwin, Charles. *The Descent of Man*. 1871. New York: Modern Library of America, 1936.

——. *The Origin of Species*. 1859. New York: Modern Library of America, 1936.

Dean, William. "Pragmatism, History, and Theology." In *Pragmatism and Religion: Classical Sources and Originally Essays*, ed. Stuart Rosenbaum, 153–175. Champaign, IL: University of Illinois Press, 2003.

Degler, Carl N. *In Search of Human Nature: The Decline and Revival of Darwinism in American Social Thought*. New York: Oxford University Press, 1992.

Deneen, Patrick J. *Democratic Faith*. Princeton: Princeton University Press, 2005.

Dewey, Jane M. "Biography of John Dewey." In *The Philosophy of John Dewey*, ed. Paul A. Schilpp and Lewis Edwin Hahn, 3–45. Evanston, IL: Northwestern University Press, 1939.

Diggins, John Patrick. "Pragmatism and Its Limits." In *The Revival of Pragmatism: New Essays on Social Thought, Law, and Culture*, ed. Morris Dickstein, 207–231. Durham: Duke University Press, 1998.

——. *The Promise of Pragmatism*. Chicago: University of Chicago Press, 1994.

Dobbs, Betty Jo Teeter, and Margaret C. Jacob. *Newton and the Culture of Newtonianism*. New York: Humanity Books, 1998.

Dryzek, John S. *Deliberative Democracy and Beyond: Liberals, Critics, Contestations*. New York: Oxford University Press, 2000.

——. *Discursive Democracy: Politics, Policy, and Political Science*. New York: Cambridge University Press, 1990.

Ducasse, Curt J. "Francis Bacon's Philosophy of Science." In *Theories of Scientific Method: The Renaissance Through the Nineteenth Century*, ed. Ralph M. Blake et al., 50–74. New York: Gordon and Breach, 1989.

Duffield, John T. "Evolutionism Respecting Man, and the Bible." *Princeton Review* 54 (1878): 150–177.

Dunne, Joseph. *Back to the Rough Ground: "Phronesis" and "Techne" in Modern Philosophy and in Aristotle*. Notre Dame: University of Notre Dame Press, 1993.

Dykhuizen, George. *The Life and Mind of John Dewey*. Carbondale: Southern Illinois University Press, 1973.

Eddy, Beth. *The Rites of Identity: The Religious Naturalism and Cultural Criticism of Kenneth Burke and Ralph Ellison*. Princeton: Princeton University Press, 2003.

Edel, Abraham. *Ethical Theory and Social Change: The Evolution of John Dewey's Ethics, 1908–1932*. New Brunswick, NJ: Transaction Publishers, 2001.

Eldridge, Michael. *Transforming Experience: John Dewey's Cultural Instrumentalism*. Nashville: Vanderbilt University Press, 1997.

Emerson, Ralph Waldo. "The American Scholar" (1837). In *Emerson: Essays and Lectures Nature: Addresses and Lectures / Essays: First and Second Series / Representative Men / English Traits / The Conduct of Life*, ed. Joel Porte, 51–71. New York: Library of America, 1983.

——. "Circles" (1841). In *Emerson: Essays and Lectures / Nature: Addresses and Lectures / Essays: First and Second Series / Representative Men / English Traits / The Conduct of Life*, ed. Joel Porte, 403–414. New York: Library of America, 1983.

——. *The Conduct of Life* (1860). In *Emerson: Essays and Lectures / Nature: Addresses and Lectures / Essays: First and Second Series / Representative Men / English Traits / The Conduct of Life*, ed. Joel Porte, 937–1112. New York: Library of America, 1983.

——. "The Conservative" (1841). In *Emerson: Essays and Lectures / Nature: Addresses and Lectures / Essays: First and Second Series / Representative Men / English Traits / The Conduct of Life*, ed. Joel Porte, 173–189. New York: Library of America, 1983.

——. "The Divinity School Address" (1838). In *Emerson: Essays and Lectures / Nature: Addresses and Lectures / Essays: First and Second Series / Representative Men / English Traits / The Conduct of Life*, ed. Joel Porte, 73–92. New York: Library of America, 1983.

——. "Man the Reformer" (1841). In *Emerson: Essays and Lectures / Nature: Addresses and Lectures / Essays: First and Second Series / Representative Men / English Traits / The Conduct of Life*, ed. Joel Porte, 135–150. New York: Library of America, 1983.

——. *Nature* (1836). In *Emerson: Essays and Lectures / Nature: Addresses and Lectures / Essays: First and Second Series / Representative Men / English Traits / The Conduct of Life*, ed. Joel Porte, 7–49. New York: Library of America, 1983.

——. "Self-Reliance" (1841). In *Emerson: Essays and Lectures / Nature: Addresses and Lectures / Essays: First and Second Series / Representative Men / English Traits / The Conduct of Life*, ed. Joel Porte, 257–283. New York: Library of America, 1983.

Farr, James. "Social Capital: A Conceptual History." *Political Theory* 32, no. 1 (2004): 6–33.

Feinberg, Waher. "The Conflict Between Intelligence and Community in Dewey's Educational Philosophy." *Educational Theory* 19, no. 3 (1969): 234–248.

Fesmire, Steven. *John Dewey and Moral Imagination: Pragmatism in Ethics*. Bloomington: Indiana University Press, 2003.

Festenstein, Matthew. *Pragmatism and Political Theory: From Dewey to Rorty*. Chicago: University of Chicago Press, 1997.

Fischer, Frank. *Citizens, Experts, and the Environment: The Politics of Local Knowledge*. Durham: Duke University Press, 2000.

Fishkin, James. *The Voice of the People: Public Opinion and Democracy*. New Haven: Yale University Press, 1997.

Fiske, John. *The Destiny of Man Viewed in the Light of His Origin*. New York: Houghton, Mifflin, and Company, 1884.

——. *Through Nature to God*. New York: Houghton, Mifflin, and Company, 1899.

Flanagan, Owen. *Varieties of Moral Personality: Ethics and Psychological Realism.* Cambridge, MA: Harvard University Press, 1991.

Floridi, Luciano. "Two Approaches to the Philosophy of Information." *Mind and Machine* 13, no. 4 (2003): 459–469.

Forst, Rainer. *Context of Justice: Political Philosophy Beyond Liberalism and Communitarianism.* Trans. John M. M. Farrell. Berkeley: University of California Press, 2002.

Fox, Richard. *Reinhold Niebuhr: A Biography*. New York: Pantheon, 1985.

Frank, Jill. *A Democracy of Distinction: Aristotle and the Work of Politics*. Chicago: University of Chicago Press, 2005.

Fraser, Nancy. *Justice Interruptus: Critical Reflections on the "PostSocialist" Condition.* New York: Routledge, 1997.

Freeman, Derek. "The Evolutionary Theories of Charles Darwin and Herbert Spencer." In *Herbert Spencer: Critical Assessments*, ed. John Offer, vol. 2, 5–26. New York: Routledge, 2000.

Friess, Horace. "Dewey's Philosophy of Religion." In *Guide to the Works of John Dewey*, ed. Jo Ann Boydston, 200–218. Carbondale: Southern Illinois University Press, 1970.

Fung, Archon. "Deliberation Before the Revolution: Toward an Ethics of Deliberative Democracy in an Unjust World." *Political Theory* 33, no. s (2005): 397–419.

——. "Deliberative Democracy, Chicago Style: Grass-Roots Governance in Policing and Public Education." In *Deepening Democracy: Institutional Innovations in Empowered Participatory Governance*, ed. Archon Fung and Erik Olin Wright, 111–143. New York: Verso, 2003.

——. *Empowered Participation: Reinventing Urban Democracy*. Princeton: Princeton University Press, 2004.

Fung, Archon, and Erik Olin Wright. "Introduction." In *Deepening Democracy: Institutional Innovations in Empowered Participatory Governance*, ed. Archon Fung and Erik Olin Wright. New York: Verso, 2003.

Gadamer, Hans-George. *Reason in the Age of Science*. Trans. Frederick G. Lawrence. Cambridge, MA: MIT Press, 1981.

——. *Truth and Method*. Trans. Joel Weinsheimer and Donald G. Marshall. 1960. 2nd ed. rev., New York: Continuum, 1989.

Garrison, Jim. *Dewey and Eros: Wisdom and Desire in the Art of Teaching*. New York: Teachers College Press, 1997.

Gastil, John, and Peter Levine, eds. *The Deliberative Democracy Handbook: Strategies for Effective Civic Engagement in the Twenty-First Century*. San Francisco: Jossey-Bass, 2005.

Gaventa, John. *Power and Powerlessness: Quiescence and Rebellion in an Appalachian Valley.* Chicago: University of Illinois Press, 1980.

Gergen, Kenneth J. *The Saturated Self: Dilemmas of Identity in Contemporary Life.* New York: Basic Books, 1991.

Ghiselin, Michael T. *The Triumph of the Darwinian Method.* Berkeley: University of California Press, 1969.

Giddens, Anthony. *The Consequences of Modernity.* Stanford: Stanford University Press, 1990.

——. *Modernity and Self-Identity.* Palo Alto, CA: Stanford University Press, 1991.

Glaude, Eddie S. *In a Shade of Blue: Pragmatism and the Politics of Black America.* Chicago: University of Chicago Press, 2007.

Gouinlock, James. "Dewey's Theory of Moral Deliberation." *Ethics* 88, no. 3 (1977): 218–228.

——. *John Dewey's Philosophy of Value.* New York: Humanities Press, 1972.

Green, John. *Darwin and the Modern World View.* Baton Rouge: Louisiana State University Press, 1961.

Green, Judith M. *Deep Democracy: Community, Diversity, and Transformation.* Lanham, MD: Rowman and Littlefield, 1999.

Gutmann, Amy, and Dennis Thompson. *Democracy and Disagreement.* Cambridge, MA: Harvard University Press, 1996.

Habermas, Jurgen. *Between Facts and Norms: Contributions to a Discourse Theory of Law and Democracy.* Trans. William Rehg. Oxford: Polity, 1998.

——. "Individuation Through Socialization: On George Herbert Mead's Theory of Subjectivity." In *Postmetaphysical Thinking: Philosophical Essays*, trans. William Mark Hohengarten, 149–204. Cambridge, MA: MIT Press, 1996.

——. "Moral Consciousness and Communicative Action." In *Moral Consciousness and Communicative Action*, trans. Christian Lenhardt and Shierry Weber Nicholsen, 116–195. Cambridge: Polity, 1990.

——. "Reconciliation Through the Public Use of Reason: Remarks on John Rawls's Political Liberalism." *Journal of Philosophy* 92, no. 3 (1995): 109–131.

——. *The Theory of Communicative Action.* Trans. Thomas McCarthy. 2 volumes. Boston: Beacon, 1984.

——. "The Unity of Reason in the Diversity of Its Voices." In *Postmetaphysical Thinking: Philosophical Essays*, trans. William Mark Hohengarten, 115–148. Cambridge, MA: MIT Press, 1996.

Hamilton, Alexander, James Madison, and John Jay. *The Federalist* (1787–1788). Ed. Jacob E. Cooke. Middletown, CT: 1961.

Hanson, Norwood Russell. *Patterns of Discovery: An Inquiry Into the Conceptual Foundations of Science.* New York: Cambridge University Press, 1958.

Harris, George. *Moral Evolution*. New York: Houghton, Mifflin, and Company, 1896.

Haskins, Casey. "Dewey's Romanticism." In *Dewey Reconfigured: Essays on Deweyan Pragmatism*, ed. Casey Haskins and David I. Seiple, 97–131. Albany: State University of New York Press, 1999.

Hauerwas, Stanley. *With the Grain of the Universe: The Church's Witness and Natural Theology*. Grand Rapids: Brazos Press, 2001.

Hayward, Clarissa Rile. *De-Facing Power*. New York: Cambridge University Press, 2000.

Henry, John. *The Scientific Revolution and the Origins of Modern Science*. New York: St. Martin's, 1997.

Hickman, Larry A. "Dewey: Pragmatic Technology and Community Life." In *Classical American Philosophy: Its Contemporary Vitality*, ed. Sandra Rosenthal, Carl Hausman, and Douglas Anderson, 99–119. Champaign: University of Illinois Press, 1999.

——. *John Dewey's Pragmatic Technology*. Bloomington: Indiana University Press, 1990.

Hodge, Charles. *Systematic Theology* (1872–1873). 3 volumes. Grand Rapids: Eerdmans, 1981.

——. *What Is Darwinism? and Other Writings on Science and Religion* (1874). Ed. Mark A. Noll and David N. Livingston. Grand Rapids: Baker Books, 1994.

Hoffecker, Andrew W. *Piety and the Princeton Theologians: Archibald Alexander, Charles Hodge, and Benjamin Warfield*. Phillipsburg, NJ: Presbyterian and Reformed Publishing Co., 1981.

Hofstadter, Richard. *Social Darwinism in American Thought*. 1944. Revised edition, Boston: Beacon, 1959.

Holifield, E. Brooks. *Theology in America: Christian Thought from the Age of the Puritans to the Civil War*. New Haven: Yale University Press, 2003.

Honneth, Axel. "Democracy as Reflexive Cooperation: John Dewey and the Theory of Democracy Today." *Political Theory* 26, no. 6 (1998): 763–783.

Hook, Sidney. *Pragmatism and the Tragic Sense of Life*. New York: Basic Books, 1974.

Hopkins, Charles Howard. *The Rise of the Social Gospel in American Protestantism, 1865–1915*. New Haven: Yale University Press, 1940.

Hovenkamp, Herbert. *Science and Religion in America, 1800–1860*. Philadelphia: University of Pennsylvania Press, 1978.

Hull, David L. *Darwin and His Critics: The Reception of Darwin's Theory of Evolution by the Scientific Community*. Chicago: University of Chicago Press, 1973.

Hume, David. *A Treatise of Human Nature* (1740). Ed. P. H. Nidditch. New York: Oxford University Press, 1978.

Hursthouse, Rosalind. *On Virtue Ethics*. New York: Oxford University Press, 1999.

Israel, Jonathan. *Enlightenment Contested: Philosophy, Modernity, and the Emancipation of Man 1670–1752*. New York: Oxford University Press, 2006.

Jackson, Philip W. *John Dewey and the Philosopher's Task*. New York: Teachers College Press, 2002.

James, William. *Essays in Radical Empiricism*. 1912; New York: Longman, Green and Company, 1922.

——. *"Lectures and Essays and Seeing and Thinking, by William K. Clifford"* (1879). In *Essays, Comments, and Reviews*, 356–361. Cambridge, MA: Harvard University Press, 1987.

——. *Pragmatism* (1907). Cambridge, MA: Harvard University Press, 1996.

——. *Psychology: Briefer Course* (1892). Cambridge, MA: Harvard University Press, 1984.

——. *The Varieties of Religious Experience* (1902). New York: Modern Library, 1999.

——. *The Will to Believe and Other Essays in Popular Philosophy* (1897). New York: Dover, 1956.

Joas, Hans. *G.H. Mead: A Contemporary Re-examination of His Thought*. Trans. Raymond Meyer. Cambridge: Polity, 1980.

——. *The Creativity of Action*. Trans. Jeremy Gains and Paul Keast. Chicago: University of Chicago Press, 1996.

——. *The Genesis of Values*. Trans. Gregory Moore. Chicago: University of Chicago Press, 2000.

Johnson, Mark. *Moral Imagination: Implications of Cognitive Science for Ethics*. Chicago: University of Chicago Press, 1994.

Kant, Immanuel. *Critique of Practical Reason* (1788). Trans. Lewis White Beck. 3rd ed. Englewood Cliffs, NJ: Prentice Hall, 1993.

——. *Critique of Pure Reason* (1787). Trans. Norman Kemp Smith. Boston: Bedford Press, 1965.

Karier, Clarence. "Making the World Safe for Democracy: An Historical Critique of John Dewey's Philosophy of the Warfare State." *Educational Theory* 27, no. 1 (1977): 12–47.

Kateb, George. *Emerson and Self-Reliance*. Thousand Oaks, CA: Sage, 1995.

——. "Wolin as a Critic of Democracy." *Democracy and Vision: Sheldon Wolin and the Vicissitudes of the Political*, ed. Aryeh Botwinick and William E. Connolly, 39–57. Princeton: Princeton University Press, 2001.

Kaufman-Osborn, Timothy. "John Dewey and the Liberal Science of Community." *Journal of Politics* 46, no. 4 (1984): 1142–1165.

Kestenbaum, Victor. *The Grace and the Severity of the Ideal: John Dewey and the Transcendent*. Chicago: University of Chicago Press, 2002.

Ketcham, Ralph. *The Idea of Democracy in the Modern Era*. Lawrence: University of Kansas Press, 2004.

——. *James Madison: A Biography*. New York: Macmillan, 1971.

Kloppenberg, James. "Pragmatism: An Old Name for Some New Ways of Thinking?" In *The Revival of Pragmatism: New Essays on Social Thought, Law, and Culture*, ed. Morris Dickstein, 83–128. Durham: Duke University Press, 1998.

——. *Uncertain Victory: Social Democracy and Progressivism in European and American Thought, 1870–1920*. New York: Oxford University Press, 1986.

——. *The Virtues of Liberalism*. New York: Oxford University Press, 1998.

Krutch, Joseph Wood. *The Modern Temper*. New York: Harcourt, Brace, and Company, 1929.

Kuklick, Bruce. "The Place of Charles Hodge in the History of Ideas in America." In *Charles Hodge Revisited: A Critical Appraisal of His Life and Work*, ed. John W. Steward and James H. Moorhead, 63–101. Grand Rapids: Eerdmans, 2002.

Laclau, Ernesto, and Chantel Mouffe. *Hegemony and Socialist Strategy*. London: Verso, 1985.

Lasch, Christopher. *The New Radicalism in America*. New York: Vintage Press, 1965.

——. *The True and Only Heaven: Progress and Its Critics*. New York: Norton, 1991.

Lear, Jonathan. *Aristotle: The Desire to Understand*. New York: Cambridge University Press, 1988.

Lears, T.J. Jackson. *No Place of Grace: Antimodernism and the Transformation of American Culture, 1880–1920*. Chicago: University of Chicago Press, 1994.

Lefort, Claude. *Democracy and Political Theory*. Minneapolis: University of Minnesota Press, 1988.

——. *The Political Forms of Modern Society: Bureaucracy, Democracy, Totalitarianism*. Oxford: Polity, 1986.

Lekan, Todd. *Making Morality: Pragmatist Reconstruction in Ethical Theory*. Nashville: Vanderbilt University Press, 2003.

Levi, Isaac. "Conflict and Inquiry." *Ethics* 102, no. 4 (1992): 814–834.

Levinson, Henry. *The Religious Investigations of William James*. Chapel Hill: University of North Carolina Press, 1981.

——. *Santayana, Pragmatism, and the Spiritual Life*. Chapel Hill: University of North Carolina Press, 1992.

——. "Stuck Between Debility and Demand: Religion and Enlightenment Traditions Among the Pragmatists." In *Knowledge and Belief in America: Enlightenment Traditions and Modern Religious Thought*, ed. William M. Shea and Peter A. Huff, 270–298. New York: Cambridge University Press, 1995.

Lindbeck, George A. *The Nature of Doctrine: Religion and Theology in a Postliberal Age*. Philadelphia: Westminster Press, 1984.

Lippmann, Walter. *Essays in the Public Philosophy.* New York: Mentor, 1955.

——. *The Phantom Public* (1927). New Brunswick, NJ: Transaction Publishers, 2004.

——. *A Preface to Morals.* New York: Time Incorporated, 1929.

——. *A Preface to Politics* (1941). Ann Arbor: University of Michigan Press, 1962.

——. *Public Opinion* (1922). New York: Free Press, 1965.

Lobkowicz, Nicholas. *Theory and Practice: History of a Concept from Aristotle to Marx.* Notre Dame: University of Notre Dame Press, 1967.

Locke, John. *An Essay Concerning Human Understanding* (1690). Ed. Peter H. Nidditch. New York: Oxford University Press, 1979.

Loewenberg, Bert James. "Darwinism Comes to America, 1859–1900." *Mississippi Valley Historical Review* 28, no. 3 (1941): 339–368.

Long, Christopher P. "The Ontological Reappropriation of Phronēsis." *Continental Philosophy Review* 35, no. 1 (2002): 35–60.

Louden, Robert B. *Morality and Moral Theory: A Reappraisal and Reaffirmation.* New York: Oxford University Press, 1992.

Lovibond, Sabina. *Ethical Formation.* Cambridge, MA: Harvard University Press, 2002.

Lovin, Robin W. *Reinhold Niebuhr and Christian Realism.* New York: Cambridge University Press, 1995.

Lukes, Steven. *Power: A Radical View.* New York: Macmillan, 1974.

MacGilvray, Eric. *Reconstructing Public Reason.* Cambridge, MA: Harvard University Press, 2004.

MacIntyre, Alasdair. *After Virtue: A Study in Moral Theory.* Notre Dame: University of Notre Dame Press, 1981.

——. *Whose Justice? Which Rationality?* Notre Dame: University of Notre Dame Press, 1988.

Mandelbaum, Maurice. *History, Man, and Reason: A Study in Nineteenth-Century Thought.* Baltimore: Johns Hopkins University Press, 1971.

Markell, Patchen. *Bound by Recognition.* Princeton: Princeton University Press, 2003.

Markoff, John. *Waves of Democracy: Social Movements and Political Change.* Thousand Oaks, CA: Pine Forge Press, 1996.

Martin, Jay. *The Education of John Dewey: A Biography.* New York: Columbia University Press, 2002.

May, Henry F. *The Enlightenment in America.* New York: Oxford University Press, 1976.

McCosh, James. "Natural Selection and the Origin of Man" (1871). In *Darwinism and Theology in America: 1850–1930,* ed. Frank X. Ryan, vol. 2, 59–73. Bristol: Thoemmes, 2002.

——. *The Religious Aspects of Evolution* (1890). In *Darwinism and Theology in America: 1850–1930*, ed. Frank X. Ryan, vol. 2, 1–49. Bristol: Thoemmes, 2002.

McDowell, John. *Mind and World*. Cambridge, MA: Harvard University Press, 1994.

——. *Mind, Value, and Reality*. Cambridge, MA: Harvard University Press, 1998.

——. "Towards Rehabilitating Objectivity." In *Rorty and His Critics*, ed. Robert Brandom, 109–123. Malden, MA: Blackwell, 2000.

Mead, George Herbert. *Mind, Self, and Society*. Ed. Charles W. Morris. 1927–1930; Chicago: University of Chicago Press, 1934.

——. "The Social Self" (1913). In *Selected Writings*, ed. Andrew J. Reck, 142–149. Chicago: University of Chicago Press, 1964.

Menand, Louis. *The Metaphysical Club: A Story of Ideas in America*. New York: Farrar, Strauss, Giroux, 2001.

Metz, Joseph G. "Democracy and the Scientific Method in the Philosophy of John Dewey." *Review of Politics* 31, no. 2 (1969): 242–262.

Meyer, D. H. "American Intellectuals and the Victorian Crisis of Faith." In *Victorian America*, ed. Daniel Walter Howe, 59–77. Philadelphia: University of Pennsylvania Press, 1976.

Miller, David. *The New Polytheism*. New York: Harper and Row, 1974.

Mills, C. Wright. *The Power Elite*. New York: Oxford University Press, 1956.

——. *Sociology and Pragmatism: The Higher Learning in America*. New York: Oxford University Press, 1969.

Misak, Cheryl. *Truth, Politics, Morality: Pragmatism and Deliberation*. New York: Routledge, 2000.

Moore, James R. *The Post-Darwinian Controversies*. New York: Cambridge University Press, 1979.

Morris, Donald. *Dewey and the Behavioristic Context of Ethics*. Bethesda, MD: International Scholars Publication, 1996.

Mouffe, Chantel. *On the Political*. New York: Routledge, 2005.

Mulgan, Richard G. *Aristotle's Political Theory: An Introduction for Students of Political Theory*. New York: Oxford University Press, 1977.

Mulhall, Stephen, and Adam Swift. *Liberals and Communitarians*. 2nd ed. Oxford: Blackwell, 1996.

Munger, Theodore T. *The Freedom of Faith*. Boston: Houghton, Mifflin, and Company, 1883.

Muntz, Diana C. *Hearing the Other Side: Deliberative Versus Participatory Democracy*. New York: Cambridge University Press, 2006.

Newfield, Christopher. *The Emerson Effect: Individualism and Submission in America*. Chicago: University of Chicago Press, 1996.

Niebuhr, Reinhold. *The Children of Light and the Children of Darkness.* New York: Charles Scribner's Sons, 1944.

——. *Moral Man and Immoral Society.* 1932; New York: Charles Scribner's Sons, 1960.

——. *The Nature and Destiny of Man: Human Nature.* Volume 1. 1941; New York: Charles Scribner's Sons, 1964.

——. "The Pathos of Liberalism." *The Nation* 141 (September 11, 1935): 303–304.

Niebuhr, Ursula, ed. *Remembering Reinhold Niebuhr: Letters of Reinhold and Ursula Niebuhr.* San Francisco: Harper, 1991.

Nietzsche, Friedrich. *Beyond Good and Evil: Prelude to a Philosophy of the Future* (1886). Trans. Walter Kaufmann. New York: Vintage, 1989.

——. *Thus Spoke Zarathustra: A Book for None and All* (1883–1885). Trans. Walter Kaufmann. New York: Penguin, 1978.

Noll, Mark. *America's God: From Jonathan Edwards to Abraham Lincoln.* New York: Oxford University Press, 2002.

——. "The Rise and Long Life of the Protestant Enlightenment in America." In *Knowledge and Belief in America: Enlightenment Traditions and Modern Religious Thought,* ed. William M. Shea and Peter A. Huff, 88–124. New York: Cambridge University Press, 1995.

Noll, Mark A., and David N. Livingston, eds. "Introduction: Charles Hodge and the Definition of 'Darwinism.'" In *What Is Darwinism? And Other Writings on Science and Religion,* 11–47. Grand Rapids: Baker Books, 1994.

Nussbaum, Martha. "Aristotelian Social Democracy." In *Liberalism and the Good,* ed. R. Bruce Douglas, 203–252. New York: Routledge, 1990.

——. *The Fragility of Goodness: Luck and Ethics in Greek Tragedy and Philosophy.* New York: Cambridge University Press, 1986.

——. *Love's Knowledge: Essays on Philosophy and Literature.* New York: Oxford University Press, 1990.

Offe, Clause. "How Can We Trust Our Fellow Citizens?" In *Democracy and Trust,* ed. Mark E. Warren, 42–88. New York: Cambridge University Press, 1999.

Pappas, Gregory Fernando. "Dewey's Moral Theory: Experience as Method." *Transactions of the Charles Peirce Society* 33, no. 3 (1997): 520–556.

——. "To Be or to Do: John Dewey and the Great Divide in Ethics." *History of Philosophy Quarterly* 14, no. 4 (1997): 447–472.

Parsons, Theophilus. *The Infinite and the Finite.* Boston: Roberts Bros., 1872.

Pateman, Carole. *Participation and Democratic Theory.* New York: Cambridge University Press, 1970.

Peirce, Charles. "The Fixation of Belief" (1877). In *The Essential Peirce: Selected Philosophical Writings*, ed. Nathan Houser and Christian Kloesel, vol. 1, 109–123. Bloomington: Indiana University Press, 1992.

——. "How to Make Our Ideas Clear" (1878). In *The Essential Peirce: Selected Philosophical Writings*, ed. Nathan Houser and Christian Kloesel, vol. 1, 124–141. Bloomington: Indiana University Press, 1992.

——. "Lessons from the History of Science" (1896). In *Collected Papers of Charles S. Peirce*, ed. Charles Hartshorne, Paul Weiss, and Arthur W. Burks, vol. 1, 19–49. Cambridge, MA: Harvard University Press, 1931.

——. "A Neglected Argument for the Reality of God" (1908). In *The Essential Peirce: Selected Philosophical Writings*, ed. Nathan Houser and Christian Kloesel, vol. 2, 434–450. Bloomington: Indiana University Press, 1998.

——. "Notes on Scientific Philosophy" (1905). In *Collected Papers of Charles S. Peirce*, ed. Charles Hartshorne, Paul Weiss, and Arthur W. Burks, vol. 1, 50–72. Cambridge, MA: Harvard University Press, 1931.

——. "Some Consequences of Four Incapacities" (1868). In *The Essential Peirce: Selected Philosophical Writings*, ed. Nathan Houser and Christian Kloesel, vol. 1, 28–55. Bloomington: Indiana University Press, 1992.

Perry, Ralph Barton. *The Thought and Character of William James*. 2 volumes. Boston. Little, Brown, and Company, 1935.

Pettit, Philip. *Republicanism: A Theory of Freedom and Government*. New York: Oxford University Press, 1997.

Pippin, Robert B. *Idealism as Modernism: Hegelian Variations*. New York: Cambridge University Press, 1997.

Plato. *Timaeus*. Trans. Donald J. Zeyl. In *Plato: Complete Works*, ed. John M. Cooper and D. S. Hutchinson. Indianapolis: Hackett, 1997.

Pocock, J. G. A. *The Machiavellian Moment: Florentine Political Thought and the Atlantic Republican Tradition*. Princeton: Princeton University Press, 1975.

Polsby, Nelson. *Community Power and Political Theory*. New Haven: Yale University Press, 1963.

Posner, Richard A. *Law, Pragmatism and Democracy*. Cambridge, MA: Harvard University Press, 2003.

Przeworski, Adam. "Minimalist Conception of Democracy: A Defense." In *Democracy's Value*, ed. Ian Shapiro and Casiano Hacker-Cordón, 23–55. New York: Cambridge University Press, 1999.

Purcell, Edward A. *The Crisis of Democratic Theory: Scientific Naturalism and the Problem of Value*. Lexington, KY: University Press of Kentucky, 1973.

Putnam, Hilary. *Enlightenment and Pragmatism*. Amsterdam: Koninklijke Van Gorcum, 2001.

——. "Pragmatism and Moral Objectivity." In Hilary Putnam, *Words and Life*, ed. James Conant, 151–158. Cambridge, MA: Harvard University Press, 1994.

——. *Pragmatism: An Open Question*. Malden, MA: Blackwell, 1995.

——. "A Reconsideration of Deweyan Democracy." In *Pragmatism in Law and Society*, ed. Michael Brint and William Weaver, 217–243. Boulder: Westview, 1991.

Putnam, Hilary, and Ruth Anna Putnam. "Dewey's Logic: Epistemology as Hypothesis." In Hilary Putnam, *Words and Life*, ed. James Conant, 198–220. Cambridge, MA: Harvard University Press.

Rancière, Jacques. *Disagreement: Politics and Philosophy*. Trans. Julie Rose. Minneapolis: University of Minnesota Press, 1999.

——. "Ten Theses on Politics." *Theory and Event* 5, no. 3 (2001): http://muse.jhu.edu/journals/theory_and_event.html.

Randall, John H., Jr. "The Changing Impact of Darwin on Philosophy." *Journal of the History of Ideas* 22, no. 4 (1961): 435–462.

——. "The Future of John Dewey's Philosophy." *Journal of Philosophy* 56, no. 26 (1959): 1005–1010.

——. *Philosophy After Darwin: Chapters for the Career of Philosophy, Volume III, and Other Essays*. Edited by Beth J. Singer. New York: Columbia University Press, 1977.

Rawls, John. *Political Liberalism*. New York: Columbia University Press, 1993.

——. *A Theory of Justice*. Cambridge, MA: Harvard University Press, 1971.

Reid, Thomas. *Inquiry and Essays* (1785). Ed. Ronald E. Beanblossom and Keith Lehrer. Indianapolis: Hackett, 1983.

Riccio, Barry D. *Walter Lippmann—Odyssey of a Liberal*. New Brunswick, NJ: Transaction Publishers, 1994.

Rice, Daniel. *Reinhold Niebuhr and John Dewey: An American Odyssey*. New York: State University of New York Press, 1993.

Richardson, Henry. *Democratic Autonomy: Public Reasoning About the Ends of Policy*. New York: Oxford University Press, 2002.

Rockefeller, Steven C. *John Dewey: Religious Faith and Democratic Humanism*. New York: Columbia University Press, 1991.

Rogers, Melvin L. "Republican Confusion and Liberal Clarification." *Philosophy and Social Criticism* 34, no. 8 (2008).

Rorty, Amelie Oksenberg, ed. "The Place of Contemplation in Aristotle's *Nicomachean Ethics*." In *Essays on Aristotle's Ethics*, 377–395. Berkeley: University of California Press, 1980.

Rorty, Richard. *The Consequences of Pragmatism*. Minneapolis: University of Minnesota Press, 1982.

——. *Contingency, Irony, and Solidarity*. New York: Cambridge University Press, 1989.

——. *Philosophy and the Mirror of Nature.* Malden, MA: Blackwell, 1980.

——. "Pragmatism as Romantic Polytheism." In *The Revival of Pragmatism: New Essays on Social Thought,* ed. Morris Dickstein, 21–36. Durham: Duke University Press, 1998.

Ross, Dorothy. *The Origins of American Social Science.* New York: Cambridge University Press, 1991.

Russell, Bertrand. *Philosophical Essays.* New York: Longmans, Green, and Co., 1910.

Ryan, Alan. *John Dewey and the High Tide of American Liberalism.* New York: Norton, 1995.

Ryan, Frank X., ed. *Darwinism and Theology in America: 1850–1930.* 4 volumes. Bristol: Thoemmes, 2002.

Salkever, Stephen. *Finding the Mean: Theory and Practice in Aristotelian Political Philosophy.* Princeton: Princeton University Press, 1990.

Sandel, Michael. *Liberalism and the Limits of Justice.* New York: Cambridge University Press, 1982.

Santayana, George. *The Life of Reason* (1905–1906). New York: Prometheus Books, 1998.

Sartori, Giovanni. *Democratic Theory.* Detroit: Wayne State University Press, 1962.

Sartre, Jean-Paul. *Existentialism and Humanism.* Trans. Philip Mairet. New York: Haskell House, 1946.

Savage, Daniel M. *John Dewey's Liberalism: Individual, Community, and Self-Development.* Carbondale: Southern Illinois University Press, 2002.

Scaff, Lawrence A. "Weber on the Cultural Situation of the Modern Age." In *The Cambridge Companion to Weber,* ed. Stephen Turner, 99–116. New York: Cambridge University Press, 2000.

Schaub, Edward L. "Dewey's Interpretation of Religion." In *The Philosophy of John Dewey,* ed. Paul Arthur Schilpp, 393–416. Evanston, IL: Northwestern University Press, 1939.

Schlesinger, Arthur Meier. "A Critical Period in American Religion, 1875–1900." *Proceedings, Massachusetts Historical Society* 64 (1932): 532–547.

Schmitt, Carl. *The Concept of the Political* (1932). Trans. George Schwab. Chicago: University of Chicago, 1996.

Schneider, Herbert W. *A History of American Philosophy.* New York: Columbia University Press, 1946.

Schumpeter, Joseph. *Capitalism, Socialism, and Democracy.* 3rd ed. New York: Harper and Row, 1950.

Seigel, Jerrold. *The Idea of the Self: Thought and Experience in Western Europe Since the Seventeenth Century.* New York: Cambridge University Press, 2005.

Shapiro, Ian. *Democratic Justice.* New Haven: Yale University Press, 1999.

——. *Political Criticism.* Berkeley: University of California Press, 1990.

——. "Revisiting *Democratic Justice*: A Response to Critics." *The Good Society* 11, no. 2 (2002): 91–97.

——. *The State of Democratic Theory*. Princeton: Princeton University Press, 2003.

Shklar, Judith. "Emerson and the Inhibitions of Democracy." In *Redeeming American Political Thought*, ed. Stanley Hoffmann and Dennis F. Thompson, 49–65. Chicago: University of Chicago Press, 1998.

Shook, John R. *Dewey's Empirical Theory of Knowledge and Reality*. Nashville: Vanderbilt University Press, 2000.

Shusterman, Richard. *Practicing Philosophy: Pragmatism and the Philosophic Life*. New York: Routledge, 1997.

——. "Pragmatism and Liberalism: Between Dewey and Rorty." *Political Theory* 22, no. 3 (1994): 391–413.

Simons, Peter. "Metaphysics." In *A Companion to Metaphysics*, ed. Jaegwon Kim and Ernest Sosa, 310–312. Malden, MA: Blackwell, 1995.

Skinner, Quentin. "The Empirical Theorists of Democracy and Their Critics." *Political Theory* 1 (1973): 287–305.

——. *Liberty Before Liberalism*. New York: Cambridge University Press, 1998.

Sleeper, Ralph W. *The Necessity of Pragmatism: John Dewey's Conception of Philosophy*. New Haven: Yale University Press, 1986.

Smiley, Marion. "Pragmatic Inquiry and Social Conflict: A Critical Reconstruction of Dewey's Model of Democracy." *Praxis International* 9, no. 4 (1990): 365–380.

Smith, Adam. *The Theory of Moral Sentiments* (1759). New York: Prometheus Books, 2000.

Smith, Barry. "Ontology." In *A Companion to Metaphysics*, ed. Jaegwon Kim and Ernest Sosa, 373–374. Malden, MA: Blackwell, 1995.

Smith, Gary Scott. *The Seeds of Secularization: Calvinism, Culture, and Pluralism in America, 1870–1915*. Grand Rapids: Christian University Press, 1985.

Smith, H. Shelton. *Changing Conceptions of Original Sin: A Study in American Theology Since 1750*. New York: Charles Scribner's Sons, 1955.

Smith, John. *Purpose and Thought: The Meaning of Pragmatism*. New Haven: Yale University Press, 1978.

Soneson, Jerome Paul. *Pragmatism and Pluralism: John Dewey's Significance for Theology*. Minneapolis: Fortress Press, 1993.

Sophocles. *Antigone*. Trans. Elizabeth Wyckoff. Ed. David Grene and Richmond Lattimore. Chicago: University of Chicago Press, 1954.

Steel, Ronald. *Walter Lippmann and the American Century*. Boston: Little, Brown, and Company, 1980.

Stocker, Michael. "The Schizophrenia of Modern Ethical Theories" (1976). *Virtue Ethics*, ed. Roger Crisp and Michael Slote, 66–78. New York: Oxford University Press, 1997.

Stout, Jeffrey. *Democracy and Tradition*. Princeton: Princeton University Press, 2004.

——. "On Our Interest in Getting Things Right: Pragmatism Without Narcissism." In *New Pragmatists*, ed. Cheryl Misak, 7–31. New York: Oxford University Press, 2007.

Strauss, Leo. *Natural Right and History*. 1953; Chicago: University of Chicago Press, 1970.

Stuhr, John J. "Dewey's Reconstruction of Metaphysics." *Transactions of Charles S. Peirce Society* 28, no. 2 (1992): 161–176.

——. *Genealogical Pragmatism: Philosophy, Experience, and Community*. Albany: State University of New York Press, 1997.

——. *Pragmatism, Postmodernism, and the Future of Philosophy*. New York: Routledge, 2003.

Talisse, Robert. *A Pragmatist Philosophy of Democracy*. New York: Routledge, 2007.

Tarrow, Sidney. *Power in Movement: Social Movements, Collective Action, and Politics*. New York: Cambridge University Press, 1994.

Taylor, Charles. *Philosophy and the Human Sciences: Philosophical Papers 2*. New York: Cambridge University Press, 1985.

——. *Sources of the Self: The Making of the Modern Identity*. Cambridge, MA: Harvard University Press, 1989.

——. *Varieties of Religion Today: William James Revisited*. Cambridge, MA: Harvard University Press, 2002.

Thayer, H. S. *Meaning and Action: A Critical History of Pragmatism*. Indianapolis: Hackett, 1981.

Tiles, J. E. *Dewey*. New York: Routledge: 1988.

Tilly, Charles. *Social Movements, 1768–2004*. Boulder: Paradigm, 2004.

Tocqueville, Alexis de. *Democracy in America* (1835–1840). Trans. Harvey C. Mansfield and Delba Winthrop. Chicago: University of Chicago Press, 2000.

Toulmin, Stephen. *Cosmopolis: The Hidden Agenda of Modernity*. Chicago: University of Chicago Press, 1990.

——. *Return to Reason*. Cambridge, MA: Harvard University Press, 2001.

Turner, James. *Without God, Without Creed: The Origins of Unbelief in America*. Baltimore: Johns Hopkins University Press, 1983.

Uslaner, Eric M. "Democracy and Social Capital." *Democracy and Trust*, ed. Mark E. Warren, 121–151. New York: Cambridge University Press, 1999.

Vernant, Jean-Pierre, and Pierre Vidal-Naquet. *Tragedy and Myth in Ancient Greece*. Trans. J. Lloyd. Atlantic Highlands, NJ: Humanities Press, 1981.

Villa, Dana. *Arendt and Heidegger: The Fate of the Political*. Princeton: Princeton University Press, 1996.

——. "Hegel, Tocqueville, and 'Individualism.'" *Review of Politics* 67, no. 4 (2005): 659–686.

Walsh, W. H. "Nature of Metaphysics." In *The Encyclopedia of Philosophy*, ed. Paul Edwards, vol. 5, 300–306. New York: Macmillan, 1972.

Ward, Keith. *Religion and Human Nature*. New York: Oxford University Press, 1998.

Weber, Max. *Economy and Society* (1922). Ed. Buenther Roth and Claus Wittich. 2 volumes. Berkeley: University of California Press, 1978.

——. *From Max Weber: Essays in Sociology* (1919). Trans. H. H. Gerth and C. Wright Mills. New York: Oxford University Press, 1946.

——. *The Protestant Ethic and the Spirit of Capitalism* (1904–1905). Trans. Talcott Parsons. New York: Routledge, 1992.

——. *Roscher and Knies: The Logical Problem of Historical Economics* (1905). Trans. Guy Oakes. New York: Free Press, 1975.

Welchman, Jennifer. *Dewey's Ethical Thought*. New York: Cornell University Press, 1995.

Wellborn, Charles. *Twentieth-Century Pilgrimage: Walter Lippmann and the Public Philosophy*. Baton Rouge: Louisiana State University Press, 1969.

West, Cornel. *The American Evasion of Philosophy: A Genealogy of Pragmatism*. Madison: University of Wisconsin Press, 1989.

——. *Democracy Matters: Winning the Fight Against Imperialism*. New York: Penguin, 2004.

——. *Keeping Faith: Philosophy and Race in America*. New York: Routledge, 1993.

Westbrook, Robert B. *Democratic Hope: Pragmatism and the Politics of Truth*. Ithaca: Cornell University Press, 2005.

——. *John Dewey and American Democracy*. Ithaca: Cornell University Press, 1991.

——. "Pragmatism and Democracy: Reconstructing the Logic of John Dewey's Faith." In *The Revival of Pragmatism: New Essays on Social Thought, Law and Culture*, ed. Morris Dickstein, 128–140. Durham: Duke University Press, 1998.

——. "An Uncommon Faith: Pragmatism and Religious Experience." In *Pragmatism and Religion: Classical Sources and Original Essays*, ed. Stuart Rosenbaum, 190–205. Champaign: University of Illinois Press, 2003.

White, Hayden. "The Value of Narrativity in the Representation of Reality." In *On Narrative*, ed. W. J. T. Mitchell, 1–23. Chicago: University of Chicago Press, 1981.

White, Stephen. *Sustaining Affirmation: The Strengths of Weak Ontology in Political Theory*. Princeton: Princeton University Press, 2000.

——. "The Very Idea of a Critical Social Science: A Pragmatist Turn." In *The Cambridge Companion to Critical Theory*, ed. Fred Rush, 310–335. New York: Cambridge University Press, 2004.

Whitman, Walt. "Democratic Vistas" (1882). In *Specimen Days and Collect*, 203–257. New York: Dover, 1995.

Williams, Bernard. *Ethics and the Limits of Philosophy*. Cambridge, MA: Harvard University Press, 1985.

——. *Moral Luck: Philosophical Papers, 1973–1980*. New York: Cambridge University Press, 1981.

Wilson, P. Eddy. "Emerson and Dewey on Natural Piety." *Journal of Religion* 75, no. 3 (1995): 329–346.

Wolin, Sheldon. "Democracy: Electoral and Athenian." *PS: Political Science and Politics* 26, no. 3 (1993): 475–477.

——. "Fugitive Democracy." In *Democracy and Difference: Contesting the Boundaries of the Political*, ed. Seyla Benhabib, 31–45. Princeton: Princeton University Press, 1996.

——. "Norm and Form: The Constitutionalizing of Democracy." In *Athenian Political Thought and the Reconstruction of American Democracy*, ed. J. Peter Euben, John R. Wallach, and Josiah Ober, 30–58. Ithaca: Cornell University Press, 1994.

——. *Politics and Vision: Continuity and Innovation in Western Political Thought*. Expanded edition. Princeton: Princeton University Press, 2004.

——. *The Presence of the Past: Essays on the State and the Constitution*. Baltimore: Johns Hopkins University Press, 1989.

——. "Transgression, Equality, Voice." In *Dēmokratia: A Conversation on Democracies, Ancient and Modern*, ed. Josiah Ober and Charles Hedrick, 63–90. Princeton: Princeton University Press, 1996.

Yack, Bernard. *The Problems of a Political Animal: Community, Justice, and Conflict in Aristotelian Political Thought*. Berkeley: University of California Press, 1993.

Young, Iris Marion. *Inclusion and Democracy*. New York: Oxford University Press, 2000.

Young, Robert M. *Darwin's Metaphor: Nature's Place in Victorian Culture*. New York: Cambridge University Press, 1985.

INDEX